Graphic Guide to
Frame
Construction

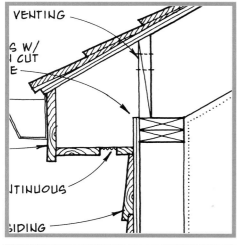
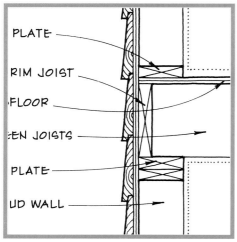

Graphic Guide to Frame Construction

Details for builders and designers

Rob Thallon

*Author's drawings
rendered by Scott Wolf*

The Taunton Press

Taunton

BOOKS & VIDEOS

for fellow enthusiasts

Printed in the United States of America
10 9 8 7 6 5 4 3 2

For Pros / By Pros™: Graphic Guide to Frame Construction
was originally published in 1991 by The Taunton Press, Inc.

For Pros / By Pros™ is a trademark of The Taunton Press,
Inc., registered in the U.S. Patent and Trademark Office.

The Taunton Press, Inc., 63 South Main Street,
PO Box 5506, Newtown, CT 06470-5506
e-mail: tp@taunton.com

Library of Congress Cataloging-in-Publication Data

Thallon, Rob.
    For Pros / By Pros™: Graphic guide to frame
construction : details for builders and designers / Rob
Thallon.
        p.   cm.
    Includes index.
    ISBN 1-56158-323-5
    1. Wooden-frame buildings—Design and construction.
2. Wooden-frame buildings—Drawings.   I. Title.
TH1101.T48   1998   91-19757
694'.2—dc20   CIP

TO DEE

ACKNOWLEDGMENTS

This book has been enriched immeasurably by the contributions of consultants throughout the country. A draft of each chapter was reviewed by the following architects and builders. Their participation has made the book more comprehensive and the process of writing it more enjoyable.

Ed Allen
South Natick, Massachusetts

Judith Capen
Washington, D.C.

Steve Kearns
Ketchum, Idaho

Scott McBride
Irvington, New York

Jud Peake
Oakland, California

Dan Rockhill
LeCompton, Kansas

Joel Schwartz
Princeton, New Jersey

Stephen Suddarth
Miami Beach, Florida

Blaine Young
Santa Fe, New Mexico

Also, I gratefully acknowledge the invaluable contributions of the following people:

Lloyd Kahn, for inspiration and support for this project long before it was realized;

Chuck Miller, for listening to my ideas and suggesting the project to the publishers in the first place;

Paul Bertorelli, for helping to define the scope of the book and the method of producing it;

Joanne Bouknight, for patient and skillful editing with just the right touch of humor;

Scott Wolf, for insightful assistance with the format and for putting as much energy into rendering the drawings as humanly possible;

Don Peting, for valuable assistance in articulating my thoughts about structural relationships in early chapters;

David Edrington, my architectural partner, for his patience and understanding;

Dee Etzwiler, my wife, for her research assistance, her loving support and her patience.

I would also like to thank the many people at the Department of Architecture at the University of Oregon and in my architectural office who made thoughtful suggestions, who accommodated my crazy schedule and who otherwise supported this project in numerous small ways.

—Rob Thallon
Eugene, Oregon
September, 1991

CONTENTS

INTRODUCTION

Lightweight wood-frame construction originated in this country over 150 years ago. When it was introduced, the system rapidly surpassed other wood building methods prevalent at the time, and to this day it is the predominant construction system for houses and other small-scale buildings. Indeed, over 90% of all new buildings in the U.S. use wood-frame construction, or a slightly modified version of it.

The wood-frame system prevails for many reasons. A primary one is its flexibility. Virtually any shape or style of building can be built easily with the studs, joists and rafters that are the components of wood-frame construction. A wood-frame building can also be easily expanded or can be altered on the interior. This is possible because the modules are small, the pieces are easily handled, the material is readily available and the skills and tools required for assembly are easily acquired. Enterprising contractors have capitalized on both the flexibility and the simplicity of the wood-frame system. Although many contractors build custom houses and others build large tracts of similar units, both often turn their building sites into virtual factories, managing specialized workers who perform highly repetitive tasks.

With all the success of the wood-frame system, one would expect at least one comprehensive reference book illustrating in detail how the components of the system fit together. Incredibly, however, no such book exists. Individual trade associations publish invaluable handbooks on specific materials and processes, and building reference books contain chapters on wood-frame construction, but I have never found a book that focuses *in detail* on how all the parts of a wood-frame building fit together. For example, what are all the good ways of connecting a porch and deck to a wall? How do the eave and rake of a roof connect at the corner? Architects and designers have had to rely on the experience of contractors. Carpenters and other tradespeople have had to rely on trade journals. Owner-builders have had to draw from myriad sources, and students haven't known what to do.

Having been a member of all of these groups myself, I saw the need for the kind of book you now have in your hands. My vision was that such a book could be a graphic reference book of the quality of *Architectural Graphic Standards,* but focused on wood-frame construction. With such a focus, each type of connection could be examined in detail and alternatives could also be explored. The book would be useful to architects as a reference during design development and for producing working drawings. Contractors and owner-builders would use it to refine their thinking while making drawings and during construction. Students would have a reference that illustrates both the principles and the fine points of how wood-frame buildings go together.

THE SCOPE OF THE BOOK

In order to provide a detailed reference, the scope of the book had to be limited. I decided to focus on the parts of a building that contribute most significantly to its longevity. Virtually all the drawings in this book, therefore, describe details relating to the structural shell or to the outer protective layers of the building. Plumbing, electrical and mechanical systems are described only as they affect the foundation and framing of the building. Interior finishes and fittings are not covered; they could be the subject of another volume (at least). The process of construction, covered adequately in so many references, has been stripped away so as to expose the details themselves as much as possible. Design, although integral with the concerns of this book, is dealt with only at the level of the detail.

The details in this book employ simple, standard materials. With these details it should be possible to build any shape wood building in just about any style. Many local variations are included.

A FOCUS ON DURABILITY

Although the details in this book have been selected partly on the basis of their widespread use, the primary focus is on durability. I believe that wood-frame buildings can and should be built to last for 200 years or more. To accomplish this, a building must be built on a solid foundation; it must be designed and built to resist moisture; it must be protected from termites, ants and other insect pests; it must be structurally stable and it must be reasonably protected from the ravages of fire. All these criteria may be met with standard construction details if care is taken in both the design and construction of the building.

There are some accepted construction practices, however, that I do not think meet the test of durability. For example, the practice in some regions of building foundations without rebar is not prudent. The small investment of placing rebar in the foundation to minimize the possibility of differential settlement is one that should be taken whether or not it is required by code. The stability of a foundation affects not only the level of the floors, but also the integrity of the structure above and the ability of the building to resist moisture. Another common practice that I discourage is the recent over-reliance on caulks and sealants for waterproofing. This practice seems counterproductive in the long run because the most sophisticated and scientifically tested sealants are warranted for only 20 to 25 years. Should we be investing time, money and materials in buildings that could be seriously damaged if someone forgets to re-caulk? It would be far better, I believe, to design buildings with adequate overhangs or with flashing and drip edges that direct water away from the structural core by means of the natural forces of gravity and surface tension.

Durability, however, does not depend entirely upon material quality and construction detailing. Durability also depends heavily upon the overall design of the building and whether its usefulness over time is sufficient to resist the wrecking ball. The more intangible design factors such as the quality of the space and the flexibility of the plan are extremely inportant, but are not a part of this book. Energy efficiency, however, has been included as it has specific effects on detailing. Insulation, air infiltration, ventilation and moisture barriers are all called out in appropriate details.

ON CODES

Every effort has been made to ensure that the details included in this book are accepted by building codes. Codes vary, however, so local codes and building departments should always be consulted to verify compliance.

Hurricane and seismic details are not included because virtually every structural connection requires additional strapping, bracing or nailing. The notes and drawings required to explain these details fully would have increased the size of this book by about one-third. Local and state building codes are the best source for such specialized details.

HOW THE BOOK WORKS

The book's five chapters follow the approximate order of construction, starting with the foundation and working up to the roof (stairs follow roofs, however). Each chapter begins with an introduction that describes general principles. The chapters are divided into subsections, also roughly ordered according to the sequence of construction. Subsections, usually with another more specific introduction and an isometric reference drawing, lead to individual drawings or notes.

Chapter titles and subsections are called out at the top of each page for easy reference. Each drawing has a title and sometimes a subtitle. The pages are numbered at the top outside corner, and the drawings are lettered. With this system, all the drawings may be cross referenced. The callout "see 43A," for example, refers to drawing A on page 43.

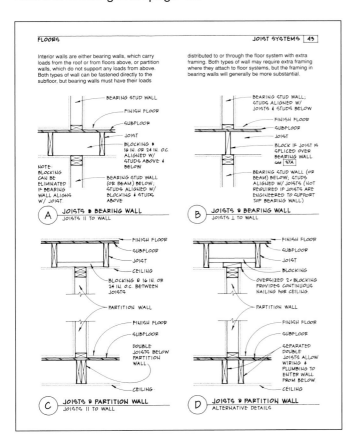

As many details as possible are drawn in the simple section format found on architectural working drawings. Most details are drawn at the scale of 1 in. equals 1 ft. or 1½ in. equals 1 ft., although the scale is not noted on the details. This format should allow the details to be transferred to architectural drawings with minor adjustments. (Details will usually have to be adjusted to allow for different size or thickness of material, for roof pitch or for positional relationships.) Those details that are not easily depicted in a simple section drawing are usually drawn isometrically in order to convey the third dimension.

Any notes included in a detail are intended to describe its most important features. The notes sometimes go a little farther than merely naming an element in a detail by describing the relationship of one element to another. Materials symbols are described on page 215, and abbreviations are spelled out on page 217.

A FINAL NOTE
It has been my intention in writing this book to assist designers and builders who are attempting to make beautiful buildings that endure. With these drawings I have tried to describe the relationship among the parts of every common connection. Alternative approaches to common details have been included. I have relied primarily on my own experiences but have also drawn significantly on the experiences of others. In order to build upon this endeavor, I encourage you, the reader, to send me your own details and critical comments. Please send them to me c/o The Taunton Press, Box 5506, Newtown, Conn. 06470-5506.

FOUNDATIONS

A foundation system has two functions. First, it supports the building structurally by keeping it level, minimizing settling, preventing uplift from the forces of frost or expansive soils and resisting horizontal forces such as winds and earthquakes. Second, a foundation system keeps the wooden parts of the building above the ground and away from the organisms and moisture in the soil that both eat wood and cause it to decay.

The foundation is the part of a building that is most likely to determine its longevity. If the foundation does not support the building adequately, cracks and openings will occur over time, even in the most finely crafted structure. No amount of repair on the structure above the foundation will compensate for an inadequate foundation; once a foundation starts to move significantly, it will continue to move. We now have developed the knowledge to design and construct durable foundations, so there is no reason to invest in a modern building that is not fully supported on a foundation that will endure for the life of the structure.

In the United States, there are three common foundation types. Each performs in different ways, but all rely on a perimeter foundation, i.e., a continuous support around the outside edge of the building.

SLAB-ON-GRADE FOUNDATIONS
Slab-on-grade systems are used mostly in warm climates, where living is close to the ground and the frost line is close to the surface. The footing is usually shallow, and the ground floor is a concrete slab. Many slab-on-grade systems allow the concrete footing, foundation and subfloor to be poured at the same time.

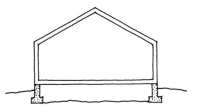

CRAWL SPACES
Crawl spaces are found in all climates but predominate in temperate regions. In this system, the insulated wooden ground floor is supported above grade on a foundation wall made of concrete or concrete block. The resulting crawl space introduces an accessible zone for ductwork, plumbing and other utilities, and allows for simplified remodeling.

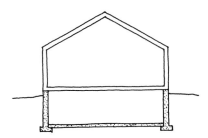

BASEMENTS
Basements are the dominant foundation system in the coldest parts of the country, where frost lines mandate deep footings in any case. Like crawl spaces, basements are accessible, and in addition they provide a large habitable space. Basement foundation systems are usually constructed of concrete or concrete-block foundation walls. Drainage is particularly critical with basement systems.

CHOOSING A FOUNDATION

Each foundation system has many variations, and it is important to select the one best suited to the climate, the soil type, the site and the building program. With all foundations, you should investigate the local soil type. Soil types, along with their bearing capacities, are often described in local soil profiles based on information from the U.S. Geological Survey (U.S.G.S.). If there is any question about matching a foundation system to the soil or to the topography of the site, consult a soil or structural engineer before construction begins. This small investment may save thousands of dollars in future repair bills.

DESIGN CHECKLIST

Because the foundation is so important to the longevity of the building and because it is so difficult to repair, it is wise to be conservative in its design and construction. Make the foundation a little stronger than you think you need to. As a minimum, even if not required by code, it is recommended that you follow this rule-of-thumb checklist:

1. Place the bottom of the footing below the frost line on solid, undisturbed soil that is free of organic material. (Local codes will prescribe frost-line depth.)
2. Use continuous horizontal rebar in the footing and at the top of foundation walls (joint reinforcing may be allowable in concrete-block walls). Tie the footing and wall together with vertical rebar.
3. Use pressure-treated or other decay-resistant wood in contact with concrete. Use a moisture barrier between all concrete and untreated wood.
4. Tie wood members to the foundation with bolts or straps embedded in the foundation. Anchoring requirements in hurricane and severe earthquake zones are not shown here, so verify such requirements with local codes.
5. Provide adequate drainage around the foundation. Slope backfill away from the building and keep soil 6 in. below all wood.

Many codes and many site conditions require measures beyond these minimum specifications. In addition, there are several other considerations important to a permanent foundation system, and these are discussed in this chapter. They include support of loads that do not fall at the perimeter wall, such as footings for point loads within the structure and at porches and decks; insulation and moisture barriers; waterproofing and drainage; protection against termites, other insects and wood-decaying organisms; and precautions against radon gas.

ABOUT THE DRAWINGS

The sizes of building elements indicated in the drawings in this section are for the purposes of illustrating principles and reminding the designer and the builder to consider their use carefully. These drawings should therefore be used only for reference. Basement walls should always be designed by an engineer or architect.

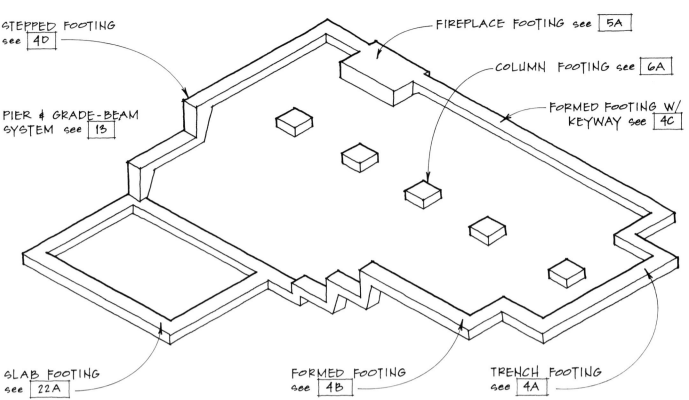

STEPPED FOOTING see 4D

PIER & GRADE-BEAM SYSTEM see 13

FIREPLACE FOOTING see 5A

COLUMN FOOTING see 6A

FORMED FOOTING W/ KEYWAY see 4C

SLAB FOOTING see 22A

FORMED FOOTING see 4B

TRENCH FOOTING see 4A

Footings are the part of a foundation that transfers the building's loads — its weight in materials, contents, occupants and snow, and possibly wind and earthquake loads — directly to the ground. Consequently, the ground upon which the footings bear should be matched by the size and type of footing.

Soil type—Concrete footings should be placed on firm, undisturbed soil that is free from organic material. Soil types are tested and rated as to their ability to support loads (bearing capacity).

Soil type	Bearing capacity (psf)
Soft clay or silt	do not build
Medium clay or silt	1,500 - 2,200
Stiff clay or silt	2,200 - 2,500
Loose sand	1,800 - 2,000
Dense sand	2,000 - 3,000
Gravel	2,500 - 3,000
Bedrock	4,000 and up

Compaction of soil may be required before footings are placed. Consult a soil engineer if the stability of the soil at a building site is unknown.

Reinforcing—Most codes require steel reinforcing rods (called rebar) in footings. Rebar is a sound investment even if it is not required because it gives tensile strength to the footing, thereby minimizing cracking and differential settling. Rebar is also the most common way to connect the footing to the foundation wall. For rebar rules of thumb, see 5B.

Size—Footing size depends mainly on soil type and the building's weight. The chart below shows footing sizes for soils with bearing capacities of 2,000 psf.

No. of stories	H	W
1	6 in.	12 in.
2	7 in.	15 in.
3	8 in.	18 in.

A rule of thumb for estimating the size of standard footings is that a footing should be 8 in. wider than the foundation wall and twice as wide as high.

Frost line—The base of the footing must be below the frost line to prevent the building from heaving as the ground swells during freezing. Frost lines range from 0 ft. to 6 ft. in the continental U.S. Check local building departments for frost-line requirements.

 FOOTINGS

LENGTH OF REBAR STUB EQUALS 30 BAR DIAMETERS (MIN.)

LOCATE VERTICAL REBAR PER LOCAL CODE & AT CENTER OF CELLS FOR BLOCK FOUNDATION.

CONCRETE OR CONCRETE-BLOCK FOUNDATION WALL

BACKFILL

KEY TOP OF FOOTING WHERE REQUIRED. see 4C

DRAINPIPE see 20A

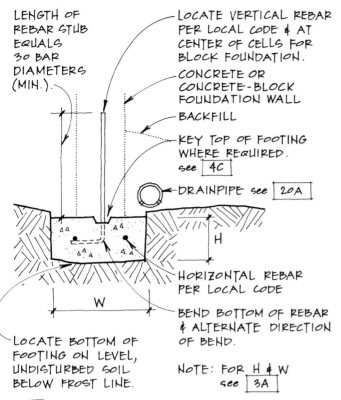

H

W

HORIZONTAL REBAR PER LOCAL CODE

BEND BOTTOM OF REBAR & ALTERNATE DIRECTION OF BEND.

LOCATE BOTTOM OF FOOTING ON LEVEL, UNDISTURBED SOIL BELOW FROST LINE.

NOTE: FOR H & W see 3A

(A) TRENCH FOOTING

LENGTH OF REBAR STUB EQUALS 30 BAR DIAMETERS (MIN.)

LOCATE VERTICAL REBAR PER LOCAL CODE & AT CENTER OF CELLS FOR BLOCK FOUNDATION.

CONCRETE OR CONCRETE-BLOCK FOUNDATION WALL

BACKFILL

BEND BOTTOM OF REBAR & ALTERNATE DIRECTION OF BEND.

DRAINPIPE see 20A

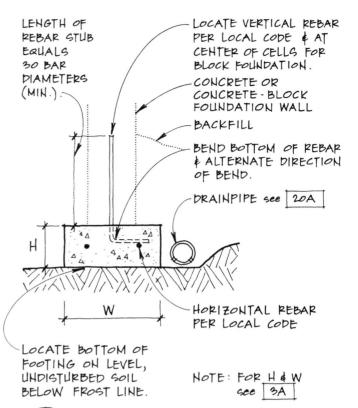

H

W

HORIZONTAL REBAR PER LOCAL CODE

LOCATE BOTTOM OF FOOTING ON LEVEL, UNDISTURBED SOIL BELOW FROST LINE.

NOTE: FOR H & W see 3A

(B) TYPICAL FORMED FOOTING

CONCRETE FOUNDATION WALL

1½-IN. BY 3-IN. (APPROX.) KEYWAY LOCKS FOOTING TO CAST-IN-PLACE CONCRETE FOUNDATION WALL.

BACKFILL

HORIZONTAL REBAR PER LOCAL CODE

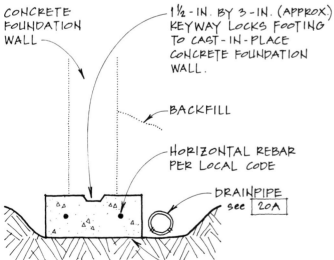

DRAINPIPE see 20A

LOCATE BOTTOM OF FOOTING ON LEVEL, UNDISTURBED SOIL BELOW FROST LINE.

NOTE:
USE KEYWAY FOOTINGS ONLY WITH CONCRETE FOUNDATION WALLS WHERE LATERAL LOADS ON FOUNDATION ARE NOT SIGNIFICANT. USE FOOTINGS DOWELED WITH VERTICAL REBAR FOR LATERAL LOADS.

(C) FORMED FOOTING W/ KEYWAY

REBAR CONTINUOUS THROUGH STEP

MULTIPLES OF 8 IN. FOR CONCRETE-BLOCK FOUNDATION WALL (MAX. DEPTH 24 IN.)

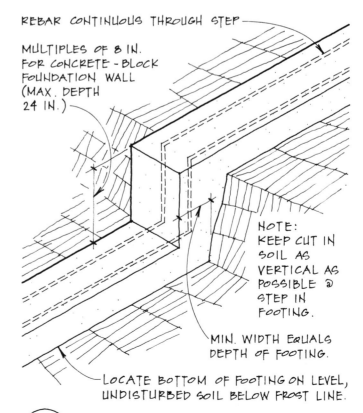

NOTE: KEEP CUT IN SOIL AS VERTICAL AS POSSIBLE @ STEP IN FOOTING.

MIN. WIDTH EQUALS DEPTH OF FOOTING.

LOCATE BOTTOM OF FOOTING ON LEVEL, UNDISTURBED SOIL BELOW FROST LINE.

(D) STEPPED FOOTING

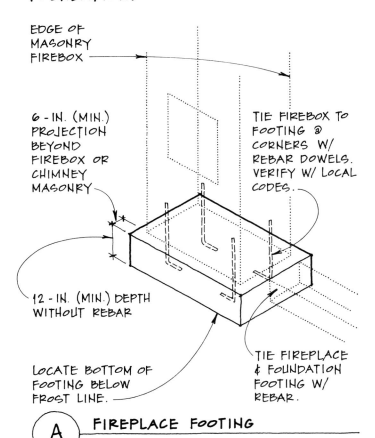

EDGE OF
MASONRY
FIREBOX

6-IN. (MIN.)
PROJECTION
BEYOND
FIREBOX OR
CHIMNEY
MASONRY

TIE FIREBOX TO
FOOTING @
CORNERS W/
REBAR DOWELS.
VERIFY W/ LOCAL
CODES.

12-IN. (MIN.) DEPTH
WITHOUT REBAR

LOCATE BOTTOM OF
FOOTING BELOW
FROST LINE.

TIE FIREPLACE
& FOUNDATION
FOOTING W/
REBAR.

(A) **FIREPLACE FOOTING**

Code requirements for rebar use may vary, but a few rules of thumb can be helpful guidelines. Verify with local codes first.

Sizes—Rebar is sized by diameter in ⅛-in. increments: #3 rebar is ⅜-in. dia., #4 is ½-in. dia., #5 is ⅝-in. dia., etc. The most common sizes for wood-frame construction foundations are #3, #4 and #5.

Overlapping—Rebar is manufactured in 20-ft. lengths. When rebar must be spliced to make it continuous or joined at corners, the length of the lap should equal 30 bar diameters, as shown below.

30 BAR DIAMETERS

Clearance—The minimum clearance between rebar and the surface of the concrete is 3 in. for footings, 2 in. for formed concrete exposed to backfill or weather, and ¾ in. for formed concrete protected from the weather.

(B) **REBAR RULES OF THUMB**

Column footings (also called pier pads) support columns in crawl spaces and under porches and decks. Place all footings on unfrozen, undisturbed soil free of organic material. The bottom of the footing must be located below the frost line unless it is within a crawl space.

Typical sizes are 12 in. to 14 in. for square footings or 16-in. to 18-in. diameter for round footings.

Extreme loads may require oversized footings. The vertical load divided by the soil bearing capacity equals the area of the footing, e.g.,

6,000 lb. ÷ 2,000 psf = 3 sq. ft.

Use a pressure-treated wood post or place a 30-lb. felt moisture barrier between an untreated wood post and a concrete footing, or use steel connectors where required (see 6B).

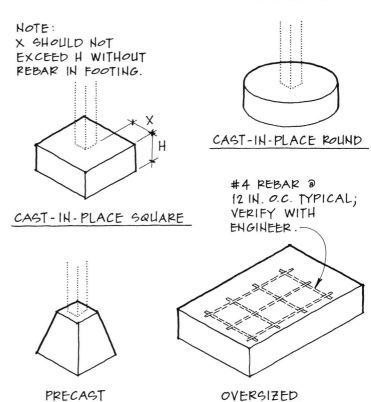

NOTE:
X SHOULD NOT EXCEED H WITHOUT REBAR IN FOOTING.

CAST-IN-PLACE ROUND

CAST-IN-PLACE SQUARE

#4 REBAR @ 12 IN. O.C. TYPICAL; VERIFY WITH ENGINEER.

PRECAST

OVERSIZED

 A COLUMN FOOTINGS

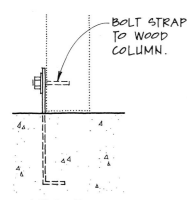 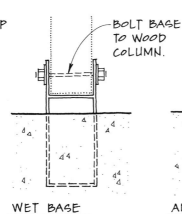 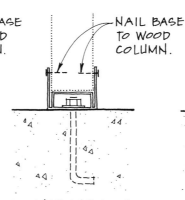 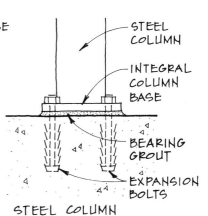

SINGLE STRAP

GALVANIZED STEEL STRAP IS OFTEN USED IN CRAWL SPACES OR UNDER PORCHES.

NOTE:
USE P.T. WOOD COLUMN OR PLACE 30-LB. FELT MOISTURE BARRIER BETWEEN UNTREATED POST & CONCRETE.

— BOLT STRAP TO WOOD COLUMN.

WET BASE

THIS GALVANIZED STEEL BASE PROVIDES THE CLEANEST CONNECTION. IT MUST BE PRECISELY LOCATED IN WET CONCRETE.

— BOLT BASE TO WOOD COLUMN.

ADJUSTABLE BASE

MULTIPLE-PIECE GALVANIZED STEEL ASSEMBLY ALLOWS FOR SOME LATERAL ADJUSTMENT BEFORE NUT IS TIGHTENED. BASE ELEVATES WOOD COLUMN ABOVE CONCRETE FOOTING.

— NAIL BASE TO WOOD COLUMN.

STEEL COLUMN

EXPANSION BOLTS ARE DRILLED INTO FOOTING OR SLAB AFTER CONCRETE IS FINISHED, ALLOWING FOR PRECISE LOCATION OF COLUMN
see | 25 D |

— STEEL COLUMN
— INTEGRAL COLUMN BASE
— BEARING GROUT
— EXPANSION BOLTS

 B COLUMN BASE CONNECTORS
IN COLUMN FOOTING OR SLAB

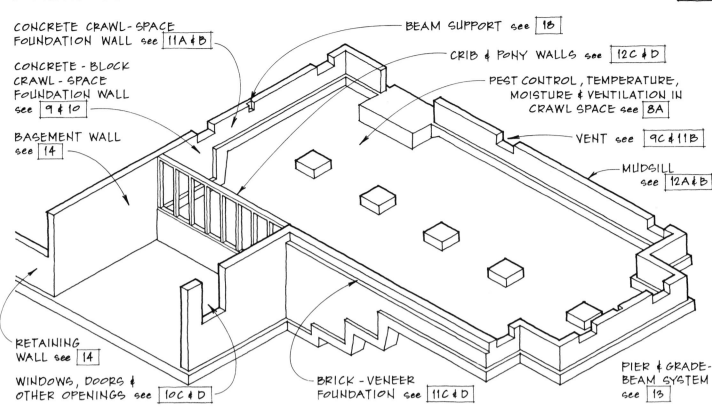

CONCRETE CRAWL-SPACE FOUNDATION WALL see | 11A & B |

CONCRETE-BLOCK CRAWL-SPACE FOUNDATION WALL see | 9 & 10 |

BASEMENT WALL see | 14 |

RETAINING WALL see | 14 |

WINDOWS, DOORS & OTHER OPENINGS see | 10C & D |

BEAM SUPPORT see | 1B |

CRIB & PONY WALLS see | 12C & D |

PEST CONTROL, TEMPERATURE, MOISTURE & VENTILATION IN CRAWL SPACE see | 8A |

VENT see | 9C & 11B |

MUDSILL see | 12A & B |

BRICK-VENEER FOUNDATION see | 11C & D |

PIER & GRADE-BEAM SYSTEM see | 13 |

Foundation walls act integrally with the footings to support the building. They also raise the building above the ground. The primary decision to make about foundation walls is what material to make them of. There are several choices:

Concrete block—Also known as concrete masonry unit or CMU construction, concrete block is the most common system for foundation walls. Its primary advantage is that it needs no formwork, making it appropriate in any situation, but especially where the foundation is complex. Concrete masonry will be used most effficiently if the foundation is planned in 8-in. increments, based on the dimensions of standard concrete blocks (8 in. by 8 in. by 16 in.).

Cast concrete—Concrete can be formed into almost any shape, but formwork is expensive. The most economical use of cast concrete, therefore, is where the formwork is simple or where the formwork can be used several times. Cast-in-place concrete is used for forming pier and grade-beam systems, which are especially appropriate for steep sites or expansive soils (see 13).

Reinforcing—Some local codes do not require reinforcing of foundation walls. Codes in severe earthquake zones are at the other extreme. As a prudent minimum, all foundation walls should be tied to the footing with vertical rebar placed at the corners, adjacent to all major openings, and at regular intervals along the wall. There should be at least one continuous horizontal bar at the top of the wall. Joint reinforcing may be an adequate substitute (see 9C).

Width—The width of the foundation wall depends on the number of stories it supports and on the depth of the backfill, which exerts a lateral force on the wall. With minimum backfill (2 ft. or less), the width of the wall can be determined from the chart below:

No. of stories	Foundation width
1	6 in.
2	8 in.
3	10 in.

The design of basement walls and foundation walls retaining more than 2 ft. of backfill should be verified by an engineer or an architect.

The minimum height of a foundation wall should allow for the adequate clearance of beams and joists from the crawl-space floor. A 12-in. to 18-in. clearance usually requires 12-in. to 24-in. foundation walls, depending on the type of floor system.

FOUNDATION WALLS
CONCRETE & CONCRETE BLOCK

Pests—Rodents and other large burrowing pests can be kept out of crawl spaces by means of a "rat slab," which is a 1-in. thick layer of concrete poured over the ground in a crawl space. A concrete-rated moisture barrier should be placed below this slab (see 22A). Termites and other insect pests are most effectively controlled by chemical treatment of the soil before construction begins.

Temperature—Heated crawl spaces must be insulated at the foundation wall. Insulation can be installed using the same details as for a basement wall (see 15C).

If the foundation wall is insulated on the inside, most codes require that the insulation be protected if it is a flammable type (such as polystyrene), or that it be a non-flammable type (such as rigid fiberglass or mineral wool).

Moisture—Even with the best drainage, the soil under crawl spaces always carries some ground moisture, which will tend to migrate up to the crawl space in the form of vapor. This vapor can be controlled with a barrier laid directly on the ground, which must first be cleared of all organic debris. In vented, unheated crawl spaces, the circulation of air through the vents will remove any excess moisture. In heated crawl spaces, the heated air that circulates through the building will absorb the excess moisture.

Crawl-space vapor barriers should be 6-mil (min.) black polyethylene. The dark plastic retards plant growth by preventing daylight from reaching the soil.

Ventilation—In an overheated crawl space, ventilation minimizes the buildup of excess moisture under the structure. In some regions, ventilation is also required to remove radon gas.

The net area of venting is related to the under-floor area and to the climatic and groundwater conditions. Most codes require that net vent area equal $\frac{1}{150}$ of the under-floor area with a reduction to $\frac{1}{1500}$ if a vapor barrier covers the ground in the crawl space. Screened vents should be rated for net venting area.

Vents should supply cross-ventilation to all areas of the crawl space. Locating vents near corners and on opposite sides of the crawl space is most effective. Access doors can provide a large area of ventilation, and wells allow vents to be placed below finished grade.

As shown in the drawing below, screened vents are available for installing in masonry, cast concrete and wood. They are available in metal or plastic, and some have operable doors for closing off the crawl space temporarily. Operable doors should be closed only during extreme weather conditions. Closing the vents for an entire season will increase moisture in the crawl space and can significantly increase the concentration of radon gas.

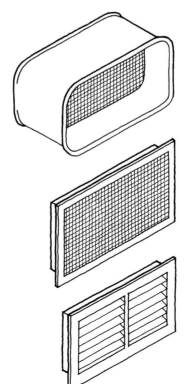

AN 8-IN. OR 10-IN. DEEP SCREENED VENT MADE TO BE CAST IN PLACE IN CONCRETE FOUNDATION WALL

AN 8-IN. × 16-IN. SCREENED VENT THAT FITS IN PLACE OF ONE CONCRETE BLOCK

ONE OF VARIOUS PLASTIC OR METAL VENTS MADE TO VENT THROUGH THE RIM JOIST AND FASTEN TO WOOD SIDING. CARE MUST BE TAKEN TO INSTALL PROPER FLASHING.

 CRAWL - SPACE CONTROLS

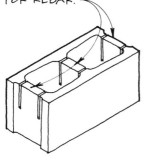

KNOCK OUT WEBS
OF BOND BLOCKS
TO FORM CHANNEL
FOR REBAR.

BOND OR LINTEL
CUT HALF, CORNER
AND OTHER BLOCKS
ON SITE TO CONTINUE
BOND BEAMS TO THE
END OF WALLS AND
AROUND CORNERS.

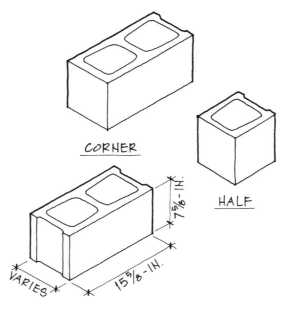

CORNER

HALF

7⅝-IN.

VARIES   15⅝-IN.

STRETCHER OR REGULAR
STANDARD WIDTHS ARE 3⅝-IN.,
5⅝-IN., 7⅝-IN., 9⅝-IN. AND
11⅝-IN. ALL DIMENSIONS
ARE ACTUAL.

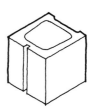

JAMB
JAMB BLOCKS ARE
AVAILABLE IN HALF
(SHOWN) AND
STRETCHER SIZES.
IN ONE SIDE A SLOT
LOCKS BASEMENT
WINDOWS IN PLACE.

NOTE:
ALMOST ANY SIZE OR SHAPE OF
MASONRY WALL CAN BE BUILT
WITH BASIC BLOCK TYPES.
CONSULT NCMA FOR CONSTRUCTION
TECHNIQUES AND FOR SPECIAL
BLOCKS WITH SPECIAL EDGE
CONDITIONS, TEXTURES, COLORS
AND SIZES.

(A) CONCRETE-BLOCK TYPES

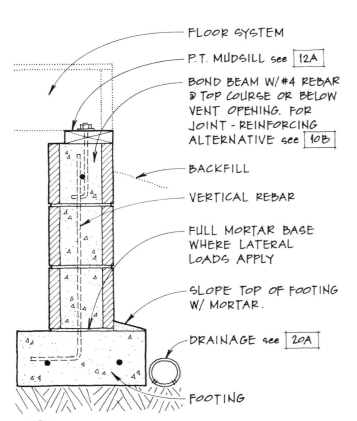

FLOOR SYSTEM

P.T. MUDSILL see 12A

BOND BEAM W/#4 REBAR
@ TOP COURSE OR BELOW
VENT OPENING. FOR
JOINT-REINFORCING
ALTERNATIVE see 10B

BACKFILL

VERTICAL REBAR

FULL MORTAR BASE
WHERE LATERAL
LOADS APPLY

SLOPE TOP OF FOOTING
W/ MORTAR.

DRAINAGE see 20A

FOOTING

(B) CRAWL-SPACE FOUNDATION WALL
CONCRETE BLOCK

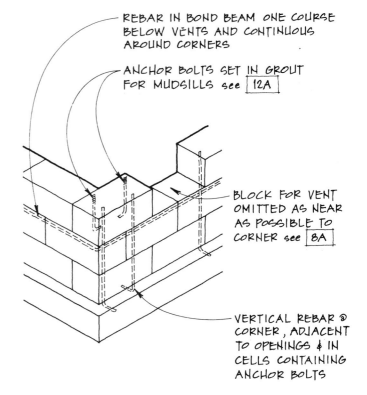

REBAR IN BOND BEAM ONE COURSE
BELOW VENTS AND CONTINUOUS
AROUND CORNERS

ANCHOR BOLTS SET IN GROUT
FOR MUDSILLS see 12A

BLOCK FOR VENT
OMITTED AS NEAR
AS POSSIBLE TO
CORNER see 8A

VERTICAL REBAR @
CORNER, ADJACENT
TO OPENINGS & IN
CELLS CONTAINING
ANCHOR BOLTS

(C) CORNER & VENT OPENING
CONCRETE-BLOCK FOUNDATION WALL

NOTE:
HORIZONTAL REBAR SHOULD BE CONTINUOUS IN A BOND BEAM AT THE TOP COURSE, OR AT THE SECOND COURSE IF FOUNDATION VENTS ARE LOCATED IN THE TOP COURSE. HORIZONTAL REBAR MAY ALSO BE LOCATED IN INTERMEDIATE BOND BEAMS IF THE HEIGHT, WIDTH & FUNCTION OF THE WALL REQUIRE IT.

NOTE:
TO REINFORCE A JOINT, A WELDED HEAVY-WIRE TRUSS MAY BE SUBSTITUTED FOR HORIZONTAL REBAR IN MANY CASES. IT IS EMBEDDED IN THE MORTAR JOINTS BETWEEN COURSES OF MASONRY.

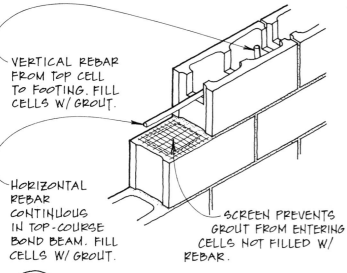

VERTICAL REBAR FROM TOP CELL TO FOOTING. FILL CELLS W/ GROUT.

HORIZONTAL REBAR CONTINUOUS IN TOP-COURSE BOND BEAM. FILL CELLS W/ GROUT.

SCREEN PREVENTS GROUT FROM ENTERING CELLS NOT FILLED W/ REBAR.

A CONCRETE-BLOCK FOUNDATION
REBAR PLACEMENT

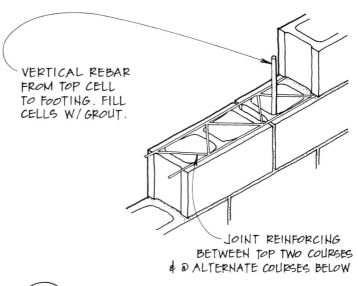

VERTICAL REBAR FROM TOP CELL TO FOOTING. FILL CELLS W/ GROUT.

JOINT REINFORCING BETWEEN TOP TWO COURSES & @ ALTERNATE COURSES BELOW

B CONCRETE-BLOCK FOUNDATION
JOINT-REINFORCING ALTERNATIVE

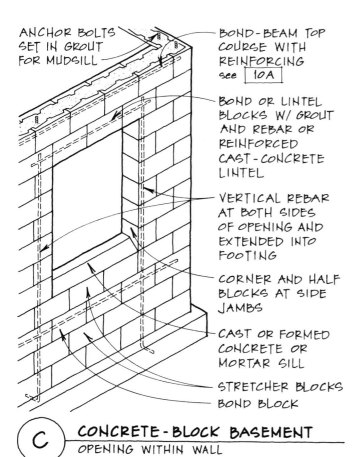

ANCHOR BOLTS SET IN GROUT FOR MUDSILL

BOND-BEAM TOP COURSE WITH REINFORCING see 10A

BOND OR LINTEL BLOCKS W/ GROUT AND REBAR OR REINFORCED CAST-CONCRETE LINTEL

VERTICAL REBAR AT BOTH SIDES OF OPENING AND EXTENDED INTO FOOTING

CORNER AND HALF BLOCKS AT SIDE JAMBS

CAST OR FORMED CONCRETE OR MORTAR SILL

STRETCHER BLOCKS
BOND BLOCK

C CONCRETE-BLOCK BASEMENT
OPENING WITHIN WALL

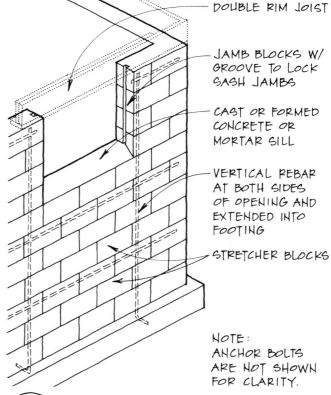

DOUBLE RIM JOIST

JAMB BLOCKS W/ GROOVE TO LOCK SASH JAMBS

CAST OR FORMED CONCRETE OR MORTAR SILL

VERTICAL REBAR AT BOTH SIDES OF OPENING AND EXTENDED INTO FOOTING

STRETCHER BLOCKS

NOTE:
ANCHOR BOLTS ARE NOT SHOWN FOR CLARITY.

D CONCRETE-BLOCK BASEMENT
OPENING @ TOP OF WALL

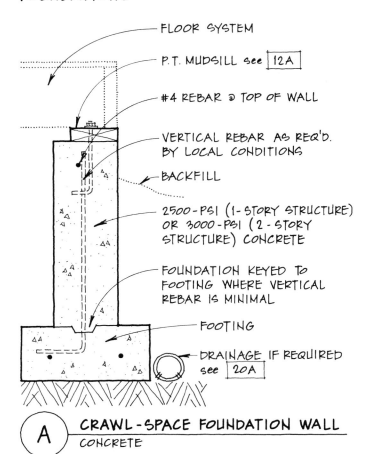

- FLOOR SYSTEM
- P.T. MUDSILL see 12A
- #4 REBAR @ TOP OF WALL
- VERTICAL REBAR AS REQ'D. BY LOCAL CONDITIONS
- BACKFILL
- 2500-PSI (1-STORY STRUCTURE) OR 3000-PSI (2-STORY STRUCTURE) CONCRETE
- FOUNDATION KEYED TO FOOTING WHERE VERTICAL REBAR IS MINIMAL
- FOOTING
- DRAINAGE IF REQUIRED see 20A

A CRAWL-SPACE FOUNDATION WALL
CONCRETE

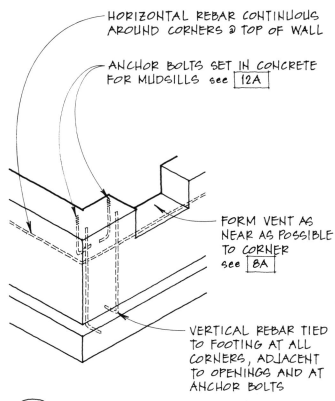

- HORIZONTAL REBAR CONTINUOUS AROUND CORNERS @ TOP OF WALL
- ANCHOR BOLTS SET IN CONCRETE FOR MUDSILLS see 12A
- FORM VENT AS NEAR AS POSSIBLE TO CORNER see 8A
- VERTICAL REBAR TIED TO FOOTING AT ALL CORNERS, ADJACENT TO OPENINGS AND AT ANCHOR BOLTS

B CORNER & VENT OPENING
CONCRETE FOUNDATION WALL

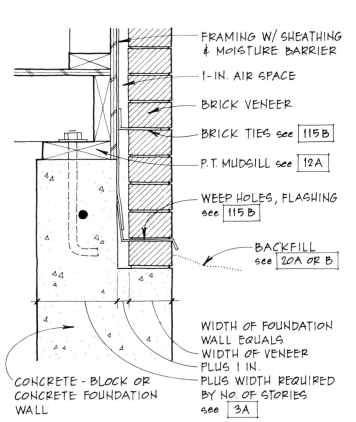

- FRAMING W/ SHEATHING & MOISTURE BARRIER
- 1-IN. AIR SPACE
- BRICK VENEER
- BRICK TIES see 115B
- P.T. MUDSILL see 12A
- WEEP HOLES, FLASHING see 115B
- BACKFILL see 20A OR B

CONCRETE-BLOCK OR CONCRETE FOUNDATION WALL

WIDTH OF FOUNDATION WALL EQUALS WIDTH OF VENEER PLUS 1 IN. PLUS WIDTH REQUIRED BY NO. OF STORIES see 3A

C BRICK-VENEER FOUNDATION
BRICK BELOW MUDSILL

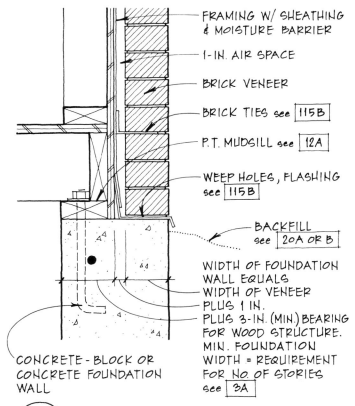

- FRAMING W/ SHEATHING & MOISTURE BARRIER
- 1-IN. AIR SPACE
- BRICK VENEER
- BRICK TIES see 115B
- P.T. MUDSILL see 12A
- WEEP HOLES, FLASHING see 115B
- BACKFILL see 20A OR B

CONCRETE-BLOCK OR CONCRETE FOUNDATION WALL

WIDTH OF FOUNDATION WALL EQUALS WIDTH OF VENEER PLUS 1 IN. PLUS 3-IN. (MIN.) BEARING FOR WOOD STRUCTURE. MIN. FOUNDATION WIDTH = REQUIREMENT FOR NO. OF STORIES see 3A

D BRICK-VENEER FOUNDATION
BRICK LEVEL W/ MUDSILL

½ - IN. STEEL ANCHOR BOLT @ 4 FT. OR 6 FT. O.C. (MAX.) & 12 - IN. (MAX.) FROM END OF EACH PIECE OF MUDSILL. VERIFY W/ LOCAL CODES.

½ - IN. STEEL NUT W/ STEEL WASHER

2 × 4 OR 2 × 6 P.T. WOOD MUDSILL

SILL GASKET OF CAULK OR FIBERGLASS @ BASEMENTS OR OTHER LIVING SPACE

CONTINUOUS TERMITE SHIELD IN TERMITE REGIONS

CONCRETE OR CONCRETE-BLOCK FOUNDATION WALL

REBAR

7 - IN. MIN. DEPTH OF ANCHOR BOLT INTO FOUNDATION WALL

NOTE: SOME CODES REQUIRE LONGER BOLTS FOR MASONRY WALLS.

(A) MUDSILL W/ ANCHOR BOLT

BEND DOUBLE-STRAP ANCHOR AROUND MUDSILL & NAIL @ SIDE & TOP, OR NAIL ONE STRAP TO MUDSILL & OTHER TO FACE OF STUD.

2 × 4 OR 2 × 6 P.T. WOOD MUDSILL

SILL GASKET OF CAULK OR FIBERGLASS AT BASEMENTS OR OTHER LIVING SPACE

PLACE SLAB ANCHORS INTO FRESH CONCRETE OR NAIL TO FORM BEFORE PLACING CONCRETE.

SLAB W/ TURNED-DOWN FOOTING see | 24 |

NOTE: VERIFY ACCEPTABILITY OF SLAB ANCHOR W/ LOCAL BUILDING CODE. THE SLAB ANCHOR ALLOWS THE ABILITY TO FINISH SLAB TO THE EDGE BUT IT IS DIFFICULT TO USE W/ TERMITE SHIELD.

(B) MUDSILL W/ SLAB ANCHOR

A CRIB WALL IS AN ALTERNATIVE TO COLUMNS & A BEAM SUPPORT FOR JOISTS IN A CRAWL SPACE. IT ALLOWS MORE CLEARANCE FOR DUCTS AND EQUIPMENT & AVOIDS THE POTENTIAL PROBLEM OF CROSS-GRAIN SHRINKAGE IN BEAMS.

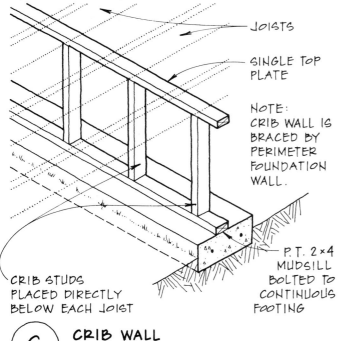

JOISTS

SINGLE TOP PLATE

NOTE: CRIB WALL IS BRACED BY PERIMETER FOUNDATION WALL.

CRIB STUDS PLACED DIRECTLY BELOW EACH JOIST

P.T. 2 × 4 MUDSILL BOLTED TO CONTINUOUS FOOTING

(C) CRIB WALL

A PONY WALL IS USEFUL IN A STEPPED FOUNDATION WALL OR IN A SLOPING PIER & GRADE-BEAM FOUNDATION. THE PONY WALL PROVIDES A LEVEL SURFACE FOR CONSTRUCTION OF THE FIRST FLOOR.

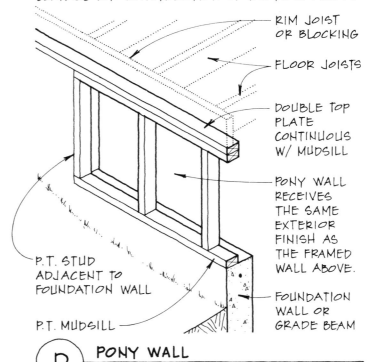

RIM JOIST OR BLOCKING

FLOOR JOISTS

DOUBLE TOP PLATE CONTINUOUS W/ MUDSILL

PONY WALL RECEIVES THE SAME EXTERIOR FINISH AS THE FRAMED WALL ABOVE.

P.T. STUD ADJACENT TO FOUNDATION WALL

P.T. MUDSILL

FOUNDATION WALL OR GRADE BEAM

(D) PONY WALL

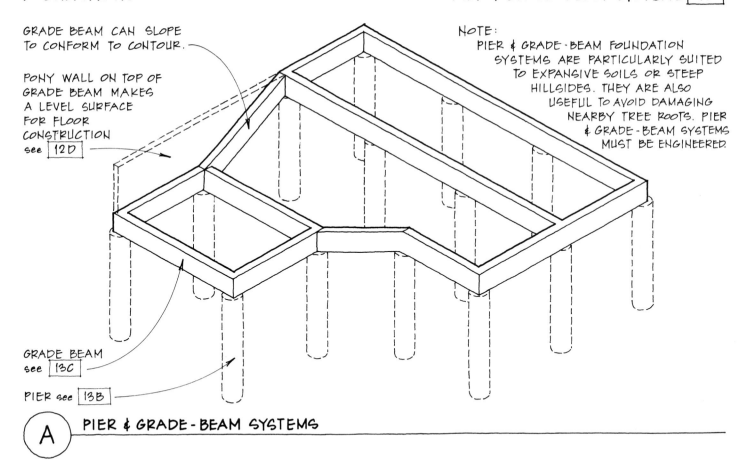

GRADE BEAM CAN SLOPE TO CONFORM TO CONTOUR.

PONY WALL ON TOP OF GRADE BEAM MAKES A LEVEL SURFACE FOR FLOOR CONSTRUCTION see 12D

NOTE:
PIER & GRADE-BEAM FOUNDATION SYSTEMS ARE PARTICULARLY SUITED TO EXPANSIVE SOILS OR STEEP HILLSIDES. THEY ARE ALSO USEFUL TO AVOID DAMAGING NEARBY TREE ROOTS. PIER & GRADE-BEAM SYSTEMS MUST BE ENGINEERED.

GRADE BEAM see 13C

PIER see 13B

A PIER & GRADE-BEAM SYSTEMS

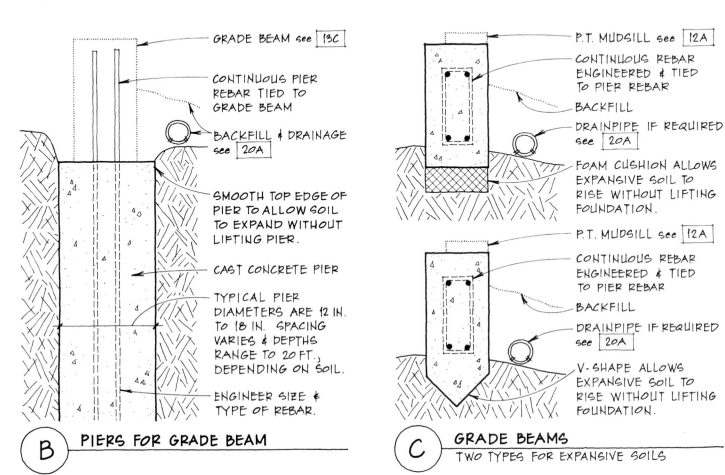

GRADE BEAM see 13C

CONTINUOUS PIER REBAR TIED TO GRADE BEAM

BACKFILL & DRAINAGE see 20A

SMOOTH TOP EDGE OF PIER TO ALLOW SOIL TO EXPAND WITHOUT LIFTING PIER.

CAST CONCRETE PIER

TYPICAL PIER DIAMETERS ARE 12 IN. TO 18 IN. SPACING VARIES & DEPTHS RANGE TO 20 FT., DEPENDING ON SOIL.

ENGINEER SIZE & TYPE OF REBAR.

B PIERS FOR GRADE BEAM

P.T. MUDSILL see 12A

CONTINUOUS REBAR ENGINEERED & TIED TO PIER REBAR

BACKFILL

DRAINPIPE IF REQUIRED see 20A

FOAM CUSHION ALLOWS EXPANSIVE SOIL TO RISE WITHOUT LIFTING FOUNDATION.

P.T. MUDSILL see 12A

CONTINUOUS REBAR ENGINEERED & TIED TO PIER REBAR

BACKFILL

DRAINPIPE IF REQUIRED see 20A

V-SHAPE ALLOWS EXPANSIVE SOIL TO RISE WITHOUT LIFTING FOUNDATION.

C GRADE BEAMS
TWO TYPES FOR EXPANSIVE SOILS

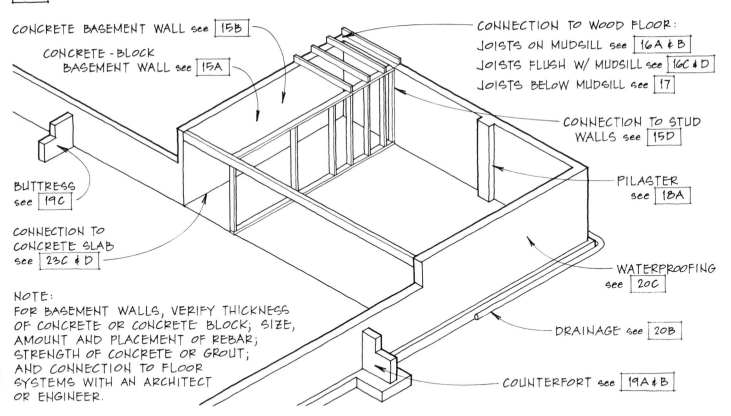

CONCRETE BASEMENT WALL see [15B]

CONCRETE - BLOCK
BASEMENT WALL see [15A]

CONNECTION TO WOOD FLOOR:
JOISTS ON MUDSILL see [16A & B]
JOISTS FLUSH W/ MUDSILL see [16C & D]
JOISTS BELOW MUDSILL see [17]

CONNECTION TO STUD
WALLS see [15D]

BUTTRESS
see [19C]

CONNECTION TO
CONCRETE SLAB
see [23C & D]

PILASTER
see [18A]

WATERPROOFING
see [20C]

DRAINAGE see [20B]

COUNTERFORT see [19A & B]

NOTE:
FOR BASEMENT WALLS, VERIFY THICKNESS
OF CONCRETE OR CONCRETE BLOCK; SIZE,
AMOUNT AND PLACEMENT OF REBAR;
STRENGTH OF CONCRETE OR GROUT;
AND CONNECTION TO FLOOR
SYSTEMS WITH AN ARCHITECT
OR ENGINEER.

Basement walls—Basement walls are one story in height (7 ft. to 9 ft.) and are generally backfilled to at least 4 ft. A basement wall must resist the lateral pressure of the backfill at both the top and bottom of the wall. Basement walls are therefore usually designed as if they were a beam spanning in the vertical direction, with the rebar located at the inside (tension) side of the wall. Because the floor must resist the lateral force of the backfill against the basement wall, the connection between the wood floor and the basement wall is especially important. For this reason, basement wall/wood-floor connections are shown in this chapter (see 16-17). The floor system should always be in place before backfilling. Basement walls can be strengthened with pilasters (see 18), which allow the wall to be designed to span between pilasters in the horizontal (as well as the vertical) direction. Pilasters are also useful as beam supports.

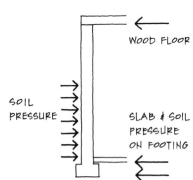

WOOD FLOOR

SOIL
PRESSURE

SLAB & SOIL
PRESSURE
ON FOOTING

Retaining walls—Retaining walls resist lateral loads from the bottom only. They rely on friction at the base of the footing and soil pressure at the outside face of

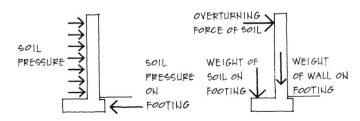

SOIL
PRESSURE

OVERTURNING
FORCE OF SOIL

SOIL
PRESSURE
ON
FOOTING

WEIGHT OF
SOIL ON
FOOTING

WEIGHT
OF WALL ON
FOOTING

FOOTING

SLIDING FORCES   OVERTURNING FORCES

the footing to resist sliding. The weight of the wall and weight of soil on the footing resist overturning.

Buttresses and counterforts strengthen retaining walls in much the same way that pilasters strengthen basement walls (see 19). Buttresses help support retaining walls from the downhill side, and counterforts from the uphill side.

Technically, retaining walls are not a part of the building, but they are included here because they are typical extensions of the building components (foundation and basement walls) into the landscape.

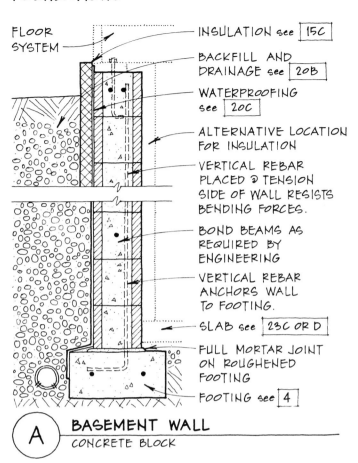

FLOOR SYSTEM — INSULATION see | 15C |
— BACKFILL AND DRAINAGE see | 20B |
— WATERPROOFING see | 20C |
— ALTERNATIVE LOCATION FOR INSULATION
— VERTICAL REBAR PLACED ⊅ TENSION SIDE OF WALL RESISTS BENDING FORCES.
— BOND BEAMS AS REQUIRED BY ENGINEERING
— VERTICAL REBAR ANCHORS WALL TO FOOTING.
— SLAB see | 23C OR D |
— FULL MORTAR JOINT ON ROUGHENED FOOTING
— FOOTING see | 4 |

(A) **BASEMENT WALL**
CONCRETE BLOCK

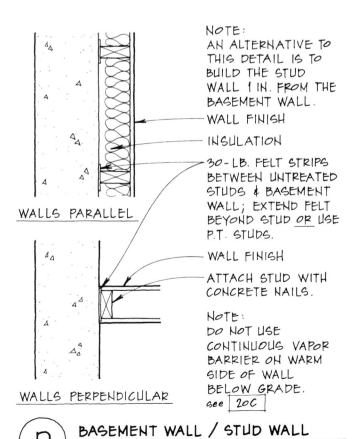

FLOOR SYSTEM — INSULATION see | 15C |
— BACKFILL AND DRAINAGE see | 20B |
— WATERPROOFING see | 20C |
— ALTERNATIVE LOCATION FOR INSULATION
— VERTICAL REBAR PLACED ⊅ TENSION SIDE OF WALL RESISTS BENDING FORCES.
— HORIZONTAL REBAR AS REQUIRED BY ENGINEERING
— VERTICAL REBAR ANCHORS WALL TO FOOTING.
— SLAB see | 23C OR D |
— FOOTING see | 4 |

(B) **BASEMENT WALL**
CONCRETE

Heated basements must be insulated at their perimeter walls. The amount of insulation required will depend on the climate. There are two ways to insulate basement walls—from the exterior or from the interior.

Exterior—Exterior insulation should be a closed-cell rigid insulation (extruded polystyrene or polyisocyanurate) that will not absorb moisture. This insulation, available in 4-ft. by 8-ft. sheets, is attached directly to the basement wall with adhesive or mechanical fasteners. It may be applied either under or over the waterproofing, depending on the type.

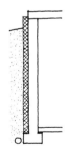

Interior—Interior insulation may be either rigid or batt type. Petroleum-based rigid types must be covered for fire protection when used in an interior location. Other rigid insulation, such as rigid mineral fiber, need not be fire-protected. Building a stud wall with batt insulation has the advantage of providing a nailing surface for interior finishes.

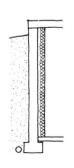

(C) **BASEMENT INSULATION**

WALLS PARALLEL

WALLS PERPENDICULAR

NOTE:
AN ALTERNATIVE TO THIS DETAIL IS TO BUILD THE STUD WALL 1 IN. FROM THE BASEMENT WALL.
— WALL FINISH
— INSULATION
— 30-LB. FELT STRIPS BETWEEN UNTREATED STUDS & BASEMENT WALL; EXTEND FELT BEYOND STUD OR USE P.T. STUDS.
— WALL FINISH
— ATTACH STUD WITH CONCRETE NAILS.

NOTE:
DO NOT USE CONTINUOUS VAPOR BARRIER ON WARM SIDE OF WALL BELOW GRADE. see | 20C |

(D) **BASEMENT WALL / STUD WALL**
PLAN VIEWS

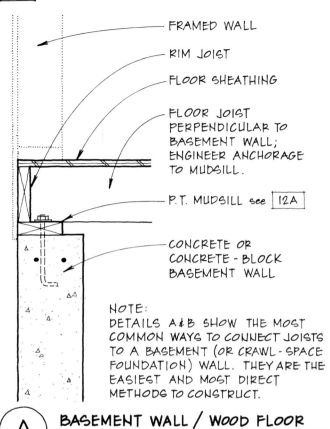

FRAMED WALL

RIM JOIST

FLOOR SHEATHING

FLOOR JOIST PERPENDICULAR TO BASEMENT WALL; ENGINEER ANCHORAGE TO MUDSILL.

P.T. MUDSILL see 12A

CONCRETE OR CONCRETE - BLOCK BASEMENT WALL

NOTE:
DETAILS A & B SHOW THE MOST COMMON WAYS TO CONNECT JOISTS TO A BASEMENT (OR CRAWL - SPACE FOUNDATION) WALL. THEY ARE THE EASIEST AND MOST DIRECT METHODS TO CONSTRUCT.

(A) BASEMENT WALL / WOOD FLOOR
JOISTS ON MUDSILL / ⊥ TO WALL

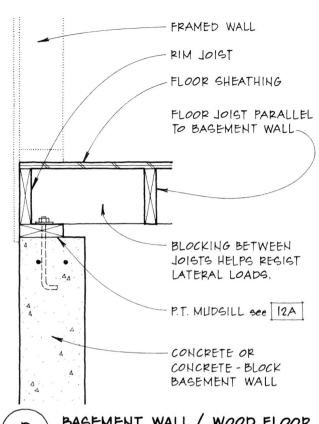

FRAMED WALL

RIM JOIST

FLOOR SHEATHING

FLOOR JOIST PARALLEL TO BASEMENT WALL

BLOCKING BETWEEN JOISTS HELPS RESIST LATERAL LOADS.

P.T. MUDSILL see 12A

CONCRETE OR CONCRETE - BLOCK BASEMENT WALL

(B) BASEMENT WALL / WOOD FLOOR
JOISTS ON MUDSILL / ‖ TO WALL

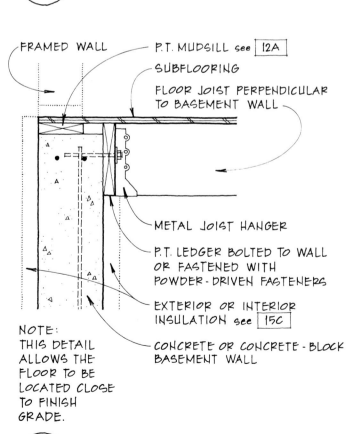

FRAMED WALL

P.T. MUDSILL see 12A

SUBFLOORING

FLOOR JOIST PERPENDICULAR TO BASEMENT WALL

METAL JOIST HANGER

P.T. LEDGER BOLTED TO WALL OR FASTENED WITH POWDER - DRIVEN FASTENERS

EXTERIOR OR INTERIOR INSULATION see 15C

CONCRETE OR CONCRETE - BLOCK BASEMENT WALL

NOTE:
THIS DETAIL ALLOWS THE FLOOR TO BE LOCATED CLOSE TO FINISH GRADE.

(C) BASEMENT WALL / WOOD FLOOR
JOISTS FLUSH W/ MUDSILL / ⊥ TO WALL

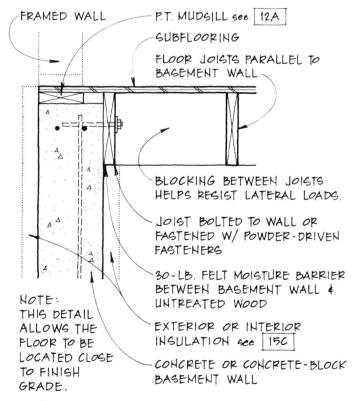

FRAMED WALL

P.T. MUDSILL see 12A

SUBFLOORING

FLOOR JOISTS PARALLEL TO BASEMENT WALL

BLOCKING BETWEEN JOISTS HELPS RESIST LATERAL LOADS.

JOIST BOLTED TO WALL OR FASTENED W/ POWDER - DRIVEN FASTENERS

30 - LB. FELT MOISTURE BARRIER BETWEEN BASEMENT WALL & UNTREATED WOOD

EXTERIOR OR INTERIOR INSULATION see 15C

CONCRETE OR CONCRETE - BLOCK BASEMENT WALL

NOTE:
THIS DETAIL ALLOWS THE FLOOR TO BE LOCATED CLOSE TO FINISH GRADE.

(D) BASEMENT WALL / WOOD FLOOR
JOISTS FLUSH W/ MUDSILL / ‖ TO WALL

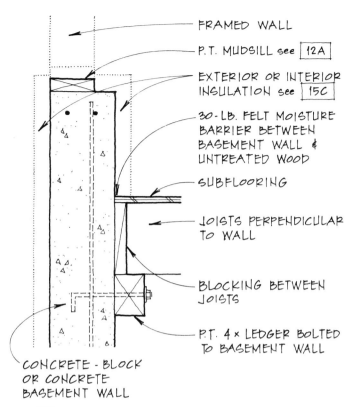

FRAMED WALL

P.T. MUDSILL see 12A

EXTERIOR OR INTERIOR INSULATION see 15C

30-LB. FELT MOISTURE BARRIER BETWEEN BASEMENT WALL & UNTREATED WOOD

SUBFLOORING

JOISTS PERPENDICULAR TO WALL

BLOCKING BETWEEN JOISTS

P.T. 4 × LEDGER BOLTED TO BASEMENT WALL

CONCRETE - BLOCK OR CONCRETE BASEMENT WALL

 A BASEMENT WALL / WOOD FLOOR
JOISTS BELOW MUDSILL / ⊥ TO WALL

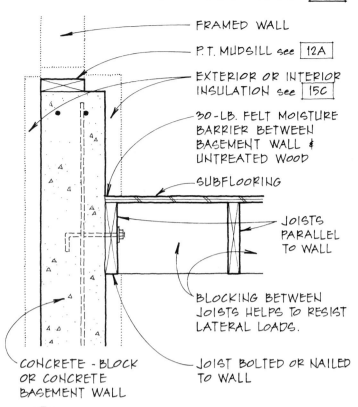

FRAMED WALL

P.T. MUDSILL see 12A

EXTERIOR OR INTERIOR INSULATION see 15C

30-LB. FELT MOISTURE BARRIER BETWEEN BASEMENT WALL & UNTREATED WOOD

SUBFLOORING

JOISTS PARALLEL TO WALL

BLOCKING BETWEEN JOISTS HELPS TO RESIST LATERAL LOADS.

JOIST BOLTED OR NAILED TO WALL

CONCRETE - BLOCK OR CONCRETE BASEMENT WALL

B BASEMENT WALL / WOOD FLOOR
JOISTS BELOW MUDSILL / ∥ TO WALL

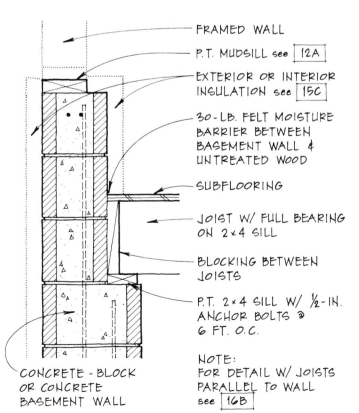

FRAMED WALL

P.T. MUDSILL see 12A

EXTERIOR OR INTERIOR INSULATION see 15C

30-LB. FELT MOISTURE BARRIER BETWEEN BASEMENT WALL & UNTREATED WOOD

SUBFLOORING

JOIST W/ FULL BEARING ON 2×4 SILL

BLOCKING BETWEEN JOISTS

P.T. 2×4 SILL W/ ½-IN. ANCHOR BOLTS @ 6 FT. O.C.

NOTE: FOR DETAIL W/ JOISTS PARALLEL TO WALL see 16B

CONCRETE - BLOCK OR CONCRETE BASEMENT WALL

 C BASEMENT WALL / WOOD FLOOR
JOISTS BELOW MUDSILL / STEPPED WALL

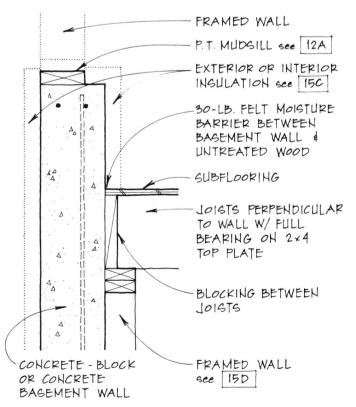

FRAMED WALL

P.T. MUDSILL see 12A

EXTERIOR OR INTERIOR INSULATION see 15C

30-LB. FELT MOISTURE BARRIER BETWEEN BASEMENT WALL & UNTREATED WOOD

SUBFLOORING

JOISTS PERPENDICULAR TO WALL W/ FULL BEARING ON 2×4 TOP PLATE

BLOCKING BETWEEN JOISTS

FRAMED WALL see 15D

CONCRETE - BLOCK OR CONCRETE BASEMENT WALL

D BASEMENT WALL / WOOD FLOOR
JOISTS BELOW MUDSILL / FRAMED WALL

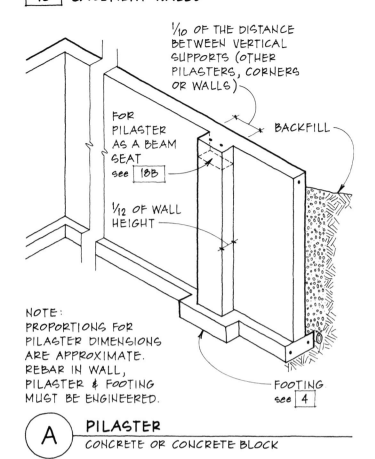

¹/₁₀ OF THE DISTANCE BETWEEN VERTICAL SUPPORTS (OTHER PILASTERS, CORNERS OR WALLS)

FOR PILASTER AS A BEAM SEAT see 18B

BACKFILL

¹/₁₂ OF WALL HEIGHT

NOTE:
PROPORTIONS FOR PILASTER DIMENSIONS ARE APPROXIMATE. REBAR IN WALL, PILASTER & FOOTING MUST BE ENGINEERED.

FOOTING see 4

A **PILASTER**
CONCRETE OR CONCRETE BLOCK

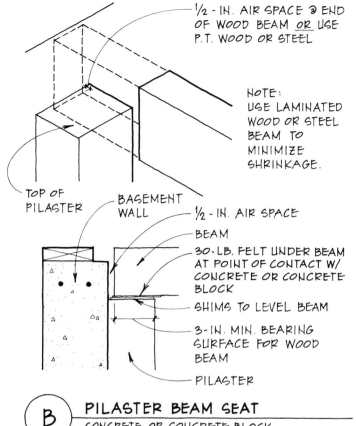

¹/₂ - IN. AIR SPACE @ END OF WOOD BEAM OR USE P.T. WOOD OR STEEL

NOTE: USE LAMINATED WOOD OR STEEL BEAM TO MINIMIZE SHRINKAGE.

TOP OF PILASTER

BASEMENT WALL

¹/₂ - IN. AIR SPACE

BEAM

30-LB. FELT UNDER BEAM AT POINT OF CONTACT W/ CONCRETE OR CONCRETE BLOCK

SHIMS TO LEVEL BEAM

3-IN. MIN. BEARING SURFACE FOR WOOD BEAM

PILASTER

B **PILASTER BEAM SEAT**
CONCRETE OR CONCRETE BLOCK

¹/₂ - IN. AIR SPACE @ END AND SIDES OF WOOD BEAM OR USE P.T. WOOD OR STEEL

NOTE: USE LAMINATED WOOD OR STEEL BEAM TO MINIMIZE SHRINKAGE.

NOTCH BEAM FOR MUDSILL IF REQUIRED. (MAX. NOTCH EQUALS ¹/₄ DEPTH OF BEAM)

¹/₂ - IN. AIR SPACE

BEAM

30-LB. FELT UNDER BEAM AT POINT OF CONTACT W/ CONCRETE OR CONCRETE BLOCK

SHIMS TO LEVEL BEAM

3-IN. MIN. BEARING SURFACE FOR WOOD BEAM

BASEMENT WALL

C **BEAM POCKET**
CONCRETE OR CONCRETE BLOCK

FRAMED WALL

¹/₂ - IN. AIR SPACE

BLOCKING AS REQUIRED

BEAM W/ 1¹/₂ - IN. DECKING see 48C & D OR BEAM & JOIST SYSTEM see 35C

ATTACH BEAM TO COLUMN

4 x 4 WOOD OR P.T. WOOD COLUMN

WOOD COLUMN BEARS ON FOOTING. IF ATTACHMENT IS REQUIRED see 6B

CONCRETE OR CONCRETE-BLOCK FOUNDATION WALL

30-LB. FELT UNDER COLUMN @ FOOTING OR USE P.T. WOOD

D **WOOD-COLUMN BEAM SUPPORT**
BASEMENT OR CRAWL - SPACE WALL

NOTE:
COUNTERFORT MUST BE PROFESSIONALLY
ENGINEERED. REINFORCEMENT IS REQUIRED
FOR TENSION AND SHEAR.

COUNTERFORT REBAR TIED TO
RETAINING WALL & FOOTING

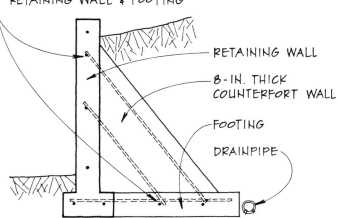

— RETAINING WALL

— 8-IN. THICK
COUNTERFORT WALL

— FOOTING

DRAINPIPE

NOTE:
FOOTING IS LARGE AND REINFORCED BECAUSE
COUNTERFORT USES ITS OWN WEIGHT PLUS
WEIGHT OF SOIL ABOVE FOOTING TO RESIST
THE HORIZONTAL FORCE ON THE WALL.

  CONCRETE COUNTERFORT

A

NOTE:
COUNTERFORT MUST BE PROFESSIONALLY
ENGINEERED.

COUNTERFORT REBAR TIED
TO RETAINING WALL
& FOOTING

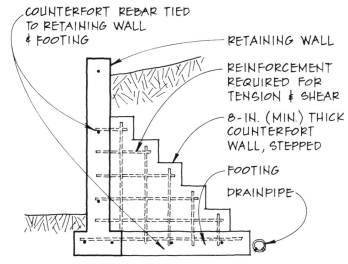

— RETAINING WALL

REINFORCEMENT
REQUIRED FOR
TENSION & SHEAR

8-IN. (MIN.) THICK
COUNTERFORT
WALL, STEPPED

FOOTING

DRAINPIPE

NOTE:
FOOTING IS LARGE AND REINFORCED BECAUSE
COUNTERFORT USES ITS OWN WEIGHT PLUS
WEIGHT OF SOIL ABOVE FOOTING TO RESIST
THE HORIZONTAL FORCE ON THE WALL.

  CONCRETE-BLOCK COUNTERFORT

B

NOTE:
BUTTRESS & RETAINING WALL MUST BE
PROFESSIONALLY ENGINEERED.

RETAINING WALL —

8-IN. (MIN.) THICK
BUTTRESS WALL,
STEPPED (SHOWN)
OR SLOPED —

BUTTRESS REBAR
REQUIRED FOR SHEAR
IS TIED TO RETAINING
WALL & FOOTING. —

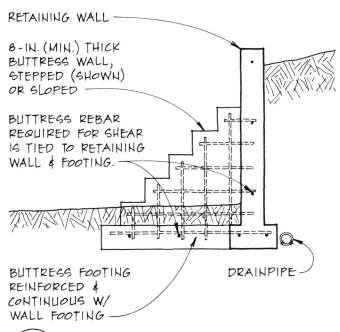

— DRAINPIPE

BUTTRESS FOOTING
REINFORCED &
CONTINUOUS W/
WALL FOOTING —

C **BUTTRESS**
CONCRETE OR CONCRETE BLOCK

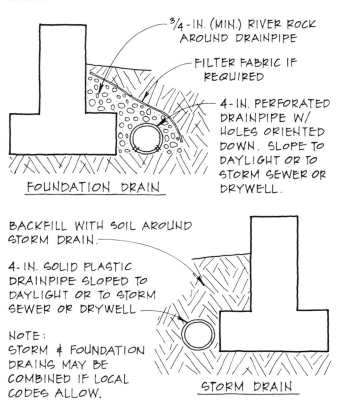

3/4-IN. (MIN.) RIVER ROCK AROUND DRAINPIPE

FILTER FABRIC IF REQUIRED

4-IN. PERFORATED DRAINPIPE W/ HOLES ORIENTED DOWN. SLOPE TO DAYLIGHT OR TO STORM SEWER OR DRYWELL.

FOUNDATION DRAIN

BACKFILL WITH SOIL AROUND STORM DRAIN.

4-IN. SOLID PLASTIC DRAINPIPE SLOPED TO DAYLIGHT OR TO STORM SEWER OR DRYWELL

NOTE: STORM & FOUNDATION DRAINS MAY BE COMBINED IF LOCAL CODES ALLOW.

STORM DRAIN

A FOUNDATION & STORM DRAINAGE

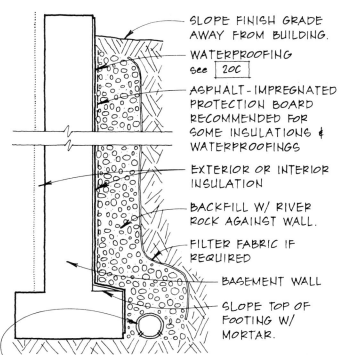

SLOPE FINISH GRADE AWAY FROM BUILDING.

WATERPROOFING see 20C

ASPHALT-IMPREGNATED PROTECTION BOARD RECOMMENDED FOR SOME INSULATIONS & WATERPROOFINGS

EXTERIOR OR INTERIOR INSULATION

BACKFILL W/ RIVER ROCK AGAINST WALL.

FILTER FABRIC IF REQUIRED

BASEMENT WALL

SLOPE TOP OF FOOTING W/ MORTAR.

4-IN. PERFORATED DRAINPIPE W/ HOLES ORIENTED DOWN & SLOPED TO DAYLIGHT OR TO STORM SEWER OR DRYWELL

B BASEMENT DRAINAGE

Drainage is essential in protecting a basement from groundwater, but waterproofing the basement wall from the outside is also vital. In selecting a waterproofing material, consider the method of application, the elasticity and the cost. Below are common waterproofing and drainage materials:

Bituminous coatings — Tar or asphalt can be rolled, sprayed, troweled or brushed on a dry surface. Often applied over a troweled-on coating of cement plaster called parging, some bituminous coatings may be fiberglass reinforced. They have minimal elasticity, and thin coats may not be impervious to standing water.

Modified portland-cement plaster — Plaster with water-repellent admixtures can look exactly like stucco. Applied with a brush or a trowel to a moistened surface, it is inelastic, and unlike parging, it is waterproof.

Bentonite — A natural clay that swells when moistened to become impervious to water, bentonite is available as panels, in rolls, or in spray-on form. It is applied to a dry surface, and is extremely elastic.

Membranes — Rubberized or plastic membranes that are mechanically applied or bonded to a moist or dry surface are moderately elastic.

Bitumin-modified urethane — The most recent development in waterproof coatings, bitumen-modified urethane is applied with a brush to a dry surface. It is elastic, protecting cracks up to 1/8 in.

Plastic air-gap materials — These drainage materials create a physical gap between the basement wall and the soil. A filter fabric incorporated in the material allows water to enter the gap and drop to the bottom of the wall. These systems are expensive, but they eliminate the need for gravel backfill.

Although waterproofing and drainage will prevent water from entering the basement, water vapor may migrate into the basement through the footing and basement wall. It's important not to trap this vapor in an insulated wall, so a vapor barrier on the warm side of a basement wall is not recommended. More common and more practical is to allow the vapor to enter the space, and to remove the vapor with ventilation or a dehumidifier.

C WATERPROOFING
PRINCIPLES & MATERIALS

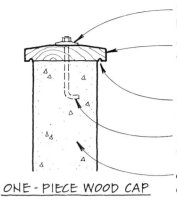

MALLEABLE OR OTHER
LARGE WASHER

WEATHER-RESISTANT
WOOD CAP BEVELED ON
TOP FOR DRAINAGE

DRIP CUT IN UNDERSIDE
OF CAP

ANCHOR BOLTS @
6 FT. O.C. MIN.

CONCRETE-BLOCK OR
CONCRETE WALL

ONE-PIECE WOOD CAP

ROWLOCK BRICK OR
PAVER CAP

MASONRY TIES @
2 FT. O.C.

CONCRETE-BLOCK OR
CONCRETE WALL

MASONRY CAP

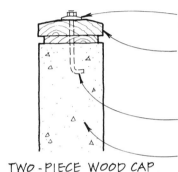

MALLEABLE OR OTHER
LARGE WASHER

WEATHER-RESISTANT
TWO-PIECE WOOD CAP;
TOP PIECE BEVELED &
W/ DRIP

ANCHOR BOLTS @
6 FT. O.C. MIN.

CONCRETE-BLOCK OR
CONCRETE WALL

TWO-PIECE WOOD CAP

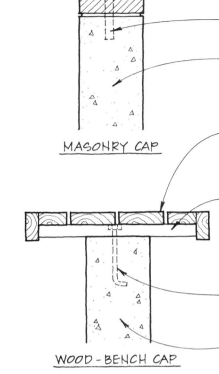

WEATHER-RESISTANT
WOOD SEAT NAILED
OR SCREWED TO
SUPPORTS

P.T. 2x OR 4x
SUPPORTS BOLTED
PERPENDICULAR TO
WALL @ 2 FT. O.C. OR
PER CAPACITY OF
FINISH SEAT MATERIAL

ANCHOR BOLTS @
2 FT. O.C. & RECESSED
FLUSH INTO SUPPORTS

CONCRETE-BLOCK OR
CONCRETE WALL

WOOD-BENCH CAP

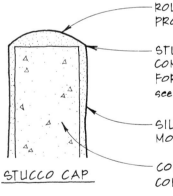

ROUNDED SHAPE
PROMOTES DRAINAGE.

STUCCO OF WALL
CONTINUOUS OVER CAP.
FOR STUCCO DETAILS
see 113A

SILICONE COATING FOR
MOISTURE PROTECTION

CONCRETE-BLOCK OR
CONCRETE WALL

STUCCO CAP

NOTES:
THESE DETAILS ARE FOR THE TOPS OF RETAINING
WALLS, WHICH ARE USUALLY EXPOSED TO THE
WEATHER. WOOD CAPS WILL ULTIMATELY DECAY,
SO THEY ARE DESIGNED FOR RELATIVE EASE OF
REPLACEMENT. THERE IS NOT MUCH POINT IN
MOISTURE BARRIERS, SINCE THEY WILL ONLY TRAP
RAINWATER AGAINST THE WOOD. RETAINING-WALL
SURFACES SHOULD BE PROTECTED FROM MOISTURE
PENETRATION TO PREVENT DAMAGE FROM THE
FREEZE-THAW CYCLE. SEAL W/ CLEAR ACRYLIC
OR SILICONE, OR WATERPROOF W/ MODIFIED
PORTLAND-CEMENT PLASTER OR
BITUMEN-MODIFIED URETHANE
see 20C

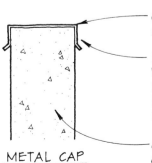

CONTINUOUS METAL
CAP W/ DRIP EDGE

FASTEN METAL CAP TO
WALL @ SIDE TO
PREVENT MOISTURE
PENETRATION OF TOP
FLAT SURFACE.

CONCRETE-BLOCK OR
CONCRETE WALL

METAL CAP

(A) CONCRETE & CONCRETE-BLOCK WALL CAPS

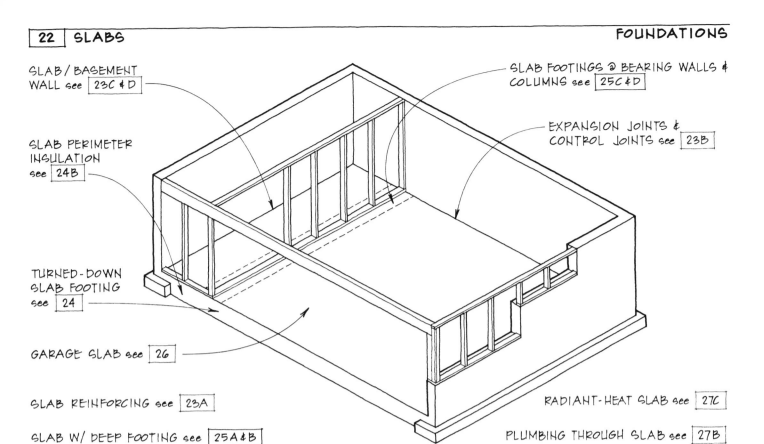

SLAB / BASEMENT WALL see 23C & D

SLAB PERIMETER INSULATION see 24B

TURNED-DOWN SLAB FOOTING see 24

GARAGE SLAB see 26

SLAB REINFORCING see 23A

SLAB W/ DEEP FOOTING see 25A & B

SLAB FOOTINGS @ BEARING WALLS & COLUMNS see 25C & D

EXPANSION JOINTS & CONTROL JOINTS see 23B

RADIANT-HEAT SLAB see 27C

PLUMBING THROUGH SLAB see 27B

Preparation before pouring a slab is critical to the quality of the slab itself. The primary goals in preparing for a slab are to provide adequate and even support, and to control ground moisture.

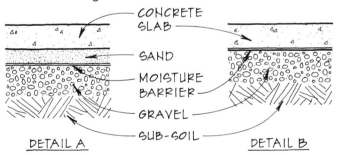

CONCRETE SLAB

SAND

MOISTURE BARRIER

GRAVEL

SUB-SOIL

DETAIL A   DETAIL B

Soil—Soil is the ultimate support of the slab. Soil must be solid and free of organic material. Some soils require compaction. In termite areas, the soil is often treated chemically. Verify compaction and soil treatment practices in your local area.

Gravel—Gravel is a leveling device that provides a porous layer for groundwater to drain through away from the slab. A minimum of 4 in. of gravel is recommended. Gravel must be clean and free from

organic matter. Crushed and ungraded gravels must be compacted. Graded gravels such as pea gravel comprised entirely of similar-sized round particles cannot and need not be compacted.

Moisture barrier—Moisture barriers prevent moisture (and retard vapor) from moving upward into a slab. Six-mil polyethylene is common and works well in Detail A. Overlap joints 12 in. and tape the joints in areas of extreme moisture. A more substantial concrete-rated moisture barrier is necessary for Detail B because the moisture barrier is in direct contact with the concrete slab. Polyethylene may deteriorate within a very short period in this situation, and it is easily punctured during slab preparation and pouring. A more substantial concrete-rated barrier is a fiber-reinforced bituminous membrane, sandwiched between two layers of polyethylene.

Sand—Sand (shown only in Detail A), allows water to escape from concrete in a downward direction during curing. This produces a stronger slab. The American Concrete Institute recommends a 2-in. layer of sand below slabs.

 SLABS

Welded wire mesh —Welded wire mesh (W.W.M.) is the most common reinforcement for light-duty slabs. The most common size is 6x6 - w1.4 x w1.4 —adequate for a residential garage, which requires a stronger slab than a house. One disadvantage to W.W.M. is that the 6-in. grid is often stepped on and forced to the bottom of the slab as the concrete is poured.

Rebar —Rebar is stronger than welded wire mesh. A grid of #3 rebar at 24 in. o.c. is also adequate for a residential garage.

Fiber reinforcement —Fiber reinforcement is a recent development in slab reinforcement. The polypropylene fiber reinforcement is mixed with the concrete at the plant and poured integrally with the slab, thereby eliminating difficulties with placement of the reinforcing material. The addition of 1.5 lb. per cubic yard of concrete produces flexural strength equal to W.W.M. in a slab.

Expansion joints —Expansion joints allow slabs to expand and contract slightly with temperature changes. They also allow slabs to act independently of building elements with which they interface. Expansion joints are appropriate at the edges of slabs that are not heated (not in the living space) or that, for some other reason, are expected to change temperature significantly over their lifetimes. Expansion joints are also used to isolate building elements that penetrate slabs such as structural columns, walls, or plumbing (see 27B).

Control joints —Control joints induce cracking to occur at selected locations. They are troweled or cut into the surface of a slab to about one-quarter of the slab depth and at 20-ft. intervals. Cold joints, which automatically occur between sections of a slab poured separately, can act as control joints.

A CONCRETE-SLAB REINFORCING

B CONCRETE-SLAB JOINTS

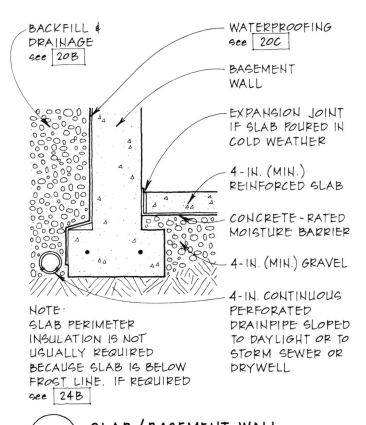

BACKFILL & DRAINAGE see 20B

WATERPROOFING see 20C

BASEMENT WALL

EXPANSION JOINT IF SLAB POURED IN COLD WEATHER

4-IN. (MIN.) REINFORCED SLAB

CONCRETE-RATED MOISTURE BARRIER

4-IN. (MIN.) GRAVEL

4-IN. CONTINUOUS PERFORATED DRAINPIPE SLOPED TO DAYLIGHT OR TO STORM SEWER OR DRYWELL

NOTE:
SLAB PERIMETER INSULATION IS NOT USUALLY REQUIRED BECAUSE SLAB IS BELOW FROST LINE. IF REQUIRED see 24B

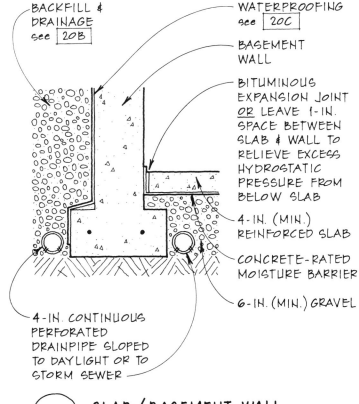

BACKFILL & DRAINAGE see 20B

WATERPROOFING see 20C

BASEMENT WALL

BITUMINOUS EXPANSION JOINT OR LEAVE 1-IN. SPACE BETWEEN SLAB & WALL TO RELIEVE EXCESS HYDROSTATIC PRESSURE FROM BELOW SLAB

4-IN. (MIN.) REINFORCED SLAB

CONCRETE-RATED MOISTURE BARRIER

6-IN. (MIN.) GRAVEL

4-IN. CONTINUOUS PERFORATED DRAINPIPE SLOPED TO DAYLIGHT OR TO STORM SEWER

C SLAB / BASEMENT WALL
WELL-DRAINED SOIL

D SLAB / BASEMENT WALL
POORLY DRAINED SOIL

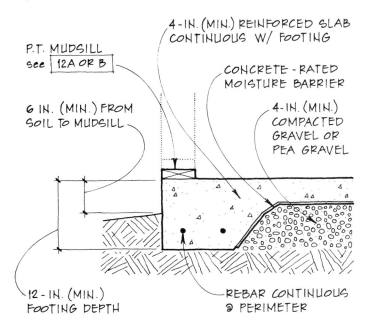

P.T. MUDSILL
see 12A OR B

6 IN. (MIN.) FROM
SOIL TO MUDSILL

4-IN. (MIN.) REINFORCED SLAB
CONTINUOUS W/ FOOTING

CONCRETE-RATED
MOISTURE BARRIER

4-IN. (MIN.)
COMPACTED
GRAVEL OR
PEA GRAVEL

12-IN. (MIN.)
FOOTING DEPTH

REBAR CONTINUOUS
@ PERIMETER

NOTE:
AN UNINSULATED & EXPOSED PERIMETER SLAB IS
APPROPRIATE ONLY @ UNHEATED SPACES OR IN
VERY WARM CLIMATES.

(A) SLAB W/ TURNED-DOWN FOOTING
WARM CLIMATE, WELL-DRAINED SOIL

NOTE:
SLABS LOSE HEAT MOST READILY AT THEIR
PERIMETERS, WHERE THEY ARE EXPOSED TO THE
AIR, SO SLABS MUST BE PROTECTED FROM HEAT
LOSS BY A CLOSED-CELL RIGID INSULATION PLACED
AT THEIR EDGES. THE AMOUNT OF INSULATION
REQUIRED WILL DEPEND ON THE CLIMATE AND ON
WHETHER THE SLAB IS HEATED.
THE POSITION OF THE INSULATION WILL DEPEND
PRIMARILY ON THE FOUNDATION TYPE. SLABS
INTEGRAL WITH TURNED-DOWN FOOTINGS ARE
INSULATED @ THE OUTSIDE BUILDING EDGE. SLABS
WITH DEEP FOOTINGS ARE OFTEN INSULATED @
THE INSIDE FACE OF THE FOUNDATION, ALTHOUGH
THEY MAY ALSO BE INSULATED @ THE OUTSIDE
BUILDING EDGE.

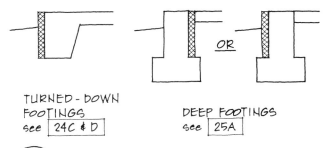

TURNED-DOWN
FOOTINGS
see 24C & D

OR

DEEP FOOTINGS
see 25A

(B) SLAB PERIMETER INSULATION

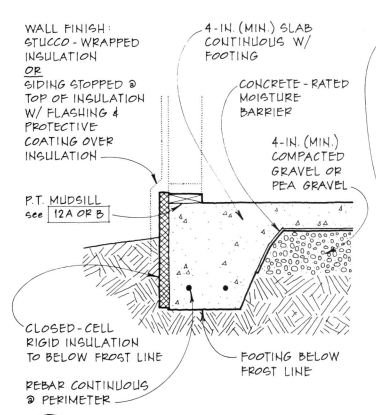

WALL FINISH:
STUCCO-WRAPPED
INSULATION
OR
SIDING STOPPED @
TOP OF INSULATION
W/ FLASHING &
PROTECTIVE
COATING OVER
INSULATION

4-IN. (MIN.) SLAB
CONTINUOUS W/
FOOTING

CONCRETE-RATED
MOISTURE
BARRIER

4-IN. (MIN.)
COMPACTED
GRAVEL OR
PEA GRAVEL

P.T. MUDSILL
see 12A OR B

CLOSED-CELL
RIGID INSULATION
TO BELOW FROST LINE

FOOTING BELOW
FROST LINE

REBAR CONTINUOUS
@ PERIMETER

(C) SLAB W/ TURNED-DOWN FOOTING
INSULATION OUTSIDE FRAMING

CEMENTITIOUS COATING PROTECTS INSULATION
FROM ULTRAVIOLET LIGHT AND MECHANICAL
ABRASION.

CLOSED-CELL RIGID INSULATION TO
BELOW FROST LINE; THICKNESS VARIES.

TERMITE SHIELD IF REQUIRED

FRAMED WALL PROJECTED OVER
INSULATION AND COATING

P.T. MUDSILL see 12A OR B

4-IN. (MIN.) SLAB
CONTINUOUS W/
FOOTING

4-IN. (MIN.) GRAVEL

CONCRETE-RATED
MOISTURE BARRIER

FOOTING BELOW
FROST LINE

(D) SLAB W/ TURNED-DOWN FOOTING
INSULATION FLUSH W/ FRAMING

FRAMED WALL

IN TERMITE REGIONS, EXTEND TERMITE SHIELD CONTINUOUSLY FROM SLAB TO EXTERIOR.

4-IN. (MIN.) REINFORCED SLAB

CONCRETE-RATED MOISTURE BARRIER

4-IN. (MIN.) COMPACTED GRAVEL OR PEA GRAVEL

CLOSED-CELL RIGID INSULATION TO BELOW FROST LINE OR 2 FT. (MIN.) see 24B

FOUNDATION WALL AND FOOTING

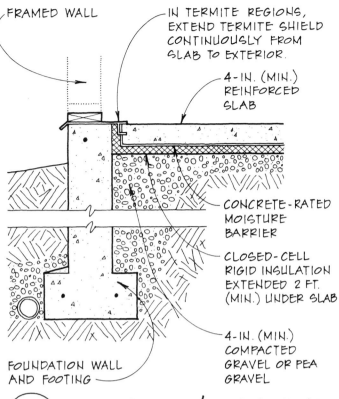

A **SLAB ON GRADE / DEEP FOOTING**
VERTICAL INTERIOR INSULATION

FRAMED WALL

IN TERMITE REGIONS, EXTEND TERMITE SHIELD CONTINUOUSLY FROM SLAB TO EXTERIOR.

4-IN. (MIN.) REINFORCED SLAB

CONCRETE-RATED MOISTURE BARRIER

CLOSED-CELL RIGID INSULATION EXTENDED 2 FT. (MIN.) UNDER SLAB

4-IN. (MIN.) COMPACTED GRAVEL OR PEA GRAVEL

FOUNDATION WALL AND FOOTING

B **SLAB ON GRADE / DEEP FOOTING**
HORIZONTAL INTERIOR INSULATION

REBAR

CONCRETE-RATED MOISTURE BARRIER

WOOD POST

GALVANIZED STEEL COLUMN BASE see 6B

WOOD POST

REBAR

CONCRETE-RATED MOISTURE BARRIER

P.T. SILL PLATE NAILED TO SLAB W/ CONCRETE NAILS

30-LB. FELT UNDER P.T. SILL

NOTE: DEPTH & FLAT BEARING SURFACE OF FOOTING MUST BE SIZED TO SUPPORT VERTICAL LOADS

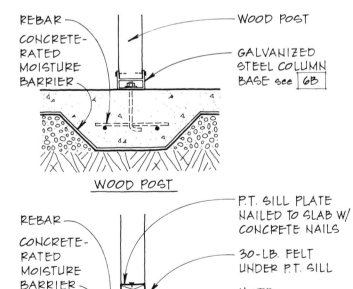

BEARING WALL

C **INTEGRAL SLAB FOOTING**
WOOD POST & BEARING WALL

NOTE: FOR ALTERNATIVE STEEL-COLUMN CONNECTION see 6B

CONCRETE-RATED MOISTURE BARRIER CONTINUOUS BETWEEN SLAB & FOOTING

STEEL COLUMN W/ STEEL BEARING PLATE @ BOTTOM BEARS ON FOOTING.

REINFORCED SLAB POURED AROUND COLUMN LOCKS COLUMN IN PLACE.

REBAR

INDEPENDENT COLUMN FOOTING UNDER SLAB

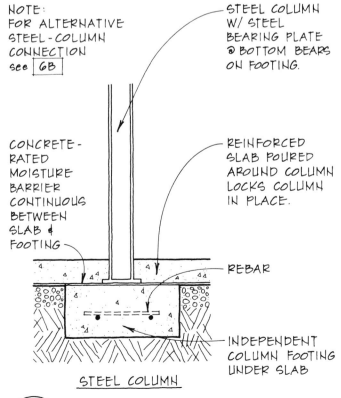

STEEL COLUMN

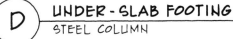

D **UNDER-SLAB FOOTING**
STEEL COLUMN

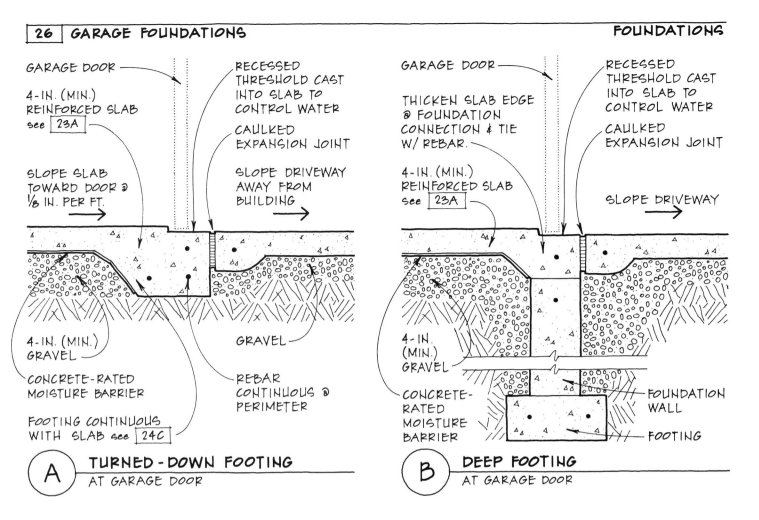

GARAGE DOOR

4-IN. (MIN.) REINFORCED SLAB see [23A]

SLOPE SLAB TOWARD DOOR @ 1/8 IN. PER FT.

4-IN. (MIN.) GRAVEL

CONCRETE-RATED MOISTURE BARRIER

FOOTING CONTINUOUS WITH SLAB see [24C]

RECESSED THRESHOLD CAST INTO SLAB TO CONTROL WATER

CAULKED EXPANSION JOINT

SLOPE DRIVEWAY AWAY FROM BUILDING

GRAVEL

REBAR CONTINUOUS @ PERIMETER

(A) TURNED-DOWN FOOTING
AT GARAGE DOOR

GARAGE DOOR

THICKEN SLAB EDGE @ FOUNDATION CONNECTION & TIE W/ REBAR.

4-IN. (MIN.) REINFORCED SLAB see [23A]

4-IN. (MIN.) GRAVEL

CONCRETE-RATED MOISTURE BARRIER

RECESSED THRESHOLD CAST INTO SLAB TO CONTROL WATER

CAULKED EXPANSION JOINT

SLOPE DRIVEWAY

FOUNDATION WALL

FOOTING

(B) DEEP FOOTING
AT GARAGE DOOR

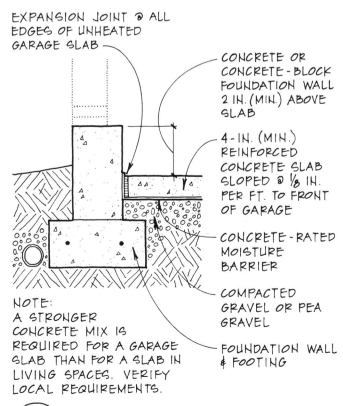

EXPANSION JOINT @ ALL EDGES OF UNHEATED GARAGE SLAB

CONCRETE OR CONCRETE-BLOCK FOUNDATION WALL 2 IN. (MIN.) ABOVE SLAB

4-IN. (MIN.) REINFORCED CONCRETE SLAB SLOPED @ 1/8 IN. PER FT. TO FRONT OF GARAGE

CONCRETE-RATED MOISTURE BARRIER

COMPACTED GRAVEL OR PEA GRAVEL

FOUNDATION WALL & FOOTING

NOTE:
A STRONGER CONCRETE MIX IS REQUIRED FOR A GARAGE SLAB THAN FOR A SLAB IN LIVING SPACES. VERIFY LOCAL REQUIREMENTS.

(C) GARAGE SLAB / FOUNDATION WALL

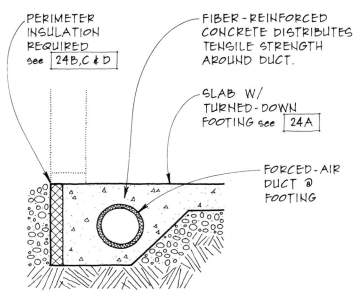

PERIMETER INSULATION REQUIRED see 24B,C & D

FIBER-REINFORCED CONCRETE DISTRIBUTES TENSILE STRENGTH AROUND DUCT.

SLAB W/ TURNED-DOWN FOOTING see 24A

FORCED-AIR DUCT @ FOOTING

NOTE:
AIR DUCTS MUST BE INSULATED AND MUST BE STRUCTURALLY CAPABLE OF SUPPORTING WET CONCRETE. AN UNREINFORCED DUCT MAY BE ALLOWED IF A LIGHT COATING OF CONCRETE IS USED TO STRENGTHEN IT BEFORE THE MAIN CONCRETE POUR.

 FORCED-AIR DUCT IN SLAB

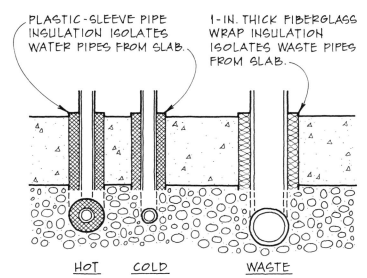

PLASTIC-SLEEVE PIPE INSULATION ISOLATES WATER PIPES FROM SLAB.

1-IN. THICK FIBERGLASS WRAP INSULATION ISOLATES WASTE PIPES FROM SLAB.

HOT   COLD   WASTE

NOTE:
USE TYPE K OR TYPE L COPPER SUPPLY PIPES. MINIMIZE BRAZED FITTINGS BELOW SLAB. HOT-PIPE INSULATION IS RECOMMENDED.

NOTE:
USE ABS PLASTIC WASTE LINES. NO CLEANOUTS ARE ALLOWED BELOW SLAB. SET CLOSET FLANGE AT F.F.L. AND ANCHOR DIRECTLY & SECURELY TO SLAB.

 PLUMBING THROUGH SLAB

PERIMETER INSULATION REQUIRED see 24B,C & D

DOUBLED SILL FOR EDGE NAILING OF WALL FINISHES & TRIM

POLYBUTYLENE TUBING @ 8 IN. O.C. (APPROX.) SET ON SLAB AND COVERED WITH 1½-IN. TOPPING SLAB W/ PEA-GRAVEL AGGREGATE

4-IN. (MIN.) REINFORCED CONCRETE SLAB

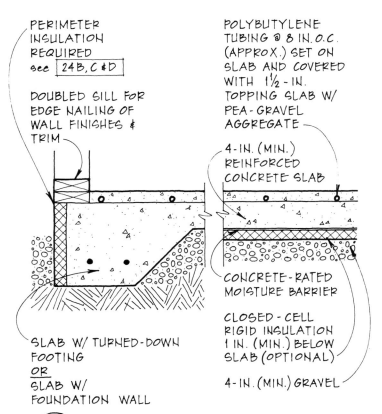

CONCRETE-RATED MOISTURE BARRIER

CLOSED-CELL RIGID INSULATION 1 IN. (MIN.) BELOW SLAB (OPTIONAL)

4-IN. (MIN.) GRAVEL

SLAB W/ TURNED-DOWN FOOTING
OR
SLAB W/ FOUNDATION WALL

NOTE:
POLYBUTYLENE TUBING HAS REPLACED COPPER TUBING AS THE CONVEYOR OF HOT WATER FOR RADIANT SLABS. THIS ELASTIC TUBING IS SUPPLIED IN LONG ROLLS & CAN COVER ABOUT 200 SQ. FT. WITHOUT ANY JOINTS BELOW THE SURFACE. THE ADDITION OF INSULATION BELOW THE SLAB WILL IMPROVE THE PERFORMANCE OF THE SYSTEM.

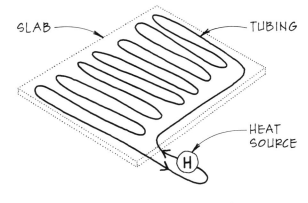

SLAB   TUBING

HEAT SOURCE

<u>DIAGRAM OF RADIANT-HEAT TUBING</u>

 RADIANT-HEAT SLAB

FLOORS

2

The floor is the part of the building with which we have most contact. We walk on the floor, and, on occasion, dance, wrestle or lie on it. We can easily tell if the floor is not level, if it is bouncy or squeaky, and this tells us something about the overall quality of the building. The floor carries the loads of our weight, all our furniture and most of our other possessions. It also acts as a diaphragm to transfer lateral loads (e.g., wind, earthquake and soil) to the walls, which resist these loads. Floors insulate us from beneath and often house ductwork, plumbing and other utilities. So a floor must be carefully designed as a system that integrates with the other systems of a wood-frame building—the foundation, walls, stairs, insulation and utilities. Once designed, the floor must be carefully built because so many subsequent parts of the construction process depend on a level and solid floor construction.

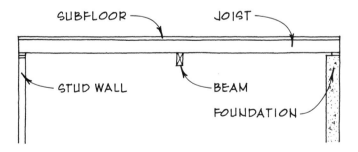

ELEMENTS OF A FLOOR SYSTEM

There are several floor-construction systems, and all of them are composed of variations of the same basic elements: support, joists and a subfloor.

Support—Wood floor systems usually span between parallel supports. These supports may be a foundation wall, a stud bearing wall or a beam. The first two are covered in Chapters 1 and 3, and beams are a subject of this chapter (see 31-33).

Joists—The primary structural members of a floor system are the joists, which span between the supports. Joists can be made of a variety of materials and usually are placed on 12-in., 16-in. or 24-in. centers.

Subfloor—The planar structural surface attached to the top of the joists is called the subfloor. The subfloor provides the level surface to which the finish floor is applied, and it also acts as a diaphragm to transfer lateral loads to the walls. Subfloors are usually made of plywood but may also be made of other materials. Some subfloors also provide mass for passive-solar heating.

FLOORS AND WALLS

It is essential to coordinate the details of a floor-framing system with those of the wall framing. There are two basic wall-framing systems from which to choose:

Balloon framing—Balloon framing is a construction system in which the studs are continuous through the floor levels. It is a mostly archaic system, but there are some situations where balloon framing is appropriate. These situations are discussed in the introduction to Chapter 3 (see 67-68). Balloon-framing details that pertain to floors are included in this chapter.

Platform framing—Platform framing is the dominant wood-floor construction system in this country. The platform-frame floor is so named because the stud-wall structure stops at each level, where the floor structure provides a platform for the construction of the walls of the next level. This chapter concentrates on platform framing, which has two basic variations: joists with plywood, and girders with decking.

Dimension-lumber joists with a plywood subfloor is the more straightforward and generally the less expensive of the two platform-frame systems and is therefore the more widely used. The details in this chapter all illustrate this system (except where noted), but the details may be extrapolated to incorporate other materials, such as composite joists. Composite joists are floor trusses, plywood joists and other composite members that are used in conjunction with plywood and other subfloor materials, often to handle long spans or heavy loads. Composite joists are more dimensionally stable than dimension-lumber joists and are deeper, which allows them to accommodate more utilities, but they are also more expensive. Composite joists are most useful when the building form is simple.

In areas where timber is plentiful, 4x girders with 2-in. tongue-and-groove subfloor decking that spans 4 ft. are often used as a floor system (see 47-49). Lower grades of decking on girders make a very economical floor over crawl spaces, and appearance grades of decking are often used for exposed ceilings. The decking itself does not technically act as a diaphragm to resist lateral loads, so it may require additional diagonal structure, especially at upper levels.

Also included in this chapter are porch and deck floors, floor insulation and vapor barriers.

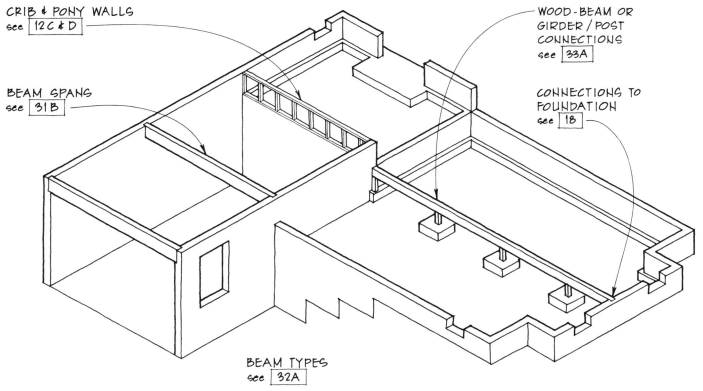

CRIB & PONY WALLS
see 12C & D

BEAM SPANS
see 31B

WOOD-BEAM OR
GIRDER / POST
CONNECTIONS
see 33A

CONNECTIONS TO
FOUNDATION
see 18

BEAM TYPES
see 32A

(A) FLOOR BEAMS

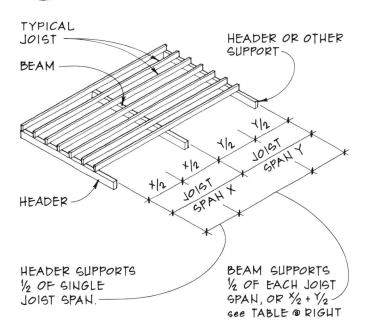

TYPICAL
JOIST

BEAM

HEADER OR OTHER
SUPPORT

HEADER

Y/2
Y/2
Y/2   JOIST
SPAN Y
X/2
X/2   JOIST
X/2   SPAN X

HEADER SUPPORTS
½ OF SINGLE
JOIST SPAN.

BEAM SUPPORTS
½ OF EACH JOIST
SPAN, OR X/2 + Y/2
see TABLE @ RIGHT

NOTE:
THE DRAWING ABOVE AND THE TABLE AT RIGHT ARE
FOR UNIFORM FLOOR LOADS ONLY. ROOF LOADS,
POINT LOADS & OTHER LOADS MUST BE ADDED
TO FLOOR LOADS WHEN CALCULATING BEAMS &
HEADERS.

Beam/span comparison				
	Joist span supported (X/2 + Y/2) in ft. for a given beam span			
Beam type	8	10	12	14
4x8 timber	8.6	7.9	7.2	6.7
(2) 2x8 built-up beam	8.1	7.3	6.7	6.2
4x12 timber	12.9	11.9	10.9	10.0
(3) ⅝x12 glue-laminated beam	15.6	14.5	13.7	13.0
4x8 steel beam (W8 x 13 A36)	19.7	17.7	16.2	15.0

This table assumes a 40-psf live load and a modulus of
elasticity of 1,400,000 for lumber beams, 2,000,000 for
laminated beams.

The table is intended only for estimating beam sizes
and comparing beam types. For calculation tables
consult the National Forest Products Association and
the Western Wood Products Association (for
addresses and phone numbers, see 219).

(B) BEAM SPANS

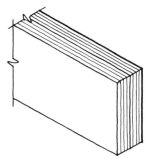

LAMINATED-VENEER LUMBER (LVL) BEAM

VERTICAL FACTORY-LAMINATED SECTIONS ARE NAILED TOGETHER. ACTUAL WIDTHS ARE MULTIPLES OF $1\frac{3}{4}$ IN. (TWO PIECES MATCH THICKNESS OF 2×4 WALL). ACTUAL HEIGHTS RANGE FROM $5\frac{1}{2}$ IN. TO 18 IN.

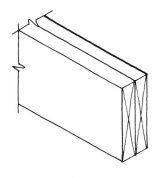

BUILT-UP BEAM

DIMENSION LUMBER IS NAILED TOGETHER TO FORM A SINGLE BEAM (4 PIECES MAX.). WIDTHS ARE MULTIPLES OF $1\frac{1}{2}$ IN. HEIGHT FOLLOWS DIMENSION LUMBER.

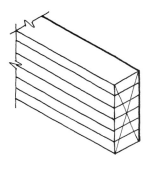

LAMINATED LUMBER BEAM

HORIZONTAL FACTORY-GLUED LAMINATIONS MAKE A KNOT-FREE & VERY STABLE BEAM. ACTUAL WIDTHS ARE $3\frac{1}{8}$ IN., $5\frac{1}{8}$ IN., $7\frac{1}{8}$ IN., ETC. HEIGHTS ARE IN MULTIPLES OF $1\frac{1}{2}$ IN.

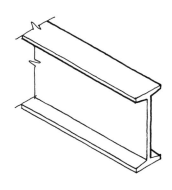

STEEL BEAM

THE STRONGEST OF THE BEAMS FOR A GIVEN SIZE, STEEL BEAMS ARE COMMONLY AVAILABLE IN VARIOUS SIZES FROM 4 IN. WIDE & 4 IN. HIGH TO 12 IN. WIDE & 36 IN. HIGH. THEY MAY BE PREDRILLED FOR BOLTING WOOD PLATE TO TOP FLANGE OR TO WEB.

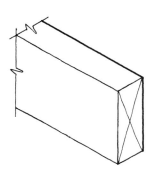

CUT TIMBER

TIMBER BEAMS ARE AVAILABLE IN A VARIETY OF SPECIES & GRADES; DOUGLAS-FIR IS THE STRONGEST. ACTUAL WIDTHS ARE $3\frac{1}{2}$ IN. AND $5\frac{1}{2}$ IN.; ACTUAL HEIGHTS ARE $5\frac{1}{2}$ IN., $7\frac{1}{2}$ IN., ETC., TO $13\frac{1}{2}$ IN.

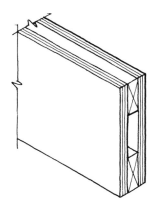

BOX BEAM

2×4 LUMBER IS SANDWICHED BETWEEN TWO PLYWOOD SKINS. PLYWOOD IS BOTH NAILED & GLUED TO 2×4s & AT ALL EDGES. PLYWOOD JOINTS MUST BE OFFSET.

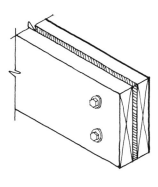

FLITCH BEAM

A STEEL PLATE SANDWICHED BETWEEN TWO PIECES OF LUMBER ADDS STRENGTH WITHOUT SUBSTANTIALLY INCREASING THE BEAM SIZE. THE LUMBER PREVENTS BUCKLING OF THE STEEL & PROVIDES A NAILING SURFACE. WIDTHS ARE 3 IN. TO $3\frac{1}{2}$ IN. HEIGHTS FOLLOW DIMENSION LUMBER.

NOTE:
BEAMS & JOISTS MUST BE DESIGNED AS A SYSTEM. CONNECTIONS BETWEEN JOISTS & BEAMS ARE SIMILAR FOR ALL WOOD-BEAM TYPES see | 37 |

FOR CONNECTIONS TO STEEL BEAMS see | 38 |

 BEAM TYPES

NOTE:
WOOD BEAMS MAY BE SPLICED OVER VERTICAL SUPPORTS & OFTEN MAY BE ATTACHED TO THE SUPPORT BY MEANS OF TOENAILING. SOME SITUATIONS & CODES, HOWEVER, REQUIRE A POSITIVE CONNECTION OF BEAM TO POST SUCH AS A PLYWOOD GUSSET OR METAL CONNECTOR. SPLICE BEAMS ONLY OVER VERTICAL SUPPORTS. SPLICE WILL DEPEND ON TYPE OF BEAM & TYPE OF SUPPORT.

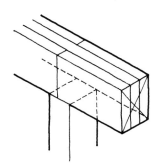 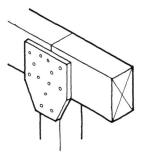 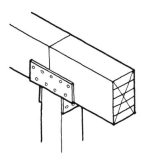 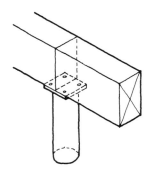

BUILT-UP BEAM

KEEP ONE MEMBER CONTINUOUS OVER POSTS. POSITION JOINTS OVER POST OR SPLICE ONE MEMBER WITHIN FIRST 30% OF SPAN FROM POST.

PLYWOOD GUSSET

PLYWOOD GUSSETS ARE APPLIED TO BOTH SIDES OF SPLICED BEAMS.

METAL CONNECTOR

METAL CONNECTORS ARE MANUFACTURED IN MANY CONFIGURATIONS FOR MOST TYPES OF WOOD BEAM & POST JOINTS.

METAL COLUMN

METAL LALLY COLUMN IS LAG-BOLTED TO BOTTOM SIDE OF SPLICED BEAM.

 A   WOOD BEAM OR GIRDER / POST CONNECTIONS

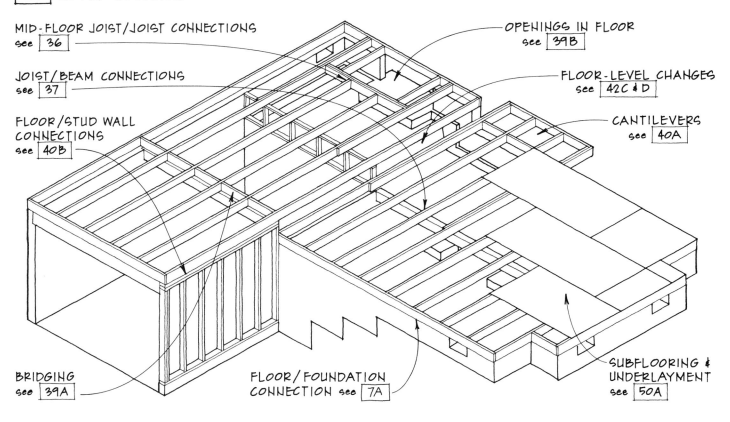

MID-FLOOR JOIST/JOIST CONNECTIONS
see | 36 |

OPENINGS IN FLOOR
see | 39B |

JOIST/BEAM CONNECTIONS
see | 37 |

FLOOR-LEVEL CHANGES
see | 42C & D |

FLOOR/STUD WALL
CONNECTIONS
see | 40B |

CANTILEVERS
see | 40A |

BRIDGING
see | 39A |

FLOOR/FOUNDATION
CONNECTION see | 7A |

SUBFLOORING &
UNDERLAYMENT
see | 50A |

A joist system is the most common floor structure in wood-frame buildings. The system is flexible and relatively inexpensive, and the materials are universally available. Species vary considerably from region to region, but sizes are uniform. The most common sizes for floors are 2x8, 2x10, and 2x12. Selection of floor-joist size depends on span; on spacing required for subflooring, flooring and ceiling finishes (usually 12 in., 16 in., or 24 in.); and on depth required for insulation (usually over a crawl space) and/or utilities (over basements and in upper floors).

The table at right compares spans at common on-center spacings for three typical species and grades of framing lumber at four different sizes of joist (2x6, 2x8, 2x10 and 2x12). For information on plywood I-joists, see 44 and 45; for information on wood trusses, see 46A.

Joist-span comparison			
	Joist span (ft.)		
Joist size, species and grade	12 in. o.c.	16 in. o.c.	24 in. o.c.
2x6 hem-fir #1	10.5	9.5	8.3
2x6 south. yellow pine #1	10.9	9.9	8.7
2x6 Douglas-fir #1	11.2	10.2	8.8
2x8 hem-fir #1	13.8	12.5	10.0
2x8 south. yellow pine	14.4	13.1	11.4
2x8 Douglas-fir #1	14.7	13.3	11.7
2x10 hem-fir #1	17.7	16.0	14.0
2x10 south. yellow pine #1	18.4	16.7	14.7
2x10 Douglas-fir #1	18.7	17.0	14.9
2x12 hem-fir #1	21.5	19.5	17.0
2x12 south. yellow pine #1	22.3	20.3	17.7
2x12 Douglas-fir #1	22.8	20.8	18.1

This table assumes a 40-psf live load, a 10-psf dead load and a deflection of L/360. The table is for estimating purposes only.

JOIST - FLOOR SYSTEMS

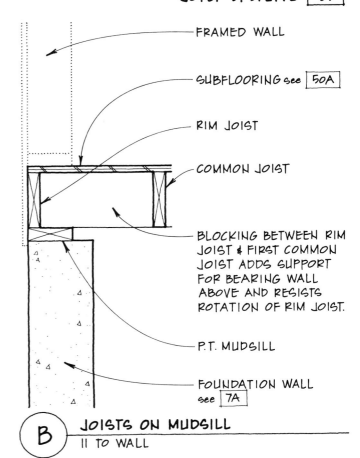

FRAMED WALL

SUBFLOORING see | 50A |

RIM JOIST

FLOOR JOIST

P.T. MUDSILL

FOUNDATION WALL
see | 7A |

NOTE:
IN EARTHQUAKE OR
HURRICANE ZONES,
SECURE FLOOR JOISTS
TO MUDSILL W/ FRAMING
ANCHORS. FOR JOIST
SPAN TABLE see | 34A |

(A) **JOISTS ON MUDSILL**
⊥ TO WALL

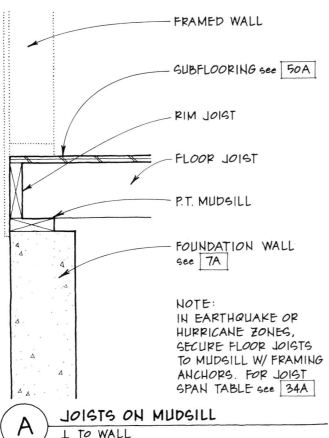

FRAMED WALL

SUBFLOORING see | 50A |

RIM JOIST

COMMON JOIST

BLOCKING BETWEEN RIM
JOIST & FIRST COMMON
JOIST ADDS SUPPORT
FOR BEARING WALL
ABOVE AND RESISTS
ROTATION OF RIM JOIST.

P.T. MUDSILL

FOUNDATION WALL
see | 7A |

(B) **JOISTS ON MUDSILL**
‖ TO WALL

FRAMED WALL

P.T. MUDSILL

SUBFLOORING see | 50A |

JOIST

METAL JOIST HANGER
AT EACH JOIST,
OR
SUPPORT W/ LEDGER
OR FRAMED WALL
see | 16C |

P.T. HEADER BOLTED TO
WALL OR ATTACHED
W/ POWDER-DRIVEN
FASTENERS

FOUNDATION WALL
see | 7A |

(C) **JOISTS FLUSH W/ MUDSILL**
⊥ TO WALL

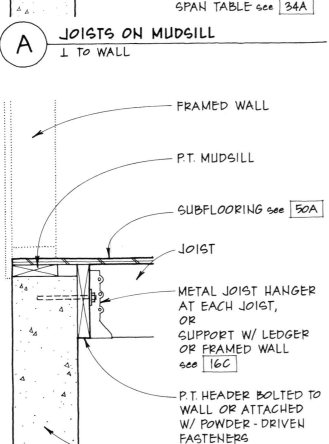

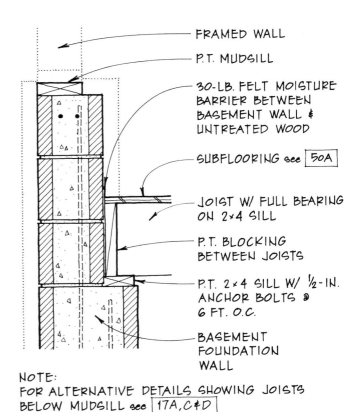

FRAMED WALL

P.T. MUDSILL

30-LB. FELT MOISTURE
BARRIER BETWEEN
BASEMENT WALL &
UNTREATED WOOD

SUBFLOORING see | 50A |

JOIST W/ FULL BEARING
ON 2×4 SILL

P.T. BLOCKING
BETWEEN JOISTS

P.T. 2×4 SILL W/ ½-IN.
ANCHOR BOLTS @
6 FT. O.C.

BASEMENT
FOUNDATION
WALL

NOTE:
FOR ALTERNATIVE DETAILS SHOWING JOISTS
BELOW MUDSILL see | 17A, C & D |

(D) **JOISTS BELOW MUDSILL**
⊥ TO WALL

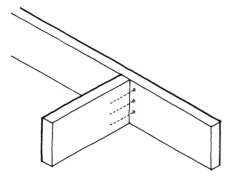

NAILED THROUGH JOIST

THE SIMPLEST BUT THE WEAKEST
METHOD IS RECOMMENDED ONLY
FOR BLOCKING.

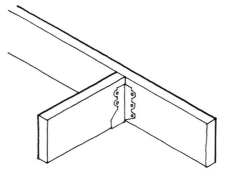

METAL JOIST HANGER

THIS IS THE STRONGEST OF
THE STANDARD METHODS.
EACH APPROVED HANGER IS
RATED IN POUNDS.

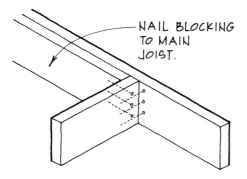

NAIL BLOCKING
TO MAIN
JOIST.

NAILED WITH BLOCKING

IN THIS FAIRLY STRONG & SIMPLE
JOINT, NAILS AT RIGHT ANGLES
EFFECTIVELY LOCK
PERPENDICULAR JOISTS IN
PLACE. IT IS RECOMMENDED
ONLY FOR SHORT JOISTS.

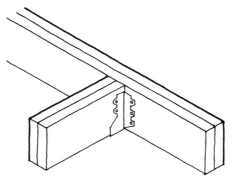

DOUBLED HANGER

DOUBLED HANGERS ARE SIZED
TO HOLD TWO PIECES OF
DIMENSION LUMBER.

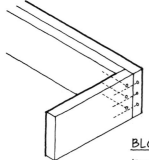

BLOCKED CORNER

DOUBLED JOISTS MAKE A
STRONG OUTSIDE CORNER.
FOR CANTILEVERS see | 40A |
AND DECKS see | 54A |

NOTES:
FOR ALL WOOD / WOOD CONNECTIONS, USE 16d
NAILS (MIN.). FOR METAL HANGERS USE ONLY
HARDENED HANGER NAILS UNLESS OTHERWISE
SPECIFIED. FOR FLOOR OPENINGS see | 39B |

(A) JOIST / JOIST CONNECTIONS

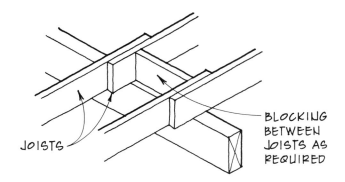

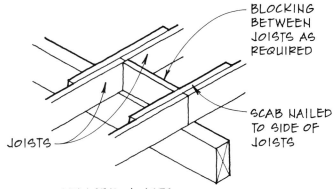

NOTE:
SCAB MUST BE LONG ENOUGH TO QUALIFY SPLICE
AS A SINGLE JOIST SO THAT ADEQUATE BEARING
ON BEAM IS ACHIEVED. VERIFY W/ LOCAL CODES.

BLOCKING
BETWEEN
JOISTS AS
REQUIRED

JOISTS

SCAB NAILED
TO SIDE OF
JOISTS

JOISTS

BLOCKING
BETWEEN
JOISTS AS
REQUIRED

LAPPED JOISTS

THIS COMMON JOINT REQUIRES
SHIFTING THE SUBFLOOR LAYOUT
1½ IN. ON OPPOSITE SIDES OF THE
BEAM TO ALLOW THE SUBFLOOR
TO BEAR ON THE JOISTS.

SPLICED JOISTS

BUTT JOISTS TO MAINTAIN
SAME SPACING FOR NAILING
THE SUBFLOOR ON EACH SIDE
OF THE BEAM.

NOTE:
LAPPED JOISTS & SPLICED JOISTS ARE COMMONLY USED OVER A CRAWL SPACE OR OTHER LOCATION WHERE
HEAD CLEARANCE BELOW THE BEAM IS NOT REQUIRED.

 A | ## JOIST / WOOD BEAM CONNECTIONS
BEAM BELOW JOISTS

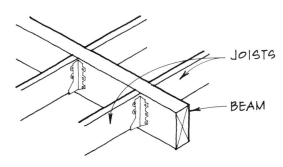

JOISTS

BEAM

JOIST HANGERS

ALIGN JOISTS ON EACH SIDE OF
BEAM TO MAINTAIN SAME SPACING
FOR SUBFLOOR NAILING.

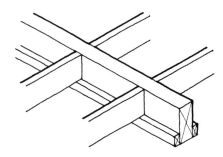

JOISTS ON LEDGER

A 2×2 OR 2×4 LEDGER NAILED TO
THE BEAM SUPPORTS THE JOISTS.
TOENAIL THE JOISTS TO THE BEAM OR
BLOCK BETWEEN JOISTS. NOTCH JOISTS
TO ⅓ OF DEPTH IF REQUIRED TO FIT
OVER THE LEDGER.

NOTE:
JOIST HANGERS & JOISTS ON LEDGER ARE USED WHERE MAXIMUM HEAD CLEARANCE IS REQUIRED BELOW THE
FLOOR. THEY WORK BEST IF THE JOISTS & BEAM ARE OF SIMILAR SPECIES & MOISTURE CONTENT SO THAT ONE
DOES NOT SHRINK MORE THAN THE OTHER.

 B | ## JOIST / WOOD BEAM CONNECTIONS
BEAM FLUSH W/ JOISTS

2×2 WOOD STRAPS NAILED TO JOISTS OVER
STEEL BEAM MAINTAIN JOIST ALIGNMENT.

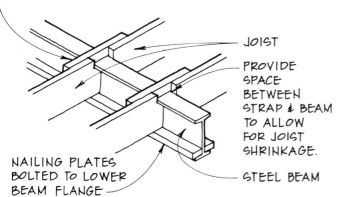

JOIST

PROVIDE
SPACE
BETWEEN
STRAP & BEAM
TO ALLOW
FOR JOIST
SHRINKAGE.

NAILING PLATES
BOLTED TO LOWER
BEAM FLANGE

STEEL BEAM

JOISTS BEARING ON STEEL FLANGE

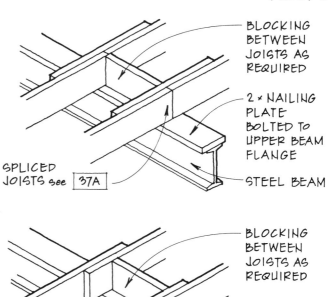

BLOCKING
BETWEEN
JOISTS AS
REQUIRED

2 × NAILING
PLATE
BOLTED TO
UPPER BEAM
FLANGE

STEEL BEAM

SPLICED
JOISTS see 37A

BLOCKING
BETWEEN
JOISTS AS
REQUIRED

2 × NAILING
PLATE
BOLTED TO
UPPER
BEAM
FLANGE

LAPPED
JOISTS see 37A

STEEL BEAM

JOISTS ON NAILING PLATE

2 × NAILING PLATE BOLTED TO
UPPER BEAM FLANGE

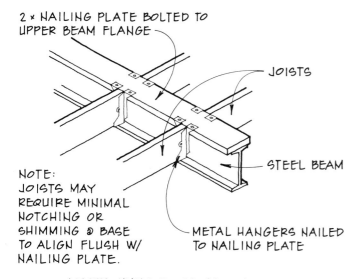

JOISTS

STEEL BEAM

NOTE:
JOISTS MAY
REQUIRE MINIMAL
NOTCHING OR
SHIMMING @ BASE
TO ALIGN FLUSH W/
NAILING PLATE.

METAL HANGERS NAILED
TO NAILING PLATE

JOISTS HUNG FROM NAILING PLATE

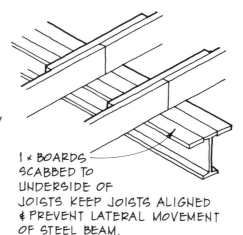

NOTE:
USE ONLY IN
CONDITIONS
WITHOUT
UPLIFT
FORCES AND
WHERE SCABS
WILL NOT
INTERFERE W/
CEILING.

1 × BOARDS
SCABBED TO
UNDERSIDE OF
JOISTS KEEP JOISTS ALIGNED
& PREVENT LATERAL MOVEMENT
OF STEEL BEAM.

JOISTS ON STEEL BEAM

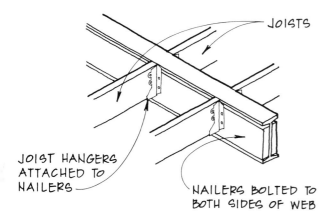

JOISTS

JOIST HANGERS
ATTACHED TO
NAILERS

NAILERS BOLTED TO
BOTH SIDES OF WEB

JOISTS HUNG FROM DOUBLE NAILER

NOTE:
THE DETAILS SHOWN IN 38A & B MAY BE
ADJUSTED FOR USE WITH OTHER TYPES OF JOISTS
& GIRDERS DISCUSSED IN THE FOLLOWING SECTIONS.

(A) JOIST/STEEL BEAM CONNECTIONS
BEAM FLUSH W/ JOISTS

(B) JOIST/STEEL BEAM CONNECTIONS
BEAM BELOW JOISTS

BLOCK BRIDGING

SOLID BLOCKING FROM
SAME MATERIAL AS
JOISTS IS STAGGERED
FOR EASE OF NAILING.

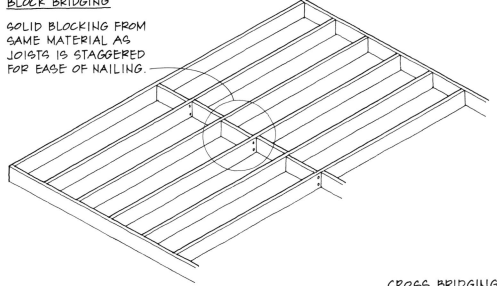

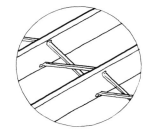

METAL BRIDGING

METAL PIECES SHOULD NOT
TOUCH EACH OTHER.

CROSS BRIDGING

$5/4 \times 3$ OR $5/4 \times 4$ OR 2×2 OR 1×4
BOARDS ARE NAILED IN A
CROSS PATTERN BETWEEN
JOISTS. PIECES SHOULD NOT
TOUCH EACH OTHER.

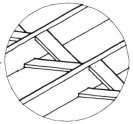

NOTE:
FOR DEEP JOISTS WITH LONG SPANS (OVER 8 FT.),
LOCAL CODES MAY REQUIRE BRIDGING TO PREVENT
ROTATION & TO DISTRIBUTE THE LOADING.

(A)　BRIDGING

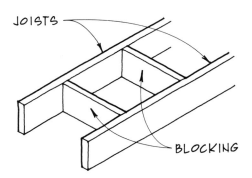

JOISTS

BLOCKING

SMALL OPENINGS

OPENINGS THAT FIT BETWEEN TWO
JOISTS FOR LAUNDRY CHUTES OR
HEATING DUCTS ARE SIMPLY MADE
BY NAILING BLOCKING BETWEEN
THE JOISTS.

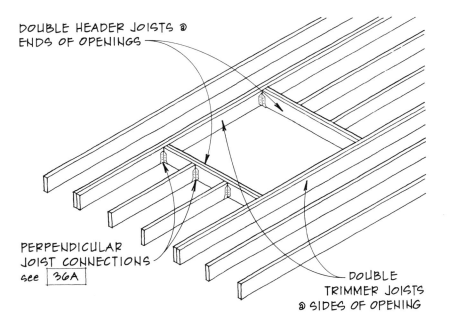

DOUBLE HEADER JOISTS @
ENDS OF OPENINGS

PERPENDICULAR
JOIST CONNECTIONS
see | 36A |

DOUBLE
TRIMMER JOISTS
@ SIDES OF OPENING

LARGE OPENINGS

IN OPENINGS THAT ARE WIDER THAN THE JOIST SPACING, SUCH AS FOR STAIRWAYS &
CHIMNEYS, THE FLOOR STRUCTURE AROUND THE OPENING MUST BE STRENGTHENED.
FOR OPENINGS UP TO THREE JOIST SPACES WIDE, DOUBLING THE JOISTS AT THE SIDES &
ENDS OF THE OPENING MAY SUFFICE. WIDER OPENINGS SHOULD BE ENGINEERED.

(B)　OPENINGS IN JOIST-FLOOR SYSTEM

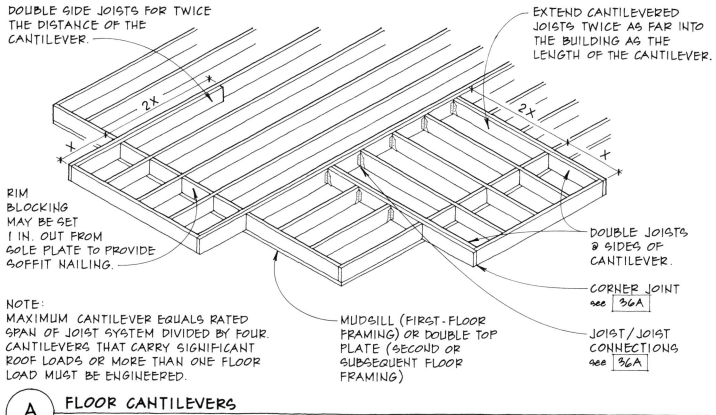

DOUBLE SIDE JOISTS FOR TWICE
THE DISTANCE OF THE
CANTILEVER.

EXTEND CANTILEVERED
JOISTS TWICE AS FAR INTO
THE BUILDING AS THE
LENGTH OF THE CANTILEVER.

2x

RIM
BLOCKING
MAY BE SET
1 IN. OUT FROM
SOLE PLATE TO PROVIDE
SOFFIT NAILING.

DOUBLE JOISTS
@ SIDES OF
CANTILEVER.

CORNER JOINT
see | 36A |

JOIST/JOIST
CONNECTIONS
see | 36A |

NOTE:
MAXIMUM CANTILEVER EQUALS RATED
SPAN OF JOIST SYSTEM DIVIDED BY FOUR.
CANTILEVERS THAT CARRY SIGNIFICANT
ROOF LOADS OR MORE THAN ONE FLOOR
LOAD MUST BE ENGINEERED.

MUDSILL (FIRST-FLOOR
FRAMING) OR DOUBLE TOP
PLATE (SECOND OR
SUBSEQUENT FLOOR
FRAMING)

(A) **FLOOR CANTILEVERS**
‖ & ⊥ TO JOIST SYSTEM

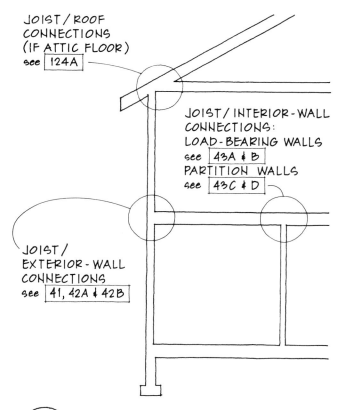

JOIST/ROOF
CONNECTIONS
(IF ATTIC FLOOR)
see | 124A |

JOIST/INTERIOR-WALL
CONNECTIONS:
LOAD-BEARING WALLS
see | 43A & B |
PARTITION WALLS
see | 43C & D |

JOIST/
EXTERIOR-WALL
CONNECTIONS
see | 41, 42A & 42B |

Joist-floor system connections to exterior walls are
straightforward. Wall framing may be one of two types.

Platform framing—Platform framing, the most
common system in use today, takes advantage of
standard materials and framing methods. The ground
floor and all upper floors can be constructed using the
same system.

Balloon framing—Balloon framing is rarely used
because it is harder to erect and requires very long
studs. It may be the system of choice, however, if the
floor structure must work with the walls to resist lateral
roof loads or if extra care is required to make the
insulation and vapor barrier continuous from floor
to floor.

Joist-floor system connections to interior walls depend
on whether the walls are load-bearing walls or partition
walls. The other factor to consider is whether edge
nailing is required for the ceiling.

(B) **JOIST/STUD-WALL CONNECTIONS**

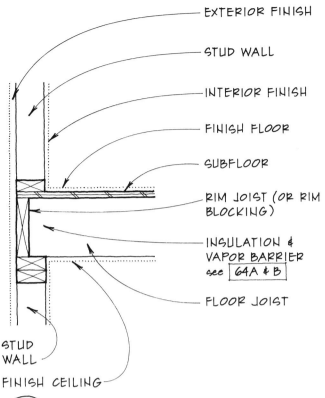

EXTERIOR FINISH

STUD WALL

INTERIOR FINISH

FINISH FLOOR

SUBFLOOR

RIM JOIST (OR RIM BLOCKING)

INSULATION & VAPOR BARRIER
see | 64A & B |

FLOOR JOIST

STUD WALL

FINISH CEILING

Ⓐ JOISTS @ EXTERIOR WALL
JOISTS ⊥ TO WALL

EXTERIOR FINISH

STUD WALL

INTERIOR FINISH

FINISH FLOOR

SUBFLOOR

RIM JOIST

INSULATION & VAPOR BARRIER
see | 64A & B |

FLOOR JOIST

2×4 BLOCKING FOR NAILING CEILING

STUD WALL

FINISH CEILING

Ⓑ JOISTS @ EXTERIOR WALL
JOISTS ‖ TO WALL

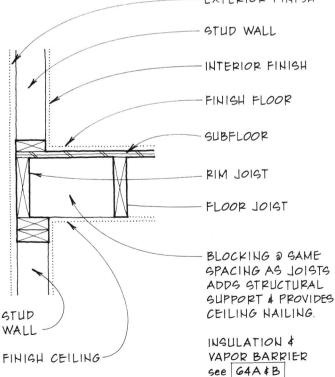

EXTERIOR FINISH

STUD WALL

INTERIOR FINISH

FINISH FLOOR

SUBFLOOR

RIM JOIST

FLOOR JOIST

BLOCKING @ SAME SPACING AS JOISTS ADDS STRUCTURAL SUPPORT & PROVIDES CEILING NAILING.

INSULATION & VAPOR BARRIER
see | 64A & B |

STUD WALL

FINISH CEILING

Ⓒ JOISTS @ EXTERIOR WALL
JOISTS ‖ TO WALL, W/ BLOCKING

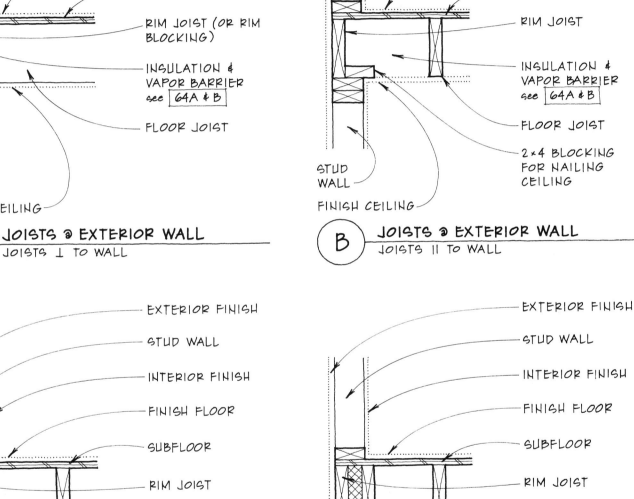

EXTERIOR FINISH

STUD WALL

INTERIOR FINISH

FINISH FLOOR

SUBFLOOR

RIM JOIST

1-IN. RIGID INSULATION

FLOOR JOIST

SECOND RIM JOIST ADDS STRUCTURAL SUPPORT & PROVIDES CEILING NAILING.

STUD WALL

FINISH CEILING

Ⓓ JOISTS @ EXTERIOR WALL
DOUBLED RIM JOISTS ‖ TO WALL

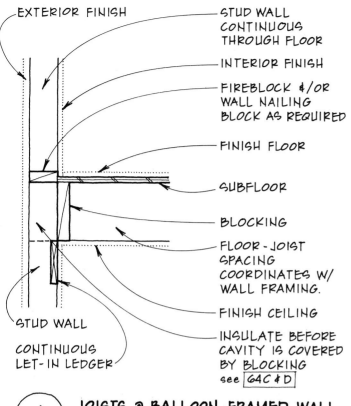

EXTERIOR FINISH

STUD WALL CONTINUOUS THROUGH FLOOR

INTERIOR FINISH

FIREBLOCK &/OR WALL NAILING BLOCK AS REQUIRED

FINISH FLOOR

SUBFLOOR

BLOCKING

FLOOR-JOIST SPACING COORDINATES W/ WALL FRAMING.

FINISH CEILING

INSULATE BEFORE CAVITY IS COVERED BY BLOCKING see 64C & D

STUD WALL

CONTINUOUS LET-IN LEDGER

Ⓐ JOISTS ⓐ BALLOON-FRAMED WALL
JOISTS ⊥ TO WALL

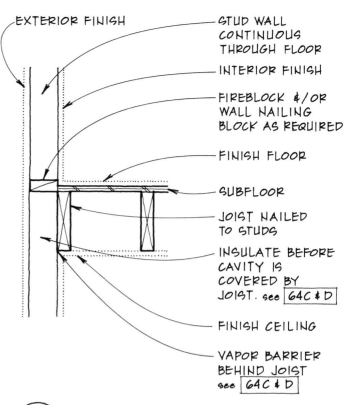

EXTERIOR FINISH

STUD WALL CONTINUOUS THROUGH FLOOR

INTERIOR FINISH

FIREBLOCK &/OR WALL NAILING BLOCK AS REQUIRED

FINISH FLOOR

SUBFLOOR

JOIST NAILED TO STUDS

INSULATE BEFORE CAVITY IS COVERED BY JOIST. see 64C & D

FINISH CEILING

VAPOR BARRIER BEHIND JOIST see 64C & D

Ⓑ JOISTS ⓐ BALLOON-FRAMED WALL
JOISTS ∥ TO WALL

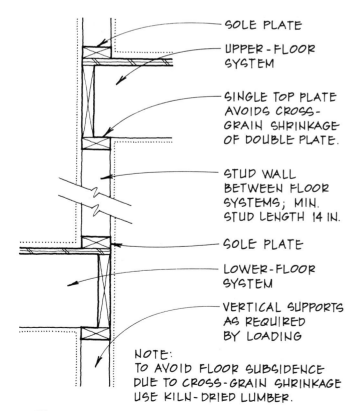

SOLE PLATE

UPPER-FLOOR SYSTEM

SINGLE TOP PLATE AVOIDS CROSS-GRAIN SHRINKAGE OF DOUBLE PLATE.

STUD WALL BETWEEN FLOOR SYSTEMS; MIN. STUD LENGTH 14 IN.

SOLE PLATE

LOWER-FLOOR SYSTEM

VERTICAL SUPPORTS AS REQUIRED BY LOADING

NOTE:
TO AVOID FLOOR SUBSIDENCE DUE TO CROSS-GRAIN SHRINKAGE USE KILN-DRIED LUMBER.

Ⓒ LEVEL CHANGE
PLATFORM FRAMING

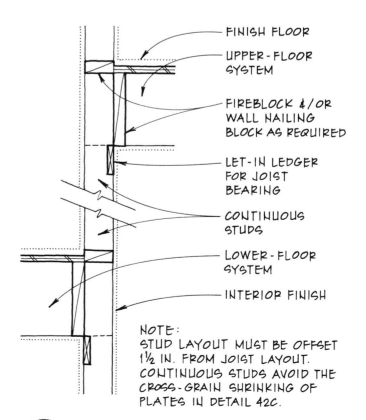

FINISH FLOOR

UPPER-FLOOR SYSTEM

FIREBLOCK &/OR WALL NAILING BLOCK AS REQUIRED

LET-IN LEDGER FOR JOIST BEARING

CONTINUOUS STUDS

LOWER-FLOOR SYSTEM

INTERIOR FINISH

NOTE:
STUD LAYOUT MUST BE OFFSET 1½ IN. FROM JOIST LAYOUT. CONTINUOUS STUDS AVOID THE CROSS-GRAIN SHRINKING OF PLATES IN DETAIL 42C.

Ⓓ LEVEL CHANGE
BALLOON FRAMING

Interior walls are either bearing walls, which carry loads from the roof or from floors above, or partition walls, which do not support any loads from above. Both types of wall can be fastened directly to the subfloor, but bearing walls must have their loads distributed to or through the floor system with extra framing. Both types of wall may require extra framing where they attach to floor systems, but the framing in bearing walls will generally be more substantial.

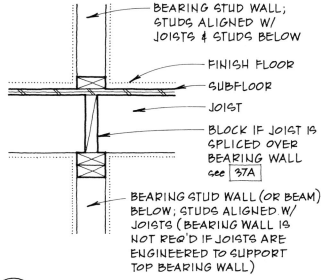

— BEARING STUD WALL

— FINISH FLOOR

— SUBFLOOR

— JOIST

— BLOCKING @ 16 IN. OR 24 IN. O.C. ALIGNED W/ STUDS ABOVE & BELOW

— BEARING STUD WALL (OR BEAM) BELOW; STUDS ALIGNED W/ BLOCKING & STUDS ABOVE

NOTE: BLOCKING CAN BE ELIMINATED IF BEARING WALL ALIGNS W/ JOIST.

A JOISTS @ BEARING WALL
JOISTS || TO WALL

— BEARING STUD WALL; STUDS ALIGNED W/ JOISTS & STUDS BELOW

— FINISH FLOOR

— SUBFLOOR

— JOIST

— BLOCK IF JOIST IS SPLICED OVER BEARING WALL see 37A

— BEARING STUD WALL (OR BEAM) BELOW; STUDS ALIGNED W/ JOISTS (BEARING WALL IS NOT REQ'D IF JOISTS ARE ENGINEERED TO SUPPORT TOP BEARING WALL)

B JOISTS @ BEARING WALL
JOISTS ⊥ TO WALL

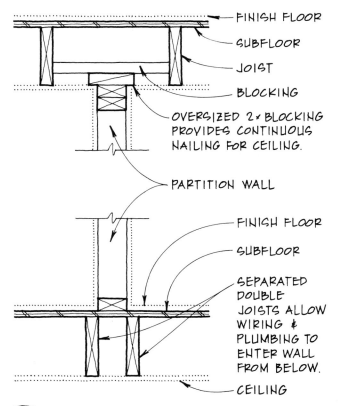

— FINISH FLOOR

— SUBFLOOR

— JOIST

— CEILING

— BLOCKING @ 16 IN. OR 24 IN. O.C. BETWEEN JOISTS

— PARTITION WALL

— FINISH FLOOR

— SUBFLOOR

— DOUBLE JOISTS BELOW PARTITION WALL

— CEILING

C JOISTS @ PARTITION WALL
JOISTS || TO WALL

— FINISH FLOOR

— SUBFLOOR

— JOIST

— BLOCKING

— OVERSIZED 2× BLOCKING PROVIDES CONTINUOUS NAILING FOR CEILING.

— PARTITION WALL

— FINISH FLOOR

— SUBFLOOR

— SEPARATED DOUBLE JOISTS ALLOW WIRING & PLUMBING TO ENTER WALL FROM BELOW.

— CEILING

D JOISTS @ PARTITION WALL
ALTERNATIVE DETAILS

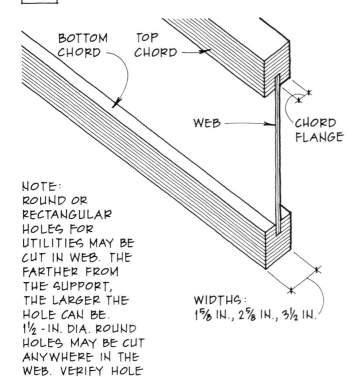

NOTE:
ROUND OR RECTANGULAR HOLES FOR UTILITIES MAY BE CUT IN WEB. THE FARTHER FROM THE SUPPORT, THE LARGER THE HOLE CAN BE. 1½-IN. DIA. ROUND HOLES MAY BE CUT ANYWHERE IN THE WEB. VERIFY HOLE SIZE AND LOCATION W/ MANUFACTURER.

BOTTOM CHORD

TOP CHORD

WEB

CHORD FLANGE

WIDTHS: 1⅝ IN., 2⅝ IN., 3½ IN.

Plywood I-joists are designed to act as a small truss and are manufactured with laminated webs and laminated or solid top and bottom chords. I-joists are straighter and more precisely sized than dimension lumber and therefore make a flatter and quieter floor. Their spanning capacity for a given depth is only slightly greater than that of dimension lumber, but because they can be manufactured much deeper and longer than lumber joists (up to 20 in. deep and 60 ft. long), they may be the floor-framing system of choice when long spans are required (16 in. I-joists can span 27 ft. with residential floor loads). Carpenters comment that plywood I-joists are practical for long spans and simple plans, but difficult for complicated buildings.

I-joists can be attached to each other with metal straps and hangers and can be cut on site. I-joists are about 50% lighter than lumber joists and do not have as much strength in compression under concentrated loads. They must therefore be stiffened under bearing walls and in other conditons as required by manufacturers' specifications and local codes.

Ⓐ PLYWOOD I-JOISTS

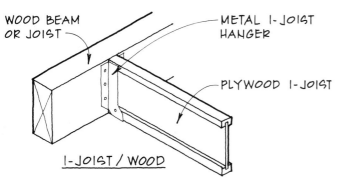

WOOD BEAM OR JOIST

METAL I-JOIST HANGER

PLYWOOD I-JOIST

I-JOIST / WOOD

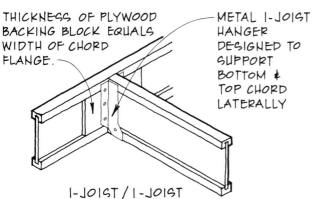

THICKNESS OF PLYWOOD BACKING BLOCK EQUALS WIDTH OF CHORD FLANGE.

METAL I-JOIST HANGER DESIGNED TO SUPPORT BOTTOM & TOP CHORD LATERALLY

I-JOIST / I-JOIST

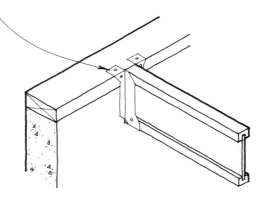

SPECIAL METAL HANGERS FOR SUCH CONDITIONS AS TOP-MOUNTED JOISTS & SKEWED JOISTS ARE AVAILABLE FOR ATTACHING I-JOISTS.

SPECIAL CONDITIONS

Ⓑ PLYWOOD I-JOIST CONNECTIONS

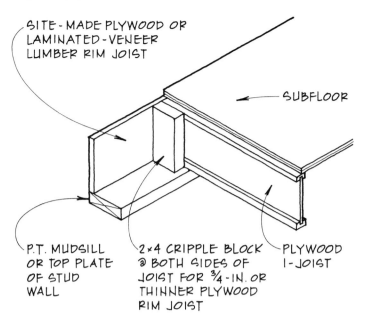

SITE-MADE PLYWOOD OR LAMINATED-VENEER LUMBER RIM JOIST

SUBFLOOR

P.T. MUDSILL OR TOP PLATE OF STUD WALL

2×4 CRIPPLE BLOCK @ BOTH SIDES OF JOIST FOR ¾-IN. OR THINNER PLYWOOD RIM JOIST

PLYWOOD I-JOIST

NOTE:
LAMINATED-VENEER LUMBER (LVL) JOISTS ARE SIZED TO CORRESPOND W/ DEPTH OF PLYWOOD I-JOIST SIZES see | 32A |

 A) PLYWOOD I-JOISTS @ RIM JOIST
PLYWOOD RIM JOIST W/ BLOCKING

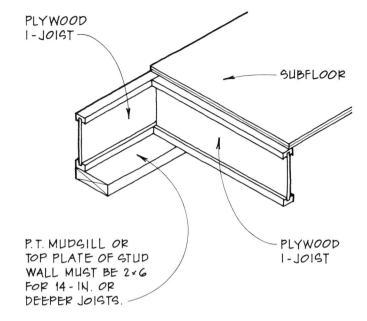

PLYWOOD I-JOIST

SUBFLOOR

P.T. MUDSILL OR TOP PLATE OF STUD WALL MUST BE 2×6 FOR 14-IN. OR DEEPER JOISTS.

PLYWOOD I-JOIST

B) PLYWOOD I-JOISTS @ RIM JOIST
I-JOIST AS RIM JOIST

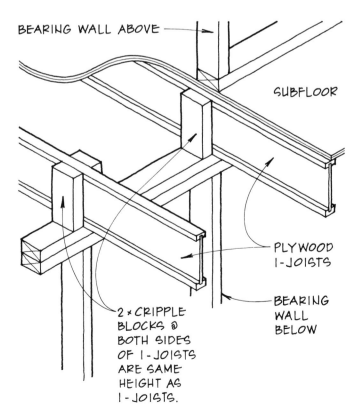

BEARING WALL ABOVE

SUBFLOOR

PLYWOOD I-JOISTS

BEARING WALL BELOW

2× CRIPPLE BLOCKS @ BOTH SIDES OF I-JOISTS ARE SAME HEIGHT AS I-JOISTS.

 **C) PLYWOOD I-JOISTS @ INTERIOR**
2× CRIPPLE BLOCKS @ BEARING WALLS

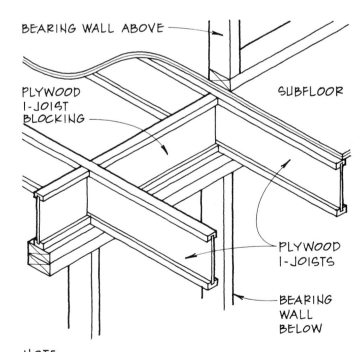

BEARING WALL ABOVE

PLYWOOD I-JOIST BLOCKING

SUBFLOOR

PLYWOOD I-JOISTS

BEARING WALL BELOW

NOTE:
SINCE I-JOISTS CAN BE MANUFACTURED IN CONTINUOUS LENGTHS UP TO 60 FT., THEY RARELY NEED TO BE SPLICED @ INTERIOR BEARING WALLS.

 **D) PLYWOOD I-JOISTS @ INTERIOR**
I-JOIST BLOCKING @ BEARING WALLS

Four-by-two wood floor trusses are made up of small members (usually 2x4s) that are connected so that they act like a single large member. The parallel top and bottom chords and the webs are made of lumber held together at the intersections with toothed metal plates.

The open web allows for utilities to run through the floor without altering the truss. Round ducts from 5 in. to 16 in. in diameter can be accommodated, depending on the depth of the truss. Truss depths vary from 10 in. to 24 in., with spans up to about 30 ft. Like plywood I-joists, floor trusses are practical for long spans and simple plans, but difficult for complicated buildings.

Floor trusses are custom manufactured for each job, and cannot be altered at the site. Bearing walls, floor openings and other departures from the simple span should always be engineered by the manufacturer.

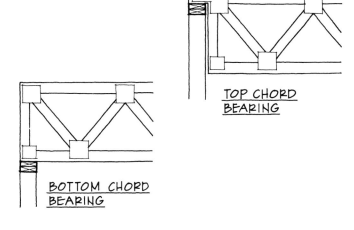

TOP CHORD
BEARING

BOTTOM CHORD
BEARING

METAL PLATE

TOP CHORD

WEB

BOTTOM CHORD

A   **WOOD FLOOR TRUSSES**

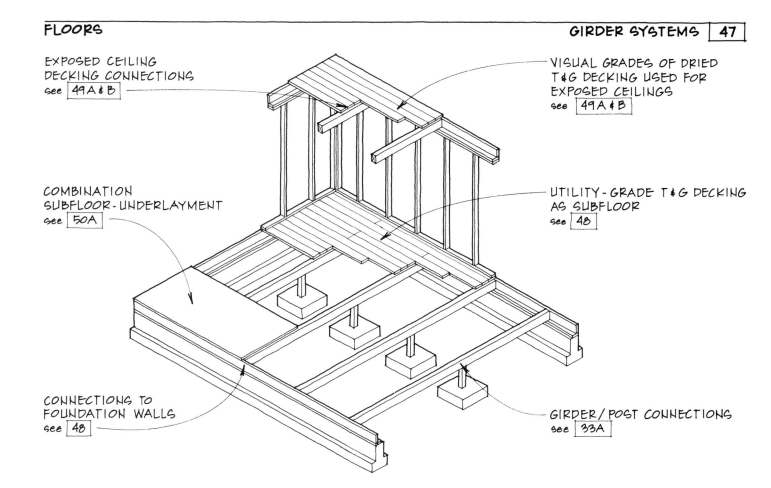

EXPOSED CEILING
DECKING CONNECTIONS
see | 49A & B |

VISUAL GRADES OF DRIED
T&G DECKING USED FOR
EXPOSED CEILINGS
see | 49A & B |

COMBINATION
SUBFLOOR-UNDERLAYMENT
see | 50A |

UTILITY-GRADE T&G DECKING
AS SUBFLOOR
see | 48 |

CONNECTIONS TO
FOUNDATION WALLS
see | 48 |

GIRDER/POST CONNECTIONS
see | 33A |

Girder systems may be designed with either dimension or laminated lumber. They are most common in the Northwest, where dimension timber is plentiful. Girder-floor systems are similar to joist-floor systems except that girders, which are wider than joists, can carry a greater load for a given span and therefore can be spaced at wider intervals than joists. Girders are typically placed on 48-in. centers, so long-spanning subfloor materials such as 2-in. T&G decking and 1⅛-in. combination subfloor-underlayment are required (see 50A).

When used over crawl spaces, girders may be supported directly on posts. Over a basement, a girder system may be supported on posts or may bear on a wall or a beam like a joist system. At upper-floor levels, girder systems are often used in conjunction with an exposed T&G decking ceiling. These exposed ceilings can make wiring, plumbing and ductwork difficult.

Girder spans	
Size, species, grade & spacing	Span (ft.)
4x6 Douglas-fir #2 @ 48 in. o.c.	8.6
4x8 Douglas-fir #2 @ 48 in. o.c.	11.3
4x10 Douglas-fir #2 @ 48 in. o.c.	14.4
4x12 Douglas-fir #2 @ 48 in. o.c.	17.6

This table assumes a 40-psf live load, a 10-psf dead load and a deflection of L/360. The table is for estimating purposes only. No. 2 Douglas-fir is most prevalent in regions where girder systems are most frequently used.

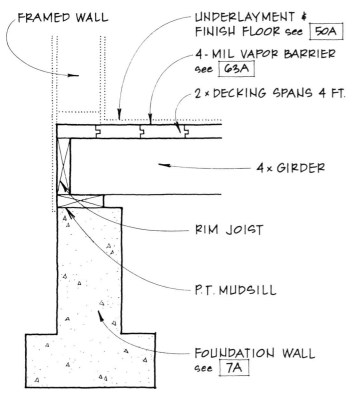

FRAMED WALL

UNDERLAYMENT &
FINISH FLOOR see 50A

4-MIL VAPOR BARRIER
see 63A

2×DECKING SPANS 4 FT.

4×GIRDER

RIM JOIST

P.T. MUDSILL

FOUNDATION WALL
see 7A

Ⓐ GIRDERS ON MUDSILL
GIRDERS ⊥ TO WALL

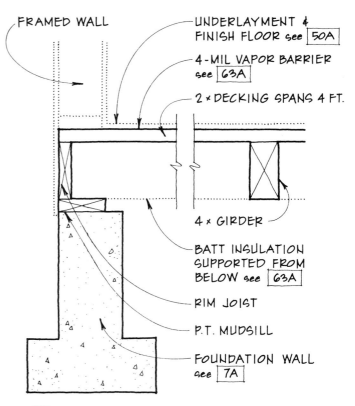

FRAMED WALL

UNDERLAYMENT &
FINISH FLOOR see 50A

4-MIL VAPOR BARRIER
see 63A

2×DECKING SPANS 4 FT.

4×GIRDER

BATT INSULATION
SUPPORTED FROM
BELOW see 63A

RIM JOIST

P.T. MUDSILL

FOUNDATION WALL
see 7A

Ⓑ GIRDERS ON MUDSILL
GIRDERS ‖ TO WALL

NOTE:
THIS DETAIL IS NOT RECOMMENDED FOR GIRDERS
OVER 4×8 BECAUSE OF POTENTIAL SHRINKAGE
PROBLEMS. FOR BEAM-POCKET DETAIL see 18C

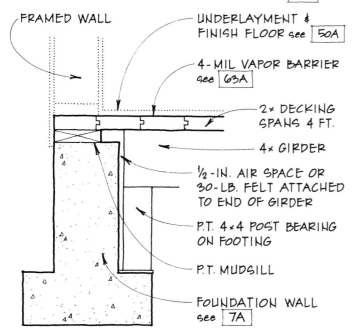

FRAMED WALL

UNDERLAYMENT &
FINISH FLOOR see 50A

4-MIL VAPOR BARRIER
see 63A

2×DECKING
SPANS 4 FT.

4×GIRDER

½-IN. AIR SPACE OR
30-LB. FELT ATTACHED
TO END OF GIRDER

P.T. 4×4 POST BEARING
ON FOOTING

P.T. MUDSILL

FOUNDATION WALL
see 7A

Ⓒ GIRDERS FLUSH W/ MUDSILL
GIRDERS ⊥ TO WALL

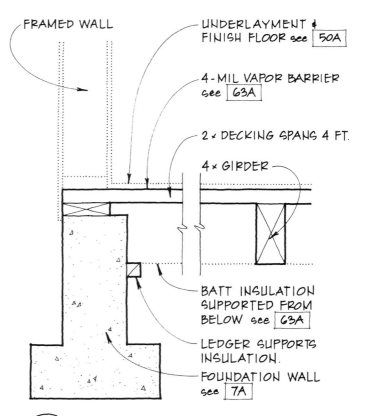

FRAMED WALL

UNDERLAYMENT &
FINISH FLOOR see 50A

4-MIL VAPOR BARRIER
see 63A

2×DECKING SPANS 4 FT.

4×GIRDER

BATT INSULATION
SUPPORTED FROM
BELOW see 63A

LEDGER SUPPORTS
INSULATION.

FOUNDATION WALL
see 7A

Ⓓ GIRDERS FLUSH W/ MUDSILL
GIRDERS ‖ TO WALL

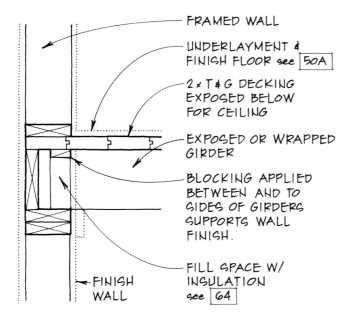

FRAMED WALL

UNDERLAYMENT & FINISH FLOOR see 50A

2 x T & G DECKING EXPOSED BELOW FOR CEILING

EXPOSED OR WRAPPED GIRDER

BLOCKING APPLIED BETWEEN AND TO SIDES OF GIRDERS SUPPORTS WALL FINISH.

FILL SPACE W/ INSULATION see 64

←FINISH WALL

NOTE:
2 x T & G DECKING MAY BE SANDED TO MAKE FINISH FLOOR, BUT THIS IS ADVISABLE ONLY W/ VERY DRY DECKING. DUST FILTRATION FROM UPPER TO LOWER FLOOR & SOUND TRANSMISSION BETWEEN FLOORS MAY OCCUR WITH THIS DETAIL.

(A) GIRDERS W/ EXPOSED DECKING
2 ND FLOOR : GIRDERS ⊥ TO WALL

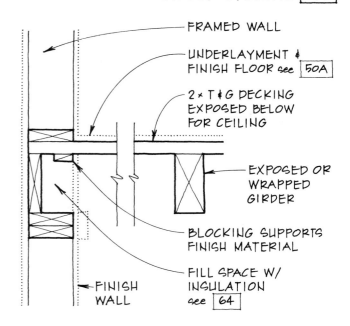

FRAMED WALL

UNDERLAYMENT & FINISH FLOOR see 50A

2 x T & G DECKING EXPOSED BELOW FOR CEILING

EXPOSED OR WRAPPED GIRDER

BLOCKING SUPPORTS FINISH MATERIAL

FILL SPACE W/ INSULATION see 64

←FINISH WALL

NOTE:
DECKING DOES NOT PROVIDE STRUCTURAL DIAPHRAGM REQUIRED @ UPPER FLOORS. USE PLYWOOD UNDERLAYMENT OR OTHER METHOD TO TRANSFER LATERAL LOADS.

(B) GIRDERS W/ EXPOSED DECKING
2 ND FLOOR : GIRDERS || TO WALL

Subflooring—Subflooring is the structural skin of a floor system. It spans between the joists and acts as a diaphragm to transfer horizontal loads to the walls of a structure. For joist systems, subflooring is typically tongue-and-groove (T&G) plywood or non-veneered panels such as waferboard, oriented-strand board (OSB) or particleboard. In girder systems, subflooring is typically T&G decking or T&G plywood combination subfloor/underlayment, which is a grade of T&G plywood that is plugged and sanded to a smooth underlayment-grade surface.

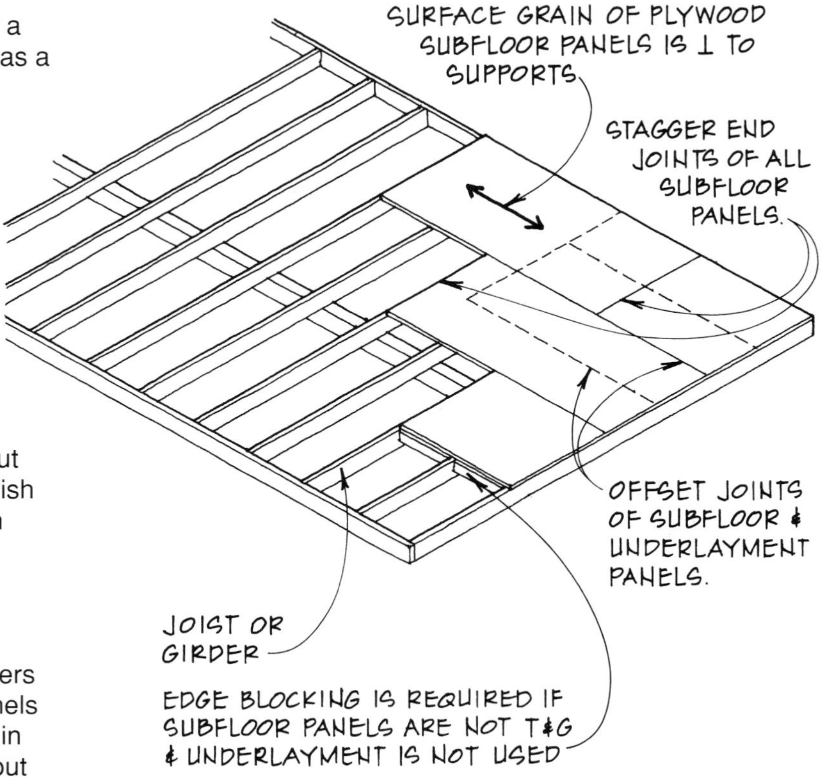
SURFACE GRAIN OF PLYWOOD SUBFLOOR PANELS IS ⊥ TO SUPPORTS
STAGGER END JOINTS OF ALL SUBFLOOR PANELS.
OFFSET JOINTS OF SUBFLOOR & UNDERLAYMENT PANELS.
JOIST OR GIRDER
EDGE BLOCKING IS REQUIRED IF SUBFLOOR PANELS ARE NOT T&G & UNDERLAYMENT IS NOT USED

Underlayment—Underlayment is not structural but provides a smooth surface necessary for some finish floors. It can also be used to fur up floors to match an adjacent finish floor of a different thickness. Underlayment is typically plywood, particleboard or hardboard.

Spacing and nailing—Most plywood manufacturers specify a space of ⅛ in. between the edges of panels to allow for expansion. Panels sized ⅛ in. smaller in each direction are available to allow a space without compromising the 4-ft. by 8-ft. module. The procedure may be successfully avoided in dry climates. Check with local contractors for accepted local practice.

A common rule of thumb is to nail panels 6 in. o.c. at edges and 12 in. o.c. in the panel field. Glues and panel adhesives can minimize squeaks and reduce the nailing requirements for panel-floor systems. Verify attachment methods with the specifications of the manufacturer. A typical plywood grade stamp is shown below.

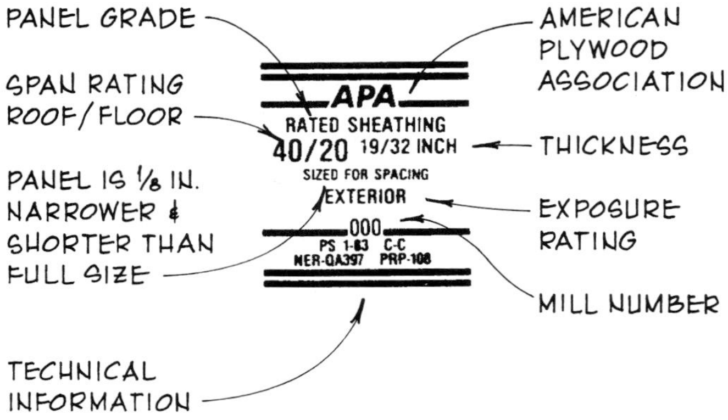
PANEL GRADE
SPAN RATING ROOF/FLOOR
PANEL IS ⅛ IN. NARROWER & SHORTER THAN FULL SIZE
TECHNICAL INFORMATION
AMERICAN PLYWOOD ASSOCIATION
THICKNESS
EXPOSURE RATING
MILL NUMBER
APA
RATED SHEATHING
40/20 19/32 INCH
SIZED FOR SPACING
EXTERIOR
000
PS 1-83 C-C
NER-QA397 PRP-108

Subflooring spans

Subfloor type	Thickness	Maximum span
Plywood sheathing or combination subfloor underlayment	½ in. to ⅝ in. ⅝ in. to ¾ in. ¾ in. to ⅞ in. 1⅛ in.	16 in. 20 in. 24 in. 48 in.
Non-veneered panels: OSB, waferboard, particleboard	⅝ in. ¾ in.	16 in. 24 in.

The values in this table are based on information from the American Plywood Association (A.P.A.) and the Uniform Building Code (UBC). Values are for panels that are continuous over two or more spans, with the long dimension of the panel perpendicular to supports. Verify span with panel rating.

A SUBFLOORING & UNDERLAYMENT
PLYWOOD & NON-VENEERED PANELS

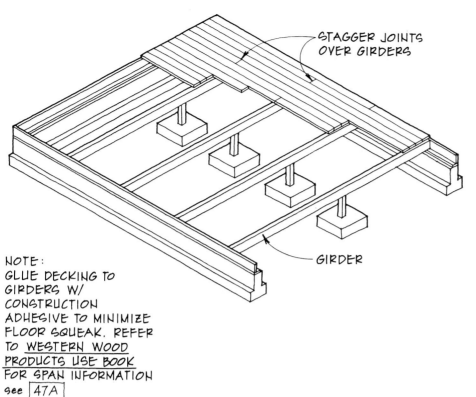

STAGGER JOINTS OVER GIRDERS

GIRDER

NOTE:
GLUE DECKING TO GIRDERS W/ CONSTRUCTION ADHESIVE TO MINIMIZE FLOOR SQUEAK. REFER TO WESTERN WOOD PRODUCTS USE BOOK FOR SPAN INFORMATION
see 47A

 A   **SUBFLOORING**
      T&G DECKING

TYPICAL T&G DECKING SECTIONS

2×6 V-JOINT IS MOST COMMONLY USED ON UPPER FLOORS TO MAKE EXPOSED CEILINGS BELOW. MOST SPECIES WILL SPAN 4 FT.

2×8 UTILITY IS USED PRIMARILY AS SUBFLOOR OVER CRAWL SPACES OR BASEMENTS, & IS OFTEN INSTALLED GREEN. IT WILL SPAN 4 FT. IN MOST FLOOR SITUATIONS.

3× & 4× LAMINATED IS USED MOSTLY AT ROOFS TO MAKE EXPOSED CEILINGS BELOW, BUT ALSO AS FLOORING. DECKING IS END MATCHED FOR RANDOM-LENGTH APPLICATION & IS AVAILABLE PREFINISHED IN 3×6, 3×8, 4×6 & 4×8 SIZES. IT SPANS UP TO 14 FT. FOR RESIDENTIAL FLOOR LOADS.

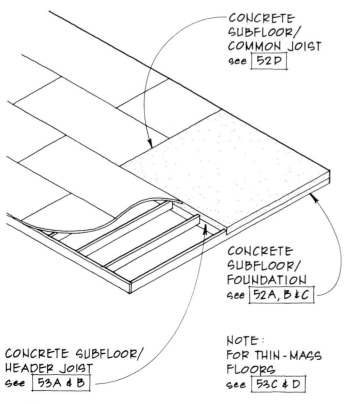

CONCRETE SUBFLOOR/ COMMON JOIST
see 52D

CONCRETE SUBFLOOR/ FOUNDATION
see 52A, B & C

CONCRETE SUBFLOOR/ HEADER JOIST
see 53A & B

NOTE:
FOR THIN-MASS FLOORS
see 53C & D

A small part of the subfloor may need to be concrete to support tiles or for a passive-solar mass floor at a south edge. The structure under the concrete must be lowered in order to accommodate the extra thickness of the concrete, typically 2¼ in. to 3 in. Use plywood that is rated to carry the load of wet concrete, usually ¾ in. (min.).

In the case of a tiled floor, the complications of adjusting the structure to accommodate a thick concrete subfloor may be avoided by using a $7/16$-in. thick glass-fiber-reinforced cement board over the surface of the typical wood subfloor. Check with the tile manufacturer for recommendations.

B   **SUBFLOORING**
      CONCRETE

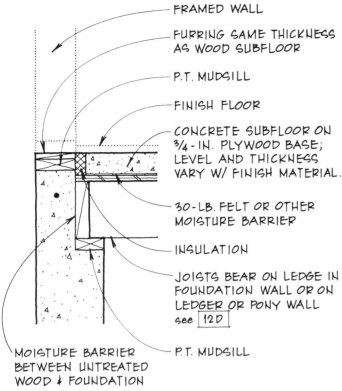

- FRAMED WALL
- FURRING SAME THICKNESS AS WOOD SUBFLOOR
- P.T. MUDSILL
- FINISH FLOOR
- CONCRETE SUBFLOOR ON ¾-IN. PLYWOOD BASE; LEVEL AND THICKNESS VARY W/ FINISH MATERIAL.
- 30-LB. FELT OR OTHER MOISTURE BARRIER
- INSULATION
- JOISTS BEAR ON LEDGE IN FOUNDATION WALL OR ON LEDGER OR PONY WALL see 12D
- MOISTURE BARRIER BETWEEN UNTREATED WOOD & FOUNDATION
- P.T. MUDSILL

A   **CONCRETE SUBFLOOR @ EXTERIOR**
FULL-DEPTH JOISTS BELOW MUDSILL

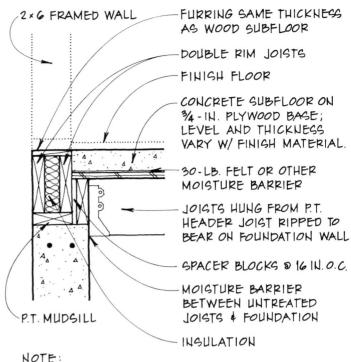

- 2×6 FRAMED WALL
- FURRING SAME THICKNESS AS WOOD SUBFLOOR
- DOUBLE RIM JOISTS
- FINISH FLOOR
- CONCRETE SUBFLOOR ON ¾-IN. PLYWOOD BASE; LEVEL AND THICKNESS VARY W/ FINISH MATERIAL.
- 30-LB. FELT OR OTHER MOISTURE BARRIER
- JOISTS HUNG FROM P.T. HEADER JOIST RIPPED TO BEAR ON FOUNDATION WALL
- SPACER BLOCKS @ 16 IN. O.C.
- MOISTURE BARRIER BETWEEN UNTREATED JOISTS & FOUNDATION
- INSULATION
- P.T. MUDSILL

NOTE:
FOR 2×4 WALL, PLACE INSULATION BETWEEN DOUBLE RIM JOIST & P.T. HEADER JOIST.

B   **CONCRETE SUBFLOOR @ EXTERIOR**
FULL-DEPTH JOISTS / ALTERNATIVE

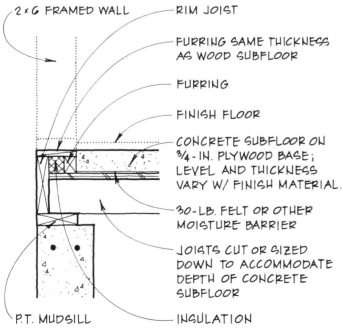

- 2×6 FRAMED WALL
- RIM JOIST
- FURRING SAME THICKNESS AS WOOD SUBFLOOR
- FURRING
- FINISH FLOOR
- CONCRETE SUBFLOOR ON ¾-IN. PLYWOOD BASE; LEVEL AND THICKNESS VARY W/ FINISH MATERIAL.
- 30-LB. FELT OR OTHER MOISTURE BARRIER
- JOISTS CUT OR SIZED DOWN TO ACCOMMODATE DEPTH OF CONCRETE SUBFLOOR
- P.T. MUDSILL
- INSULATION

NOTE:
DECREASE SPAN &/OR SPACING OF SIZED-DOWN JOISTS SUPPORTING CONCRETE.

C   **CONCRETE SUBFLOOR @ EXTERIOR**
CUT-DOWN JOISTS ON MUDSILL

NOTE:
FOR CONDITION @ EXTERIOR WALL see 52A OR B

NOTE:
FOR CONDITION @ EXTERIOR WALL see 52C

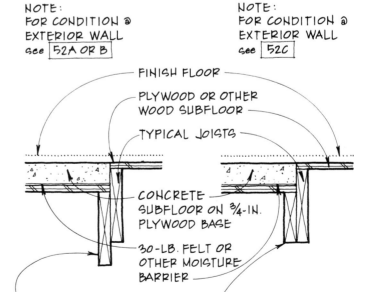

- FINISH FLOOR
- PLYWOOD OR OTHER WOOD SUBFLOOR
- TYPICAL JOISTS
- CONCRETE SUBFLOOR ON ¾-IN. PLYWOOD BASE
- 30-LB. FELT OR OTHER MOISTURE BARRIER
- LOWERED JOISTS MAY NEED TO BE SIZED DEEPER THAN TYPICAL FULL-DEPTH JOIST TO SUPPORT CONCRETE SUBFLOOR.
- CUT OR SIZED-DOWN JOIST; DECREASE SPAN &/OR SPACING TO SUPPORT CONCRETE SUBFLOOR.

D   **CONCRETE SUBFLOOR @ INTERIOR**
EDGE ‖ TO JOISTS / 2 DETAILS

NOTE:
FOR CONDITION @ EXTERIOR WALL
see 52A OR B

PLYWOOD OR OTHER
WOOD SUBFLOOR

FINISH
FLOOR

CONCRETE SUBFLOOR
ON ¾-IN. PLYWOOD
BASE

30-LB. FELT OR OTHER
MOISTURE BARRIER

JOIST ON JOIST HANGER

DOUBLE HEADER JOIST

SINGLE HEADER JOIST
NAILED TO DOUBLE
HEADER JOIST

JOIST ON
JOIST
HANGER

VERTICAL SUPPORT
AS REQUIRED

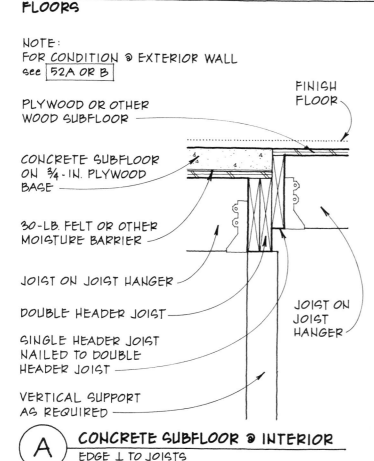

A CONCRETE SUBFLOOR @ INTERIOR
EDGE ⊥ TO JOISTS

FINISH FLOOR

CONCRETE
SUBFLOOR ON ¾-IN.
PLYWOOD BASE

CUT-DOWN JOIST

VERTICAL SUPPORT
AS REQUIRED

FINISH FLOOR

CONCRETE
SUBFLOOR ON ¾-IN.
PLYWOOD BASE

30-LB. FELT OR OTHER
MOISTURE BARRIER

NOTCHED JOIST

BLOCKING

BEAM OR STUD-WALL
SUPPORT AS REQUIRED

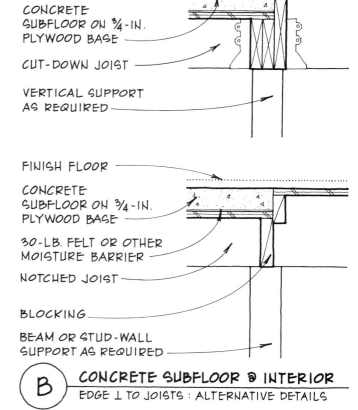

B CONCRETE SUBFLOOR @ INTERIOR
EDGE ⊥ TO JOISTS : ALTERNATIVE DETAILS

STUD WALL FRAMED
AFTER CONCRETE IS
FINISHED

DOUBLE 2× P.T. PLATE
SERVES AS SCREED.

3-IN. CONCRETE
SUBFLOOR ON ¾-IN.
PLYWOOD BASE

30-LB. FELT OR OTHER
MOISTURE BARRIER

JOIST

P.T. MUDSILL (OR TOP
PLATE IF THIN-MASS
SUBFLOOR IS AT
UPPER STORY)

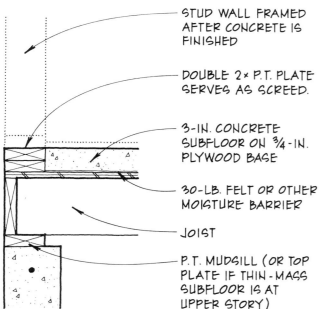

NOTE:
THIS DETAIL IS USED TO PROVIDE MASS TO A LARGE
AREA OF FLOOR FOR SOLAR GAIN.

C THIN-MASS SUBFLOOR
@ EXTERIOR WALL

STUD WALL FRAMED
AFTER CONCRETE IS
FINISHED

DOUBLE 2× P.T. PLATE
SERVES AS SCREED &
ALLOWS UTILITIES TO
PASS THROUGH FLOOR
SYSTEM @ WALL

3-IN. CONCRETE
SUBFLOOR ON ¾-IN.
PLYWOOD BASE

30-LB. FELT OR OTHER
MOISTURE BARRIER

JOIST

BLOCKING

STRUCTURE BELOW
AS REQUIRED

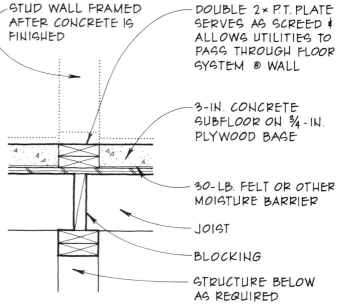
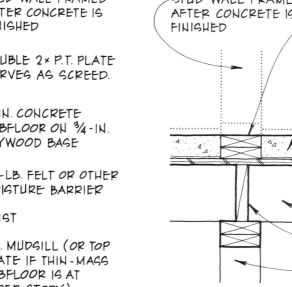

NOTE:
IF THE CONCRETE IS TO BE EXPOSED, THE DOUBLE
PLATE MAY BE OMITTED FOR EASE OF TROWELING.
THE STUD WALL MAY THEN BE SHOT TO CONCRETE
see 25C

D THIN-MASS SUBFLOOR
@ INTERIOR WALL

Porches and decks are traditional and useful additions to wood-frame structures. They provide a transition between indoors and out, allowing people to pause upon entering or leaving, and they extend the building to include the out-of-doors. Porch and deck floors must be constructed differently from interior floors in order to withstand the weather. The connection between porch and deck floors and the building itself is especially critical in keeping moisture out of the main structure. Because of constant exposure to the weather, this connection must be detailed in such a way that it can be repaired or replaced.

Waterproof porch—A waterproof porch or deck floor can be treated like a flat roof. As shown in the drawing below, flashing (or the roofing material itself) must be tucked under the siding to catch water running down the side of the building, and the floor (roof) surface must be sloped away from the building (see 58A). The framing for waterproof decks over living spaces needs proper ventilation (see 193A).

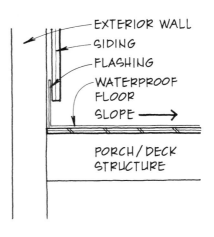

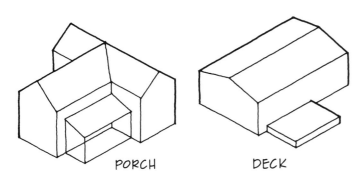

PORCH   DECK

The floors of porches and decks can be grouped into two major types: those that are waterproof and thus act as a roof protecting the area below them, and those that are open and allow water to pass through them.

Open porch—In an open porch or deck floor, the parts that connect it to the main structure are exposed to the weather, yet need to penetrate the skin of the wall. This connection can be accomplished by keeping the porch/deck structure away from the exterior wall and attaching it only at intervals with spaced connectors (see 56B & C).

Alternatively, a continuous ledger may be bolted to the wall and flashed (see 57A).

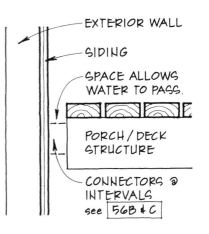

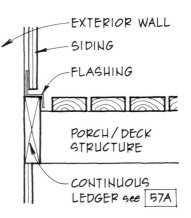

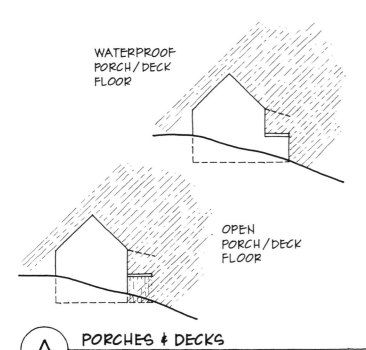

WATERPROOF PORCH/DECK FLOOR

OPEN PORCH/DECK FLOOR

Porches and decks are exposed directly to the weather in ways that the main part of the structure is not. Consequently, the wood used in porches and decks is much more susceptible to expansion and contraction, twisting, checking and rotting. A special strategy for building porches and decks is therefore appropriate.

Weather resistance—Elements of porches and decks that are likely to get wet should be constructed of weather-resistant materials. Virtually all the material required to make a new porch or deck including T&G flooring is now available in pressure-treated lumber. Weather-resistant woods like cedar and redwood are also appropriate. Flat-grain boards oriented horizontally, such as rail caps and decking, should be placed with the bark side up (as shown) so if they cup, the boards will shed water.

Connectors—At least once a year, joints exposed to the weather will shrink and swell, causing nails to withdraw and the joints to weaken. Joints made with screws or bolts will outlast those made with nails. For joist connections, use joist hangers and angle clips.

Air circulation—Areas between adjacent wood members collect moisture and are especially prone to rot. Even pressure-treated lumber can rot in this situation. Avoid doubling up members in exposed situations. It is better to use a single large timber where extra strength is required, as shown in the drawing at right.   POOR   GOOD

Where wood must touch another surface, make the area of contact as small as possible and allow for air circulation around the joint.

Painting—Sealers and preservatives will extend the life of porches and decks. Special attention should be given to end grain and to areas likely to hold moisture. Stains will outlast paints. Special porch and deck paints are available for use where exposure to the weather is not severe.

(A) **PORCH & DECK CONSTRUCTION**

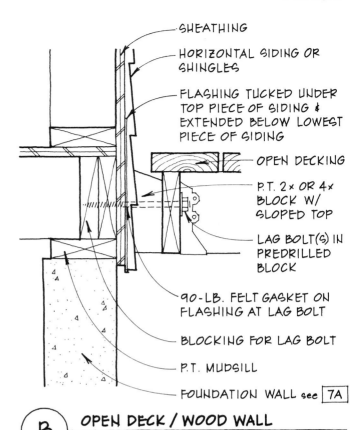

SHEATHING

SIDING

P.T. MUDSILL

MAINTAIN 1-IN. GAP BELOW WOOD SIDING.

OPEN DECKING

DECK JOIST

P.T. HEADER JOIST BOLTED TO FOUNDATION WALL

FOUNDATION WALL see 7A

(A) OPEN DECK / FOUNDATION WALL

SHEATHING

HORIZONTAL SIDING OR SHINGLES

FLASHING TUCKED UNDER TOP PIECE OF SIDING & EXTENDED BELOW LOWEST PIECE OF SIDING

OPEN DECKING

P.T. 2× OR 4× BLOCK W/ SLOPED TOP

LAG BOLT(S) IN PREDRILLED BLOCK

90-LB. FELT GASKET ON FLASHING AT LAG BOLT

BLOCKING FOR LAG BOLT

P.T. MUDSILL

FOUNDATION WALL see 7A

(B) OPEN DECK / WOOD WALL
1ST FLOOR : HORIZONTAL SIDING OR SHINGLES

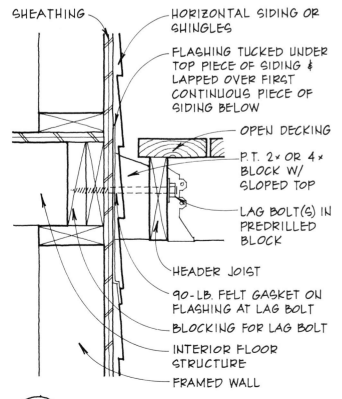

SHEATHING

HORIZONTAL SIDING OR SHINGLES

FLASHING TUCKED UNDER TOP PIECE OF SIDING & LAPPED OVER FIRST CONTINUOUS PIECE OF SIDING BELOW

OPEN DECKING

P.T. 2× OR 4× BLOCK W/ SLOPED TOP

LAG BOLT(S) IN PREDRILLED BLOCK

HEADER JOIST

90-LB. FELT GASKET ON FLASHING AT LAG BOLT

BLOCKING FOR LAG BOLT

INTERIOR FLOOR STRUCTURE

FRAMED WALL

(C) OPEN DECK / WOOD WALL
2ND FLOOR : HORIZONTAL SIDING OR SHINGLES

NOTES :
FLASHING EXTENDS 8 IN. MIN. PAST BOTH SIDES OF BLOCK SPACERS. INSTALL SPACER BLOCKS SIMULTANEOUSLY W/ SIDING & FLASHING, THEN INSTALL DECK.
OPEN DECKING LAID DIAGONALLY ACROSS JOIST SYSTEM ACTS AS A DIAPHRAGM, WHICH MAY ELIMINATE THE NEED FOR BRACING PORCH SUPPORTS.
DETAILS SHOW LEVEL OF DECK SLIGHTLY BELOW LEVEL OF FINISH FLOOR. IN SNOW COUNTRY, ADJUST DECK LEVEL TO ACCOUNT FOR SNOW BUILDUP.

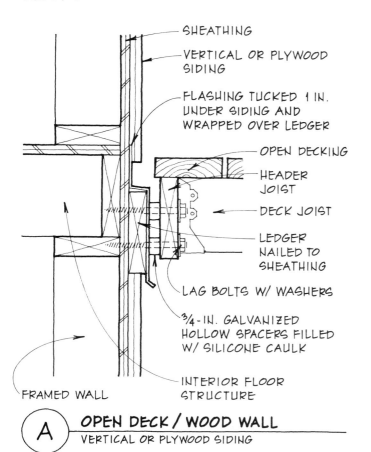

SHEATHING

VERTICAL OR PLYWOOD SIDING

FLASHING TUCKED 1 IN. UNDER SIDING AND WRAPPED OVER LEDGER

OPEN DECKING

HEADER JOIST

DECK JOIST

LEDGER NAILED TO SHEATHING

LAG BOLTS W/ WASHERS

¾-IN. GALVANIZED HOLLOW SPACERS FILLED W/ SILICONE CAULK

INTERIOR FLOOR STRUCTURE

FRAMED WALL

(A) **OPEN DECK / WOOD WALL**
VERTICAL OR PLYWOOD SIDING

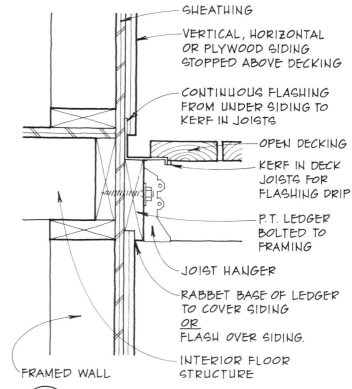

SHEATHING

VERTICAL, HORIZONTAL OR PLYWOOD SIDING STOPPED ABOVE DECKING

CONTINUOUS FLASHING FROM UNDER SIDING TO KERF IN JOISTS

OPEN DECKING

KERF IN DECK JOISTS FOR FLASHING DRIP

P.T. LEDGER BOLTED TO FRAMING

JOIST HANGER

RABBET BASE OF LEDGER TO COVER SIDING OR FLASH OVER SIDING.

INTERIOR FLOOR STRUCTURE

FRAMED WALL

(B) **OPEN DECK / WOOD WALL**
VERTICAL, HORIZONTAL OR PLYWOOD SIDING

OPEN RAILING BOLTED TO JOISTS OR AS EXTENSION OF VERTICAL SUPPORT
see 61A

OPEN DECKING

DECK JOIST SUPPORTED BY JOIST HANGER ON HEADER JOIST

HEADER JOIST BOLTED TO VERTICAL SUPPORTS

SKIRTING

STUD WALL, WOOD POST OR OTHER VERTICAL SUPPORT

(C) **OPEN DECK / OPEN RAILING**

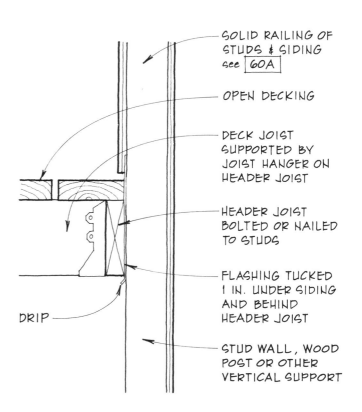

SOLID RAILING OF STUDS & SIDING
see 60A

OPEN DECKING

DECK JOIST SUPPORTED BY JOIST HANGER ON HEADER JOIST

HEADER JOIST BOLTED OR NAILED TO STUDS

FLASHING TUCKED 1 IN. UNDER SIDING AND BEHIND HEADER JOIST

STUD WALL, WOOD POST OR OTHER VERTICAL SUPPORT

DRIP

(D) **OPEN DECK / SOLID RAILING**

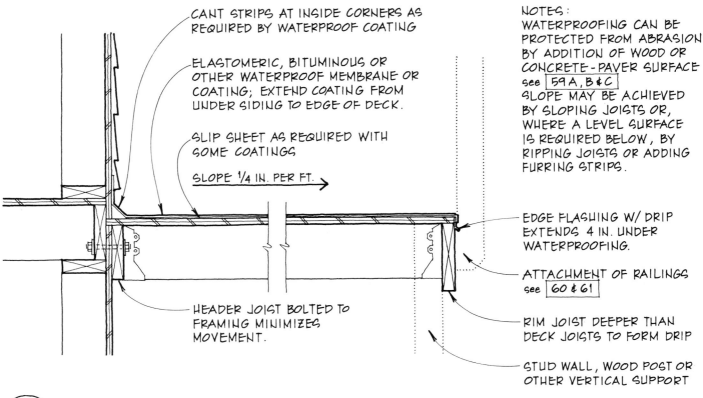

CANT STRIPS AT INSIDE CORNERS AS REQUIRED BY WATERPROOF COATING

ELASTOMERIC, BITUMINOUS OR OTHER WATERPROOF MEMBRANE OR COATING; EXTEND COATING FROM UNDER SIDING TO EDGE OF DECK.

SLIP SHEET AS REQUIRED WITH SOME COATINGS

SLOPE 1/4 IN. PER FT. →

NOTES:
WATERPROOFING CAN BE PROTECTED FROM ABRASION BY ADDITION OF WOOD OR CONCRETE - PAVER SURFACE see 59 A, B & C
SLOPE MAY BE ACHIEVED BY SLOPING JOISTS OR, WHERE A LEVEL SURFACE IS REQUIRED BELOW, BY RIPPING JOISTS OR ADDING FURRING STRIPS.

EDGE FLASHING W/ DRIP EXTENDS 4 IN. UNDER WATERPROOFING.

ATTACHMENT OF RAILINGS see 60 & 61

RIM JOIST DEEPER THAN DECK JOISTS TO FORM DRIP

HEADER JOIST BOLTED TO FRAMING MINIMIZES MOVEMENT.

STUD WALL, WOOD POST OR OTHER VERTICAL SUPPORT

(A) WATERPROOF DECKS
GENERAL CHARACTERISTICS

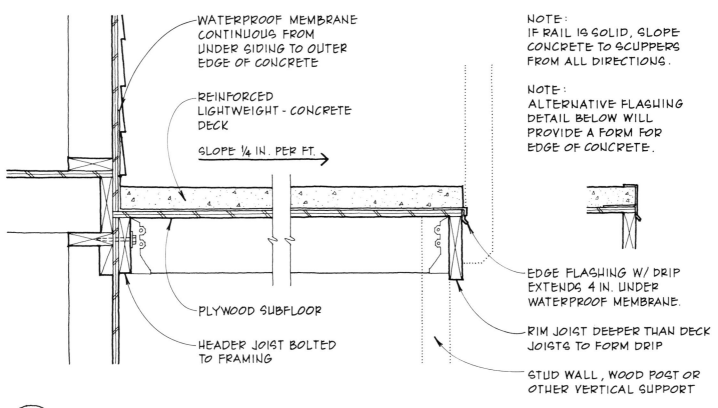

WATERPROOF MEMBRANE CONTINUOUS FROM UNDER SIDING TO OUTER EDGE OF CONCRETE

REINFORCED LIGHTWEIGHT - CONCRETE DECK

SLOPE 1/4 IN. PER FT. →

NOTE:
IF RAIL IS SOLID, SLOPE CONCRETE TO SCUPPERS FROM ALL DIRECTIONS.

NOTE:
ALTERNATIVE FLASHING DETAIL BELOW WILL PROVIDE A FORM FOR EDGE OF CONCRETE.

EDGE FLASHING W/ DRIP EXTENDS 4 IN. UNDER WATERPROOF MEMBRANE.

RIM JOIST DEEPER THAN DECK JOISTS TO FORM DRIP

PLYWOOD SUBFLOOR

HEADER JOIST BOLTED TO FRAMING

STUD WALL, WOOD POST OR OTHER VERTICAL SUPPORT

(B) LIGHTWEIGHT - CONCRETE PORCH DECK

OPEN RAIL (SHOWN) OR SOLID RAIL & SCUPPER see | 59D & 60A |

WATERPROOF MEMBRANE CONTINUOUS FROM UNDER SIDING TO FLASHING @ EDGE OF DECK

DUCKBOARDS see | 59B |

SLOPE 1/4 IN. PER FT.

EDGE FLASHING W/ DRIP

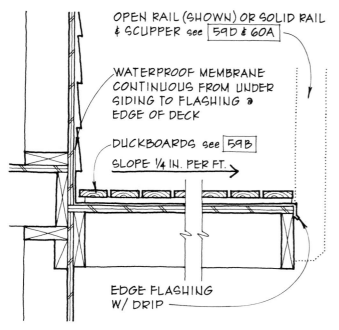

NOTE:
DUCKBOARD DECKS ARE GENERALLY HELD IN PLACE BY GRAVITY. THEY SHOULD NOT BE USED IN AREAS OF EXTREMELY HIGH WINDS.

(A) DUCKBOARD DECK
OPEN RAIL SHOWN

RECESSED SLEEPERS AT EDGES AGAINST WALL ALLOW WATER PASSAGE.

1x4 CEDAR, P.T. OR OTHER WEATHER-RESISTANT BOARDS SPACED 3/16 IN. APART

3/16 IN.

SLOPE OF DECK SURFACE

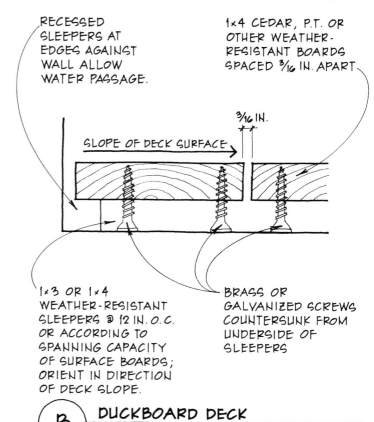

1x3 OR 1x4 WEATHER-RESISTANT SLEEPERS @ 12 IN. O.C. OR ACCORDING TO SPANNING CAPACITY OF SURFACE BOARDS; ORIENT IN DIRECTION OF DECK SLOPE.

BRASS OR GALVANIZED SCREWS COUNTERSUNK FROM UNDERSIDE OF SLEEPERS

(B) DUCKBOARD DECK
DETAIL

WATERPROOF MEMBRANE CONTINUOUS FROM UNDER SIDING TO SCUPPER THROUGH WALL

CONCRETE PAVERS SET ON 30-LB. OR 90-LB. FELT

CEDAR SLEEPER PROVIDES GUTTER @ SOLID RAIL & RETAINS PAVERS @ OPEN RAIL & ALLOWS FOR EXPANSION OF PAVERS.

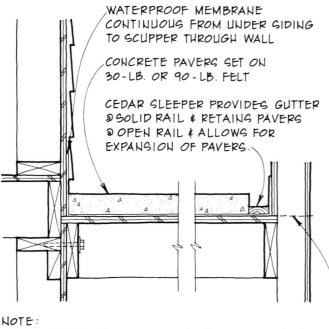

NOTE:
THIS DETAIL IS NOT RECOMMENDED IN AREAS OF SEVERE FREEZING WEATHER.

SCUPPER THROUGH SOLID RAIL see | 59D |

(C) CONCRETE-PAVER DECK
SOLID RAIL SHOWN

THROUGH-WALL FLASHING

SCUPPER

OVERFLOW OPENING

DRIP

DOWNSPOUT

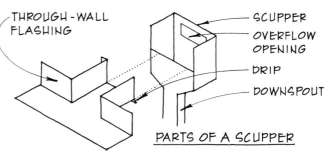

PARTS OF A SCUPPER

THROUGH-WALL FLASHING EXTENDS 4 IN. (MIN.) PAST WALL

LOW POINT IN DECK FLOOR

SIDING FORMS DRIP OVER WALL OPENING

EXTEND FLASHING DRIP BEYOND SIDING

SCUPPER

DOWNSPOUT

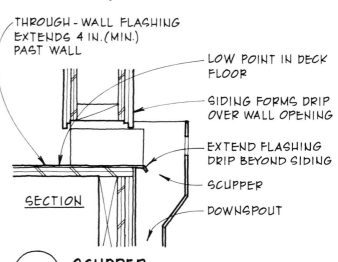

SECTION

(D) SCUPPER

Solid railings are relatively simple to design and construct to resist overturning due to lateral force because they make continuous contact with the porch or deck floor. For short railings (up to 8 ft. long) supported at both ends by a column, a wall or a corner, the simplest framing (see the drawing below) will suffice because the top edge may be made stiff enough to span between its two rigid ends.

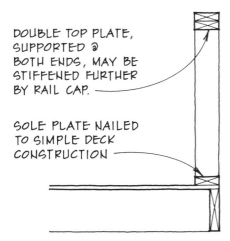

DOUBLE TOP PLATE, SUPPORTED @ BOTH ENDS, MAY BE STIFFENED FURTHER BY RAIL CAP.

SOLE PLATE NAILED TO SIMPLE DECK CONSTRUCTION

Longer railings or railings with one or both ends unsupported must be designed to resist lateral forces by means of a series of vertical supports firmly secured to the porch or deck floor framing (see the drawing below). This means, of course, that the porch floor framing itself must be solidly constructed.

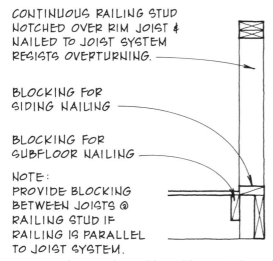

CONTINUOUS RAILING STUD NOTCHED OVER RIM JOIST & NAILED TO JOIST SYSTEM RESISTS OVERTURNING.

BLOCKING FOR SIDING NAILING

BLOCKING FOR SUBFLOOR NAILING

NOTE: PROVIDE BLOCKING BETWEEN JOISTS @ RAILING STUD IF RAILING IS PARALLEL TO JOIST SYSTEM.

The same results may be achieved in a porch or deck built over a living space by using a balloon-frame system with porch-rail studs continuous through to the wall below (see 61A).

Waterproof deck with solid railing—Waterproof decks surrounded by a solid railing must be sloped to an opening in the railing. This opening can be a flashed hole in the wall, or scupper, as shown here, or it can be a gap in the wall that accommodates a stairway or walk. (Avoid directing water to walkways in climates with freezing temperatures.) The opening should be located away from the main structure of the building, and the floor should pitch toward the opening from all directions. In some cases, a second opening or overflow should be provided to guarantee that water won't build up if the primary drain clogs.

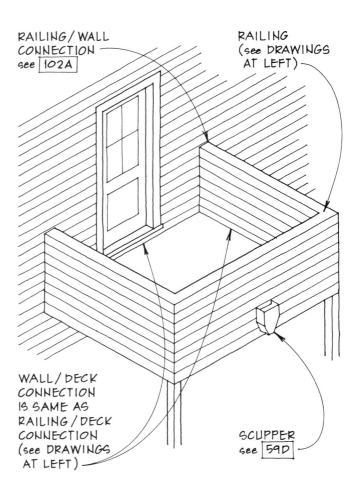

RAILING/WALL CONNECTION see 102A

RAILING (see DRAWINGS AT LEFT)

WALL/DECK CONNECTION IS SAME AS RAILING/DECK CONNECTION (see DRAWINGS AT LEFT)

SCUPPER see 59D

Open deck with solid railing—Open decks surrounded by a solid railing are simple to drain since water will pass through the floor surface (see 61A). Care should be taken to provide adequate drainage from the surface below the deck.

(A) SOLID RAILING @ PORCH OR DECK

Open railings are connected to the floor of a porch or deck only intermittently, where the vertical supports occur. It is through these supports that open railings gain their rigidity. When the end of the railing is supported at a wall or a column, no special connections are required. When the vertical support does not coincide with a rigid part of the structure, however, a rigid connection must be made with the floor system of the porch or deck. One logical place to locate this connection is at the inside edge of the rim joist (see the drawing below).

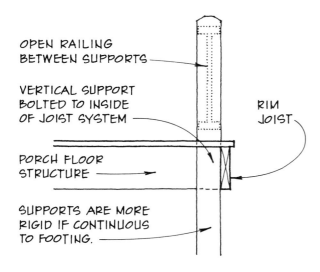

OPEN RAILING
BETWEEN SUPPORTS

VERTICAL SUPPORT
BOLTED TO INSIDE
OF JOIST SYSTEM

RIM
JOIST

PORCH FLOOR
STRUCTURE

SUPPORTS ARE MORE
RIGID IF CONTINUOUS
TO FOOTING.

Another logical place to secure the railing to the porch floor is at the outside of the rim joist (see the drawing below). This is usually the most practical choice for waterproof decks, since the railing does not have to penetrate the waterproof surface.

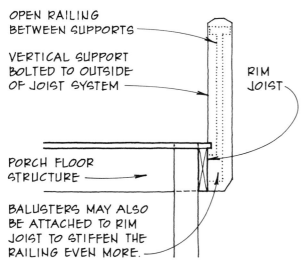

OPEN RAILING
BETWEEN SUPPORTS

VERTICAL SUPPORT
BOLTED TO OUTSIDE
OF JOIST SYSTEM

RIM
JOIST

PORCH FLOOR
STRUCTURE

BALUSTERS MAY ALSO
BE ATTACHED TO RIM
JOIST TO STIFFEN THE
RAILING EVEN MORE.

Waterproof deck with open railing—However the railing is attached to the porch, its rigidity depends ultimately on the solid construction of the porch framing. Pressure-treated joists will contribute to the floor's longevity, and metal hangers and clips will add rigidity. Block between joist bays when the railing is parallel to the joist system.

Waterproof decks surrounded by an open railing should be sloped away from the wall(s) of the building. Drainage may be distributed around all open edges, as shown below, or it can be collected in a scupper.

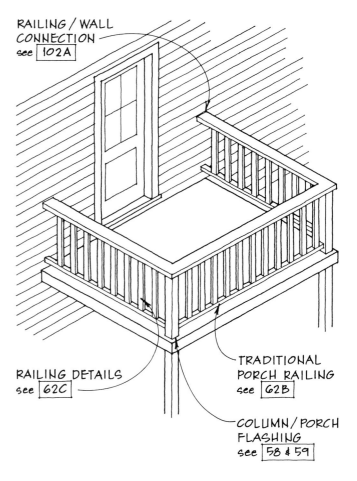

RAILING / WALL
CONNECTION
see | 102A |

RAILING DETAILS
see | 62C |

TRADITIONAL
PORCH RAILING
see | 62B |

COLUMN / PORCH
FLASHING
see | 58 & 59 |

Open deck with open railing—Open decks surrounded by an open railing are relatively simple to drain. Be sure to provide adequate drainage from the surface below the deck.

 A   OPEN RAILING @ PORCH OR DECK

A wood porch with an open railing and a tongue-and-groove wood floor has been a tradition throughout the U.S. for the entire history of wood-frame construction and is still in demand. A tongue-and-groove porch floor is actually a hybrid between a waterproof deck and an open deck because although it is not waterproof, it is also not truly open like the spaced decking of open porch or deck floors. Moisture is likely to get trapped in the tongue-and-groove joint between floor boards and cause decay. For this reason, the floors of these porches are often painted annually. Weather-resistant species or wood that has been pressure-treated will provide the most maintenance-free porch.

The tongue-and-groove wood porch was traditionally built without flashing. But for a longer lasting porch, the connection between the porch floor and the main structure should be flashed for the same reason as for all open porch and deck floors.

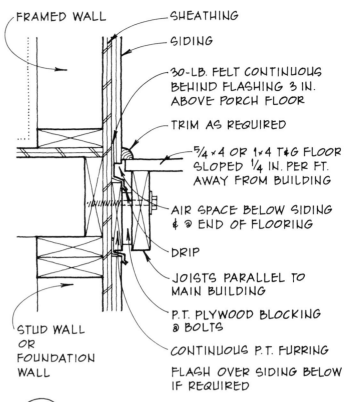

FRAMED WALL
SHEATHING
SIDING
30-LB. FELT CONTINUOUS BEHIND FLASHING 3 IN. ABOVE PORCH FLOOR
TRIM AS REQUIRED
⁵/₄ × 4 OR 1×4 T&G FLOOR SLOPED ¼ IN. PER FT. AWAY FROM BUILDING
AIR SPACE BELOW SIDING & @ END OF FLOORING
DRIP
JOISTS PARALLEL TO MAIN BUILDING
P.T. PLYWOOD BLOCKING @ BOLTS
CONTINUOUS P.T. FURRING
FLASH OVER SIDING BELOW IF REQUIRED
STUD WALL OR FOUNDATION WALL

(A) TRADITIONAL WOOD PORCH
FLOOR CHARACTERISTICS

(B) TRADITIONAL WOOD PORCH
CONNECTION TO MAIN STRUCTURE

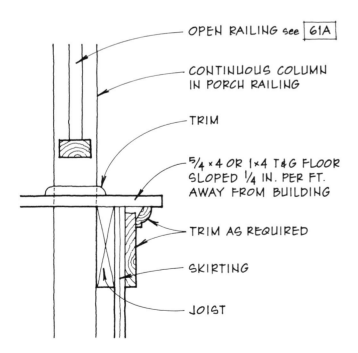

OPEN RAILING see 61A
CONTINUOUS COLUMN IN PORCH RAILING
TRIM
⁵/₄ × 4 OR 1×4 T&G FLOOR SLOPED ¼ IN. PER FT. AWAY FROM BUILDING
TRIM AS REQUIRED
SKIRTING
JOIST

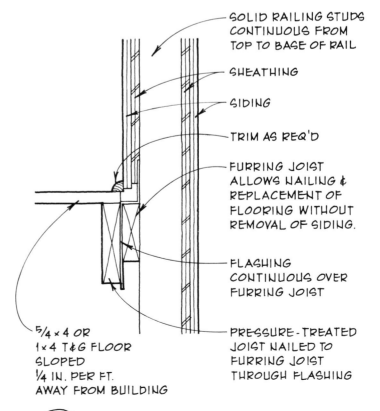

SOLID RAILING STUDS CONTINUOUS FROM TOP TO BASE OF RAIL
SHEATHING
SIDING
TRIM AS REQ'D
FURRING JOIST ALLOWS NAILING & REPLACEMENT OF FLOORING WITHOUT REMOVAL OF SIDING.
⁵/₄ × 4 OR 1×4 T&G FLOOR SLOPED ¼ IN. PER FT. AWAY FROM BUILDING
FLASHING CONTINUOUS OVER FURRING JOIST
PRESSURE-TREATED JOIST NAILED TO FURRING JOIST THROUGH FLASHING

(C) TRADITIONAL WOOD PORCH
OPEN RAILING

(D) TRADITIONAL WOOD PORCH
CLOSED RAILING

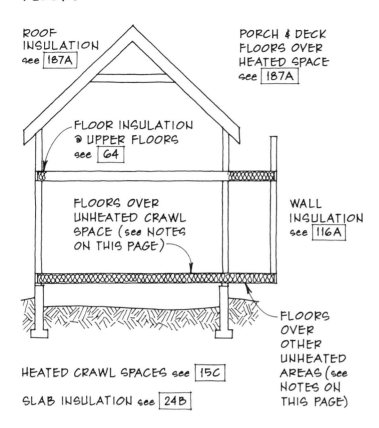

ROOF
INSULATION
see | 187A |

PORCH & DECK
FLOORS OVER
HEATED SPACE
see | 187A |

FLOOR INSULATION
@ UPPER FLOORS
see | 64 |

FLOORS OVER
UNHEATED CRAWL
SPACE (see NOTES
ON THIS PAGE)

WALL
INSULATION
see | 116A |

FLOORS
OVER
OTHER
UNHEATED
AREAS (see
NOTES ON
THIS PAGE)

HEATED CRAWL SPACES see | 15C |

SLAB INSULATION see | 24B |

Floor insulation—Building codes in most climates require at least R-11 for floors over unheated spaces.

Installation—Floors over vented crawl spaces and other unheated areas are typically insulated with fiberglass batts because the ample depth of the floor structure can accommodate this cost-effective but relatively bulky type of insulation. The batts are easiest to install if weather and other considerations permit them to be dropped in from above. To support the batts, a wire or plastic mesh or wood lath can first be stapled to the underside of the joists, or plastic mesh can be draped very loosely over the joists.

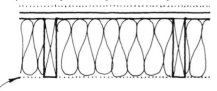

SUPPORT FIBERGLASS-BATT INSULATION
W/ WIRE OR PLASTIC MESH, OR W/
WOOD LATH OR WIRE @ 12 IN. O.C.

When crawl-space floor insulation must be installed from below, spring wires are cheap, easy and effective.

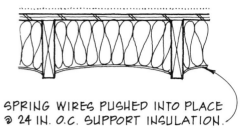

SPRING WIRES PUSHED INTO PLACE
@ 24 IN. O.C. SUPPORT INSULATION.

Floor insulation over open areas that are exposed to varmints and house pets should be covered from below with solid sheathing.

Vapor barriers—A vapor barrier is not always required over a crawl space because the temperature differential between the interior space and the crawl space is not enough to cause condensation. When a vapor barrier is required or when an air-infiltration barrier is desired at the floor, a 4-mil vapor barrier may be placed on the warm side of the insulation, as shown in the drawing below.

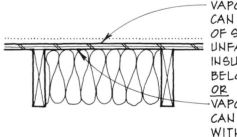

VAPOR BARRIER
CAN GO ON TOP
OF SUBFLOOR IF
UNFACED BATT
INSULATION IS
BELOW,
OR
VAPOR BARRIER
CAN BE INTEGRAL
WITH OR ON TOP
SIDE OF INSULATION.

A vapor barrier placed on the subfloor is more continuous than a vapor barrier on the top side of the batts, and it also will not trap rainwater during construction. For more on vapor barriers, see 116A.

(A)　**FLOOR INSULATION**

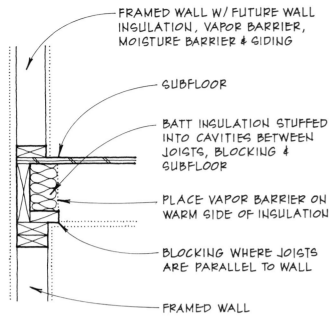

FRAMED WALL W/ FUTURE WALL INSULATION, VAPOR BARRIER, MOISTURE BARRIER & SIDING

SUBFLOOR

BATT INSULATION STUFFED INTO CAVITIES BETWEEN JOISTS, BLOCKING & SUBFLOOR

PLACE VAPOR BARRIER ON WARM SIDE OF INSULATION

BLOCKING WHERE JOISTS ARE PARALLEL TO WALL

FRAMED WALL

NOTE:
BECAUSE JOISTS PERPENDICULAR TO THE WALL PENETRATE THE WALL CAVITY, IT IS DIFFICULT TO GET A TIGHT SEAL AGAINST AIR INFILTRATION. FOR ALTERNATIVE DETAIL see 64B

(A) UPPER-FLOOR INSULATION
PLATFORM FRAMING

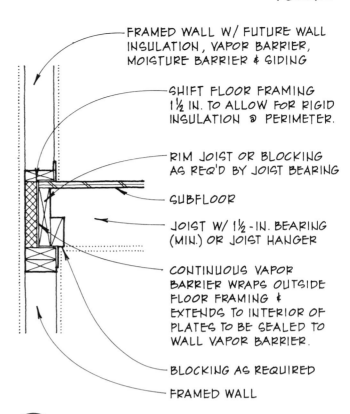

FRAMED WALL W/ FUTURE WALL INSULATION, VAPOR BARRIER, MOISTURE BARRIER & SIDING

SHIFT FLOOR FRAMING 1½ IN. TO ALLOW FOR RIGID INSULATION @ PERIMETER.

RIM JOIST OR BLOCKING AS REQ'D BY JOIST BEARING

SUBFLOOR

JOIST W/ 1½-IN. BEARING (MIN.) OR JOIST HANGER

CONTINUOUS VAPOR BARRIER WRAPS OUTSIDE FLOOR FRAMING & EXTENDS TO INTERIOR OF PLATES TO BE SEALED TO WALL VAPOR BARRIER.

BLOCKING AS REQUIRED

FRAMED WALL

(B) UPPER-FLOOR INSULATION
PLATFORM FRAME : ALTERNATIVE DETAIL

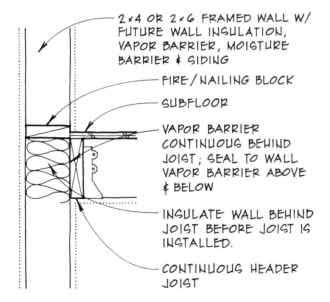

2×4 OR 2×6 FRAMED WALL W/ FUTURE WALL INSULATION, VAPOR BARRIER, MOISTURE BARRIER & SIDING

FIRE/NAILING BLOCK

SUBFLOOR

VAPOR BARRIER CONTINUOUS BEHIND JOIST; SEAL TO WALL VAPOR BARRIER ABOVE & BELOW

INSULATE WALL BEHIND JOIST BEFORE JOIST IS INSTALLED.

CONTINUOUS HEADER JOIST

NOTE:
BECAUSE THE JOISTS DO NOT PENETRATE THE WALL CAVITY, IT IS POSSIBLE TO PROVIDE A GOOD SEAL AGAINST AIR INFILTRATION. HOWEVER, THIS DETAIL DOES NOT PROVIDE THE LATERAL STRUCTURAL STRENGTH OF ALTERNATIVE DETAIL 64D.

(C) UPPER-FLOOR INSULATION
BALLOON FRAMING / JOISTS ⊥ TO WALL

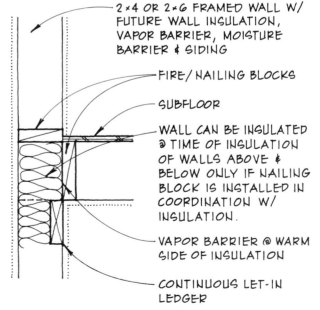

2×4 OR 2×6 FRAMED WALL W/ FUTURE WALL INSULATION, VAPOR BARRIER, MOISTURE BARRIER & SIDING

FIRE/NAILING BLOCKS

SUBFLOOR

WALL CAN BE INSULATED @ TIME OF INSULATION OF WALLS ABOVE & BELOW ONLY IF NAILING BLOCK IS INSTALLED IN COORDINATION W/ INSULATION.

VAPOR BARRIER @ WARM SIDE OF INSULATION

CONTINUOUS LET-IN LEDGER

NOTE:
BECAUSE JOISTS PERPENDICULAR TO THE WALL PENETRATE THE WALL CAVITY, IT IS DIFFICULT TO GET A TIGHT SEAL AGAINST AIR INFILTRATION. FOR ALTERNATIVE DETAIL see 64C

(D) UPPER-FLOOR INSULATION
BALLOON FRAME : ALTERNATIVE DETAIL

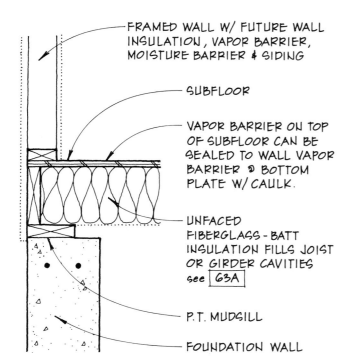

FRAMED WALL W/ FUTURE WALL INSULATION, VAPOR BARRIER, MOISTURE BARRIER & SIDING

SUBFLOOR

VAPOR BARRIER ON TOP OF SUBFLOOR CAN BE SEALED TO WALL VAPOR BARRIER @ BOTTOM PLATE W/ CAULK.

UNFACED FIBERGLASS-BATT INSULATION FILLS JOIST OR GIRDER CAVITIES see 63A

P.T. MUDSILL

FOUNDATION WALL

A **FLOOR INSULATION @ FOUNDATION**
JOISTS ⊥ TO WALL

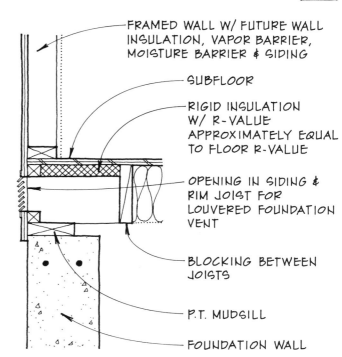

FRAMED WALL W/ FUTURE WALL INSULATION, VAPOR BARRIER, MOISTURE BARRIER & SIDING

SUBFLOOR

RIGID INSULATION W/ R-VALUE APPROXIMATELY EQUAL TO FLOOR R-VALUE

OPENING IN SIDING & RIM JOIST FOR LOUVERED FOUNDATION VENT

BLOCKING BETWEEN JOISTS

P.T. MUDSILL

FOUNDATION WALL

NOTE:
BLOCK TO FIRST JOIST WHERE JOISTS ARE PARALLEL TO WALL.

B **FLOOR INSULATION @ FOUNDATION**
JOISTS ⊥ TO WALL / VENT IN RIM JOIST

WALLS

3

T he walls of a building serve several important functions: they define the spaces within the building to provide privacy and zoning, and they enclose the building itself, keeping the weather out and the heat or cold in. Walls provide the vertical structure that supports the upper floors and roof of the building, and the lateral structure that stiffens the building. Walls also enclose the mechanical systems (electrical wiring, plumbing and heating). To incorporate all of this within a 4-in. or 6-in. deep wood-framed panel is quite an achievement, and numerous decisions need to be made in the course of designing a wall system for a wood-frame building. There are two preliminary decisions to make that establish the framework for the remaining decisions.

WALL THICKNESS

Should the walls be framed with 2x4s or 2x6s? The 2x6 wall has become increasingly popular in recent years, primarily because it provides more space for insulation and allows for other minor energy-saving advantages (such as the ability to run electricity in a notched base, as shown in 78A). These advantages all come at some cost. A 2x6 wall with studs spaced 24 in. o.c. (the maximum spacing allowed by codes) uses about 20% more material for studs and plates than a 2x4 wall with studs with a code-allowed spacing of 16 in. o.c. On the outside, the sheathing has to be ½ in. thick (⅛ in. thicker than sheathing on a standard 2x4 wall), and inside the drywall also has to be ⅛ in. thicker to span the 24-in. spacing between 2x6 studs. Thicker insulation costs more too. So, overall, 2x6 framing makes a superior wall, but one that costs more. Framing the exterior walls with 2x6s and interior walls with 2x4s is a typical combination when the energy-efficient 2x6 wall is selected. Stud spacing of 2x4 and 2x6 walls may vary with loading, lumber grades and finish materials; in this book, however, studs are assumed to be 16 in. o.c. in 2x4 walls and 24 in. o.c. in 2x6 walls unless noted otherwise.

FRAMING STYLE

Should the walls be built using platform framing or balloon framing? Balloon framing, with studs continuous from mudsill to top plate and continuous between floors, was developed in the 1840s and is the antecedent of the framed wall. In recent years, balloon framing has been almost completely superseded by the more labor-efficient and fire-resistant platform-frame construction, with studs extending only between floors. There are still situations, however, where a variation of the balloon-frame system is useful. One such situation is where the continuity of studs longer than the normal ceiling height is essential to the strength of a wall. Examples include parapet walls and eave (side) walls that must resist the lateral thrust of a vaulted roof (as in a 1½-story building).

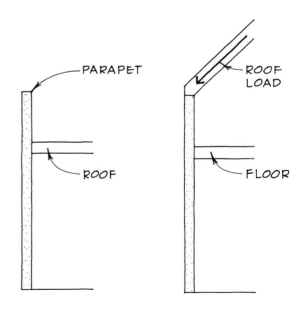

PARAPET

ROOF

ROOF LOAD

FLOOR

Another reason for using balloon framing is to minimize the effects of shrinkage that occurs across the grain of joists in a platform-framed building. This could be important with continuous stucco siding that spans two floors without a control joint, or in a multiple-story hybrid building system where the floors in the balloon-framed part would not shrink equally with the floors in the platform-framed part.

DESIGNING A WALL SYSTEM

Once the stud size and spacing and the framing system have been selected, it is time to consider how to brace the building to resist the forces of wind, earthquakes and eccentric loading. Will diagonal bracing be adequate, or should the building be braced with structural sheathing? This question is best answered in the context of the design of the building as a whole, considering the other materials that complete the wall system. How is the wall to be insulated? Where are the openings in the wall for doors and windows? Will there be an air infiltration barrier? What material will be used for the exterior finish? The details relating to these issues are addressed in this chapter, along with some suggestions for their appropriate use. How these various details are assembled into a complete wall system depends on local climate, codes, tradition and the talent of the designer.

SIZING HEADERS

Header size depends on wood species and grade, loading, header design and rough-opening span. Following is a rule of thumb for sizing a common header type, the 4x header (see 71C):

For a single-story building with a 30-lb. live load on the roof and 2x4 bearing walls, the span in feet of the rough opening should equal the depth (nominal) in inches of a 4x header. For example, openings up to 4 ft. wide require a 4x4 header.

ABOUT THE DRAWINGS

Construction terms vary regionally, and the names for the components that frame wall openings (see 70A) are the least cast in stone. Consult local builders and architects for common usage.

For clarity, insulation is not shown in the exterior walls except in the insulation section (116-117).

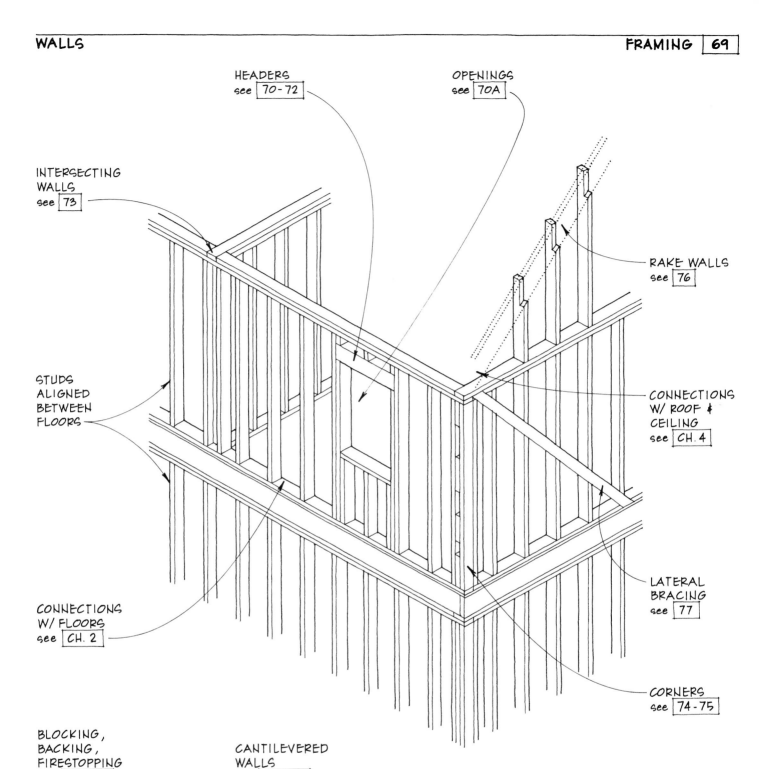

HEADERS
see | 70-72 |

OPENINGS
see | 70A |

INTERSECTING
WALLS
see | 73 |

RAKE WALLS
see | 76 |

STUDS
ALIGNED
BETWEEN
FLOORS

CONNECTIONS
W/ ROOF &
CEILING
see | CH. 4 |

CONNECTIONS
W/ FLOORS
see | CH. 2 |

LATERAL
BRACING
see | 77 |

CORNERS
see | 74-75 |

BLOCKING,
BACKING,
FIRESTOPPING
see | 78A & B |

CANTILEVERED
WALLS
see | 78C & D |

NOTE:
IN THIS CHAPTER ALL 2×4 WALLS ARE SHOWN
WITH STUDS @ 16 IN. O.C.; ALL 2×6 WALLS ARE
SHOWN WITH STUDS @ 24 IN. O.C.; UNLABELED
WALLS MAY BE EITHER 2×4 OR 2×6.

 WALL FRAMING

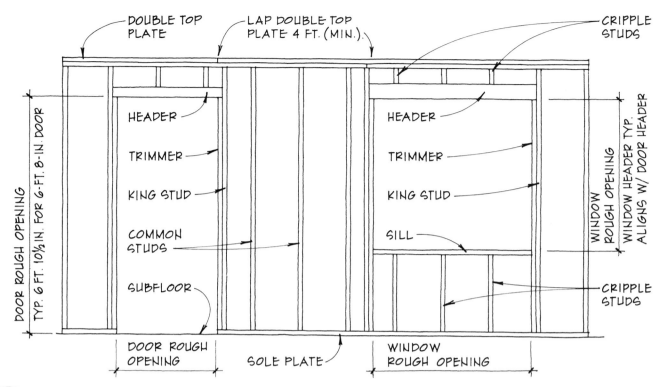

DOUBLE TOP PLATE

LAP DOUBLE TOP PLATE 4 FT. (MIN.).

CRIPPLE STUDS

DOOR ROUGH OPENING TYP. 6 FT. 10½ IN. FOR 6-FT. 8-IN. DOOR

HEADER

TRIMMER

KING STUD

COMMON STUDS

SUBFLOOR

DOOR ROUGH OPENING

SOLE PLATE

HEADER

TRIMMER

KING STUD

SILL

WINDOW ROUGH OPENING

WINDOW ROUGH OPENING

WINDOW HEADER TYP. ALIGNS W/ DOOR HEADER

CRIPPLE STUDS

(A) OPENINGS IN A STUD WALL

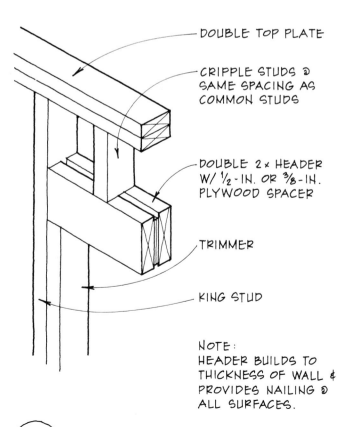

DOUBLE TOP PLATE

CRIPPLE STUDS @ SAME SPACING AS COMMON STUDS

DOUBLE 2× HEADER W/ ½-IN. OR ⅜-IN. PLYWOOD SPACER

TRIMMER

KING STUD

NOTE: HEADER BUILDS TO THICKNESS OF WALL & PROVIDES NAILING @ ALL SURFACES.

(B) TYPICAL DOUBLE 2× HEADER
2×4 BEARING WALL

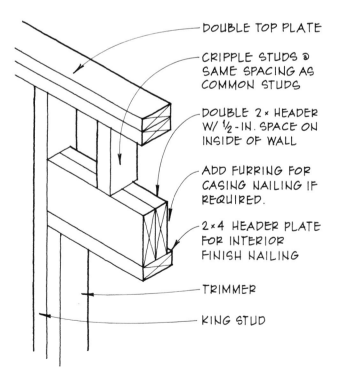

DOUBLE TOP PLATE

CRIPPLE STUDS @ SAME SPACING AS COMMON STUDS

DOUBLE 2× HEADER W/ ½-IN. SPACE ON INSIDE OF WALL

ADD FURRING FOR CASING NAILING IF REQUIRED.

2×4 HEADER PLATE FOR INTERIOR FINISH NAILING

TRIMMER

KING STUD

(C) ALTERNATIVE DOUBLE 2× HEADER
2×4 BEARING WALL

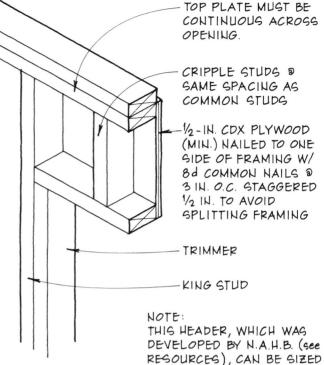

DOUBLE TOP PLATE

DOUBLE 2×10 HEADER W/ 2×4 SCABBED TO BOTTOM (ELIMINATES THE NEED FOR CRIPPLE STUDS IN AN 8-FT. WALL)

½-IN. PLYWOOD OR WOOD LATH SHIMS @ INSIDE SURFACE

TRIMMER

KING STUD

TOP PLATE MUST BE CONTINUOUS ACROSS OPENING.

CRIPPLE STUDS @ SAME SPACING AS COMMON STUDS

½-IN. CDX PLYWOOD (MIN.) NAILED TO ONE SIDE OF FRAMING W/ 8d COMMON NAILS @ 3 IN. O.C. STAGGERED ½ IN. TO AVOID SPLITTING FRAMING

TRIMMER

KING STUD

NOTE:
THIS HEADER, WHICH WAS DEVELOPED BY N.A.H.B. (see RESOURCES), CAN BE SIZED TO SPAN UP TO 8 FT.

A **DOUBLE 2×10 HEADER**
2×4 BEARING WALL

B **OPEN-BOX PLYWOOD HEADER**
2×4 BEARING WALL

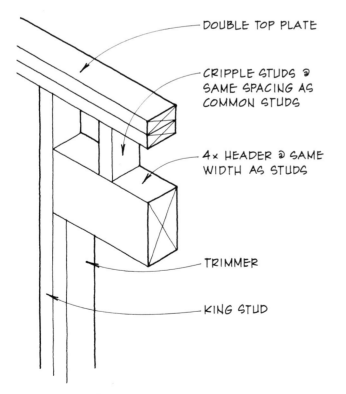

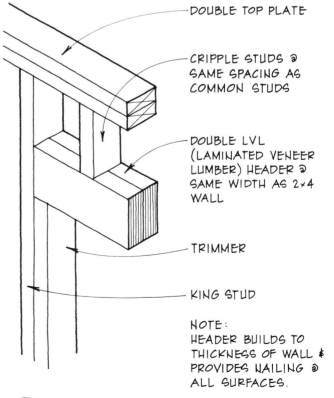

DOUBLE TOP PLATE

CRIPPLE STUDS @ SAME SPACING AS COMMON STUDS

4× HEADER @ SAME WIDTH AS STUDS

TRIMMER

KING STUD

DOUBLE TOP PLATE

CRIPPLE STUDS @ SAME SPACING AS COMMON STUDS

DOUBLE LVL (LAMINATED VENEER LUMBER) HEADER @ SAME WIDTH AS 2×4 WALL

TRIMMER

KING STUD

NOTE:
HEADER BUILDS TO THICKNESS OF WALL & PROVIDES NAILING @ ALL SURFACES.

C **4× HEADER**
2×4 BEARING WALL

D **LVL HEADER**
2×4 BEARING WALL

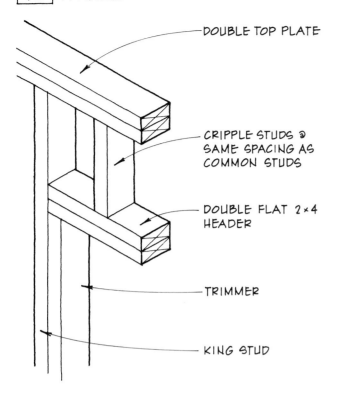

DOUBLE TOP PLATE

CRIPPLE STUDS @ SAME SPACING AS COMMON STUDS

DOUBLE FLAT 2×4 HEADER

TRIMMER

KING STUD

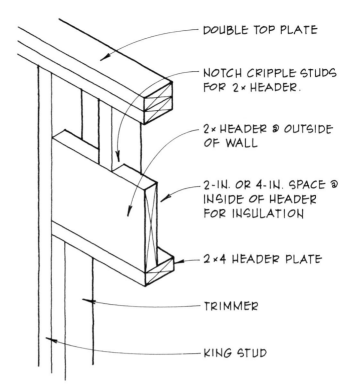

DOUBLE TOP PLATE

NOTCH CRIPPLE STUDS FOR 2× HEADER.

2× HEADER @ OUTSIDE OF WALL

2-IN. OR 4-IN. SPACE @ INSIDE OF HEADER FOR INSULATION

2×4 HEADER PLATE

TRIMMER

KING STUD

A FLAT 2×4 HEADER
2×4 PARTITION WALL

B INSULATED HEADER
2×4 OR 2×6 EXTERIOR WALL

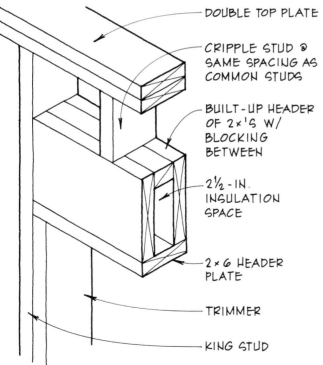

DOUBLE TOP PLATE

CRIPPLE STUD @ SAME SPACING AS COMMON STUDS

BUILT-UP HEADER OF 2×'S W/ BLOCKING BETWEEN

2½-IN. INSULATION SPACE

2×6 HEADER PLATE

TRIMMER

KING STUD

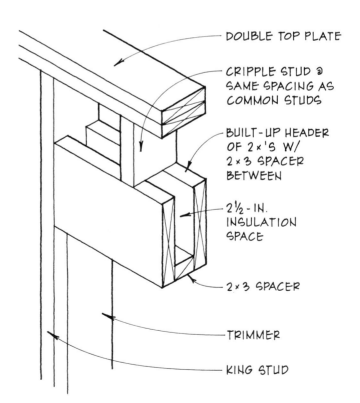

DOUBLE TOP PLATE

CRIPPLE STUD @ SAME SPACING AS COMMON STUDS

BUILT-UP HEADER OF 2×'S W/ 2×3 SPACER BETWEEN

2½-IN. INSULATION SPACE

2×3 SPACER

TRIMMER

KING STUD

C INSULATED DOUBLE 2× HEADER
2×6 BEARING WALL

D INSULATED DOUBLE 2× HEADER
2×6 BEARING WALL/ALTERNATIVE DETAIL

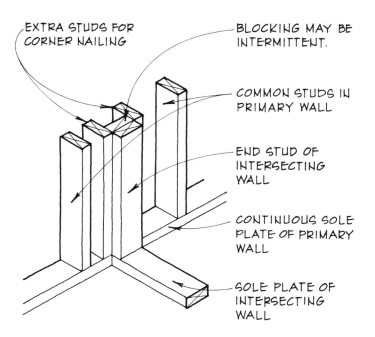

EXTRA STUDS FOR CORNER NAILING

BLOCKING MAY BE INTERMITTENT.

COMMON STUDS IN PRIMARY WALL

END STUD OF INTERSECTING WALL

CONTINUOUS SOLE PLATE OF PRIMARY WALL

SOLE PLATE OF INTERSECTING WALL

NOTE:
INSULATE CAVITY BEHIND INTERSECTING WALL BEFORE SHEATHING IS APPLIED IF PRIMARY WALL IS ON EXTERIOR.

(A) INTERSECTING 2× WALLS

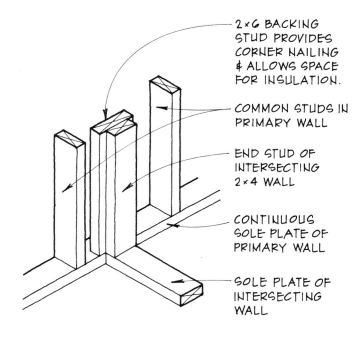

2×6 BACKING STUD PROVIDES CORNER NAILING & ALLOWS SPACE FOR INSULATION.

COMMON STUDS IN PRIMARY WALL

END STUD OF INTERSECTING 2×4 WALL

CONTINUOUS SOLE PLATE OF PRIMARY WALL

SOLE PLATE OF INTERSECTING WALL

NOTE:
FOR A TIGHTER SEAL AGAINST AIR INFILTRATION, APPLY VAPOR BARRIER (& GYPSUM WALLBOARD) BEFORE FRAMING THE INTERSECTING WALL.

(B) INTERSECTING 2× WALLS
ALTERNATIVE DETAIL

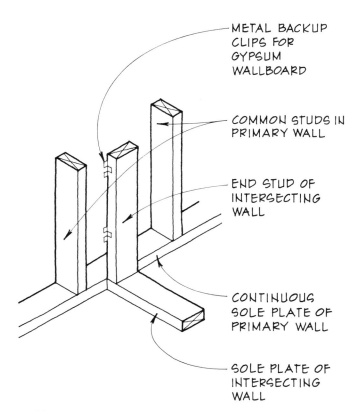

METAL BACKUP CLIPS FOR GYPSUM WALLBOARD

COMMON STUDS IN PRIMARY WALL

END STUD OF INTERSECTING WALL

CONTINUOUS SOLE PLATE OF PRIMARY WALL

SOLE PLATE OF INTERSECTING WALL

(C) INTERSECTING 2× WALLS
W/ GYPSUM WALLBOARD CLIPS

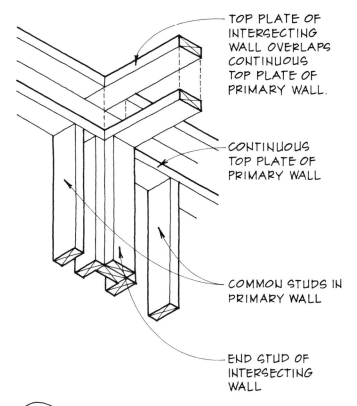

TOP PLATE OF INTERSECTING WALL OVERLAPS CONTINUOUS TOP PLATE OF PRIMARY WALL.

CONTINUOUS TOP PLATE OF PRIMARY WALL

COMMON STUDS IN PRIMARY WALL

END STUD OF INTERSECTING WALL

(D) INTERSECTING 2× WALLS
@ DOUBLE TOP PLATE

CORNER STUDS BUILT UP W/
2×4 BLOCKING BETWEEN
PROVIDES NAILING @
INSIDE CORNER.

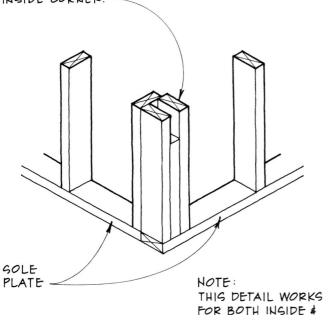

SOLE
PLATE

NOTE:
THIS DETAIL WORKS
FOR BOTH INSIDE &
OUTSIDE CORNERS.

Ⓐ 2×4 CORNER
W/ BLOCKING

EXTRA STUD ADDED PERPENDICULAR
TO CORNER STUD PROVIDES NAILING @
INSIDE CORNER & ALLOWS SPACE FOR
INSULATION @ CORNER.

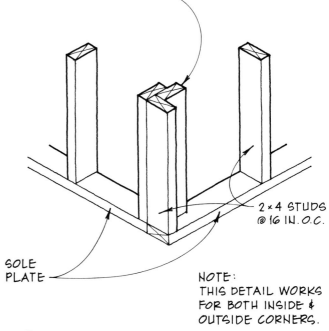

SOLE
PLATE

2×4 STUDS
@ 16 IN. O.C.

NOTE:
THIS DETAIL WORKS
FOR BOTH INSIDE &
OUTSIDE CORNERS.

Ⓑ 2×4 CORNER
W/ INSULATION @ CORNER

DOUBLE TOP PLATE OVERLAPS
@ CORNERS TO LOCK TWO
WALLS TOGETHER.

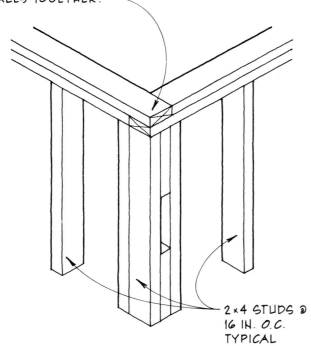

2×4 STUDS @
16 IN. O.C.
TYPICAL

Ⓒ 2×4 CORNER
@ DOUBLE TOP PLATE

EXTRA STUD ADDED PERPENDICULAR
TO CORNER STUD PROVIDES NAILING @
INSIDE CORNER & ALLOWS SPACE FOR
4-IN. THICK INSULATION @ CORNER.

DOUBLE TOP PLATE
OVERLAPS @ CORNERS,
LOCKING TWO WALLS
TOGETHER.

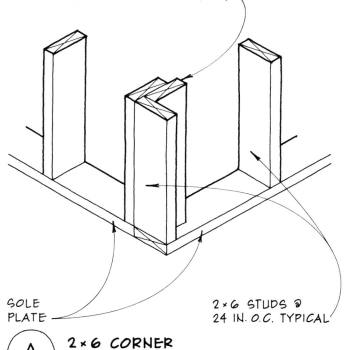

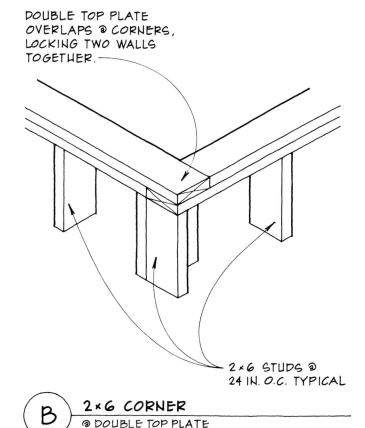

SOLE
PLATE

2×6 STUDS @
24 IN. O.C. TYPICAL

2×6 STUDS @
24 IN. O.C. TYPICAL

(A) 2×6 CORNER
W/ INSULATION @ CORNER

(B) 2×6 CORNER
@ DOUBLE TOP PLATE

METAL BACKUP CLIPS @ INSIDE CORNERS
OF GYPSUM WALLBOARD ELIMINATE NEED
FOR EXTRA STUD, ALLOWING FOR FULL
THICKNESS OF INSULATION.

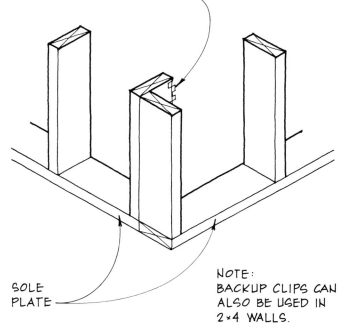

SOLE
PLATE

NOTE:
BACKUP CLIPS CAN
ALSO BE USED IN
2×4 WALLS.

(C) SUPERINSULATED 2×6 CORNER
OUTSIDE CORNER ONLY

A wall that extends to a sloped roof or ceiling is called a rake wall and may be built one of two ways:

Platform framing is commonly the method of choice when a horizontal structural element such as a floor or ceiling ties the structure together at the level of the top plate or when the top plate itself is short enough to provide the necessary lateral strength (see 76B).

Balloon framing allows for ease of construction and economy of material and stabilizes a tall wall where there is no horizontal structure at the level of the top plate (see 76C).

For details of rake walls with truss-framed roofs, see 149.

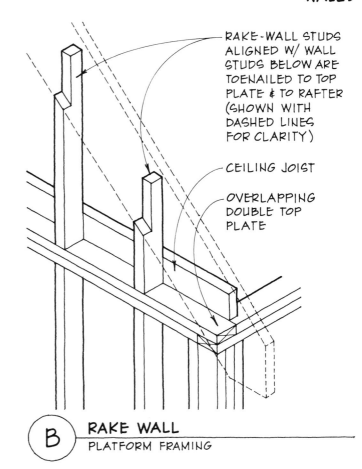

RAKE-WALL STUDS ALIGNED W/ WALL STUDS BELOW ARE TOENAILED TO TOP PLATE & TO RAFTER (SHOWN WITH DASHED LINES FOR CLARITY)

CEILING JOIST

OVERLAPPING DOUBLE TOP PLATE

A **RAKE WALL**
NOTES

B **RAKE WALL**
PLATFORM FRAMING

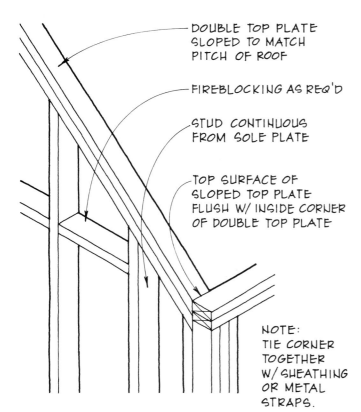

DOUBLE TOP PLATE SLOPED TO MATCH PITCH OF ROOF

FIREBLOCKING AS REQ'D

STUD CONTINUOUS FROM SOLE PLATE

TOP SURFACE OF SLOPED TOP PLATE FLUSH W/ INSIDE CORNER OF DOUBLE TOP PLATE

NOTE:
TIE CORNER TOGETHER W/ SHEATHING OR METAL STRAPS.

C **RAKE WALL**
BALLOON FRAMING

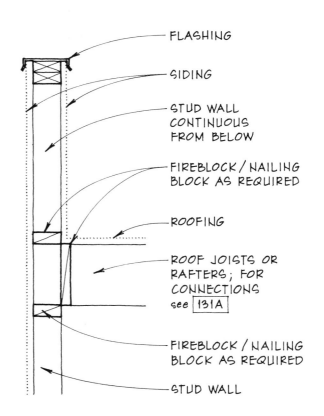

FLASHING

SIDING

STUD WALL CONTINUOUS FROM BELOW

FIREBLOCK / NAILING BLOCK AS REQUIRED

ROOFING

ROOF JOISTS OR RAFTERS; FOR CONNECTIONS see 131A

FIREBLOCK / NAILING BLOCK AS REQUIRED

STUD WALL

D **PARAPET WALL FRAMING**
ROOF JOISTS SHOWN ⊥ TO WALL

The walls of a wood-frame structure must provide lateral resistance to counteract the forces of wind, earthquakes and eccentric loading. Most wood buildings are sheathed or sided with plywood or another structural sheet material that will provide the necessary lateral stability when fastened directly to the stud frame (see 79-81). When this is not the case, there are two good methods of bracing the building for lateral stability. These are the let-in wood brace (see 77B) and the kerfed-in metal brace (see 77C).

The method of bracing with diagonal blocking between studs is not recommended because the nails may withdraw under tension and the many joints tend to open up as the blocking shrinks.

Bracing is often referred to as "corner bracing," but there is really no need to locate the braces only at corners. Braces may be located anywhere along a wall, and the bracing effect will be transferred to the rest of the wall through the continuous top and bottom plates. The methods shown here are located at a corner only for ease of illustration.

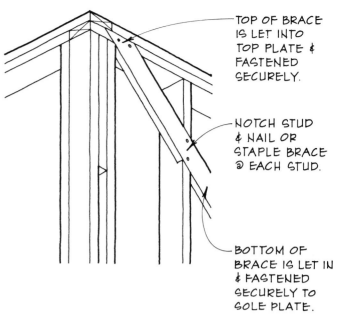

TOP OF BRACE IS LET INTO TOP PLATE & FASTENED SECURELY.

NOTCH STUD & NAIL OR STAPLE BRACE @ EACH STUD.

BOTTOM OF BRACE IS LET IN & FASTENED SECURELY TO SOLE PLATE.

NOTE:
LET-IN BRACES SHOULD BE MADE OF STRUCTURALLY SOUND 1x4 LUMBER. THEY SHOULD BE CONTINUOUS FROM TOP PLATE TO SOLE PLATE & @ 45° TO 60° FROM THE HORIZONTAL.

A LATERAL BRACING
NOTES

B LET-IN WOOD BRACE

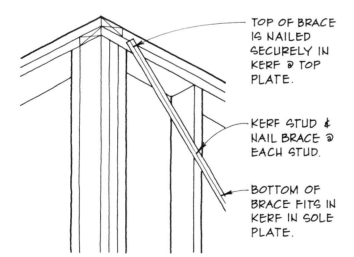

TOP OF BRACE IS NAILED SECURELY IN KERF @ TOP PLATE.

KERF STUD & NAIL BRACE @ EACH STUD.

BOTTOM OF BRACE FITS IN KERF IN SOLE PLATE.

NOTE:
METAL BRACING SET IN A SAW KERF & NAILED TO EACH STUD IS NOT AS GOOD AS LET-IN WOOD BRACING. BECAUSE OF ITS THIN PROFILE, THE METAL MAY BUCKLE UNDER EXTREME COMPRESSION. IN ADDITION, THE METAL WILL NOT SHRINK & SWELL ALONG W/ THE WOOD FRAMING, AS THE LET-IN WOOD BRACE WILL.

C KERFED-IN METAL BRACE

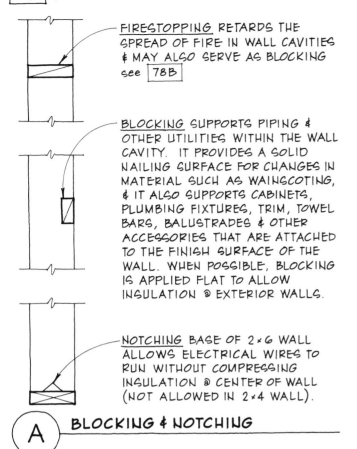

FIRESTOPPING RETARDS THE SPREAD OF FIRE IN WALL CAVITIES & MAY ALSO SERVE AS BLOCKING see 78B

BLOCKING SUPPORTS PIPING & OTHER UTILITIES WITHIN THE WALL CAVITY. IT PROVIDES A SOLID NAILING SURFACE FOR CHANGES IN MATERIAL SUCH AS WAINSCOTING, & IT ALSO SUPPORTS CABINETS, PLUMBING FIXTURES, TRIM, TOWEL BARS, BALUSTRADES & OTHER ACCESSORIES THAT ARE ATTACHED TO THE FINISH SURFACE OF THE WALL. WHEN POSSIBLE, BLOCKING IS APPLIED FLAT TO ALLOW INSULATION @ EXTERIOR WALLS.

NOTCHING BASE OF 2×6 WALL ALLOWS ELECTRICAL WIRES TO RUN WITHOUT COMPRESSING INSULATION @ CENTER OF WALL (NOT ALLOWED IN 2×4 WALL).

A   BLOCKING & NOTCHING

FIRESTOPPING MAY BE STAGGERED FOR EASE OF NAILING.

CONTINUOUS STUDS

NOTE:
CODES VARY, BUT FIRESTOPPING IS USUALLY REQUIRED: AT STAIRS ALONGSIDE THE STRINGERS; BETWEEN FLOORS & BETWEEN THE TOP FLOOR AND THE ATTIC IN BALLOON-FRAME BUILDINGS (THE PLATES IN PLATFORM-FRAME BUILDINGS AUTOMATICALLY PROVIDE FIREBLOCKING BETWEEN FLOORS); BETWEEN WALL CAVITIES & CONCEALED HORIZONTAL SPACES SUCH AS SOFFITS & DROP CEILINGS; IN TALL WALLS EVERY 10 FT. VERTICALLY.

FIRESTOPPING IS USUALLY 2× FRAMING LUMBER BUT CAN ALSO BE OTHER MATERIALS SUCH AS LAYERS OF PLYWOOD OR GYPSUM WALLBOARD WHEN APPROVED BY LOCAL CODES.

B   FIRESTOPPING

IT IS OCCASIONALLY DIFFICULT OR IMPOSSIBLE TO CANTILEVER THE FLOOR FRAMING TO SUPPORT A PROJECTION FROM THE BUILDING. WHERE LOADS ARE NOT GREAT, IT IS POSSIBLE TO SUPPORT THE PROJECTION WITH CANTILEVERED WALLS.

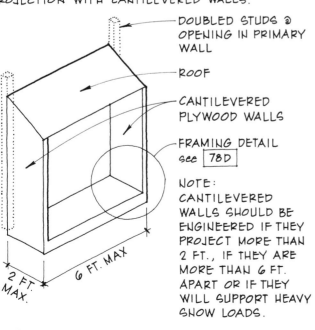

DOUBLED STUDS @ OPENING IN PRIMARY WALL

ROOF

CANTILEVERED PLYWOOD WALLS

FRAMING DETAIL see 78D

NOTE:
CANTILEVERED WALLS SHOULD BE ENGINEERED IF THEY PROJECT MORE THAN 2 FT., IF THEY ARE MORE THAN 6 FT. APART OR IF THEY WILL SUPPORT HEAVY SNOW LOADS.

2 FT. MAX.

6 FT. MAX

C   CANTILEVERED WALLS

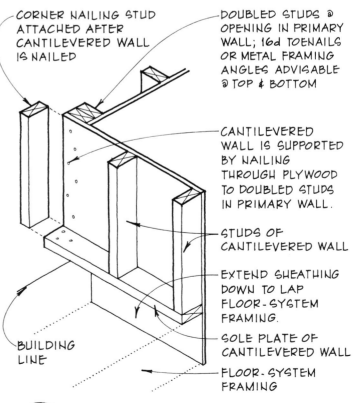

CORNER NAILING STUD ATTACHED AFTER CANTILEVERED WALL IS NAILED

DOUBLED STUDS @ OPENING IN PRIMARY WALL; 16d TOENAILS OR METAL FRAMING ANGLES ADVISABLE @ TOP & BOTTOM

CANTILEVERED WALL IS SUPPORTED BY NAILING THROUGH PLYWOOD TO DOUBLED STUDS IN PRIMARY WALL.

STUDS OF CANTILEVERED WALL

EXTEND SHEATHING DOWN TO LAP FLOOR-SYSTEM FRAMING.

SOLE PLATE OF CANTILEVERED WALL

FLOOR-SYSTEM FRAMING

BUILDING LINE

D   CANTILEVERED-WALL FRAMING
DETAIL @ BASE

Plywood and other panel materials may be used as structural sheathing or as finish siding (in single-wall construction, these functions are combined in one layer, as in 81A, B and C). Structural-sheathing panels resist lateral loads and contribute to the overall stiffness of the building, thereby eliminating the need for let-in bracing. In earthquake or hurricane zones or where walls are very tall or penetrated by many openings, structural sheathing may require engineering.

Panels may be installed either vertically or horizontally. Vertically applied sheathing does not usually require blocking because all edges are aligned with framing members. Horizontally applied plywood sheathing is stronger because the highest-quality veneers and the most plies are oriented with the length of the plywood panel. This horizontal strength acts in concert with the vertical strength of the studs. Horizontal orientation is used when the stiffness of plywood is required for the backing of siding materials, such as shingles or stucco.

The capacity of plywood panels to span between studs is related to thickness and to the orientation and number of plies. The spanning capacity of composite panels, like oriented strand board, is generally slightly less than plywood and is related to panel thickness. The following chart applies as a rule of thumb:

Stud spacing	Panel thickness
16 in. o.c.	3/8 in.
24 in. o.c.	1/2 in.

Nails or other approved fasteners should be sized and spaced according to the following schedule. Verify with manufacturer and local codes.

Panel thickness	Nail size	Panel edge nailing	Field nailing
1/2 in. or less	6d	6 in. o.c.	12 in. o.c.
over 1/2 in.	8d		

Composite panels expand more than plywood when exposed to moisture. For this reason, adequate spacing between non-plywood panels is critical.

A   STRUCTURAL SHEATHING
     NOTES

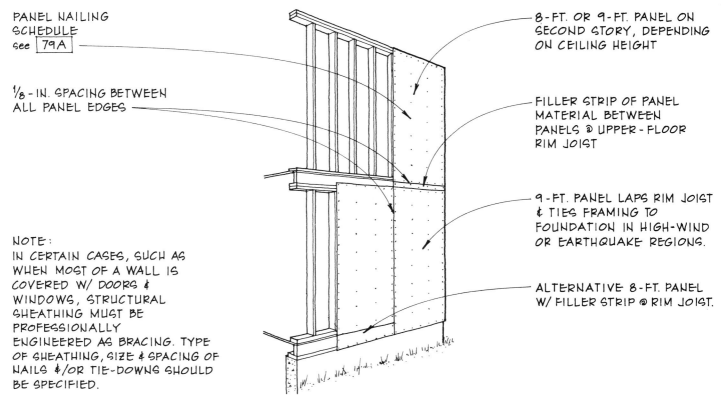

PANEL NAILING SCHEDULE see 79A

1/8 - IN. SPACING BETWEEN ALL PANEL EDGES

8-FT. OR 9-FT. PANEL ON SECOND STORY, DEPENDING ON CEILING HEIGHT

FILLER STRIP OF PANEL MATERIAL BETWEEN PANELS @ UPPER - FLOOR RIM JOIST

9-FT. PANEL LAPS RIM JOIST & TIES FRAMING TO FOUNDATION IN HIGH-WIND OR EARTHQUAKE REGIONS.

ALTERNATIVE 8-FT. PANEL W/ FILLER STRIP @ RIM JOIST.

NOTE:
IN CERTAIN CASES, SUCH AS WHEN MOST OF A WALL IS COVERED W/ DOORS & WINDOWS, STRUCTURAL SHEATHING MUST BE PROFESSIONALLY ENGINEERED AS BRACING. TYPE OF SHEATHING, SIZE & SPACING OF NAILS &/OR TIE-DOWNS SHOULD BE SPECIFIED.

B   STRUCTURAL SHEATHING
     MULTIPLE - STORY BUILDING

NOTE:
IN REGIONS NOT
SUBJECT TO HIGH RISK
OF HURRICANE OR
EARTHQUAKE,
HORIZONTAL PANELS
WITHOUT BLOCKING & W/
FILLER STRIPS @ BASE
MAY BE ACCEPTABLE.

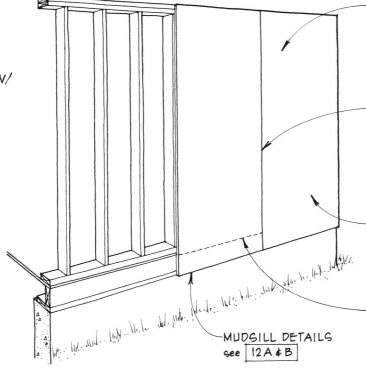

PANEL NAILING SCHEDULE
see [79A]

LEAVE ⅛-IN. SPACE
BETWEEN ALL PANEL
EDGES.

IN HIGH-WIND OR
HIGH-RISK SEISMIC ZONES,
USE 9-FT. VERTICAL PANEL
CUT TO EXTEND FROM TOP
OF FRAMING TO MUDSILL.

IN OTHER REGIONS, 8-FT.
VERTICAL PANEL TO RIM
JOIST W/ FILLER STRIP
BELOW IS ADEQUATE.

MUDSILL DETAILS
see [12A & B]

 A STRUCTURAL SHEATHING / SINGLE-STORY BUILDING
DISTANCE FROM MUDSILL TO TOP PLATE OVER 8 FT.

STAGGER VERTICAL
JOINTS BETWEEN
STRUCTURAL PANELS.

WHEN NOT ENGINEERED
AS BRACING, SHEATHING
PANELS MAY SPAN
BETWEEN STUDS WITHOUT
BLOCKING DEPENDING ON
STUD SPACING, PANEL
THICKNESS & SIDING
MATERIAL. ⅜-IN.
SHEATHING IS
RECOMMENDED FOR
STUDS @ 16 IN. O.C. & ½-IN.
SHEATHING FOR STUDS @
24 IN. O.C. VERIFY SPAN
RATING ON PANELS.

NOTE:
HORIZONTAL PANELS
SHOWN IN THIS DETAIL
MAY BE REPLACED W/
VERTICAL PANELS
see [80A]

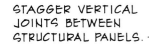

PANEL NAILING SCHEDULE
see [79A]

UPPER EDGE OF PANEL
ALIGNS W/ LOWER TOP
PLATE.

LEAVE ⅛-IN. SPACE @ ALL
PANEL EDGES.

BLOCKING BEHIND
PANEL JOINTS IS
REQUIRED WHEN
HORIZONTAL PANELS ARE
ENGINEERED FOR
LATERAL BRACING.

NOTE:
THIS DETAIL IS APPROPRIATE
ONLY IF STUDS ARE PRECUT
@ 90¾ IN. OR LESS & THE
SUBFLOOR SITS DIRECTLY ON
THE MUDSILL see [16A & B]
OR IF A SLAB FOUNDATION
IS USED see [22A]

MUDSILL DETAILS
see [12A & B]

 B STRUCTURAL SHEATHING / SINGLE-STORY BUILDING
DISTANCE FROM MUDSILL TO TOP PLATE 8 FT. OR LESS

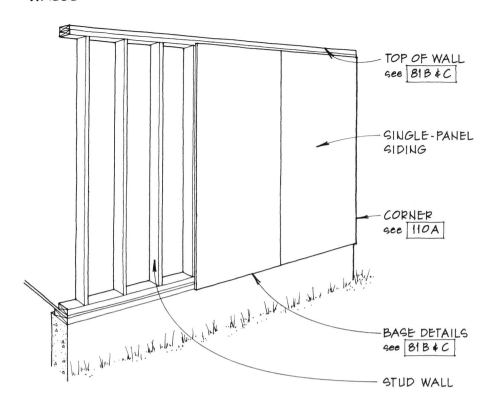

In single-wall construction, a single panel of plywood or composite board siding provides both structural and weathering functions. This is an inexpensive, low-quality type of construction most appropriate for garages and sheds, but also used for residential construction. Panels are installed vertically, often over a moisture barrier.

Precut studs (from 88½ in. to 92⅜ in.) allow 8-ft. panels to cover the framing on the exterior if the subfloor sits directly on the mudsill (see 81B) or if there is a slab floor. Adding trim to the base allows the use of 8-ft. panels with taller studs and/or different subfloor connections (see 81C).

Taller (9-ft. and 10-ft.) plywood panels are also available.

(A) SINGLE-WALL CONSTRUCTION
STRUCTURAL SHEATHING

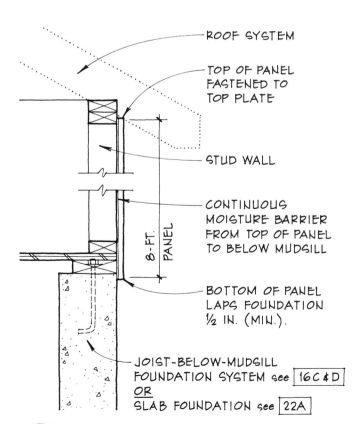

(B) SINGLE-WALL CONSTRUCTION
8-FT. PANEL TYPICAL

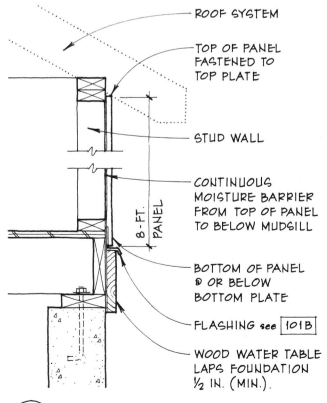

(C) SINGLE-WALL CONSTRUCTION
8-FT. PANEL W/ WATER TABLE

SHEATHING PANELS MAY SPAN
BETWEEN STUDS WITHOUT
BLOCKING SINCE SIDING MUST BE
NAILED TO STUDS IN ANY CASE.

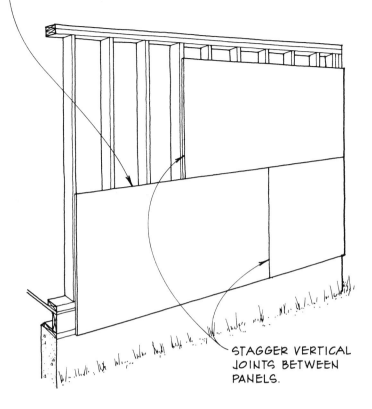

STAGGER VERTICAL
JOINTS BETWEEN
PANELS.

Many sheet materials that can be used for sheathing do not provide adequate lateral bracing. In addition to providing a base for a moisture barrier and siding, such non-structural sheathings may also provide insulation or fire protection.

Insulative sheathings range in thickness from ½ in. to 1½ in. They include fiberboards, foam plastic and rigid fiberglass boards. R-values vary. Verify that the perm rating of the sheathing is lower than the perm rating of the vapor barrier (see 83A).

Fire-protective sheathings are often required at walls on or near property lines, between attached dwellings and to separate garages from living space. Type-X gypsum wallboard applied directly to the studs will satisfy most codes.

Siding must be nailed through non-structural sheathings directly into the studs beneath them. These sheathings do not produce an adequate base for shingles or brick. The need for lateral bracing is often satisfied by applying plywood or other structural panels to the corners of a building, with less expensive non-structural sheathing elsewhere.

 NON-STRUCTURAL SHEATHING

Once the walls are framed and sheathed, they must be insulated and protected from moisture. This must be a coordinated effort involving a moisture barrier, vapor barrier, insulation and possibly an air barrier.

A moisture barrier is a membrane directly under the siding that prevents any water penetrating the siding from reaching the sheathing or the framing. An effective moisture barrier stops liquid water but lets water vapor through, thereby letting the wall breathe.

A vapor barrier is a membrane on the warm side of the wall (usually the interior) that retards the passage of water vapor from the warm inside air into the cooler wall, where it could condense. A vapor barrier may be integral with the insulation or it may be a separate item.

An air barrier is a membrane that limits the infiltration of air through the wall. Either a moisture barrier or a vapor barrier may be detailed to seal the wall against air infiltration, thereby becoming an air barrier as well.

For a discussion of insulation, see 116-117.

Coordinating these components is critical to avoid trapping water vapor in the wall cavity. The principle to follow is that the permeability (the degree to which water vapor will pass through a material) must be higher for materials on the cool side of the wall (usually the outside) than for materials on the warm side of the wall (usually the inside). For example, foil-faced rigid insulation, which has a very low permeability, should not be placed on the exterior of a wall in a cool climate. The following chart rates the permeability of several common materials:

Material	Permeability (perms per ASTM-E96)
Foil-faced insulation	0
4-mil PVC	0.08
Extruded polystyrene	0.3-1.0
½-in. CDX plywood	0.4-1.2
Kraft paper	1.8
15-lb. felt	5.6
½-in. fiberboard	50-90
Building or house wraps	88-107

A MOISTURE, VAPOR & AIR BARRIERS
        NOTES

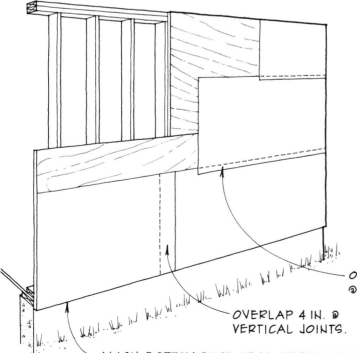

OVERLAP 2 IN. TO 4 IN.
@ HORIZONTAL JOINTS.

OVERLAP 4 IN. @
VERTICAL JOINTS.

ALIGN BOTTOM EDGE OF MOISTURE BARRIER W/ BOTTOM EDGE
OF SHEATHING. SEE SPECIFIC SIDING TYPE FOR DETAILS.

A moisture barrier under the siding is a sensible second line of defense to prevent water from reaching the frame of the building. Many suitable products such as 15-lb. felt and bitumin-impregnated paper come in 3-ft. wide rolls, as shown here.

A moisture barrier acting also as an air infiltration barrier under the siding must retard the passage of air and be impermeable to water, but allow vapor to pass. Chemically derived membranes, commonly called building or house wraps, have been developed recently that meet these specifications. They are very lightweight and come in rolls up to 12 ft. wide, allowing a single-story building to be covered in one pass. Building wraps can provide better protection against air infiltration than felt and Kraft paper because the wide rolls require fewer joints, and these joints are taped.

B MOISTURE & AIR INFILTRATION BARRIERS
        INSTALLATION

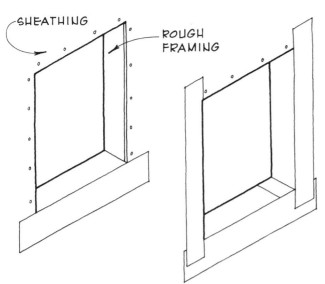
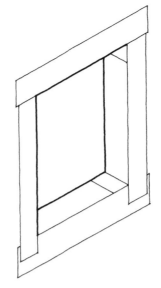

NOTE:
IT IS EXTREMELY IMPORTANT TO WRAP ROUGH OPENINGS WITH A MOISTURE BARRIER BECAUSE THIS IS WHERE LEAKS ARE MOST LIKELY TO OCCUR & BECAUSE THE FRAMING IS MOST VULNERABLE AT OPENINGS. THIS PROCEDURE IS ADEQUATE FOR MOST EXPOSED SITUATIONS BECAUSE ALL LAYERS OVERLAP IN AN ORDER THAT DIRECTS WATER AWAY FROM THE STRUCTURAL FRAME OF THE BUILDING. SIMPLER METHODS MAY BE EMPLOYED WHERE EXPOSURE TO RAIN IS NOT LIKELY TO OCCUR. FOR THE METHOD SHOWN, MANY BUILDERS PREFER TO USE THIN MOISTURE BARRIERS (SUCH AS KRAFT PAPER) THAT WILL NOT BUILD UP W/ THE FOLDS & W/ SEVERAL LAYERS.

1. STAPLE MOISTURE BARRIER TO SILL & FOLD 6 IN. DOWN, EXTENDING 6 IN. TO EACH SIDE. DO NOT STAPLE LOWER EDGE; IT WILL LAP WALL MOISTURE BARRIER.

2. STAPLE MOISTURE BARRIER TO JAMBS OF ROUGH OPENING & FOLD 6 IN. OVER SHEATHING & 6 IN. ABOVE & BELOW ROUGH OPENING.

3. REPEAT STEP 2, BUT FOR TOP OF ROUGH OPENING. LEAVE OUTER EDGES UNSTAPLED FOR FUTURE INTEGRATION W/ WALL MOISTURE BARRIER.

(A) WINDOW / DOOR ROUGH - OPENING WRAP

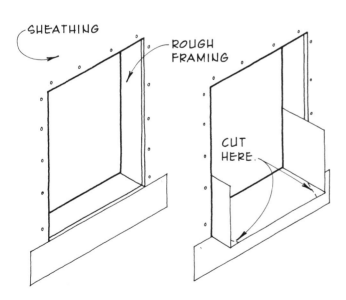
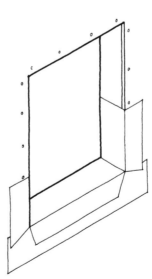
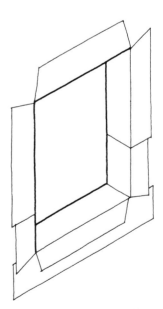

1. STAPLE 6-IN. MOISTURE-BARRIER PAPER @ BOTTOM EDGE OF ROUGH OPENING & EXTENDING 6 IN. TO EACH SIDE.

2. STAPLE MOISTURE BARRIER, WHICH EXTENDS 6 IN. PAST BUILDING'S FACE, AROUND FRAMING @ BOTTOM OF ROUGH OPENING. CUT AS SHOWN.

3. FOLD MOISTURE BARRIER INSTALLED IN STEP 2 AGAINST FACE OF BUILDING.

4. REPEAT STEPS 2 & 3 BUT FOR UPPER PART OF ROUGH OPENING.

(B) WINDOW / DOOR ROUGH - OPENING WRAP
ALTERNATIVE DETAIL FOR SEVERE EXPOSURE TO RAIN

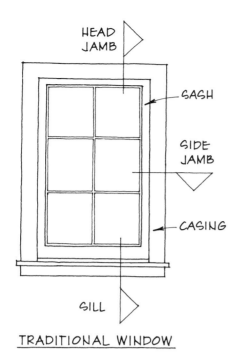

HEAD
JAMB

SASH

SIDE
JAMB

CASING

SILL

TRADITIONAL WINDOW

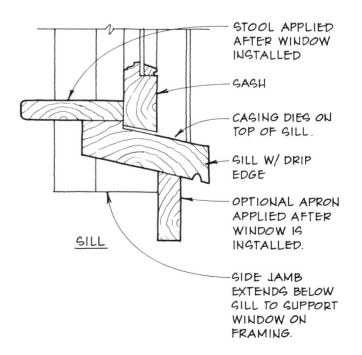

CASING ATTACHES
TO EXTERIOR
FRAME OF
BUILDING.

JAMB

SASH

STOP

JAMB EXTENDER
ADJUSTS JAMB
WIDTH TO WALL
THICKNESS.

HEAD JAMB

SILL (see BELOW)

CASING

JAMB

SASH

STOP

JAMB
EXTENDER

SIDE JAMB

STOOL APPLIED
AFTER WINDOW
INSTALLED

SASH

CASING DIES ON
TOP OF SILL.

SILL W/ DRIP
EDGE

OPTIONAL APRON
APPLIED AFTER
WINDOW IS
INSTALLED.

SIDE JAMB
EXTENDS BELOW
SILL TO SUPPORT
WINDOW ON
FRAMING.

SILL

Modern windows derive from the traditional wooden window shown above. Older windows have a wooden sash that holds the glass, which is usually divided into small panes by muntin bars. This sash is hinged within a wooden frame that is fixed to an opening in the wall. At the bottom of the frame is a wood sill, sloped to shed water, and the sides and top of the frame are called jambs.

These components and their terminology have been handed down to the modern window, but modern windows are better insulated and better sealed, and usually need less maintenance than the traditional prototypes.

Today's window is made in a factory and is usually assembled there and shipped ready to install in a rough opening. Several popular types, classified by their method of operation, include casement, double-hung, sliding, hopper, awning and fixed. Each of these types is made in wood, metal, vinyl or a combination of two materials. Sizes and details vary with the manufacturer. Double-hung, sliding and fixed windows are generally made in larger sizes than the hinged types. Optional trim packages are available with most.

 A WINDOW TERMINOLOGY

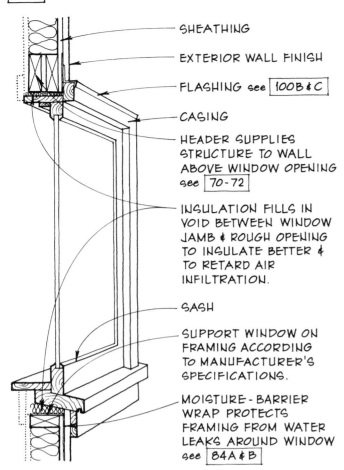

SHEATHING

EXTERIOR WALL FINISH

FLASHING see 100B & C

CASING

HEADER SUPPLIES STRUCTURE TO WALL ABOVE WINDOW OPENING see 70-72

INSULATION FILLS IN VOID BETWEEN WINDOW JAMB & ROUGH OPENING TO INSULATE BETTER & TO RETARD AIR INFILTRATION.

SASH

SUPPORT WINDOW ON FRAMING ACCORDING TO MANUFACTURER'S SPECIFICATIONS.

MOISTURE - BARRIER WRAP PROTECTS FRAMING FROM WATER LEAKS AROUND WINDOW see 84A & B

All windows require a coordinated installation in wood-frame walls, as follows:

Header—Size the header so that loads from above do not bear on the window itself and restrict its operation.

Window wrap—Wrap the framing at the rough opening with a moisture barrier to protect it from the occasional leaks that are most likely to occur around the edges of windows and doors.

Shim and support—Shim the window at the sill and affix the shims to the framing so that the window is level and rests firmly on the framing.

Insulation—Place batt or spray foam insulation around the edges of the installed window to reduce both heat loss and air infiltration.

Air barrier—An air barrier, if used, must be sealed to the window unit. The moisture/air barrier may be sealed to the window nailing flange at the wall's outside surface, or the vapor/air barrier may be sealed to the jamb's inside edge at the wall's inside surface.

Wood windows—Wood windows (see 87-89 and 91) are pleasing for their warm, natural look. Along with the excellent thermal properties of wood, the aesthetic appeal of the wood window is its strongest asset.

The major disadvantages of wood windows are the initial high cost and the ongoing need for maintenance. Wood is susceptible to deterioration from the weather, so periodically refinishing the exterior surfaces is necessary. Every effort should be made to protect all-wood windows from rain by locating them under overhangs. Wood windows that are exposed to the rain in existing structures will have their lives extended significantly by the protection of a storm sash.

Aluminum and vinyl-clad wood windows were developed to minimize maintenance. The cladding on these windows decreases their need for maintenance, yet retains the aesthetic and thermal advantages of wood on the interior. The availability of custom shapes is limited compared to all-wood windows, however.

Metal windows—Metal windows (see 89A and 90A) are made of extruded aluminum that is screwed or welded together at mitered corners. A wide range of quality and profiles is available. Metal windows are known for their low maintenance and low cost. Higher-quality units are available with thermal breaks built into the extrusion. These thermal breaks are recommended in cold climates to reduce heat loss and condensation.

Metal windows are not available with exterior casings, so their potential to act as strong visual elements on the exterior of a building is limited. Decorative casings are often added, however (see 87A). A wide variety of finishes is available on metal and metal-clad windows, with colors ranging from polished aluminum and anodized bronze to a full spectrum of baked-enamel colors.

Vinyl windows—Vinyl windows (see 89A and 90B) are made of extruded PVC. The extrusions are either screwed or heat-welded at the mitered corners to make both frames and jambs. Some units are manufactured with abbreviated casings; others are made to trim to the siding without casings.

Vinyl windows have not been used extensively in this country, but they look promising. Both their cost and their expected maintenance are low, while their insulative properties are relatively high. They are available in all operating types. Color is integral and is available in white, greys and shades of brown.

 WINDOW INSTALLATION

 WINDOW MATERIALS

Unclad wood windows are attached to the building through the casing. This is the traditional way that windows have been fastened to wood buildings. The nail holes are typically filled and the casings painted. It is also possible to cover the nails with a dripmold or with a backband that may be nailed from the side or the face, depending on the profile of the backband. The backband is mitered at the corners and dies on the sill.

TYPICAL BACKBAND PROFILES

When attaching a window through the casing, it is important to support the weight of the window unit from below. Shim the sill and/or the extensions of the side jambs below the sill.

Some manufacturers also recommend blocking and nailing the units through the jamb. In this case, the nails can be covered by the stops.

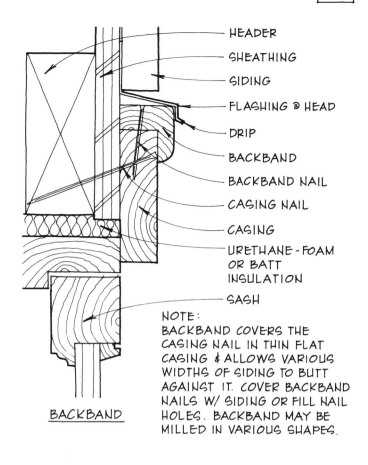

- HEADER
- SHEATHING
- SIDING
- FLASHING @ HEAD
- DRIP
- BACKBAND
- BACKBAND NAIL
- CASING NAIL
- CASING
- URETHANE - FOAM OR BATT INSULATION
- SASH

NOTE:
BACKBAND COVERS THE CASING NAIL IN THIN FLAT CASING & ALLOWS VARIOUS WIDTHS OF SIDING TO BUTT AGAINST IT. COVER BACKBAND NAILS W/ SIDING OR FILL NAIL HOLES. BACKBAND MAY BE MILLED IN VARIOUS SHAPES.

BACKBAND

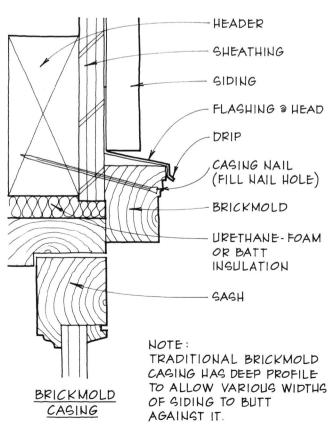

- HEADER
- SHEATHING
- SIDING
- FLASHING @ HEAD
- DRIP
- CASING NAIL (FILL NAIL HOLE)
- BRICKMOLD
- URETHANE - FOAM OR BATT INSULATION
- SASH

NOTE:
TRADITIONAL BRICKMOLD CASING HAS DEEP PROFILE TO ALLOW VARIOUS WIDTHS OF SIDING TO BUTT AGAINST IT.

BRICKMOLD CASING

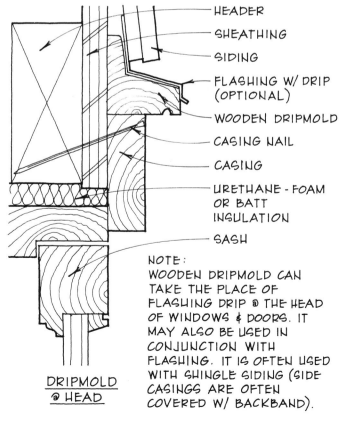

- HEADER
- SHEATHING
- SIDING
- FLASHING W/ DRIP (OPTIONAL)
- WOODEN DRIPMOLD
- CASING NAIL
- CASING
- URETHANE - FOAM OR BATT INSULATION
- SASH

NOTE:
WOODEN DRIPMOLD CAN TAKE THE PLACE OF FLASHING DRIP @ THE HEAD OF WINDOWS & DOORS. IT MAY ALSO BE USED IN CONJUNCTION WITH FLASHING. IT IS OFTEN USED WITH SHINGLE SIDING (SIDE CASINGS ARE OFTEN COVERED W/ BACKBAND).

DRIPMOLD @ HEAD

 A   **WOOD WINDOWS**
ATTACHMENT THROUGH CASING

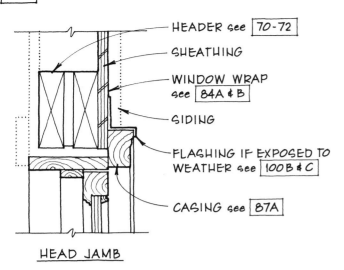

HEADER see 70-72

SHEATHING

WINDOW WRAP
see 84A & B

SIDING

FLASHING IF EXPOSED TO
WEATHER see 100B & C

CASING see 87A

HEAD JAMB

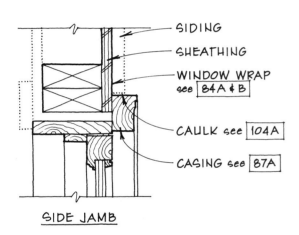

SIDING

SHEATHING

WINDOW WRAP
see 84A & B

CAULK see 104A

CASING see 87A

SIDE JAMB

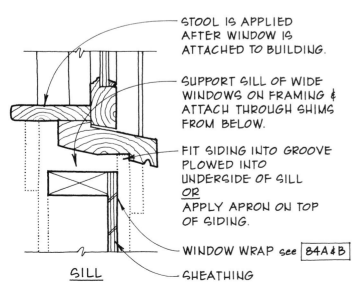

STOOL IS APPLIED
AFTER WINDOW IS
ATTACHED TO BUILDING.

SUPPORT SILL OF WIDE
WINDOWS ON FRAMING &
ATTACH THROUGH SHIMS
FROM BELOW.

FIT SIDING INTO GROOVE
PLOWED INTO
UNDERSIDE OF SILL
OR
APPLY APRON ON TOP
OF SIDING.

WINDOW WRAP see 84A & B

SHEATHING

SILL

 A   **UNCLAD WOOD WINDOWS**
ATTACHMENT THROUGH CASING

METAL, VINYL & CLAD WOOD WINDOWS ARE USUALLY MANUFACTURED W/ NAILING FINS THAT ACT AS FLASHING & PROVIDE NAILING FOR ATTACHING THE WINDOW TO THE BUILDING. CLAD UNITS W/ NAILING FINS CAN BE USED BOTH WITH & WITHOUT CASINGS.

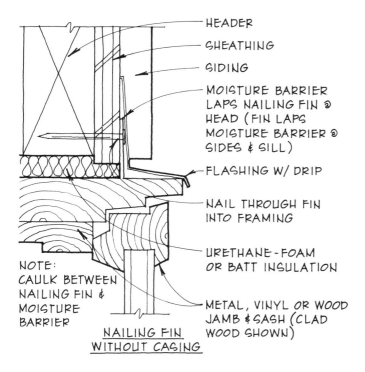

- HEADER
- SHEATHING
- SIDING
- MOISTURE BARRIER LAPS NAILING FIN @ HEAD (FIN LAPS MOISTURE BARRIER @ SIDES & SILL)
- FLASHING W/ DRIP
- NAIL THROUGH FIN INTO FRAMING
- URETHANE-FOAM OR BATT INSULATION

NOTE: CAULK BETWEEN NAILING FIN & MOISTURE BARRIER

- METAL, VINYL OR WOOD JAMB & SASH (CLAD WOOD SHOWN)

<u>NAILING FIN WITHOUT CASING</u>

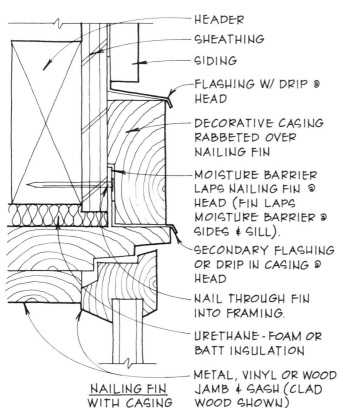

- HEADER
- SHEATHING
- SIDING
- FLASHING W/ DRIP @ HEAD
- DECORATIVE CASING RABBETED OVER NAILING FIN
- MOISTURE BARRIER LAPS NAILING FIN @ HEAD (FIN LAPS MOISTURE BARRIER @ SIDES & SILL).
- SECONDARY FLASHING OR DRIP IN CASING @ HEAD
- NAIL THROUGH FIN INTO FRAMING.
- URETHANE-FOAM OR BATT INSULATION
- METAL, VINYL OR WOOD JAMB & SASH (CLAD WOOD SHOWN)

<u>NAILING FIN WITH CASING</u>

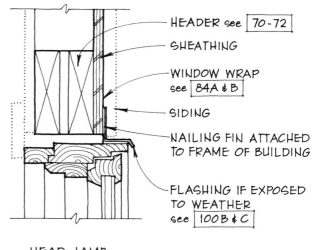

- HEADER see 70-72
- SHEATHING
- WINDOW WRAP see 84A & B
- SIDING
- NAILING FIN ATTACHED TO FRAME OF BUILDING
- FLASHING IF EXPOSED TO WEATHER see 100B & C

<u>HEAD JAMB</u>

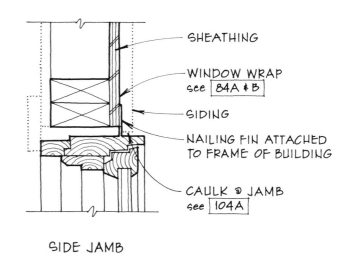

- SHEATHING
- WINDOW WRAP see 84A & B
- SIDING
- NAILING FIN ATTACHED TO FRAME OF BUILDING
- CAULK @ JAMB see 104A

<u>SIDE JAMB</u>

- SHIM WINDOW TO BOTTOM OF ROUGH OPENING FOR LEVELING & SUPPORT.
- NAILING FIN ATTACHED TO FRAME OF BUILDING
- SHEATHING
- WINDOW WRAP see 84A & B
- SIDING

<u>SILL</u>

(A) **WOOD, METAL OR VINYL WINDOWS**
ATTACHMENT THROUGH NAILING FIN

(B) **CLAD WOOD WINDOWS**
ATTACHMENT THROUGH NAILING FIN

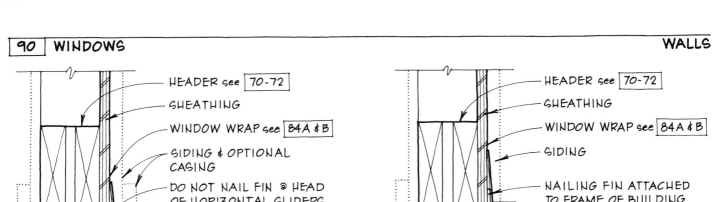

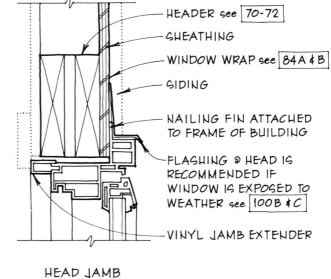

HEADER see [70-72]

SHEATHING

WINDOW WRAP see [84A & B]

SIDING & OPTIONAL CASING

DO NOT NAIL FIN @ HEAD OF HORIZONTAL SLIDERS.

FLASHING @ HEAD IF WINDOW IS EXPOSED TO WEATHER see [100B & C]

WOOD JAMB W/ CASING <u>OR</u> WRAP INTERIOR FINISH TO WINDOW.

<u>HEAD JAMB</u>

HEADER see [70-72]

SHEATHING

WINDOW WRAP see [84A & B]

SIDING

NAILING FIN ATTACHED TO FRAME OF BUILDING

FLASHING @ HEAD IS RECOMMENDED IF WINDOW IS EXPOSED TO WEATHER see [100B & C]

VINYL JAMB EXTENDER

<u>HEAD JAMB</u>

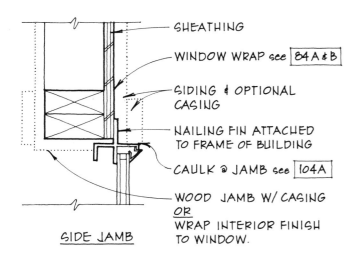

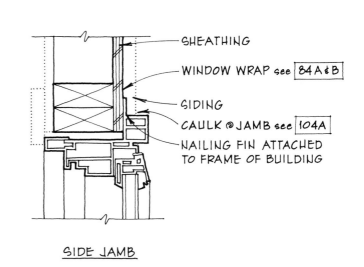

SHEATHING

WINDOW WRAP see [84A & B]

SIDING & OPTIONAL CASING

NAILING FIN ATTACHED TO FRAME OF BUILDING

CAULK @ JAMB see [104A]

WOOD JAMB W/ CASING <u>OR</u> WRAP INTERIOR FINISH TO WINDOW.

<u>SIDE JAMB</u>

SHEATHING

WINDOW WRAP see [84A & B]

SIDING

CAULK @ JAMB see [104A]

NAILING FIN ATTACHED TO FRAME OF BUILDING

<u>SIDE JAMB</u>

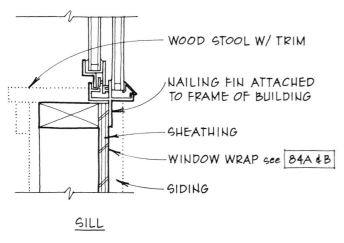

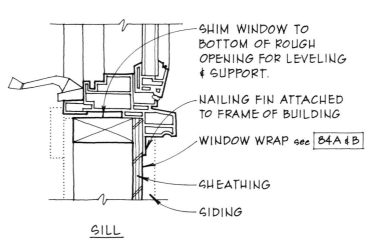

WOOD STOOL W/ TRIM

NAILING FIN ATTACHED TO FRAME OF BUILDING

SHEATHING

WINDOW WRAP see [84A & B]

SIDING

<u>SILL</u>

SHIM WINDOW TO BOTTOM OF ROUGH OPENING FOR LEVELING & SUPPORT.

NAILING FIN ATTACHED TO FRAME OF BUILDING

WINDOW WRAP see [84A & B]

SHEATHING

SIDING

<u>SILL</u>

 (A)   **METAL WINDOWS**

 (B)   **VINYL WINDOWS**

Where fixed windows are acceptable, a great deal of expense may be saved by custom-building the windows on the job without sash. In this case, the glass is stopped directly into the window frame, and caulk or glazing tape seals the glass to the casing just as it would to sash. Ventilation must be provided for the space by means other than operable windows.

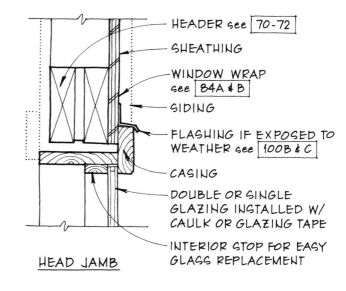

- HEADER see 70-72
- SHEATHING
- WINDOW WRAP see 84A & B
- SIDING
- FLASHING IF EXPOSED TO WEATHER see 100B & C
- CASING
- DOUBLE OR SINGLE GLAZING INSTALLED W/ CAULK OR GLAZING TAPE
- INTERIOR STOP FOR EASY GLASS REPLACEMENT

HEAD JAMB

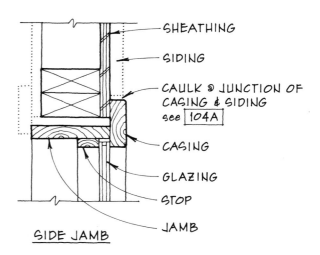

- SHEATHING
- SIDING
- CAULK @ JUNCTION OF CASING & SIDING see 104A
- CASING
- GLAZING
- STOP
- JAMB

SIDE JAMB

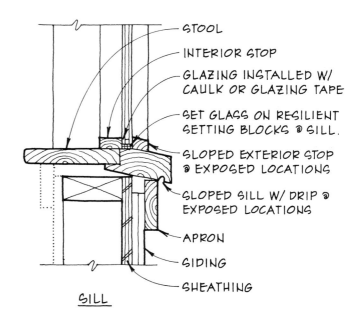

- STOOL
- INTERIOR STOP
- GLAZING INSTALLED W/ CAULK OR GLAZING TAPE
- SET GLASS ON RESILIENT SETTING BLOCKS @ SILL.
- SLOPED EXTERIOR STOP @ EXPOSED LOCATIONS
- SLOPED SILL W/ DRIP @ EXPOSED LOCATIONS
- APRON
- SIDING
- SHEATHING

SILL

NOTES:
ALLOW 1/8-IN. (MIN.) CLEARANCE AT TOP AND SIDES OF GLASS.
REST BASE OF GLASS ON SETTING BLOCKS SPACED ONE-QUARTER OF THE WIDTH FROM EACH END.
STOOL & SILL CAN BE ONE SINGLE FLAT PIECE @ PROTECTED LOCATIONS.
GLASS CAN BE SET CLOSER TO INTERIOR OF BUILDING W/ EXTRA EXTERIOR STOP IF DESIRED.
SUPPORT SILL OF WIDE WINDOWS ON FRAMING & ATTACH THROUGH SHIMS FROM BELOW.

(A) SITE-BUILT FIXED WINDOWS

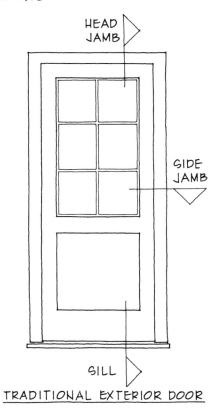

HEAD JAMB

SIDE JAMB

SILL

TRADITIONAL EXTERIOR DOOR

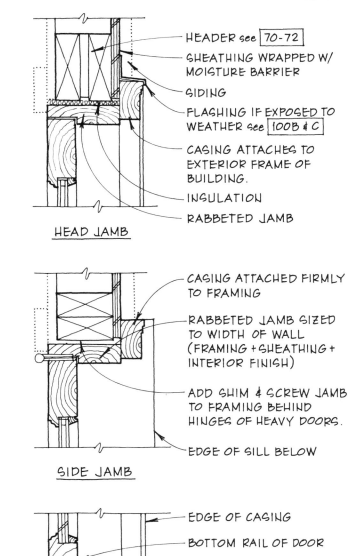

HEADER see 70-72

SHEATHING WRAPPED W/ MOISTURE BARRIER

SIDING

FLASHING IF EXPOSED TO WEATHER see 100B & C

CASING ATTACHES TO EXTERIOR FRAME OF BUILDING.

INSULATION

RABBETED JAMB

HEAD JAMB

CASING ATTACHED FIRMLY TO FRAMING

RABBETED JAMB SIZED TO WIDTH OF WALL (FRAMING + SHEATHING + INTERIOR FINISH)

ADD SHIM & SCREW JAMB TO FRAMING BEHIND HINGES OF HEAVY DOORS.

EDGE OF SILL BELOW

SIDE JAMB

Modern doors have been derived from traditional prototypes; they are better insulated and better sealed, and usually require less maintenance than their ancestors. The material of choice for exterior doors is wood (plywood, composite or solid wood), but insulated metal panel doors are making inroads into the market. Most exterior doors swing inward to protect them from the weather. Nearly all manufacturers sell their doors prehung (hinged to a jamb and with exterior casing attached). Sills and thresholds are the most variable elements in manufactured prehung doors.

Most doors come with an extruded metal sill and integral threshold, which is installed on top of the subfloor (see 96B). Wood sills must be thicker for strength, so they are installed lower than metal sills, flush with the floor framing (see 96A).

Because of the torsional forces exerted by the hinges on the jamb when the door is open, doors that swing need to have their jambs fastened directly and securely to the building's frame. The best way to accomplish this is to nail the jamb directly to the supporting stud, using shims to make the jamb plumb. To do this, remove the casing on the hinged side of a prehung exterior door or find a way to shim the jamb with the casings in place. It is common practice to attach a prehung door through the casing with long screws through the hinge and jamb into the stud.

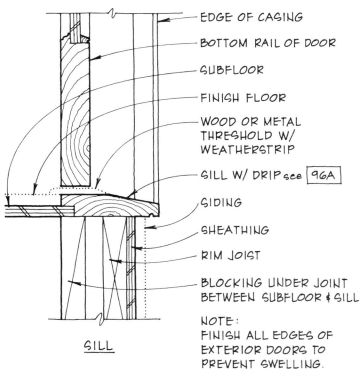

EDGE OF CASING

BOTTOM RAIL OF DOOR

SUBFLOOR

FINISH FLOOR

WOOD OR METAL THRESHOLD W/ WEATHERSTRIP

SILL W/ DRIP see 96A

SIDING

SHEATHING

RIM JOIST

BLOCKING UNDER JOINT BETWEEN SUBFLOOR & SILL

NOTE:
FINISH ALL EDGES OF EXTERIOR DOORS TO PREVENT SWELLING.

SILL

A EXTERIOR SWINGING DOORS
ATTACHMENT TO WALLS

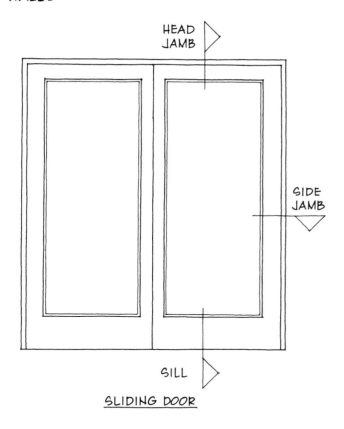

HEAD JAMB

SIDE JAMB

SILL

SLIDING DOOR

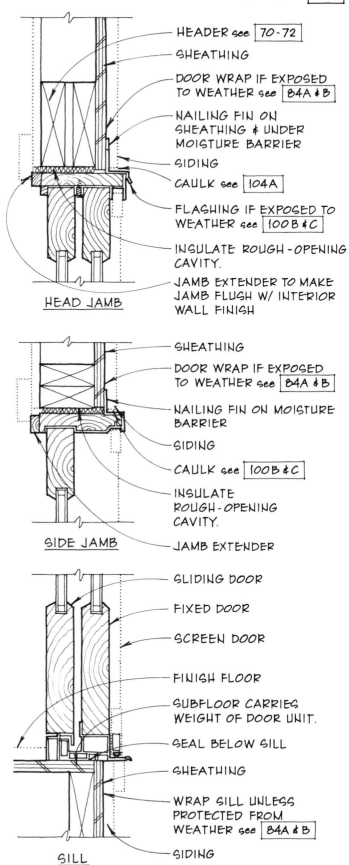

HEADER see 70-72

SHEATHING

DOOR WRAP IF EXPOSED
TO WEATHER see 84A & B

NAILING FIN ON
SHEATHING & UNDER
MOISTURE BARRIER

SIDING

CAULK see 104A

FLASHING IF EXPOSED TO
WEATHER see 100B & C

INSULATE ROUGH-OPENING
CAVITY.

JAMB EXTENDER TO MAKE
JAMB FLUSH W/ INTERIOR
WALL FINISH

HEAD JAMB

SHEATHING

DOOR WRAP IF EXPOSED
TO WEATHER see 84A & B

NAILING FIN ON MOISTURE
BARRIER

SIDING

CAULK see 100B & C

INSULATE
ROUGH-OPENING
CAVITY.

JAMB EXTENDER

SIDE JAMB

SLIDING DOOR

FIXED DOOR

SCREEN DOOR

FINISH FLOOR

SUBFLOOR CARRIES
WEIGHT OF DOOR UNIT.

SEAL BELOW SILL

SHEATHING

WRAP SILL UNLESS
PROTECTED FROM
WEATHER see 84A & B

SIDING

SILL

Sliding doors, whether they are wood or aluminum, fasten to a building more like a window than like a swinging door. Because the weight of a sliding door remains within the plane of the wall, there is no lateral loading on the jamb of the door unit. Sliding doors are therefore supported on the sill and can be attached to the building like windows, through the casing or with a nailing fin.

Sliding doors are trimmed to the finish materials of the wall in the same way as swinging doors and windows (see 87-90).

A **SLIDING DOORS**
ATTACHMENT TO WALLS

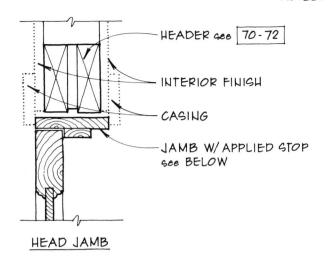

HEAD JAMB

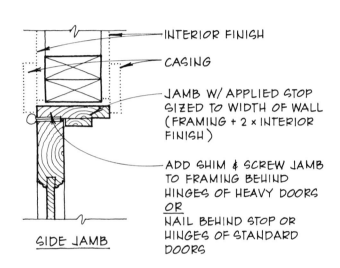

SIDE JAMB

INTERIOR DOOR

Because they do not have to be sealed against the weather, interior doors are much simpler than exterior doors. Interior doors are used primarily for privacy and to control air flow. The doors themselves are typically made of wood. They are 1⅜ in. thick, and have either six or four panels, like the one shown above, or a flush plywood veneer over a hollow core or solid core.

Hinged doors are usually prehung on a jamb without casings. The jamb on the hinged side is first nailed to the frame of the building using shims to make it plumb. The jambs at the head and opposite side are then shimmed for proper clearance and nailed.

Some doors are hinged to a split jamb that well expand to accommodate some variation in wall thickness. Interior doors do not have sills and rarely have a threshold unless the floor material changes at the door.

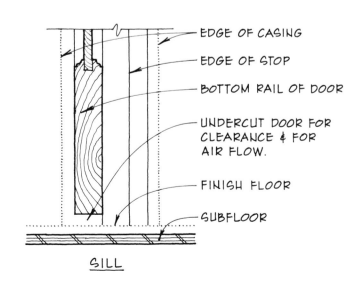

SILL

INTERIOR HINGED DOORS

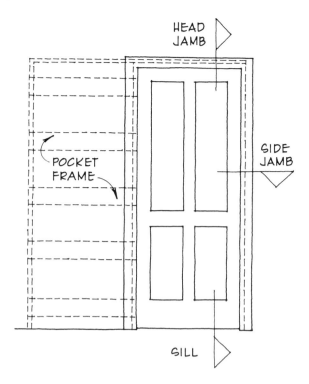

HEAD JAMB

SIDE JAMB

POCKET FRAME

SILL

POCKET DOOR

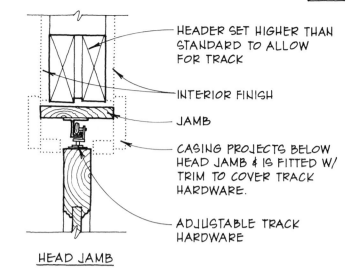

HEADER SET HIGHER THAN STANDARD TO ALLOW FOR TRACK

INTERIOR FINISH

JAMB

CASING PROJECTS BELOW HEAD JAMB & IS FITTED W/ TRIM TO COVER TRACK HARDWARE.

ADJUSTABLE TRACK HARDWARE

HEAD JAMB

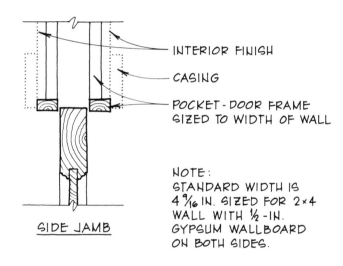

INTERIOR FINISH

CASING

POCKET-DOOR FRAME SIZED TO WIDTH OF WALL

NOTE:
STANDARD WIDTH IS 4 9/16 IN. SIZED FOR 2×4 WALL WITH ½-IN. GYPSUM WALLBOARD ON BOTH SIDES.

SIDE JAMB

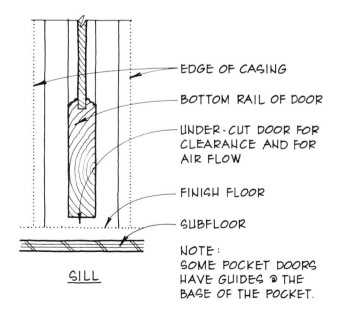

EDGE OF CASING

BOTTOM RAIL OF DOOR

UNDER-CUT DOOR FOR CLEARANCE AND FOR AIR FLOW

FINISH FLOOR

SUBFLOOR

NOTE:
SOME POCKET DOORS HAVE GUIDES @ THE BASE OF THE POCKET.

SILL

Pocket doors—Pocket doors slide on a track attached to the head jamb and are sold as a kit with the door and pocket separate and the pocket broken-down for ease of transport. The pocket is assembled at the site, and the head jamb (which much be set higher than 6 ft. 8 in. to allow for the track) is leveled, shimmed and attached to the frame of the building. Next the pocket itself and the opposite jamb are shimmed and nailed. The heavier and wider the door and the better the quality of the hardware, the less likely the door is to derail. Pocket doors can't be made to seal as tightly as hinged doors. The walls are flimsy at the pocket, and wiring or plumbing can't be put in this section of wall.

Bypass doors—Bypass doors, such as sliding closet doors, slide on a track like pocket doors, but have a double track and two doors that are not concealed in a pocket in the wall. Nylon guides on the floor keep the bottom of the doors in line. As with pocket doors, the header of a bypass door should be set higher than normal, and the casing should be designed to cover the track hardware. The jambs are like those for hinged doors but without stops.

Bifold doors—Bifold doors have two hinged halves that fold to one side, with a track at the top. Installation notes for bypass doors apply, except that casing trim must be kept above the top of the doors to allow the doors to fold.

 A POCKET DOORS, BYPASS DOORS & BIFOLD DOORS

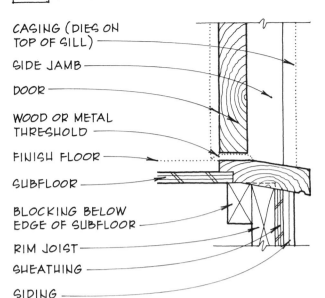

CASING (DIES ON TOP OF SILL)
SIDE JAMB
DOOR
WOOD OR METAL THRESHOLD
FINISH FLOOR
SUBFLOOR
BLOCKING BELOW EDGE OF SUBFLOOR
RIM JOIST
SHEATHING
SIDING

TRADITIONAL WOOD SILL W/ DRIP SLOPES @ 10° & REQUIRES THAT TOP OF RIM JOIST & COMMON JOISTS BE SHAVED OFF FOR INSTALLATION. SILL EXTENDS TO OUTSIDE EDGES OF DOOR CASINGS.

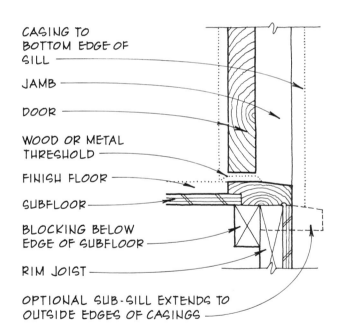

CASING TO BOTTOM EDGE OF SILL
JAMB
DOOR
WOOD OR METAL THRESHOLD
FINISH FLOOR
SUBFLOOR
BLOCKING BELOW EDGE OF SUBFLOOR
RIM JOIST

OPTIONAL SUB-SILL EXTENDS TO OUTSIDE EDGES OF CASINGS

FLATTENED WOOD SILL SLOPES @ 7° & IS INSTALLED ON TOP OF JOIST SYSTEM. OUTSIDE EDGE IS FLUSH W/ JAMB (SHOWN) OR CASING.

NOTES:
ADJUST PROFILE OF SILLS FOR OUTSWINGING DOORS.
WEATHERSTRIP BOTTOM OF DOOR.
WOOD SILLS ARE NOT COMPATIBLE W/ SLAB SUBFLOORS.

 WOOD SILLS

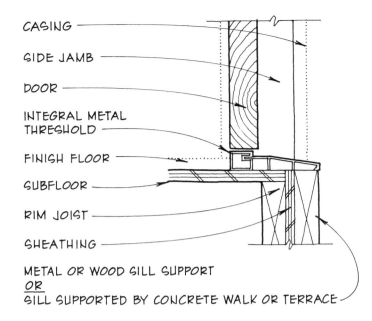

CASING
SIDE JAMB
DOOR
INTEGRAL METAL THRESHOLD
FINISH FLOOR
SUBFLOOR
RIM JOIST
SHEATHING

METAL OR WOOD SILL SUPPORT
OR
SILL SUPPORTED BY CONCRETE WALK OR TERRACE

EXTRUDED SILLS OF ALUMINUM OR POLYCARBONATE ARE THE MOST COMMON FOR ALL MODERN DOORS. THE THRESHOLD IS INTEGRAL. THE SILL MUST BE SUPPORTED @ OUTER EDGE. EXTRUDED SILLS MAY ALSO BE USED IN SLAB-ON-GRADE CONSTRUCTION.

 EXTRUDED SILLS

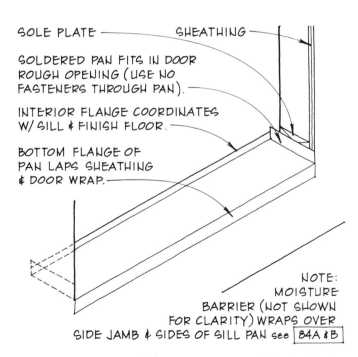

SOLE PLATE   SHEATHING
SOLDERED PAN FITS IN DOOR ROUGH OPENING (USE NO FASTENERS THROUGH PAN).
INTERIOR FLANGE COORDINATES W/ SILL & FINISH FLOOR.
BOTTOM FLANGE OF PAN LAPS SHEATHING & DOOR WRAP.

NOTE: MOISTURE BARRIER (NOT SHOWN FOR CLARITY) WRAPS OVER SIDE JAMB & SIDES OF SILL PAN see 84A & B

AT DOOR LOCATIONS EXPOSED TO THE WEATHER, A GALVANIZED METAL DOOR-SILL PAN FIT INTO THE DOOR ROUGH OPENING WILL PROTECT THE STRUCTURE OF A WOODEN FLOOR SYSTEM BELOW.

 DOOR-SILL PAN

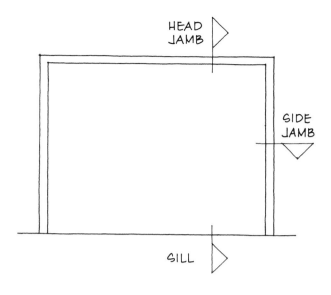

HEAD JAMB

SIDE JAMB

SILL

GARAGE DOOR

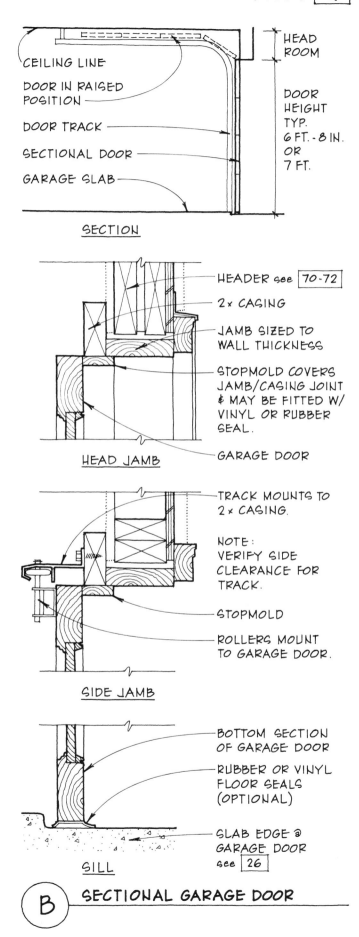

CEILING LINE

DOOR IN RAISED POSITION

DOOR TRACK

SECTIONAL DOOR

GARAGE SLAB

HEAD ROOM

DOOR HEIGHT TYP. 6 FT. - 8 IN. OR 7 FT.

SECTION

HEADER see 70-72

2 x CASING

JAMB SIZED TO WALL THICKNESS

STOPMOLD COVERS JAMB/CASING JOINT & MAY BE FITTED W/ VINYL OR RUBBER SEAL.

GARAGE DOOR

HEAD JAMB

TRACK MOUNTS TO 2 x CASING.

NOTE: VERIFY SIDE CLEARANCE FOR TRACK.

STOPMOLD

ROLLERS MOUNT TO GARAGE DOOR.

SIDE JAMB

BOTTOM SECTION OF GARAGE DOOR

RUBBER OR VINYL FLOOR SEALS (OPTIONAL)

SLAB EDGE @ GARAGE DOOR see 26

SILL

Residential garage doors have evolved from swinging and sliding types to almost exclusively the overhead variety. They are manufactured primarily with a solid-wood frame and plywood or particleboard panels. Paneled metal, fiberglass and vinyl doors are available in some regions. There are two operating types, sectional and one-piece, both which can be manual or fitted with automatic openers.

Sectional doors—Sectional doors are the more common (see 97B). They are hinged horizontally—usually in four sections—and roll up overhead. The advantages are that a sectional door is totally protected by the structure when in the open position, and that it closes to the inside face of the jamb, making the design of the jamb opening somewhat flexible.

One-piece doors—One-piece doors pivot up (see 98A). The door usually fits within the jamb and extends to the outside of the building when in the open position. This exposes the open door to the weather. The advantage of this type of door is the greater flexibility of design afforded by the one-piece door.

 A GARAGE DOORS

B SECTIONAL GARAGE DOOR

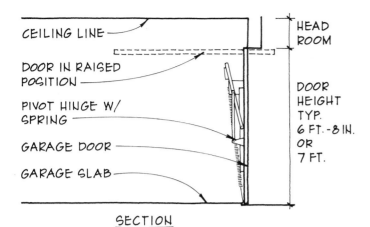

CEILING LINE

DOOR IN RAISED
POSITION

PIVOT HINGE W/
SPRING

GARAGE DOOR

GARAGE SLAB

HEAD
ROOM

DOOR
HEIGHT
TYP.
6 FT. - 8 IN.
OR
7 FT.

SECTION

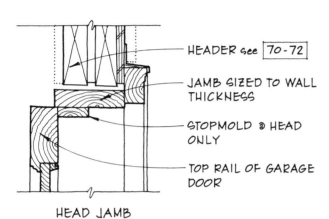

HEADER see [70-72]

JAMB SIZED TO WALL
THICKNESS

STOPMOLD @ HEAD
ONLY

TOP RAIL OF GARAGE
DOOR

HEAD JAMB

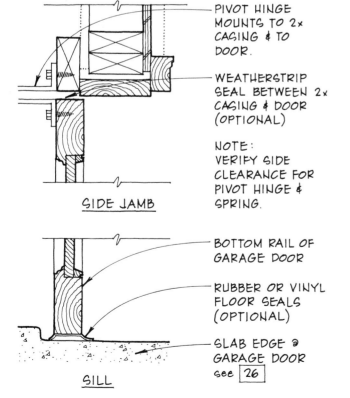

PIVOT HINGE
MOUNTS TO 2x
CASING & TO
DOOR.

WEATHERSTRIP
SEAL BETWEEN 2x
CASING & DOOR
(OPTIONAL)

NOTE:
VERIFY SIDE
CLEARANCE FOR
PIVOT HINGE &
SPRING.

SIDE JAMB

BOTTOM RAIL OF
GARAGE DOOR

RUBBER OR VINYL
FLOOR SEALS
(OPTIONAL)

SLAB EDGE @
GARAGE DOOR
see [26]

SILL

A | ONE - PIECE GARAGE DOOR

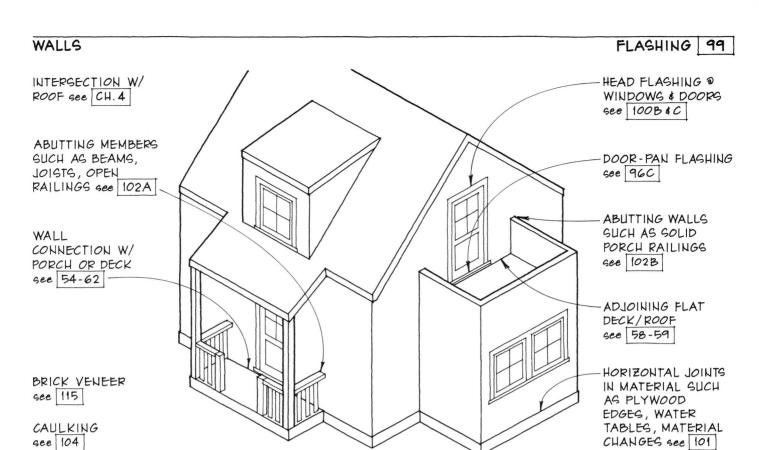

INTERSECTION W/
ROOF see | CH.4 |

ABUTTING MEMBERS
SUCH AS BEAMS,
JOISTS, OPEN
RAILINGS see | 102A |

WALL
CONNECTION W/
PORCH OR DECK
see | 54-62 |

BRICK VENEER
see | 115 |

CAULKING
see | 104 |

HEAD FLASHING @
WINDOWS & DOORS
see | 100B & C |

DOOR-PAN FLASHING
see | 96C |

ABUTTING WALLS
SUCH AS SOLID
PORCH RAILINGS
see | 102B |

ADJOINING FLAT
DECK/ROOF
see | 58-59 |

HORIZONTAL JOINTS
IN MATERIAL SUCH
AS PLYWOOD
EDGES, WATER
TABLES, MATERIAL
CHANGES see | 101 |

Flashing is essential to keeping water away from the structure and the interior of a building. It is used wherever there is a horizontal or sloped penetration of the outer building skin or a juncture of dissimilar materials that is likely to be exposed to the weather. Flashing provides a permanent barrier to the water and directs it to the outer surface of the building, where gravity carries the water down to the ground. Of course, the best protection against water penetration of walls is an adequate eave, but wind-driven rain may make this strategy occasionally unreliable.

Wall flashing, which provides the first line of defense against water, should be taken very seriously, especially since walls, unlike roofs, are not intended to be replaced regularly. Wall flashing is likely to be in place for the life of the building.

Two physical properties affect the flow of water on vertical surfaces. The first property, gravity, can be used to advantage in directing water down the wall of a building. The other property, surface tension, creates capillary action that results in water migrating in all directions along cracks in and between materials. In many cases, the negative effects of surface tension can be avoided by the proper use of a drip.

A drip is a thin edge or undercut at the bottom of a material placed far enough away from the building surface so that a drop of water forming on it will not touch the wall but will drop away. Drips may be made of flashing or may be cut into the building material itself.

In the case of vertical joints, a sealant may be required to counter the effects of surface tension. Caulk (sealant) should be used primarily as an air barrier, not a water barrier (see 104A). Except for vertical joints that cannot be flashed effectively, a well-designed flashing (see 100-102) is always preferable to a bead of caulk.

Common flashing materials include galvanized steel, baked enamel steel, aluminum, copper, stainless steel, and lead. Because flashing materials may be affected in different ways by different climates, air pollutants and building materials, the selection of appropriate materials is specific to each job. It is also important to isolate different metals when flashing to prevent corrosive interaction (galvanic action) between them. Consult with local sheet-metal shops for appropriate materials for specific applications.

 WALL FLASHING

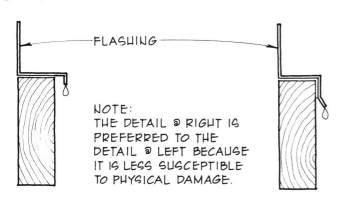

FLASHING

NOTE:
THE DETAIL ⓐ RIGHT IS PREFERRED TO THE DETAIL ⓐ LEFT BECAUSE IT IS LESS SUSCEPTIBLE TO PHYSICAL DAMAGE.

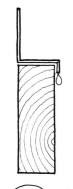

PAINT TENDS TO CLOG FLASHING DRIPS, BUT IT ALSO TENDS TO SEAL THE CRACK BETWEEN FLASHING & THE MATERIAL THE FLASHING COVERS. FLASHING OVER PAINTED WOOD, THEREFORE, IS OFTEN MADE WITHOUT A DRIP, AS SHOWN ⓐ LEFT.

Ⓐ FLASHING DRIPS

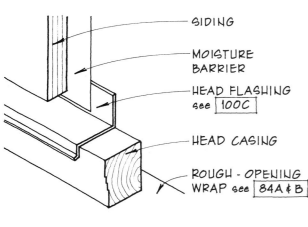

- SIDING
- MOISTURE BARRIER
- HEAD FLASHING see | 100C |
- HEAD CASING
- ROUGH - OPENING WRAP see | 84A & B |

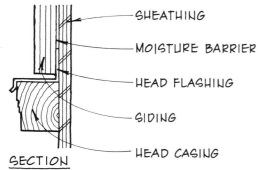

- SHEATHING
- MOISTURE BARRIER
- HEAD FLASHING
- SIDING
- HEAD CASING

SECTION

Ⓑ WINDOW/DOOR HEAD FLASHING

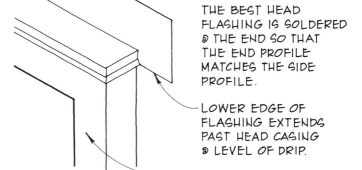

THE BEST HEAD FLASHING IS SOLDERED ⓐ THE END SO THAT THE END PROFILE MATCHES THE SIDE PROFILE.

LOWER EDGE OF FLASHING EXTENDS PAST HEAD CASING ⓐ LEVEL OF DRIP.

CASING

SOLDERED HEAD FLASHING

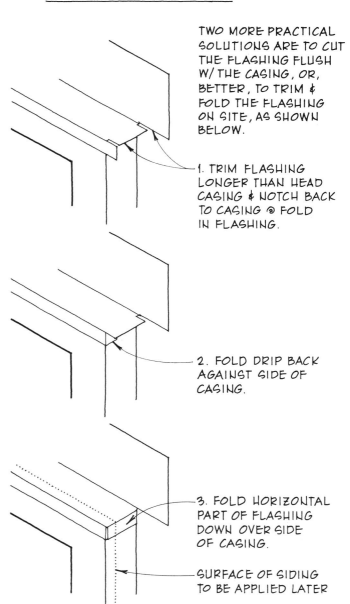

TWO MORE PRACTICAL SOLUTIONS ARE TO CUT THE FLASHING FLUSH W/ THE CASING, OR, BETTER, TO TRIM & FOLD THE FLASHING ON SITE, AS SHOWN BELOW.

1. TRIM FLASHING LONGER THAN HEAD CASING & NOTCH BACK TO CASING ⓐ FOLD IN FLASHING.

2. FOLD DRIP BACK AGAINST SIDE OF CASING.

3. FOLD HORIZONTAL PART OF FLASHING DOWN OVER SIDE OF CASING.

SURFACE OF SIDING TO BE APPLIED LATER

FOLDED HEAD FLASHING

Ⓒ WINDOW/DOOR HEAD FLASHING
ⓐ END OF FLASHING

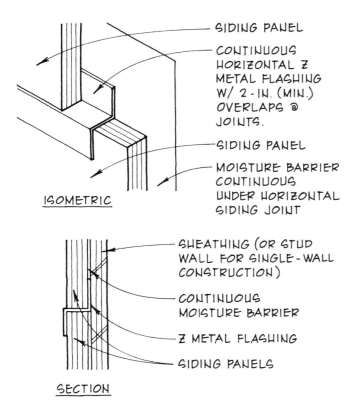

SIDING PANEL

CONTINUOUS HORIZONTAL Z METAL FLASHING W/ 2-IN. (MIN.) OVERLAPS @ JOINTS.

SIDING PANEL

MOISTURE BARRIER CONTINUOUS UNDER HORIZONTAL SIDING JOINT

ISOMETRIC

SHEATHING (OR STUD WALL FOR SINGLE-WALL CONSTRUCTION)

CONTINUOUS MOISTURE BARRIER

Z METAL FLASHING

SIDING PANELS

SECTION

(A) **HORIZONTAL WALL FLASHING**
Z METAL @ PANEL JOINT

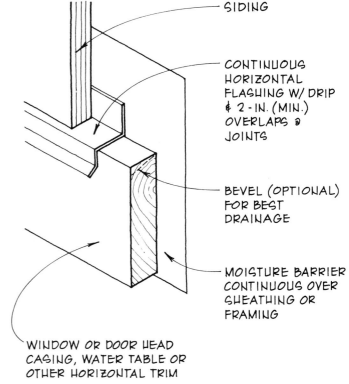

SIDING

CONTINUOUS HORIZONTAL FLASHING W/ DRIP & 2-IN. (MIN.) OVERLAPS @ JOINTS

BEVEL (OPTIONAL) FOR BEST DRAINAGE

MOISTURE BARRIER CONTINUOUS OVER SHEATHING OR FRAMING

WINDOW OR DOOR HEAD CASING, WATER TABLE OR OTHER HORIZONTAL TRIM

(B) **HORIZONTAL WALL FLASHING**
JOINT BETWEEN DISSIMILAR MATERIALS

STEP 1   STEP 2

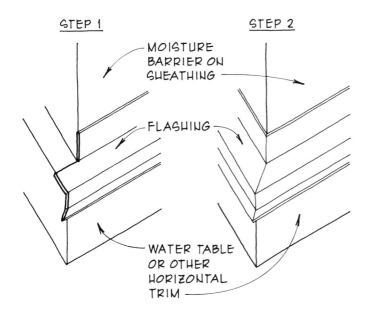

MOISTURE BARRIER ON SHEATHING

FLASHING

WATER TABLE OR OTHER HORIZONTAL TRIM

OUTSIDE CORNER

STEP 1   STEP 2

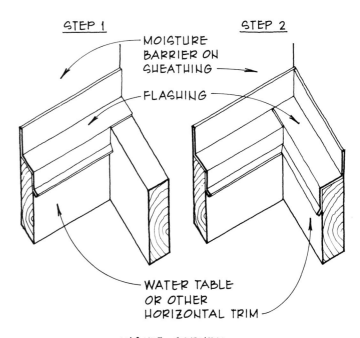

MOISTURE BARRIER ON SHEATHING

FLASHING

WATER TABLE OR OTHER HORIZONTAL TRIM

INSIDE CORNER

NOTE:
IT IS PRUDENT TO COVER THE VERTICAL END OF THE FLASHING W/ A SMALL PIECE OF MOISTURE BARRIER OR A DAB OF CAULK TO MINIMIZE THE POTENTIAL FOR LEAKS.

(C) **HORIZONTAL WALL FLASHING**
CORNER DETAILS

Any horizontal member such as a handrail, a trellis or a joist that butts into an exterior wall poses an inherently difficult flashing problem at the top edge of the abutting members. Where such a connection is likely to get wet, the best approach is to avoid the problem by supporting the member independent of the wall. A handrail, for example, could be supported by a column near the wall but not touching it. A trellis could be self-supported.

If a horizontal member must be connected to a wall in a location exposed to the weather, two things can be done to protect the structure of the wall. First, do not puncture the surface of the siding with the member, and do everything possible to attach the member to the surface of the siding with a minimum number of fasteners. Second, place an adequate gasket, such as 30-lb. or 90-lb. felt, behind the siding at the location of attachment. This will help seal nails or screws that pass through the siding to the structure of the wall.

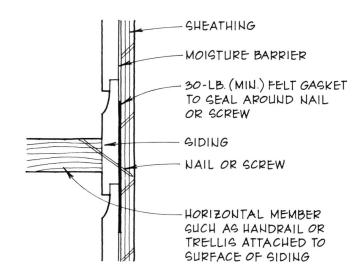

- SHEATHING
- MOISTURE BARRIER
- 30-LB. (MIN.) FELT GASKET TO SEAL AROUND NAIL OR SCREW
- SIDING
- NAIL OR SCREW
- HORIZONTAL MEMBER SUCH AS HANDRAIL OR TRELLIS ATTACHED TO SURFACE OF SIDING

 A   FLASHING ABUTTING MEMBERS

THIS HORIZONTAL JOINT IS BEST PROTECTED W/ A FLASHING MADE TO FIT OVER THE SHEATHING & MOISTURE BARRIER OF THE FRAMED WALL.

- HORIZONTAL JOINT (DETAIL @ RIGHT)
- WALL CAP see | 103A |

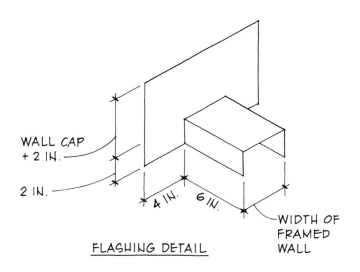

WALL CAP + 2 IN.

2 IN.

4 IN.   6 IN.

WIDTH OF FRAMED WALL

FLASHING DETAIL

LAP FLASHING OVER MOISTURE BARRIERS THAT HAVE BEEN WRAPPED OVER THE ABUTTING WALL & JOINED TO THE MOISTURE BARRIER ON THE PRIMARY WALL. THEN LAP THE TOP EDGE OF THE FLASHING W/ THE MOISTURE BARRIER ON THE PRIMARY WALL.

 B   FLASHING ABUTTING WALLS

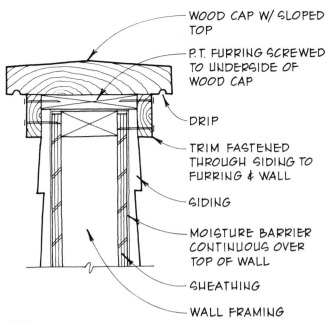

WOOD CAP W/ SLOPED TOP

P.T. FURRING SCREWED TO UNDERSIDE OF WOOD CAP

DRIP

TRIM FASTENED THROUGH SIDING TO FURRING & WALL

SIDING

MOISTURE BARRIER CONTINUOUS OVER TOP OF WALL

SHEATHING

WALL FRAMING

NOTE:
THIS DETAIL HAS A CONTINUOUS MOISTURE BARRIER OVER THE TOP OF THE WALL WITHOUT PENETRATIONS. THE MOISTURE BARRIER MAY BE REPLACED W/ METAL FLASHING.

 A   **WOOD WALL CAP**

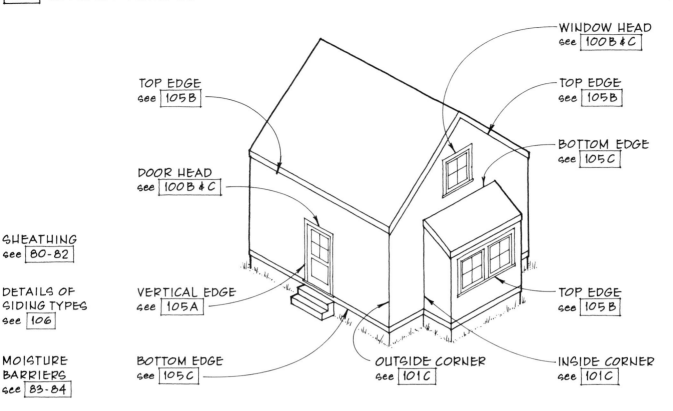

SHEATHING
see 80-82

DETAILS OF
SIDING TYPES
see 106

MOISTURE
BARRIERS
see 83-84

TOP EDGE
see 105B

DOOR HEAD
see 100B & C

VERTICAL EDGE
see 105A

BOTTOM EDGE
see 105C

WINDOW HEAD
see 100B & C

TOP EDGE
see 105B

BOTTOM EDGE
see 105C

TOP EDGE
see 105B

OUTSIDE CORNER
see 101C

INSIDE CORNER
see 101C

With the exceptions of recently developed plywood, hardboard and vinyl sidings, most of today's common exterior wall finishes have been protecting walls from the weather for hundreds of years. Applied properly, each is capable of protecting the building for as long as the finish material itself lasts.

If possible, the best way to protect both the exterior finish and the building from the weather is with adequate overhangs. But even with overhangs, wind-driven rain will occasionally get the building wet. It is important, therefore, to detail exterior wall finishes carefully at all but the most protected locations.

The introduction of effective moisture barriers under the siding has the potential to prolong the life of walls beyond the life of the siding alone. While the siding is still the first line of defense against weather, it is possible to view one of its primary functions as keeping sunlight from causing the moisture barrier to deteriorate, which ultimately protects the walls of the building.

Where the moisture barrier stops—at the edges and the openings through the wall—special attention must be paid to the detailing of exterior wall finishes.

Caulks—In this country alone, there are more than 200 manufacturers of 20 different types of caulks and sealants. (The term "caulk" is commonly applied to sealant, which is more resilient than actual caulk and more properly used in good-quality construction.) However, the appropriate use of caulks for wood-frame buildings is limited for two reasons. First, caulking is not needed—there are 200-year-old wooden buildings still in good condition that were built without caulks. Second, the lifespan of caulk is limited— manufacturers claim only 20 to 25 years for the longest-lasting caulks and sealants.

However, some situations in wood-frame construction do call for the use of caulking. These are mostly cases where the caulk is a second or third line of defense against water intrusion or where the caulk is used to retard the infiltration of air into the building. In all instances, it is recommended that the caulk not be exposed to the sunlight.

A EXTERIOR WALL FINISHES

A VERTICAL EDGE IS A LIKELY PLACE FOR WATER TO LEAK AROUND THE EXTERIOR WALL FINISH INTO THE STRUCTURE OF A BUILDING. A CONTINUOUS MOISTURE BARRIER BEHIND THE VERTICAL JOINT IS CRUCIAL. CAULKING CAN HELP DETER THE MOISTURE, BUT WILL DETERIORATE IN THE ULTRAVIOLET LIGHT UNLESS PLACED BEHIND THE WALL FINISH, WHERE IT WILL BE PROTECTED.

AT THE UPPER EDGES OF WALL FINISHES (@ EAVES & RAKES, UNDER WINDOWS & DOORS, & @ OTHER HORIZONTAL BREAKS), DIRECT MOISTURE AWAY FROM THE TOP EDGE OF THE FINISH MATERIAL TO THE FACE OF THE WALL.

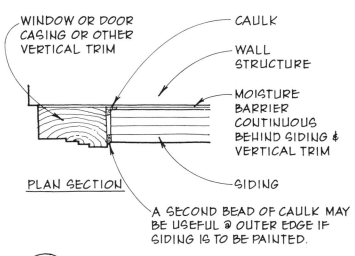

WINDOW OR DOOR CASING OR OTHER VERTICAL TRIM

CAULK

WALL STRUCTURE

MOISTURE BARRIER CONTINUOUS BEHIND SIDING & VERTICAL TRIM

SIDING

PLAN SECTION

A SECOND BEAD OF CAULK MAY BE USEFUL @ OUTER EDGE IF SIDING IS TO BE PAINTED.

(A) EXTERIOR WALL FINISHES
@ VERTICAL EDGES

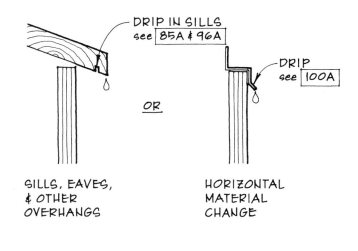

DRIP IN SILLS see 85A & 96A

DRIP see 100A

OR

SILLS, EAVES, & OTHER OVERHANGS

HORIZONTAL MATERIAL CHANGE

(B) EXTERIOR WALL FINISHES
@ TOP EDGES

THE BOTTOM EDGE OF THE WALL FINISH IS MORE LIKELY TO GET WET THAN THE TOP. ALLOW WATER TO FALL FROM THE BOTTOM EDGE OF THE WALL FINISH IN A WAY THAT AVOIDS CAPILLARY ACTION.

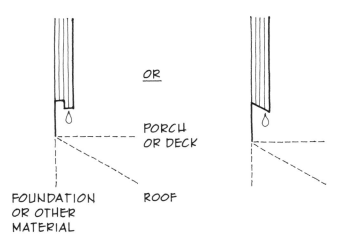

OR

PORCH OR DECK

FOUNDATION OR OTHER MATERIAL

ROOF

(C) EXTERIOR WALL FINISHES
@ BOTTOM EDGES

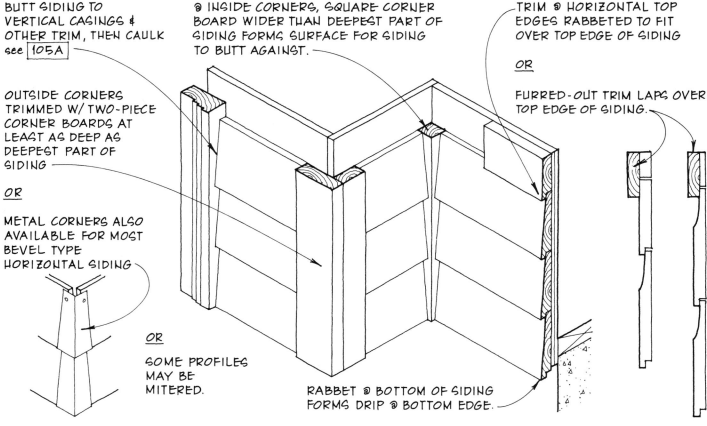

BUTT SIDING TO VERTICAL CASINGS & OTHER TRIM, THEN CAULK see 105A

OUTSIDE CORNERS TRIMMED W/ TWO-PIECE CORNER BOARDS AT LEAST AS DEEP AS DEEPEST PART OF SIDING

OR

METAL CORNERS ALSO AVAILABLE FOR MOST BEVEL TYPE HORIZONTAL SIDING

OR

SOME PROFILES MAY BE MITERED.

@ INSIDE CORNERS, SQUARE CORNER BOARD WIDER THAN DEEPEST PART OF SIDING FORMS SURFACE FOR SIDING TO BUTT AGAINST.

RABBET @ BOTTOM OF SIDING FORMS DRIP @ BOTTOM EDGE.

TRIM @ HORIZONTAL TOP EDGES RABBETED TO FIT OVER TOP EDGE OF SIDING

OR

FURRED-OUT TRIM LAPS OVER TOP EDGE OF SIDING.

Horizontal wood siding is common in both historic and modern buildings. The boards cast a horizontal shadow line unique to this type of siding.

Materials—Profiles are commonly cut from 4-in., 6-in. and 8-in. boards. Cedar, redwood and pine are the most typical. Clear grades are available in cedar and redwood. Many profiles are also made from composite hardboard. This material is much less expensive than siding milled from lumber and is almost indistinguishable from it when painted.

Types—Siding joints may be tongue and groove, rabbeted or lapped. Common profiles (names may vary regionally) are illustrated at bottom right.

Application—Boards are typically applied over a moisture barrier and sheathing, and should be backprimed before installation. Boards are face nailed with a single nail near the bottom of each board but above the board below to allow movement. Siding is joined end to end with miter or scarf joints and caulk over a stud.

Finish—Horizontal wood siding is usually painted or stained. Clear lumber siding is sometimes treated with a semi-transparent stain.

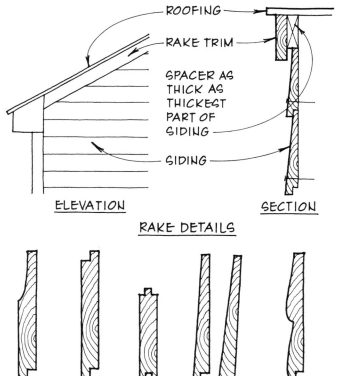

ROOFING

RAKE TRIM

SPACER AS THICK AS THICKEST PART OF SIDING

SIDING

ELEVATION

SECTION

RAKE DETAILS

DROP   SHIPLAP   T&G   BEVEL   CLAPBOARD

HORIZONTAL SIDING PROFILES

A   HORIZONTAL WOOD SIDING

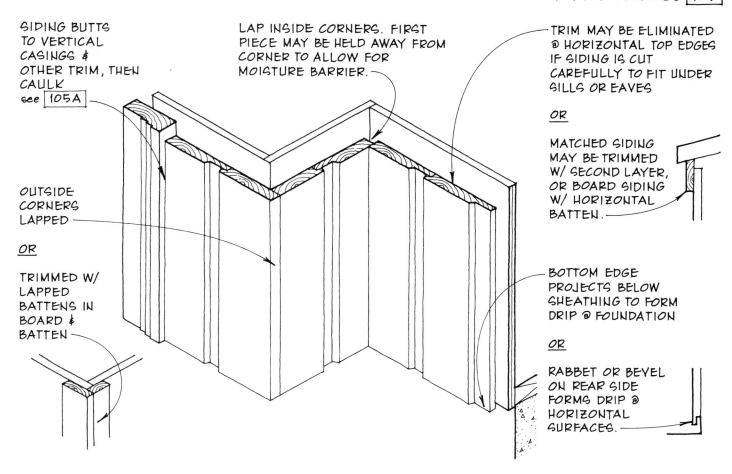

SIDING BUTTS TO VERTICAL CASINGS & OTHER TRIM, THEN CAULK
see | 105A |

LAP INSIDE CORNERS. FIRST PIECE MAY BE HELD AWAY FROM CORNER TO ALLOW FOR MOISTURE BARRIER.

TRIM MAY BE ELIMINATED @ HORIZONTAL TOP EDGES IF SIDING IS CUT CAREFULLY TO FIT UNDER SILLS OR EAVES

OR

MATCHED SIDING MAY BE TRIMMED W/ SECOND LAYER, OR BOARD SIDING W/ HORIZONTAL BATTEN.

OUTSIDE CORNERS LAPPED

OR

TRIMMED W/ LAPPED BATTENS IN BOARD & BATTEN

BOTTOM EDGE PROJECTS BELOW SHEATHING TO FORM DRIP @ FOUNDATION

OR

RABBET OR BEVEL ON REAR SIDE FORMS DRIP @ HORIZONTAL SURFACES.

Vertical wood siding falls into two major groups. One group, such as the tongue-and groove and channel patterns shown below, has its side edges rabbeted or grooved and lies flat on the wall, one board thick. The other group, including board and batten, has square edges and uses a second layer to cover the edges of the first layer. The thicker patterns in the second group may require careful coordination with casings and trim. Both groups require ⅝-in. (min.) plywood sheathing or horizontal nailing strips to strengthen the wall. Where end joints occur, siding is sealed and joined with a scarf joint or a miter joint sloped to the exterior.

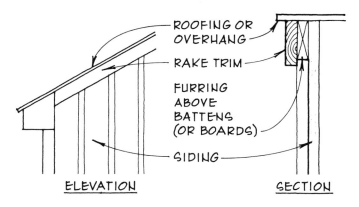

ROOFING OR OVERHANG

RAKE TRIM

FURRING ABOVE BATTENS (OR BOARDS)

SIDING

ELEVATION   SECTION

RAKE DETAILS
(BOARD & BATTEN)

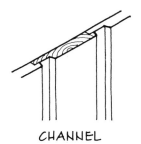

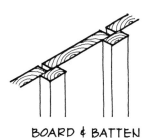

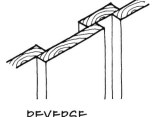

CHANNEL

TONGUE & GROOVE FLUSH (SHOWN) & V-GROOVE

BOARD & BATTEN

REVERSE BOARD & BATTEN

 A   VERTICAL WOOD SIDING

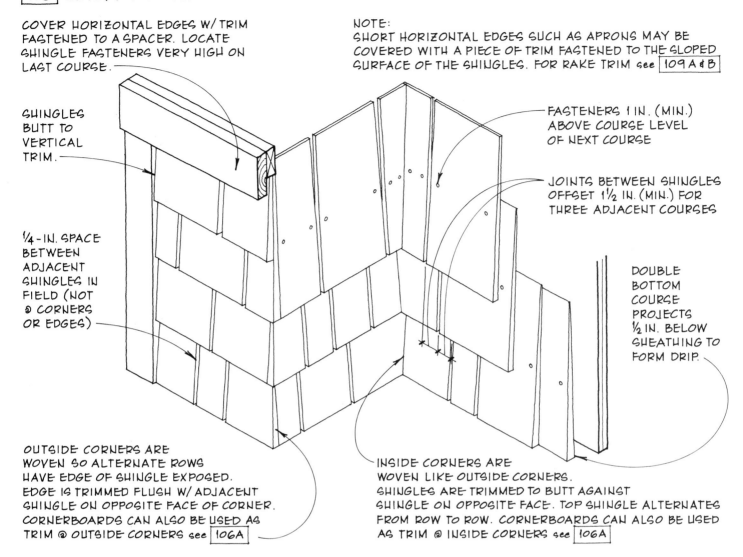

COVER HORIZONTAL EDGES W/ TRIM FASTENED TO A SPACER. LOCATE SHINGLE FASTENERS VERY HIGH ON LAST COURSE.

SHINGLES BUTT TO VERTICAL TRIM.

1/4-IN. SPACE BETWEEN ADJACENT SHINGLES IN FIELD (NOT @ CORNERS OR EDGES)

NOTE:
SHORT HORIZONTAL EDGES SUCH AS APRONS MAY BE COVERED WITH A PIECE OF TRIM FASTENED TO THE SLOPED SURFACE OF THE SHINGLES. FOR RAKE TRIM see | 109 A & B |

FASTENERS 1 IN. (MIN.) ABOVE COURSE LEVEL OF NEXT COURSE

JOINTS BETWEEN SHINGLES OFFSET 1 1/2 IN. (MIN.) FOR THREE ADJACENT COURSES

DOUBLE BOTTOM COURSE PROJECTS 1/2 IN. BELOW SHEATHING TO FORM DRIP.

OUTSIDE CORNERS ARE WOVEN SO ALTERNATE ROWS HAVE EDGE OF SHINGLE EXPOSED. EDGE IS TRIMMED FLUSH W/ ADJACENT SHINGLE ON OPPOSITE FACE OF CORNER. CORNERBOARDS CAN ALSO BE USED AS TRIM @ OUTSIDE CORNERS see | 106A |

INSIDE CORNERS ARE WOVEN LIKE OUTSIDE CORNERS. SHINGLES ARE TRIMMED TO BUTT AGAINST SHINGLE ON OPPOSITE FACE. TOP SHINGLE ALTERNATES FROM ROW TO ROW. CORNERBOARDS CAN ALSO BE USED AS TRIM @ INSIDE CORNERS see | 106A |

Shingles are popular because they can provide a durable, low-maintenance siding with a refined natural appearance. Shadow lines are primarily horizontal but are complemented with minor verticals. Material costs are relatively moderate but installation costs may be very high.

Materials—Shingles are available in a variety of sizes, grades and patterns. The most typical is a western red cedar shingle 16 in. long. Redwood and cypress shingles are also available. Because shingles are relatively small, they are extremely versatile, with a wide variety of coursings and patterns.

Installation—Shingles are applied over a moisture barrier to a plywood or composite wall sheathing so at least two layers of shingles always cover the

wall. Standard coursing allows nail or staple fasteners to be concealed by subsequent courses. With shingles there is less waste than with other wood sidings.

Finish—Enough moisture gets between and behind shingles that paint will not adhere to them reliably. Left unfinished, they endure extremely well, but may weather differentially, especially between those places exposed to the rain and those that are protected. Stains and bleaching stains will produce more even weathering.

Pre-assembled shingles—Shingles are also available mounted to boards. These shingle boards increase material cost, decrease installation cost and are most appropriate for large, uninterrupted surfaces. Corner boards are required at corners.

 WOOD SHINGLE SIDING

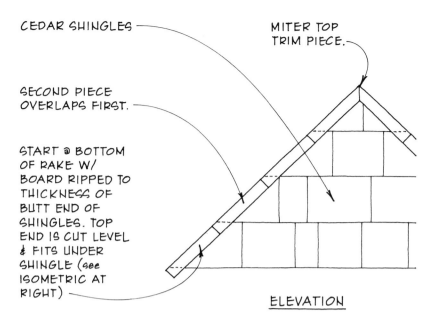

CEDAR SHINGLES

MITER TOP TRIM PIECE.

SECOND PIECE OVERLAPS FIRST.

START @ BOTTOM OF RAKE W/ BOARD RIPPED TO THICKNESS OF BUTT END OF SHINGLES. TOP END IS CUT LEVEL & FITS UNDER SHINGLE (see ISOMETRIC AT RIGHT)

ELEVATION

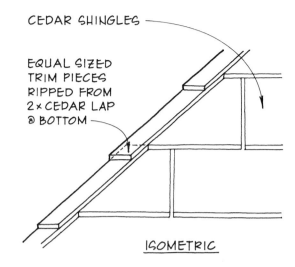

CEDAR SHINGLES

EQUAL SIZED TRIM PIECES RIPPED FROM 2× CEDAR LAP @ BOTTOM

ISOMETRIC

ONE METHOD OF FINISHING THE TOP EDGE OF A SHINGLE WALL IS TO LAP THE SHINGLE COURSES WITH TRIM PIECES RIPPED FROM A CEDAR 2×. IF THE COURSING IS EQUAL, ALL THE TRIM PIECES, EXCEPT FOR THE MITERED TOP PIECES, WILL ALSO BE EQUAL.

Ⓐ SHINGLE SIDING @ RAKE
LAPPED TRIM

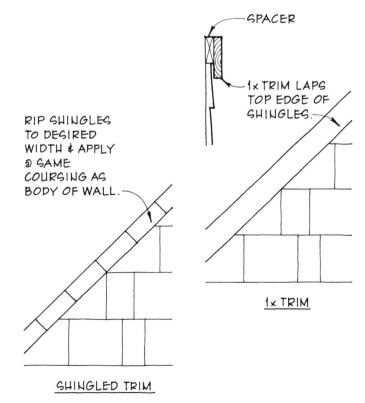

RIP SHINGLES TO DESIRED WIDTH & APPLY @ SAME COURSING AS BODY OF WALL.

SPACER

1× TRIM LAPS TOP EDGE OF SHINGLES.

1× TRIM

SHINGLED TRIM

Ⓑ SHINGLE SIDING @ RAKE
SHINGLED & 1× TRIM

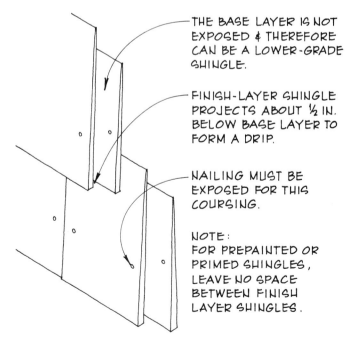

THE BASE LAYER IS NOT EXPOSED & THEREFORE CAN BE A LOWER-GRADE SHINGLE.

FINISH-LAYER SHINGLE PROJECTS ABOUT ½ IN. BELOW BASE LAYER TO FORM A DRIP.

NAILING MUST BE EXPOSED FOR THIS COURSING.

NOTE: FOR PREPAINTED OR PRIMED SHINGLES, LEAVE NO SPACE BETWEEN FINISH LAYER SHINGLES.

DOUBLE COURSING, AN ALTERNATIVE COURSING METHOD, CALLS FOR TWO LAYERS APPLIED @ THE SAME COURSE. A PREPAINTED OR PRIMED SHINGLE CALLED "SIDEWALL SHAKE" IS COMMONLY USED.

Ⓒ DOUBLE-COURSED SHINGLES

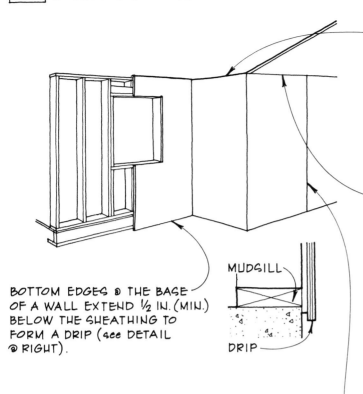

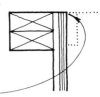

TOP EDGES ARE SOMETIMES LEFT WITHOUT TRIM BECAUSE THEY CAN EASILY BE CUT TO A CLEAN SQUARE EDGE THAT IS BUTTED AGAINST A SOFFIT, EAVE, OR OTHER HORIZONTAL SURFACE, OR TRIM MAY BE ADDED.

BOTTOM EDGES @ THE BASE OF A WALL EXTEND ½ IN. (MIN.) BELOW THE SHEATHING TO FORM A DRIP (see DETAIL @ RIGHT).

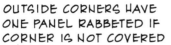

MUDSILL

DRIP

HORIZONTAL JOINTS BETWEEN SIDING PANELS OR BETWEEN PANELS & OTHER MATERIAL SHOULD BE BLOCKED IF THEY DO NOT OCCUR OVER A PLATE OR FLOOR FRAMING.

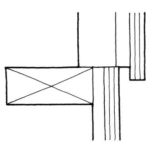

LAP PANELS TO FORM A DRIP EDGE   OR

BUTT PANELS AND FLASH W/ METAL Z FLASHING see 101A

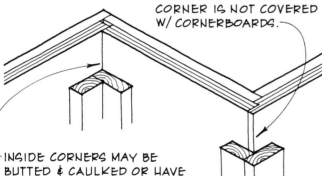

OUTSIDE CORNERS HAVE ONE PANEL RABBETED IF CORNER IS NOT COVERED W/ CORNERBOARDS.

INSIDE CORNERS MAY BE BUTTED & CAULKED OR HAVE CORNER BOARDS ADDED.

VERTICAL JOINTS BETWEEN SIDING PANELS SHOULD ALWAYS FALL OVER A STUD.

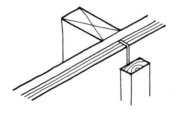

BUTT JOINT COVERED WITH BATTEN

MANUFACTURED LAP JOINT

Materials—Plywood siding is available in 4-ft. wide panels, 8 ft., 9 ft. and 10 ft. tall. Typical thicknesses are ⅜ in., ½ in. and ⅝ in. The panels are usually installed vertically to avoid horizontal joints, which require blocking and flashing. Textures and patterns can be cut into the face of the plywood to resemble vertical wood-siding patterns.

Installation—Manufacturers suggest leaving a ⅛-in. gap at panel edges to allow for expansion. All edges should be treated with water repellent before

installation. It is wise to plan for window and door trim because of the difficulty of cutting panels precisely around openings. Fasten panels to framing following the manufacturer's recommendation.

Single-wall construction—Since plywood, even in a vertical orientation, will provide lateral bracing for a building, it is often applied as the only surface to cover a building. This is called single-wall construction and has some unique details. (see 81A, B & C and 111A).

 PLYWOOD SIDING

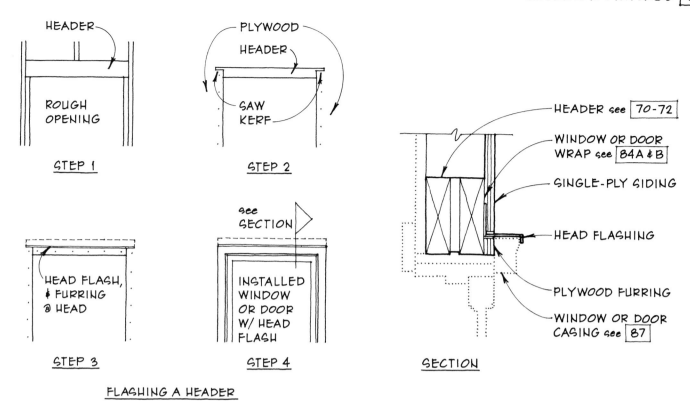

HEADER

ROUGH OPENING

STEP 1

PLYWOOD

HEADER

SAW KERF

STEP 2

HEAD FLASH, & FURRING @ HEAD

STEP 3

see SECTION

INSTALLED WINDOW OR DOOR W/ HEAD FLASH

STEP 4

FLASHING A HEADER

HEADER see | 70-72 |

WINDOW OR DOOR WRAP see | 84A & B |

SINGLE-PLY SIDING

HEAD FLASHING

PLYWOOD FURRING

WINDOW OR DOOR CASING see | 87 |

SECTION

Most of the details for double-wall plywood construction also apply to single-wall construction. But with single-wall construction, the moisture barrier is applied directly to the framing, making it more difficult to achieve a good seal. The wide-roll, chemically derived moisture/air infiltration barriers work best (see 83B). Also, the bottom edge of the plywood is flush against the foundation, so a drip detail is impossible (see below).

MUDSILL

NO SHEATHING BENEATH PLYWOOD, SO PLYWOOD DOES NOT FORM DRIP @ BOTTOM EDGE. CAULK MAY BE BETTER THAN NOTHING IN SOME SITUATIONS.

Flashing—Windows and doors that are attached through the casing and need head flashing because of exposure to rain or snow are very difficult to flash. As shown in the drawings above, a saw kerf must be cut into the siding at the precise location of the flashing. The flashing and siding must be installed simultaneously before the door or window is attached.

 A SINGLE-WALL PLYWOOD SIDING

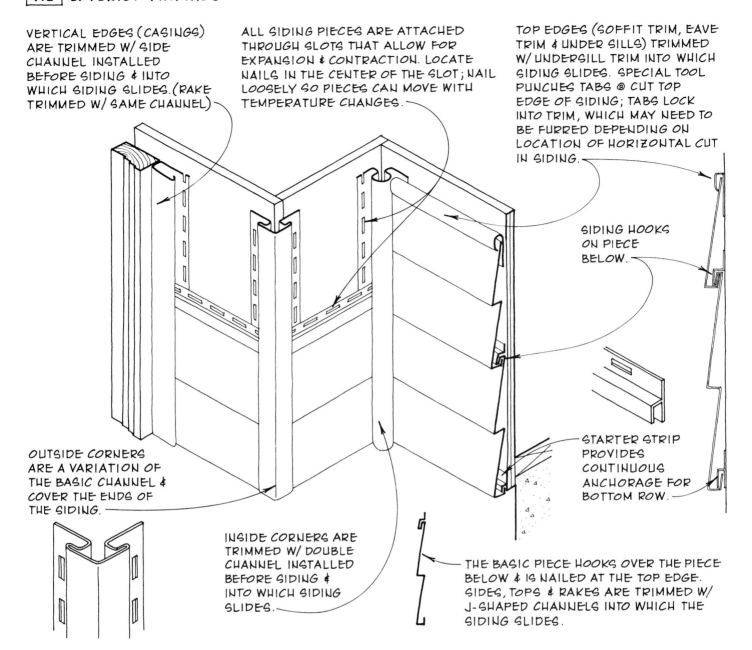

VERTICAL EDGES (CASINGS) ARE TRIMMED W/ SIDE CHANNEL INSTALLED BEFORE SIDING & INTO WHICH SIDING SLIDES. (RAKE TRIMMED W/ SAME CHANNEL)

ALL SIDING PIECES ARE ATTACHED THROUGH SLOTS THAT ALLOW FOR EXPANSION & CONTRACTION. LOCATE NAILS IN THE CENTER OF THE SLOT; NAIL LOOSELY SO PIECES CAN MOVE WITH TEMPERATURE CHANGES.

TOP EDGES (SOFFIT TRIM, EAVE TRIM & UNDER SILLS) TRIMMED W/ UNDERSILL TRIM INTO WHICH SIDING SLIDES. SPECIAL TOOL PUNCHES TABS @ CUT TOP EDGE OF SIDING; TABS LOCK INTO TRIM, WHICH MAY NEED TO BE FURRED DEPENDING ON LOCATION OF HORIZONTAL CUT IN SIDING.

SIDING HOOKS ON PIECE BELOW.

OUTSIDE CORNERS ARE A VARIATION OF THE BASIC CHANNEL & COVER THE ENDS OF THE SIDING.

INSIDE CORNERS ARE TRIMMED W/ DOUBLE CHANNEL INSTALLED BEFORE SIDING & INTO WHICH SIDING SLIDES.

STARTER STRIP PROVIDES CONTINUOUS ANCHORAGE FOR BOTTOM ROW.

THE BASIC PIECE HOOKS OVER THE PIECE BELOW & IS NAILED AT THE TOP EDGE. SIDES, TOPS & RAKES ARE TRIMMED W/ J-SHAPED CHANNELS INTO WHICH THE SIDING SLIDES.

Vinyl sidings were developed in an attempt to eliminate the maintenance required of wood sidings. Most aluminum-siding manufacturers are moving to vinyl.

Material—There are several shapes available. Most imitate horizontal wood bevel patterns, but there are some vertical patterns as well. Lengths are generally about 12 ft., and widths are 8 in. to 12 in. The ends of panels are factory-notched to allow for lapping at end joints, which accommodates expansion and contraction. Color is integral with the material and ranges mostly in the whites, greys and imitation wood

colors. The vinyl will not dent like metal, but will shatter on sharp impact, especially when cold. Most manufacturers also make vinyl soffit material, and some also make decorative trim.

Installation—Vinyl has little structural strength, so most vinyl sidings must be installed over solid sheathing. Proper nailing with corrosion-resistant nails is essential to allow for expansion and contraction. Because vinyl trim pieces are rather narrow, many architects use vinyl siding in conjunction with wood trim, as suggested in the isometric drawing above.

 VINYL SIDING

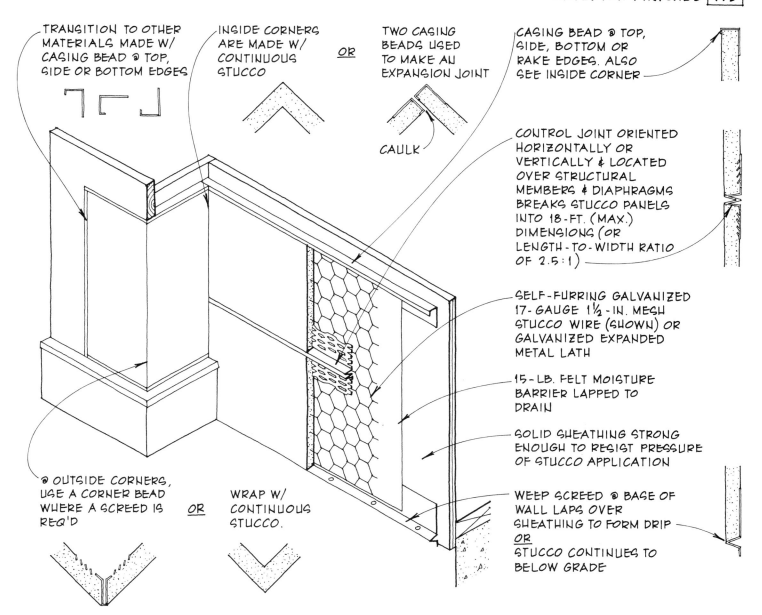

TRANSITION TO OTHER MATERIALS MADE W/ CASING BEAD @ TOP, SIDE OR BOTTOM EDGES

INSIDE CORNERS ARE MADE W/ CONTINUOUS STUCCO

OR

TWO CASING BEADS USED TO MAKE AN EXPANSION JOINT

CAULK

CASING BEAD @ TOP, SIDE, BOTTOM OR RAKE EDGES. ALSO SEE INSIDE CORNER

CONTROL JOINT ORIENTED HORIZONTALLY OR VERTICALLY & LOCATED OVER STRUCTURAL MEMBERS & DIAPHRAGMS BREAKS STUCCO PANELS INTO 18-FT. (MAX.) DIMENSIONS (OR LENGTH-TO-WIDTH RATIO OF 2.5:1)

SELF-FURRING GALVANIZED 17-GAUGE 1½-IN. MESH STUCCO WIRE (SHOWN) OR GALVANIZED EXPANDED METAL LATH

15-LB. FELT MOISTURE BARRIER LAPPED TO DRAIN

SOLID SHEATHING STRONG ENOUGH TO RESIST PRESSURE OF STUCCO APPLICATION

@ OUTSIDE CORNERS, USE A CORNER BEAD WHERE A SCREED IS REQ'D

OR

WRAP W/ CONTINUOUS STUCCO.

WEEP SCREED @ BASE OF WALL LAPS OVER SHEATHING TO FORM DRIP OR STUCCO CONTINUES TO BELOW GRADE

Stucco is made of cement, sand and lime. It is usually applied in three coats, building to a minimum thickness of ¾ in. Cost may be moderate in areas with high use, but high where skilled workers are few.

Materials—Reinforcing materials through which the plaster is forced are either stucco wire or metal lath. This reinforcing is fastened either to sheathing or directly to the framing (without sheathing). When sheathing is used, it must be rigid enough to remain stiff during the process of applying the stucco—⅝-in. plywood is typical.

Application—The first (scratch) coat has a raked finish, the second (brown) coat has a floated finish,

and the final (color) coat may have a variety of finishes. Applying stucco takes skill, and stucco is the least appropriate of all the exterior wall finishes for owner-builders to attempt.

Finish—Textures ranging from smooth to rustic are achieved by troweling the final coat. Color may be integral in the final coat or may be painted on the surface. Stucco is not very moisture resistant and must be sealed or painted.

Synthetic stucco—Synthetic stucco is a relatively flexible material that is applied over rigid insulation board without wire or lath according to manufacturer's specifications. Synthetic stucco is gaining in popularity.

 STUCCO WALL SYSTEM

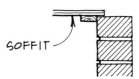

FASCIA

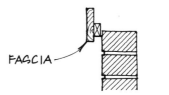

SOFFIT

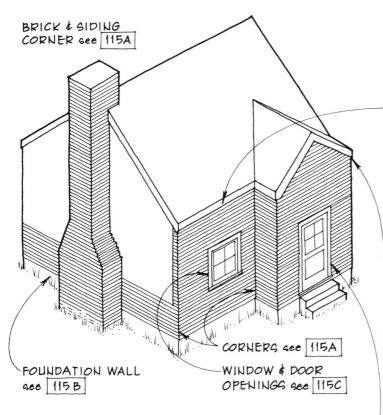

BRICK & SIDING CORNER see 115A

FOUNDATION WALL see 115B

CORNERS see 115A

WINDOW & DOOR OPENINGS see 115C

TOP OF WALL IS DETAILED TO KEEP WATER OFF THE HORIZONTAL SURFACE OF THE TOP BRICK. THIS CAN USUALLY BE ACCOMPLISHED WITH THE DETAILING OF THE ROOF ITSELF. COVER THE JOINT BETWEEN BRICK & ROOF WITH WOOD TRIM. CAULK THE JOINT AS FOR VERTICAL JOINTS, BELOW.

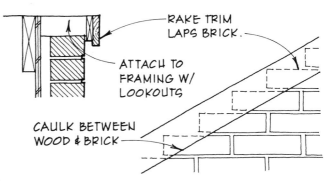

RAKE TRIM LAPS BRICK.

ATTACH TO FRAMING W/ LOOKOUTS

CAULK BETWEEN WOOD & BRICK

RAKE IS USUALLY TRIMMED WITH WOOD SUFFICIENTLY WIDE TO COVER STEPPING OF BRICK CAUSED BY SLOPE. DETAIL AS FOR TOP OF WALL.

Brick veneer covers wood-frame construction across the country. Where it is not subjected to moisture and severe freezing, it is the most durable exterior finish.

Materials—Bricks come in a wide variety of sizes, with the most common (and the smallest) being the modular brick (2¼ in. by 3⅝ in. by 7⅝ in.). These bricks, when laid in mortar, can follow 8-in. modules both horizontally and vertically. Colors vary from cream and yellows to browns and reds, depending on the clay color and method of firing. Bricks should be selected for their history of durability in a given region.

Installation—Bricks are laid in mortar that should be tooled at the joints to compress it for increased resistance to the weather. Because both brick and mortar are porous (increasingly so as they weather over the years), they must be detailed to allow for ventilation and drainage of the unexposed surface. A 1-in. air space between the brick and the wood framing with weep holes located at the base of the wall typically suffices (see 115B). It is important to keep this space and the weep holes clean and free of mortar droppings to ensure proper drainage.

Finish—A number of clear sealers and masonry paints can be applied to the finished masonry to improve weather resistance, but re-application is required every few years.

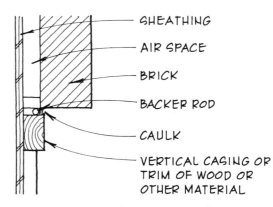

SHEATHING

AIR SPACE

BRICK

BACKER ROD

CAULK

VERTICAL CASING OR TRIM OF WOOD OR OTHER MATERIAL

VERTICAL JOINTS SUCH AS WINDOW & DOOR CASINGS AND @ TRANSITIONS TO OTHER MATERIALS MUST BE CAREFULLY CAULKED TO SEAL AGAINST THE WEATHER. BACKPRIME WOOD COVERED BY OR IN CONTACT W/ BRICK.

(A) **BRICK VENEER**

BOTH INSIDE & OUTSIDE
CORNERS CAN BE MADE
SIMPLY W/ THE BRICKS
THEMSELVES.

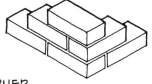

BRICK CORNER

- SHEATHING
- AIR SPACE
- BRICK
- CAULK
- BRICKMOLD
- SIDING

OUTSIDE CORNER   INSIDE CORNER

BRICK AND
SIDING CORNERS

(A) BRICK VENEER
CORNERS

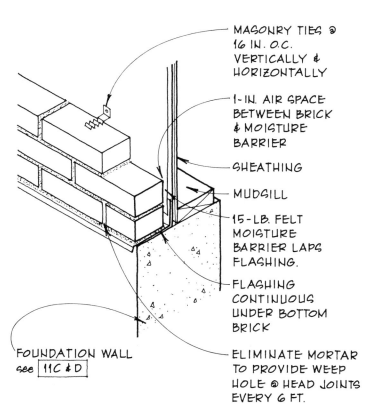

- MASONRY TIES @ 16 IN. O.C. VERTICALLY & HORIZONTALLY
- 1-IN. AIR SPACE BETWEEN BRICK & MOISTURE BARRIER
- SHEATHING
- MUDSILL
- 15-LB. FELT MOISTURE BARRIER LAPS FLASHING.
- FLASHING CONTINUOUS UNDER BOTTOM BRICK
- ELIMINATE MORTAR TO PROVIDE WEEP HOLE @ HEAD JOINTS EVERY 6 FT.

FOUNDATION WALL
see | 11C & D |

(B) BRICK VENEER
WALL CONSTRUCTION

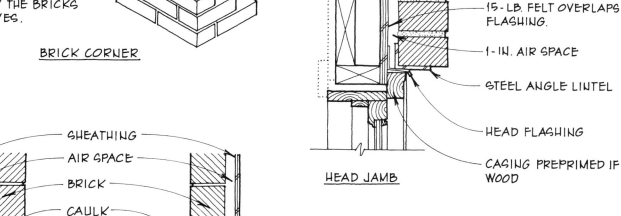

HEAD JAMB

- SHEATHING
- 15-LB. FELT OVERLAPS FLASHING.
- 1-IN. AIR SPACE
- STEEL ANGLE LINTEL
- HEAD FLASHING
- CASING PREPRIMED IF WOOD

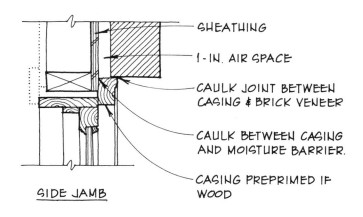

SIDE JAMB

- SHEATHING
- 1-IN. AIR SPACE
- CAULK JOINT BETWEEN CASING & BRICK VENEER
- CAULK BETWEEN CASING AND MOISTURE BARRIER.
- CASING PREPRIMED IF WOOD

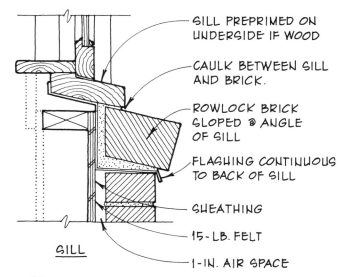

SILL

- SILL PREPRIMED ON UNDERSIDE IF WOOD
- CAULK BETWEEN SILL AND BRICK.
- ROWLOCK BRICK SLOPED @ ANGLE OF SILL
- FLASHING CONTINUOUS TO BACK OF SILL
- SHEATHING
- 15-LB. FELT
- 1-IN. AIR SPACE

(C) BRICK VENEER @ WINDOW/DOOR
ATTACHMENT TO CASING & SILL

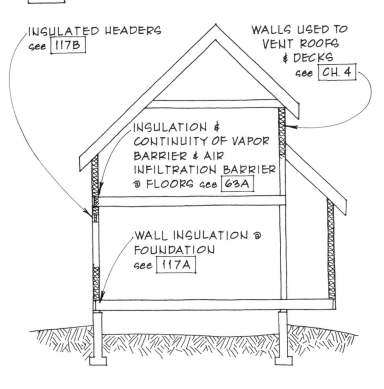

INSULATED HEADERS
see 117B

WALLS USED TO
VENT ROOFS
& DECKS
see CH. 4

INSULATION &
CONTINUITY OF VAPOR
BARRIER & AIR
INFILTRATION BARRIER
@ FLOORS see 63A

WALL INSULATION @
FOUNDATION
see 117A

RIGID
INSULATION
see THIS PAGE

FRAMING FOR
INSULATION @
CORNERS see 73-74

Wall insulation is typically provided by fiberglass batts. Building codes in most climates allow 2x4 walls with 3½ in. of insulation (R-11) or 2x6 walls with 5½ in. of insulation (R-19).

Vapor barriers—Vapor barriers are installed concurrently with wall insulation. This membrane, located on the warm side of the insulation, prevents vaporized (gaseous) moisture from entering the insulated wall cavity, where it can condense.

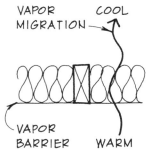

VAPOR
MIGRATION

COOL

VAPOR
BARRIER

WARM

The vapor barrier can be further used to seal the building against the infiltration of outside air, which is done by carefully overlapping and sealing the vapor barrier at all joints, openings and around electrical boxes. When this is done, the vapor barrier may also be properly called an air infiltration barrier.

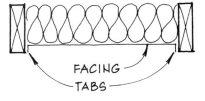

Faced batts—Batt insulation is often faced with a vapor barrier or with paper, which should be applied toward the warm living space. The facing material has tabs that are stapled in place between the studs.

FACING
TABS

If the facing is being used as a vapor barrier, it is better to staple the tabs to the face of the studs to make a better seal. This interferes, however, with the installation of interior finish materials because it builds up unevenly on the face of the studs.

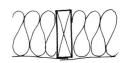

With foil-faced batts it is necessary to staple the tabs to the sides of the studs in order to provide the air space required for the foil to act as a reflector of radiant heat.

AIR SPACE

INTERIOR
FINISH

Unfaced batts—The most effective method of insulating and stopping vapor is to use unfaced batts, which are fit between studs, and to cover the studs on the inside with a continuous vapor barrier such as 4-mil polyethylene. The advantages to this system are that the wall cavities get completely filled without any voids and the vapor barrier is continuous.

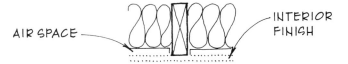

UNFACED BATT INSULATION

CONTINUOUS VAPOR BARRIER

INTERIOR FINISH

Rigid insulation—Rigid insulation can increase the thermal performance of walls beyond the typically accepted standards. Rigid insulation is usually added to the outside of the walls on top of the structural sheathing, or the sheathing may itself be rigid insulation. Insulation may also be added to the inside of the wall before the vapor barrier and interior finish. Rigid insulation should be less permeable than the vapor barrier to prevent moisture that finds its way into the wall cavity from being trapped (see 82A).

EXTERIOR FINISH

RIGID INSULATION

SHEATHING

A INSULATION

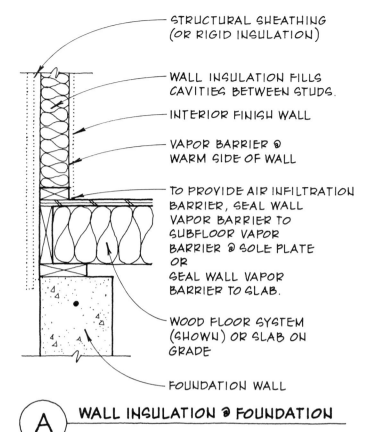

STRUCTURAL SHEATHING
(OR RIGID INSULATION)

WALL INSULATION FILLS
CAVITIES BETWEEN STUDS.

INTERIOR FINISH WALL

VAPOR BARRIER @
WARM SIDE OF WALL

TO PROVIDE AIR INFILTRATION
BARRIER, SEAL WALL
VAPOR BARRIER TO
SUBFLOOR VAPOR
BARRIER @ SOLE PLATE
OR
SEAL WALL VAPOR
BARRIER TO SLAB.

WOOD FLOOR SYSTEM
(SHOWN) OR SLAB ON
GRADE

FOUNDATION WALL

(A) WALL INSULATION @ FOUNDATION

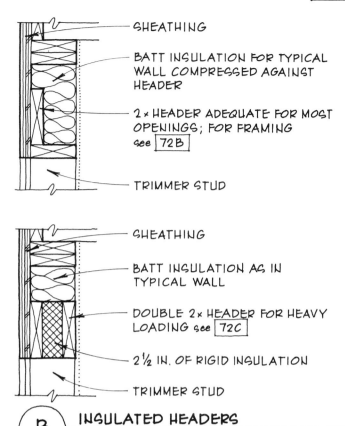

SHEATHING

BATT INSULATION FOR TYPICAL
WALL COMPRESSED AGAINST
HEADER

2 x HEADER ADEQUATE FOR MOST
OPENINGS; FOR FRAMING
see 72B

TRIMMER STUD

SHEATHING

BATT INSULATION AS IN
TYPICAL WALL

DOUBLE 2 x HEADER FOR HEAVY
LOADING see 72C

2½ IN. OF RIGID INSULATION

TRIMMER STUD

(B) INSULATED HEADERS
2 ALTERNATIVES FOR 2 x 6 EXTERIOR WALL

ROOFS

4

The roof is the part of the wood-frame structure that varies most widely across the country. This is because the roof plays the most active role of all the parts of a building in protecting against the weather, and in the U.S., variations in weather are extreme. Some roofs protect primarily against the heat of the sun; others must shelter the inhabitants under tons of snow.

SELECTION OF ROOF SLOPE
One of the most obvious variations of roof form has to do with the slope or pitch of the roof. The main factors affecting the slope of a roof are stylistic considerations, the type of roofing material to be used and the space desired beneath the roof. The climate also has a strong influence on roof slope. Areas of significant rainfall have roofs pitched to shed the rain; warm, arid climates tend to favor flatter roofs.

The slope or pitch of a roof is measured as a proportion of rise to run. A roof that rises 4 in. in 1 ft. (12 in.) is said to have a 4-in-12 pitch (or 4:12). The second number in the roof-pitch proportion is always 12.

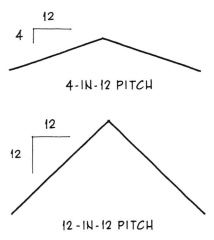

4-IN-12 PITCH

12-IN-12 PITCH

THE SHAPE OF ROOFS
Roof shapes tend to have a regional character that reflects not only climatic variation, but also historical and material influences. All roof forms are derived from four basic roof shapes shown below: the flat roof, the shed roof, the gable roof and the hip roof.

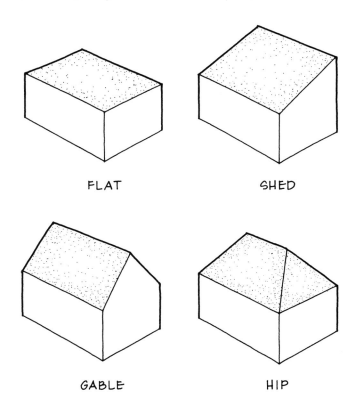

FLAT   SHED

GABLE   HIP

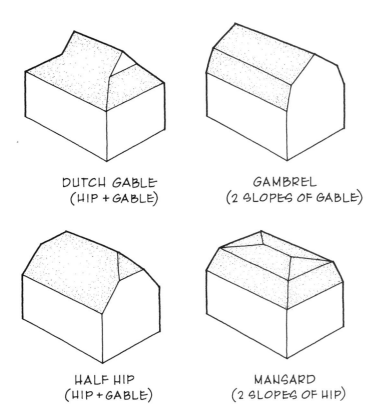

DUTCH GABLE
(HIP + GABLE)

GAMBREL
(2 SLOPES OF GABLE)

HALF HIP
(HIP + GABLE)

MANSARD
(2 SLOPES OF HIP)

Virtually any roof form may be made by combining the four basic shapes with the connections illustrated in this chapter. Some of these composite shapes are so common they have their own names. For example, the hip and gable shapes can combine to form a Dutch gable. Two different slopes of gable roof can combine to form a gambrel roof. A shed dormer may be added to a gable roof, and so forth. Four common combinations are shown above.

WHAT TYPE OF CONSTRUCTION SYSTEM?

Roofs are constructed either with rafters (stick-framed roofs) or with trusses. Stick-framed roofs are usually made with dimension lumber but may also use composite materials such as plywood I-rafters (which are simply plywood I-joists).

Stick framing originated before the development of wood-frame construction in the 19th century. Antecedents of the modern stick-framed roof can be seen on ancient roofs around the world, and modern stick-frame roofing remains popular because it is the most flexible roof-framing system and the materials are least expensive.

Trusses are made of a number of small members (usually 2x4s) joined in a factory or shop to make one long structural assembly. Only in very simple buildings does the labor savings of a truss system compete with stick framing.

Stick framing—One advantage of stick framing is that the space within the roof structure can become living space or storage. Vaulted (cathedral) ceilings, half-story living spaces on upper floors, and true storage attics are all examples. A second advantage is that complex roofs may be stick framed more economically than truss framed. For this reason stick framing may be attractive to owner-builders when the cost of labor is not a factor.

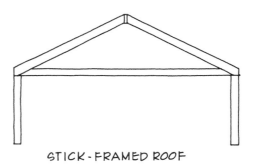

STICK-FRAMED ROOF

Truss framing—Trusses can span much farther than stick-framed roofs, leaving large open areas below them or permitting partition walls to be relocated without consideration for the roof structure above. Trusses go up quickly, usually resulting in a cost saving over stick-framed roofs on simply shaped buildings. A big disadvantage of trusses is that the truss roof is almost impossible to remodel, since trusses should never be cut.

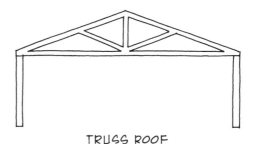

TRUSS ROOF

OTHER CONSIDERATIONS

In addition to the choices about pitch, shape and structure discussed above, many other decisions contribute to the overall performance of the roof. These include selection of sheathing, underlayment and roofing material; eave, rake and flashing details; gutters and downspouts; and insulation and ventilation of the roof assembly.

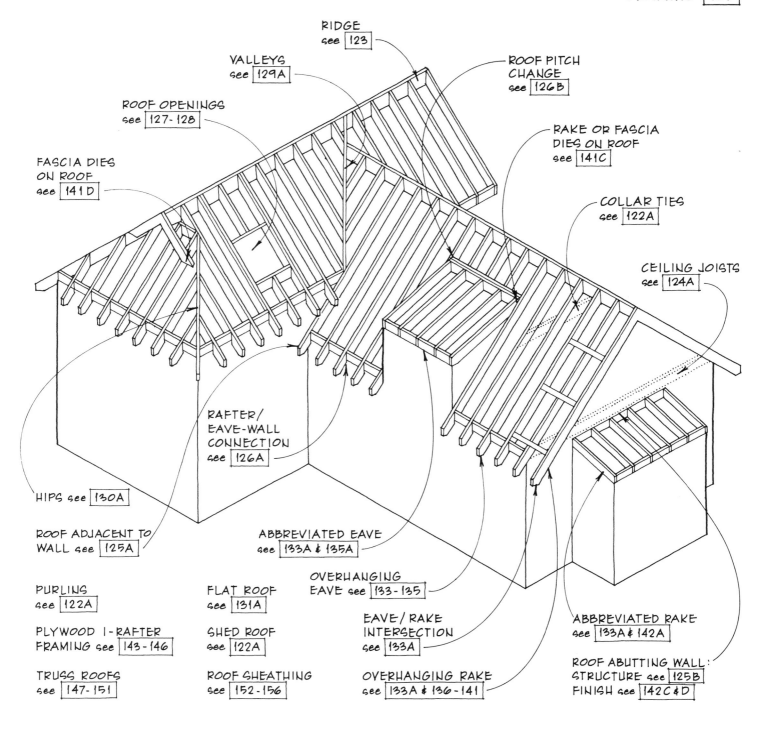

RIDGE see 123

VALLEYS see 129A

ROOF PITCH CHANGE see 126B

ROOF OPENINGS see 127-128

RAKE OR FASCIA DIES ON ROOF see 141C

FASCIA DIES ON ROOF see 141D

COLLAR TIES see 122A

CEILING JOISTS see 124A

RAFTER/ EAVE-WALL CONNECTION see 126A

HIPS see 130A

ROOF ADJACENT TO WALL see 125A

ABBREVIATED EAVE see 133A & 135A

PURLINS see 122A

FLAT ROOF see 131A

OVERHANGING EAVE see 133-135

ABBREVIATED RAKE see 133A & 142A

PLYWOOD I-RAFTER FRAMING see 143-146

SHED ROOF see 122A

EAVE/RAKE INTERSECTION see 133A

ROOF ABUTTING WALL: STRUCTURE see 125B FINISH see 142C&D

TRUSS ROOFS see 147-151

ROOF SHEATHING see 152-156

OVERHANGING RAKE see 133A & 136-141

Rafter sizes are usually 2x6, 2x8, 2x10 or 2x12, and spacing is usually 16 in. or 24 in. o.c. Species vary from region to region. Rafter sizing depends primarily on span, spacing, roof loads and sometimes on required insulation depth.

For rafter-span table, see 123A.

 ROOF FRAMING

Stick-framed rafters may be supported by the walls of the building, by a structural ridge beam or by purlins.

Simple-span roof—The simplest sloped roof—the shed roof—has rafters that span from one wall to another, as shown at right. These rafters must be strong enough to carry the dead-load weight of the roof itself and subsequent layers of re-roofing, plus the live-load weight of snow. The rafters must usually be deep enough to contain adequate insulation.

The total roof load is transferred to the ends of the rafters, where it is supported by the walls. In the simple example at right, each wall carries part of the roof load.

Triangulated roof—Common (full-length) rafters are paired and usually joined to a ridge board, as shown in the drawing at right. Each rafter spans only half the distance between the two walls (the gable roof, shown in the drawing at right, is the simplest version). Horizontal ties—either ceiling joists or collar ties— form a triangle with the rafters. Ceiling joists are generally located on the top plate of the walls but may also be located higher to form a partially vaulted ceiling. Collar ties are usually nailed near the top of the roof between opposing rafters and spaced at 4 ft. o.c. Collar ties are not sufficient by themselves to resist the outward thrust of the rafters.

Rafters in triangulated roofs are shallower than those in shed roofs of equal width because they span only half the distance of the shed rafters and because they do not usually contain insulation.

Structural ridge beam—The horizontal ties that are required in a triangulated roof may be avoided if the rafters are attached at the ridge to a structural ridge beam (or a wall), which effectively changes the triangulated roof into two simple-span roofs, as shown in the drawing below.

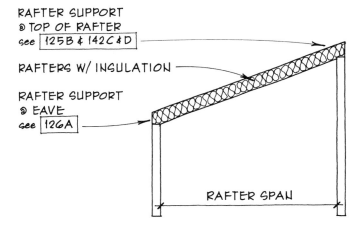

RAFTER SUPPORT
@ TOP OF RAFTER
see [125B & 142C & D]

RAFTERS W/ INSULATION

RAFTER SUPPORT
@ EAVE
see [126A]

RAFTER SPAN

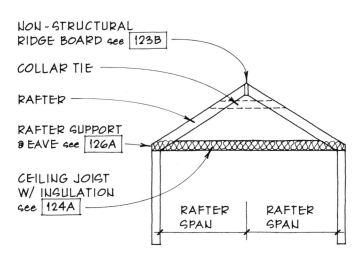

NON-STRUCTURAL
RIDGE BOARD see [123B]

COLLAR TIE

RAFTER

RAFTER SUPPORT
@ EAVE see [126A]

CEILING JOIST
W/ INSULATION
see [124A]

RAFTER SPAN | RAFTER SPAN

Purlin—A purlin is a horizontal member that supports several rafters—usually at mid-span. Purlins were commonly used to help support the long slender rafters of pioneer houses and barns. Today they are also used occasionally to reduce the span of a set of rafters, but the purlins must themselves be supported by the frame of the structure, as shown in the drawing below.

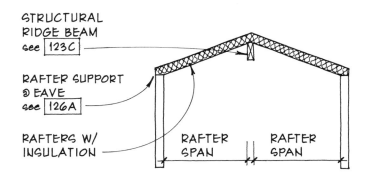

STRUCTURAL
RIDGE BEAM
see [123C]

RAFTER SUPPORT
@ EAVE
see [126A]

RAFTERS W/
INSULATION

RAFTER SPAN | RAFTER SPAN

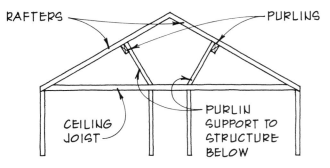

RAFTERS — PURLINS

CEILING JOIST

PURLIN SUPPORT TO STRUCTURE BELOW

NOTE:
THE NAME "PURLIN" IS ALSO GIVEN TO A MEMBER THAT SPANS ACROSS RAFTERS TO SUPPORT ROOF DECKING see [142C]

A **STICK FRAMING**
TERMINOLOGY

Rafter size, species and grade	On-center spacing		
	12 in.	16 in.	24 in.
2x6 hem-fir #1	11.5	10.5	9.2
2x6 south. pine #1	12.0	10.9	9.6
2x6 Douglas-fir #1	12.2	11.1	9.7
2x8 hem-fir #1	15.2	13.8	12.1
2x8 south. pine #1	15.8	14.4	12.6
2x8 Douglas-fir #1	16.2	14.7	12.8
2x10 hem-fir #1	19.4	17.7	16.4
2x10 south. pine #1	20.3	18.4	17.1
2x10 Douglas-fir #1	20.6	18.7	17.4
2x12 hem-fir #1	23.6	21.5	18.7
2x12 south. pine #1	24.6	22.4	19.5
2x12 Douglas-fir #1	25.1	22.8	19.8

This table compares three species for a roof with a 30-psf live load. The table is for estimating purposes only. For roof-sheathing span table, see 153A.

 A RAFTER-SPAN COMPARISON TABLE

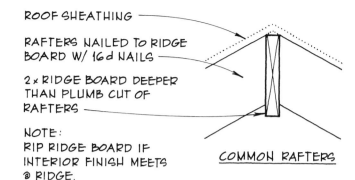

ROOF SHEATHING

RAFTERS NAILED TO RIDGE BOARD W/ 16d NAILS

2 x RIDGE BOARD DEEPER THAN PLUMB CUT OF RAFTERS

NOTE: RIP RIDGE BOARD IF INTERIOR FINISH MEETS @ RIDGE.

COMMON RAFTERS

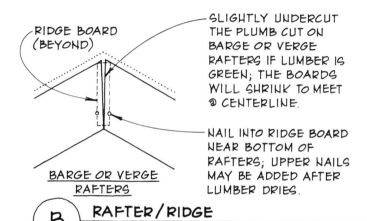

RIDGE BOARD (BEYOND)

SLIGHTLY UNDERCUT THE PLUMB CUT ON BARGE OR VERGE RAFTERS IF LUMBER IS GREEN; THE BOARDS WILL SHRINK TO MEET @ CENTERLINE.

NAIL INTO RIDGE BOARD NEAR BOTTOM OF RAFTERS; UPPER NAILS MAY BE ADDED AFTER LUMBER DRIES.

BARGE OR VERGE RAFTERS

B RAFTER/RIDGE
NON-STRUCTURAL RIDGE BOARD

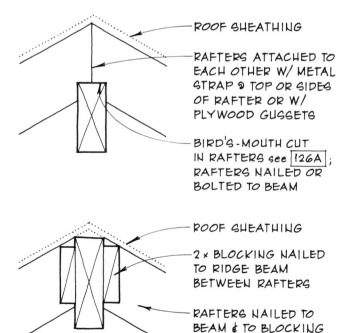

ROOF SHEATHING

RAFTERS ATTACHED TO EACH OTHER W/ METAL STRAP @ TOP OR SIDES OF RAFTER OR W/ PLYWOOD GUSSETS

BIRD'S-MOUTH CUT IN RAFTERS see 126A ; RAFTERS NAILED OR BOLTED TO BEAM

ROOF SHEATHING

2 x BLOCKING NAILED TO RIDGE BEAM BETWEEN RAFTERS

RAFTERS NAILED TO BEAM & TO BLOCKING

NOTE:
AS AN ALTERNATIVE, USE METAL RIDGE HANGERS FOR SMALL RAFTERS UP TO 7-IN-12 PITCH.

 C RAFTER/RIDGE
STRUCTURAL RIDGE BEAM: 4 ALTERNATIVES

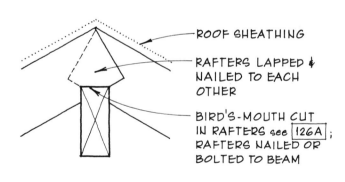

ROOF SHEATHING

RAFTERS LAPPED & NAILED TO EACH OTHER

BIRD'S-MOUTH CUT IN RAFTERS see 126A ; RAFTERS NAILED OR BOLTED TO BEAM

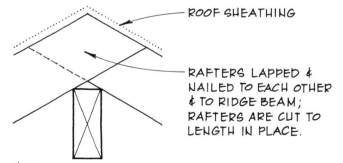

ROOF SHEATHING

RAFTERS LAPPED & NAILED TO EACH OTHER & TO RIDGE BEAM; RAFTERS ARE CUT TO LENGTH IN PLACE.

NOTE:
RAFTERS IN THESE DETAILS LAP @ RIDGE, SO @ THE END RAFTERS, FUR OUT INNER RAFTER TO ALIGN W/ OUTER RAFTER.

Ceiling joists are very similar to floor joists. In fact, the second-floor joists of a two-story building act as the ceiling joists for the story below. Ceiling joists are distinguished from floor joists only when there is no floor (except an attic floor) above the joists.

Ceiling joists are sized like floor joists. The span of the joists depends on spacing and whether the attic above the joists will be used for storage.

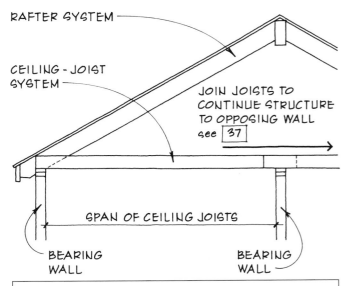

RAFTER SYSTEM

CEILING - JOIST SYSTEM

JOIN JOISTS TO CONTINUE STRUCTURE TO OPPOSING WALL see 37

SPAN OF CEILING JOISTS

BEARING WALL

BEARING WALL

The joists can function as ties to resist the lateral forces of rafters. For this purpose, it is important to attach the joists securely to the rafters.

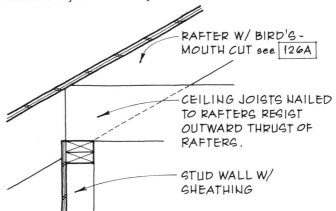

RAFTER W/ BIRD'S-MOUTH CUT see 126A

CEILING JOISTS NAILED TO RAFTERS RESIST OUTWARD THRUST OF RAFTERS.

STUD WALL W/ SHEATHING

NOTE:
CHECK CODES FOR NAILING REQUIREMENTS & ANGLE NAILS THROUGH JOISTS INTO RAFTERS TOWARD CENTER OF BUILDING.

The underside of ceiling joists is often furred down with a layer of 1x lumber to resist plaster or drywall cracking due to movement of the joists. The drawing below illustrates furring parallel to the joists to resist cracking along a beam that interrupts the continuity of the joists. Furring perpendicular to the joists, usually called strapping, is also common.

Ceiling-joist span table			
Joist size and species	On-center spacing		
	12 in.	16 in.	24 in.
2x6 hem-fir #1	13.2	12.0	10.5
2x6 south. pine #1	13.7	12.5	11.0
2x6 Douglas-fir #1	14.0	12.7	11.1
2x8 hem-fir #1	17.5	15.8	13.8
2x8 south. pine #1	18.2	16.5	14.5
2x8 Douglas-fir #1	18.5	16.7	14.7
2x10 hem-fir #1	22.2	20.2	17.7
2x10 south. pine #1	23.2	21.0	18.4
2x10 Douglas-fir #1	23.6	21.5	18.7
2x12 hem-fir #1	27.0	24.5	21.5
2x12 south. pine #1	28.1	25.6	22.4
2x12 Douglas-fir #1	28.7	26.0	22.8

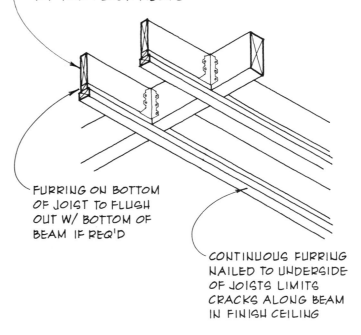

DISCONTINUOUS CEILING JOIST HUNG FROM STRUCTURAL BEAM FLUSH @ TOP FOR FLOOR ABOVE

FURRING ON BOTTOM OF JOIST TO FLUSH OUT W/ BOTTOM OF BEAM IF REQ'D

CONTINUOUS FURRING NAILED TO UNDERSIDE OF JOISTS LIMITS CRACKS ALONG BEAM IN FINISH CEILING

This table is based on a light attic load of 20 psf and a deflection of L/360. The table is for estimating purposes only.

 A RAFTERS/CEILING JOISTS

The end rafters of a gable or a shed roof are supported by the walls under them, called rake walls. The framing of the rake should be coordinated with the detailing of the rake. Of the three drawings below, the first example is the simplest method of support and is used with all types of rake, often in conjunction with an unfinished attic. The second example is best for supporting lookouts for an exposed or boxed-in rake. The third example provides nailing for a boxed-in rake or an exposed ceiling. Elements from the three examples may be combined differently for specific situations. For rake-wall framing see 76A, B & C.

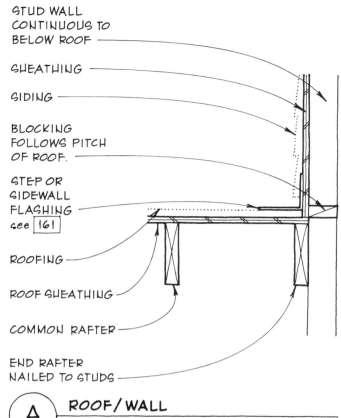

STUD WALL CONTINUOUS TO BELOW ROOF

SHEATHING

SIDING

BLOCKING FOLLOWS PITCH OF ROOF.

STEP OR SIDEWALL FLASHING see 161

ROOFING

ROOF SHEATHING

COMMON RAFTER

END RAFTER NAILED TO STUDS

(A) ROOF / WALL
RAFTERS || TO WALL

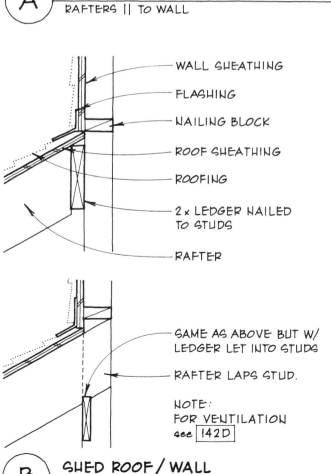

WALL SHEATHING

FLASHING

NAILING BLOCK

ROOF SHEATHING

ROOFING

2 × LEDGER NAILED TO STUDS

RAFTER

SAME AS ABOVE BUT W/ LEDGER LET INTO STUDS

RAFTER LAPS STUD.

NOTE: FOR VENTILATION see 142D

(B) SHED ROOF / WALL
RAFTERS ⊥ TO WALL

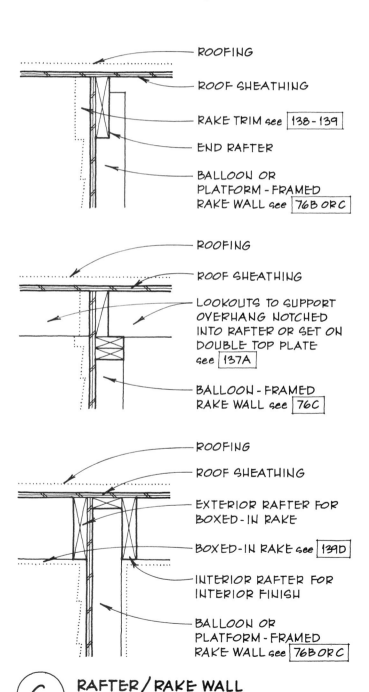

ROOFING

ROOF SHEATHING

RAKE TRIM see 138-139

END RAFTER

BALLOON OR PLATFORM-FRAMED RAKE WALL see 76B OR C

ROOFING

ROOF SHEATHING

LOOKOUTS TO SUPPORT OVERHANG NOTCHED INTO RAFTER OR SET ON DOUBLE TOP PLATE see 137A

BALLOON-FRAMED RAKE WALL see 76C

ROOFING

ROOF SHEATHING

EXTERIOR RAFTER FOR BOXED-IN RAKE

BOXED-IN RAKE see 139D

INTERIOR RAFTER FOR INTERIOR FINISH

BALLOON OR PLATFORM-FRAMED RAKE WALL see 76B OR C

(C) RAFTER / RAKE WALL
3 ALTERNATIVES

At supporting eave walls or beams, rafters are cut at the point of support with a notch called a bird's mouth.

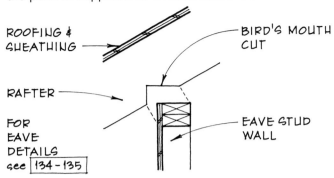

ROOFING & SHEATHING

BIRD'S MOUTH CUT

RAFTER

FOR EAVE DETAILS see 134-135

EAVE STUD WALL

The width of the bird's mouth is equal to the width of the sheathed stud wall (or unsheathed wall if sheathing is to be applied later). The underside of the rafters should meet the inside corner of the top of the wall (as shown below) if the ceiling is vaulted and a smooth transition between wall and ceiling is desired.

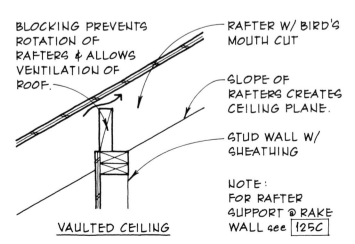

BLOCKING PREVENTS ROTATION OF RAFTERS & ALLOWS VENTILATION OF ROOF.

RAFTER W/ BIRD'S MOUTH CUT

CEILING JOISTS see 123

STUD WALL W/ SHEATHING

FLAT CEILING

BLOCKING PREVENTS ROTATION OF RAFTERS & ALLOWS VENTILATION OF ROOF.

RAFTER W/ BIRD'S MOUTH CUT

SLOPE OF RAFTERS CREATES CEILING PLANE.

STUD WALL W/ SHEATHING

NOTE: FOR RAFTER SUPPORT @ RAKE WALL see 125C

VAULTED CEILING

(A) RAFTER / EAVE WALL
BIRD'S MOUTH CUT

Wherever the pitch of a roof changes from shallow to steep (as in a gambrel roof) or from steep to shallow (as in a shed dormer) the two ends of the rafters must be supported. If the pitch change occurs over a wall, the wall itself will provide the support.

If the pitch change does not occur over a wall, the support will have to be provided by a purlin or a beam (header).

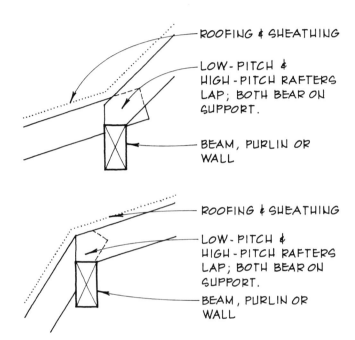

ROOFING & SHEATHING

LOW-PITCH & HIGH-PITCH RAFTERS LAP; BOTH BEAR ON SUPPORT.

BEAM, PURLIN OR WALL

ROOFING & SHEATHING

LOW-PITCH & HIGH-PITCH RAFTERS LAP; BOTH BEAR ON SUPPORT.

BEAM, PURLIN OR WALL

PITCH CHANGES WITH SUPPORT BELOW.

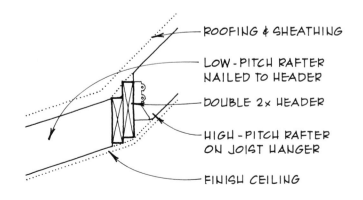

ROOFING & SHEATHING

LOW-PITCH RAFTER NAILED TO HEADER

DOUBLE 2x HEADER

HIGH-PITCH RAFTER ON JOIST HANGER

FINISH CEILING

PITCH CHANGE WITHOUT SUPPORT BELOW

(B) ROOF PITCH CHANGE

Framing the elements that project through the roof of a building—skylights, chimneys and dormers—begins with a rectangular opening in the framing. For openings that fall within a single roof plane framed entirely with common rafters, framing is relatively easy. An opening three rafter spaces wide or less can be made by heading off the interrupted rafters and doubling the side rafters, as shown below. Obviously, it is more efficient if the width and placement of the opening correspond to the rafter spacing. Larger openings should be engineered. Openings that straddle hips, valleys or pitch changes must have special support, special framing and special flashing.

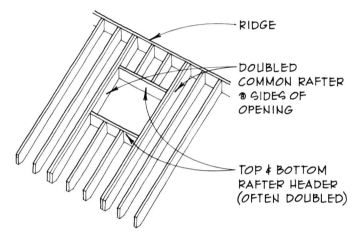

Headers for simple openings are, in most cases, either plumb or perpendicular to the rafters, as shown in the drawing below. Plumb openings require a header deeper than the rafters.

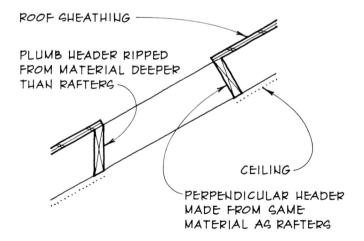

FOR DORMER OPENINGS see 127B
FOR SKYLIGHT OPENINGS see 128A & B
FOR CHIMNEY OPENINGS see 128C

A — ROOF OPENINGS
GENERAL

Dormers are often more than three rafter spaces wide so their structure cannot be calculated by rules of thumb. The opening in the roof may be structured to support all or part of the loads imposed by the dormer. The dormer walls and roof are framed like the walls and roof of the main building.

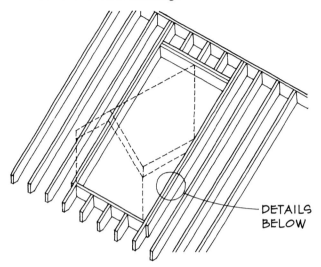

If the dormer walls do not extend below ceiling level, the roof structure at the edge of the opening must support the dormer.

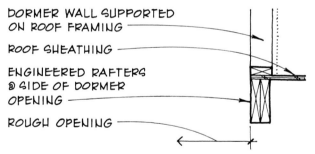

If the dormer has side walls that extend to the floor, the floor may be used to support the dormer, and the rafters at the side of the opening may be single.

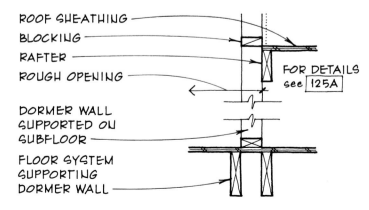

B — DORMER OPENING

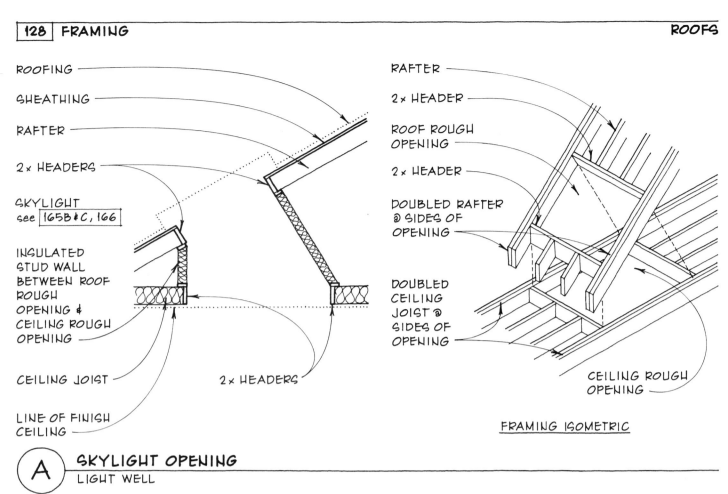

ROOFING

SHEATHING

RAFTER

2× HEADERS

SKYLIGHT
see 165B & C, 166

INSULATED
STUD WALL
BETWEEN ROOF
ROUGH
OPENING &
CEILING ROUGH
OPENING

CEILING JOIST

LINE OF FINISH
CEILING

2× HEADERS

RAFTER

2× HEADER

ROOF ROUGH
OPENING

2× HEADER

DOUBLED RAFTER
@ SIDES OF
OPENING

DOUBLED
CEILING
JOIST @
SIDES OF
OPENING

CEILING ROUGH
OPENING

FRAMING ISOMETRIC

(A) SKYLIGHT OPENING
LIGHT WELL

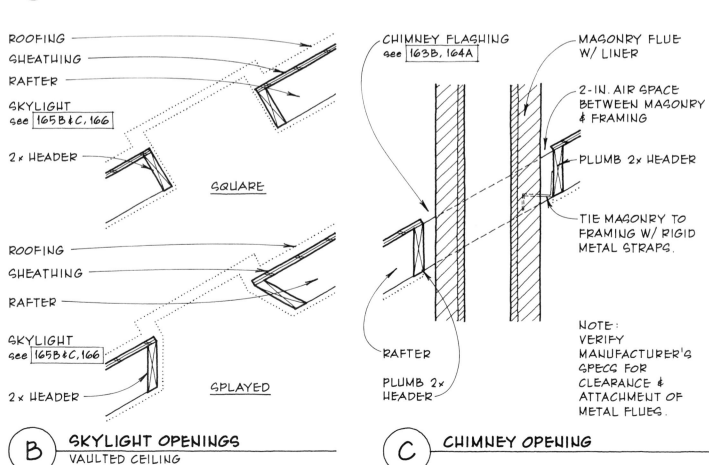

ROOFING
SHEATHING
RAFTER
SKYLIGHT
see 165B & C, 166

2× HEADER

SQUARE

ROOFING
SHEATHING
RAFTER

SKYLIGHT
see 165B & C, 166

2× HEADER

SPLAYED

(B) SKYLIGHT OPENINGS
VAULTED CEILING

CHIMNEY FLASHING
see 163B, 164A

MASONRY FLUE
W/ LINER

2-IN. AIR SPACE
BETWEEN MASONRY
& FRAMING

PLUMB 2× HEADER

TIE MASONRY TO
FRAMING W/ RIGID
METAL STRAPS.

RAFTER

PLUMB 2×
HEADER

NOTE:
VERIFY
MANUFACTURER'S
SPECS FOR
CLEARANCE &
ATTACHMENT OF
METAL FLUES.

(C) CHIMNEY OPENING

The inside corner of two intersecting roof planes is called a valley. In most cases, valleys are supported by a valley rafter that extends from the outside wall of the building to the ridge or to a header. These valley rafters support large loads and should be engineered. Jack rafters support the area between the valley rafter and the ridge or header.

As shown at right, valley rafters can be supported at the top by a ridge or by a header. The ridge support system is more practical when the ridges of the intersecting roofs are close together; the header support system is better when the lower ridge intersects the main roof near or below the center of the rafter span.

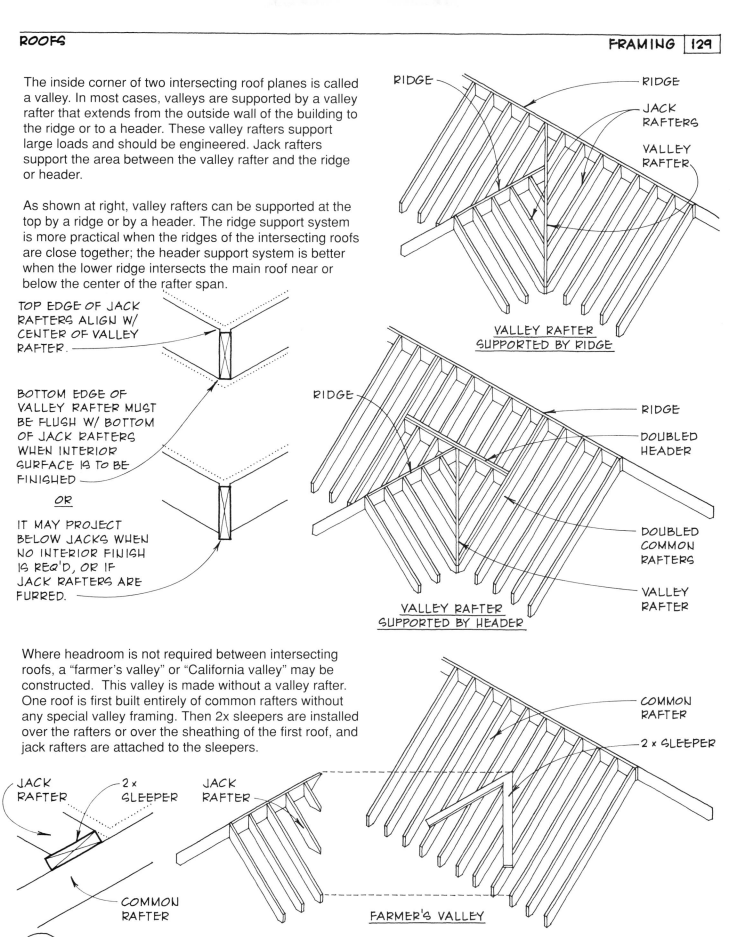

TOP EDGE OF JACK RAFTERS ALIGN W/ CENTER OF VALLEY RAFTER.

BOTTOM EDGE OF VALLEY RAFTER MUST BE FLUSH W/ BOTTOM OF JACK RAFTERS WHEN INTERIOR SURFACE IS TO BE FINISHED

OR

IT MAY PROJECT BELOW JACKS WHEN NO INTERIOR FINISH IS REQ'D, OR IF JACK RAFTERS ARE FURRED.

RIDGE — RIDGE
JACK RAFTERS
VALLEY RAFTER

VALLEY RAFTER SUPPORTED BY RIDGE

RIDGE
RIDGE
DOUBLED HEADER
DOUBLED COMMON RAFTERS
VALLEY RAFTER

VALLEY RAFTER SUPPORTED BY HEADER

Where headroom is not required between intersecting roofs, a "farmer's valley" or "California valley" may be constructed. This valley is made without a valley rafter. One roof is first built entirely of common rafters without any special valley framing. Then 2x sleepers are installed over the rafters or over the sheathing of the first roof, and jack rafters are attached to the sleepers.

JACK RAFTER
2 x SLEEPER
COMMON RAFTER

JACK RAFTER

COMMON RAFTER
2 x SLEEPER

FARMER'S VALLEY

(A) VALLEY FRAMING

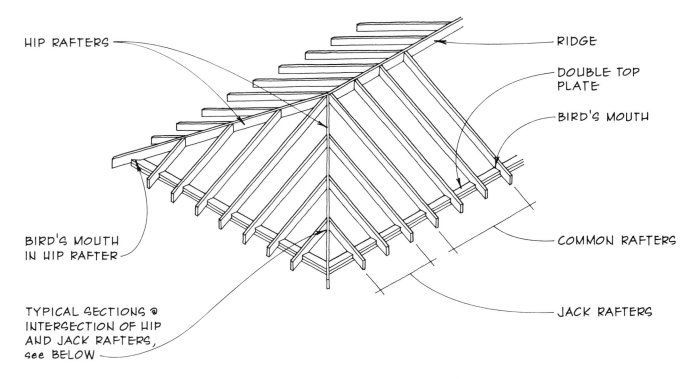

HIP RAFTERS

RIDGE

DOUBLE TOP PLATE

BIRD'S MOUTH

BIRD'S MOUTH IN HIP RAFTER

COMMON RAFTERS

JACK RAFTERS

TYPICAL SECTIONS @ INTERSECTION OF HIP AND JACK RAFTERS, see BELOW

A hip is the outside corner where two planes of a roof meet. It is comprised of a hip rafter at the corner and jack rafters from the hip to the eave. The hip rafter is supported at its lower end by the wall at plate level (or by a post) and at its upper end by the ridge (or by a wall).

Most codes require that the hip rafter project below the bottom edge of the jack rafters (see the top drawing at right). This is not very logical because, unlike a valley rafter, a hip rafter does not support much roof load. The extra depth presents no problem in an attic space, but if the inside face of the roof is to be made into a finish ceiling, the hip rafter will have to be ripped to allow the planes of the finish ceiling to meet (middle drawing at right). If codes will not permit ripping the hip rafter, furring may be added to the underside of the jack and common rafters to allow the finish ceiling to clear the hip rafter.

The top ends of the jack rafters may be cut off to permit venting at the top of the hip roof (bottom drawing at right).

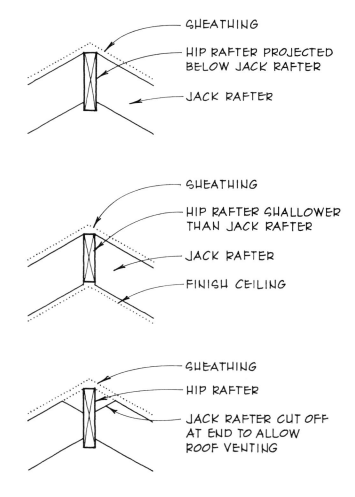

SHEATHING

HIP RAFTER PROJECTED BELOW JACK RAFTER

JACK RAFTER

SHEATHING

HIP RAFTER SHALLOWER THAN JACK RAFTER

JACK RAFTER

FINISH CEILING

SHEATHING

HIP RAFTER

JACK RAFTER CUT OFF AT END TO ALLOW ROOF VENTING

A HIP FRAMING

The framing of a flat roof is more like a floor than it is like a pitched roof. The joists are level or nearly level and support the ceiling below and the live loads above. Connections to walls are like those for floors (see 34A), as are the framing details for openings (see 39B) and cantilevers (see 40A). As for floors, the structure of a flat roof may be a joist system (dimension lumber or laminated), a girder system or a truss system. Blocking and bridging (see 39A) must be considered at the appropriate locations.

Flat roofs are unlike floors, however, in that they are not really flat. They might be more properly called "low-slope" roofs because they must slope at least ¼ in. per ft. in order to eliminate standing water. This minimal slope may be achieved in several ways:
   1. The joists themselves may slope if the ceiling below does not have to be level, or if the ceiling is furred to level.
   2. Trusses may be manufactured with a built-in slope.
   3. Shims may be added to the top of the joists.
   4. Tapered rigid insulation may be added to the top of the sheathing.
   5. The joists may be oversized and tapered on top.
   6. Sloped rafters can be scabbed alongside level ceiling joists.

The easiest and most direct way to support an overhang at the corner of a flat roof is with a beam below the joists cantilevered from the top of a bearing wall, as shown in the drawing below.

A traditional framing method for a cantilevered corner without a beam is with joists that radiate from a doubled central diagonal joist, as shown below. A strong fascia board is advisable here, as with all framing using cantilevered joists.

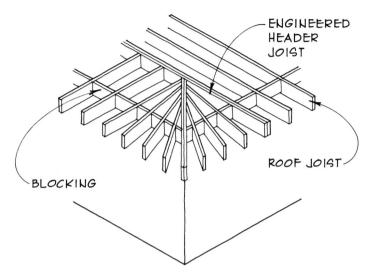

A third option for framing a cantilevered corner is shown below. All methods illustrated should be engineered by a professional.

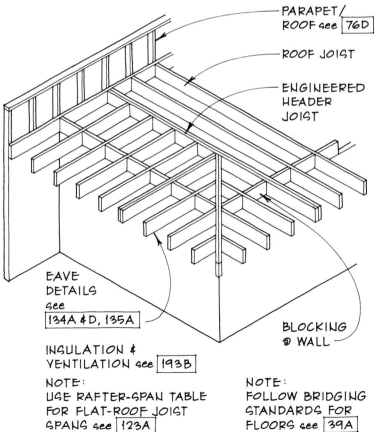

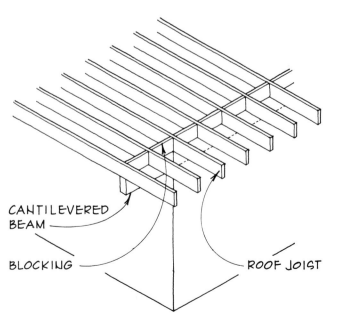

FLAT-ROOF FRAMING

Designing the basic shape of the roof and designing the configuration of eaves and rakes are the most critical tasks in roof design. Stylistically, the selection of eave and rake types should complement both the roof form and the roofing material.

Functionally, the eave and rake should help protect the building from the elements. The shape of the roof will suggest certain eave and/or rake shapes (see 132B), and certain eave types work best with particular rake types (see 133A).

Eave—The eave is the level connection between the roof and the wall. Eaves are common to all sloped roofs and often to flat roofs. There are four basic types of eave (see 133A). For eave support, see 134 and 135A & B.

Rake—The rake is the sloped connection between the roof and the wall. Only shed and gable roof types and their derivatives have a rake. There are three basic types of rake (see 133A).

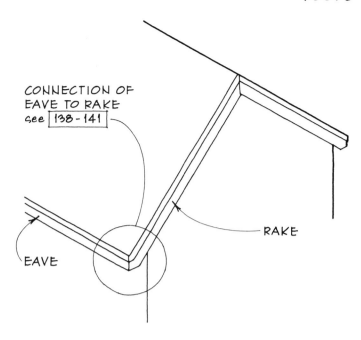

CONNECTION OF EAVE TO RAKE see 138-141

RAKE

EAVE

A EAVES & RAKES

INTRODUCTION

The basic shape and structure of a roof system need to be coordinated with the finish of the roof at the edges. The shape of the roof affects the treatment of the edges, and vice versa. A hip roof, for example, is easier to finish with a soffited eave than is a gable roof. The basic roof shapes are best suited for the following finish treatment at the edges:

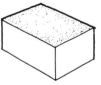

HIP ROOF

HIP ROOFS HAVE ONLY EAVES, WHICH MAY BE ABBREVIATED, BOXED, SOFFITED OR EXPOSED W/ ALMOST EQUAL EASE.

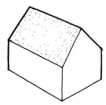

SHED ROOF

SHED ROOFS HAVE BOTH A RAKE & AN EAVE. ALL EAVE TYPES EXCEPT FOR SOFFITS CAN BE COMBINED W/ ALL RAKE TYPES. A SPECIAL EAVE DETAIL IS REQ'D FOR THE TOP EDGE see 135B

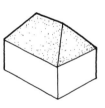

FLAT ROOF

FLAT ROOFS HAVE NO RAKES. OVERHANGING EAVES CAN BE DETAILED W/ A SOFFIT OR W/ EXPOSED RAFTERS. WHEN THERE ARE NO OVERHANGS, THERE IS AN ABBREVIATED EAVE OR A PARAPET see 76D

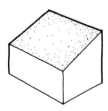

GABLE ROOF

GABLE ROOFS, LIKE SHED ROOFS, HAVE BOTH EAVES & RAKES. EXCEPT FOR SOFFITED EAVES, ALL EAVE & RAKE TYPES CAN BE COMBINED. A SPECIAL DETAIL IS REQ'D @ THE RIDGE, WHERE THE TWO RAKES MEET see 126B & 136C

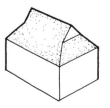

COMBINATION TYPES

COMBINATION ROOF TYPES USUALLY HAVE BOTH RAKES & EAVES. THEY FOLLOW THE GUIDELINES OF THE INDIVIDUAL ROOF TYPES.

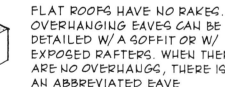

 B ROOF SHAPE & EAVE/RAKE SELECTION

The way in which one edge of a roof is finished affects the detailing of other edges. For example, a soffited eave on a gable-roofed building is easier to build with an abbreviated rake than with an exposed rake. The designer should attempt to match the level edge of the roof (the eave) to the sloped edge (the rake).

In examining the details of the eave and rake, therefore, the two must be considered as a set. It is logical to start with the eave, because all sloped roof types have eaves, but not all have rakes.

There are four basic sloped-roof eave types. All four types are appropriate for hip roofs, and all but the soffited type can make a simple and elegant transition from eave to rake on gable and shed roofs. The eave types and their most appropriate companion rakes are diagrammed below.

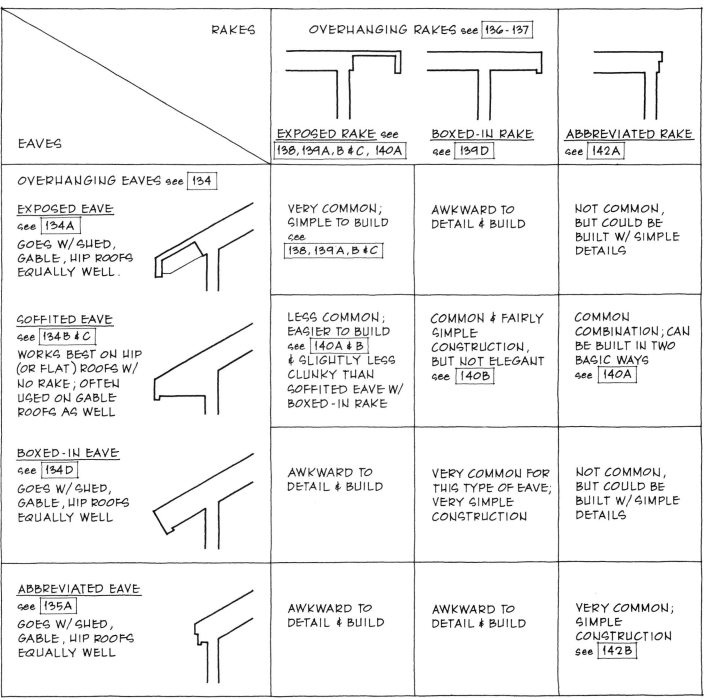

EAVES \ RAKES	OVERHANGING RAKES see 136-137		
	EXPOSED RAKE see 138, 139A, B & C, 140A	BOXED-IN RAKE see 139D	ABBREVIATED RAKE see 142A
OVERHANGING EAVES see 134 **EXPOSED EAVE** see 134A GOES W/ SHED, GABLE, HIP ROOFS EQUALLY WELL.	VERY COMMON; SIMPLE TO BUILD see 138, 139A, B & C	AWKWARD TO DETAIL & BUILD	NOT COMMON, BUT COULD BE BUILT W/ SIMPLE DETAILS
SOFFITED EAVE see 134B & C WORKS BEST ON HIP (OR FLAT) ROOFS W/ NO RAKE; OFTEN USED ON GABLE ROOFS AS WELL	LESS COMMON; EASIER TO BUILD see 140A & B & SLIGHTLY LESS CLUNKY THAN SOFFITED EAVE W/ BOXED-IN RAKE	COMMON & FAIRLY SIMPLE CONSTRUCTION, BUT NOT ELEGANT see 140B	COMMON COMBINATION; CAN BE BUILT IN TWO BASIC WAYS see 140A
BOXED-IN EAVE see 134D GOES W/ SHED, GABLE, HIP ROOFS EQUALLY WELL	AWKWARD TO DETAIL & BUILD	VERY COMMON FOR THIS TYPE OF EAVE; VERY SIMPLE CONSTRUCTION	NOT COMMON, BUT COULD BE BUILT W/ SIMPLE DETAILS
ABBREVIATED EAVE see 135A GOES W/ SHED, GABLE, HIP ROOFS EQUALLY WELL	AWKWARD TO DETAIL & BUILD	AWKWARD TO DETAIL & BUILD	VERY COMMON; SIMPLE CONSTRUCTION see 142B

(A) EAVE / RAKE COMBINATIONS

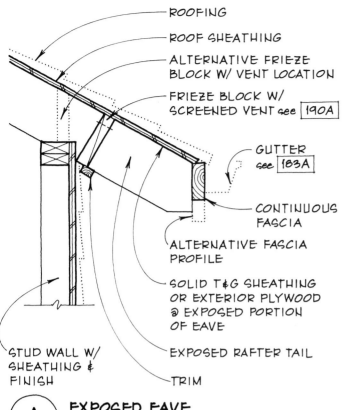

ROOFING

ROOF SHEATHING

ALTERNATIVE FRIEZE
BLOCK W/ VENT LOCATION

FRIEZE BLOCK W/
SCREENED VENT see | 190A |

GUTTER
see | 183A |

CONTINUOUS
FASCIA

ALTERNATIVE FASCIA
PROFILE

SOLID T&G SHEATHING
OR EXTERIOR PLYWOOD
@ EXPOSED PORTION
OF EAVE

EXPOSED RAFTER TAIL

STUD WALL W/
SHEATHING &
FINISH

TRIM

(A) EXPOSED EAVE

ROOFING

ROOF SHEATHING

BLOCKING AS REQ'D W/
SPACE FOR VENTILATION

2 × SOFFIT JOIST NAILED
TO RAFTERS

GUTTER
see | 183A |

CONTINUOUS
FASCIA

CONTINUOUS SOFFIT OF
EXTERIOR PLYWOOD OR
OTHER EXTERIOR - RATED
FINISH

CONTINUOUS SCREENED
VENT W/ TRIM see | 190B |

STUD WALL W/
SHEATHING &
FINISH

CONTINUOUS LEDGER
FOR SOFFIT JOISTS

(B) SOFFITED EAVE

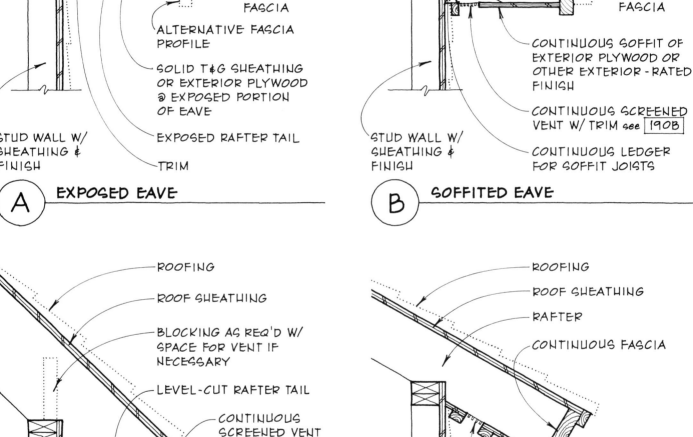

ROOFING

ROOF SHEATHING

BLOCKING AS REQ'D W/
SPACE FOR VENT IF
NECESSARY

LEVEL-CUT RAFTER TAIL

CONTINUOUS
SCREENED VENT
see | 190B |

1 × 4 OR 1 × 6

SOLID T&G SHEATHING OR
EXTERIOR PLYWOOD

STUD WALL W/ SHEATHING
& FINISH

NOTE:
THIS DETAIL WORKS WELL ON STEEP ROOFS,
WHERE A FASCIA MAY APPEAR TOO BULKY.

(C) SOFFITED EAVE
ALTERNATIVE DETAIL

ROOFING

ROOF SHEATHING

RAFTER

CONTINUOUS FASCIA

EXTERIOR PLYWOOD OR
OTHER EXTERIOR-GRADE
FINISH

STUD WALL W/
SHEATHING & FINISH

CONTINUOUS SCREENED
VENT W/ TRIM see | 190B |

NOTE:
NO GUTTER SHOWN. HANG GUTTER FROM STRAP
see | 185C |
OR USE VERTICAL FASCIA ON PLUMB-CUT RAFTERS
TO ACCOMMODATE STANDARD GUTTERS.

(D) BOXED-IN EAVE

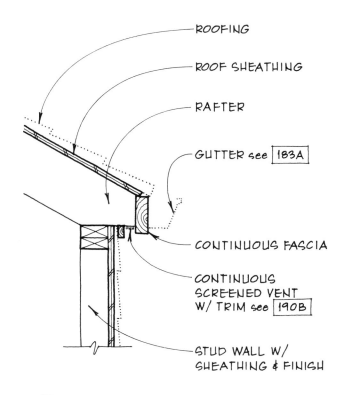

ROOFING

ROOF SHEATHING

RAFTER

GUTTER see [183A]

CONTINUOUS FASCIA

CONTINUOUS
SCREENED VENT
W/ TRIM see [190B]

STUD WALL W/
SHEATHING & FINISH

(A) ABBREVIATED EAVE

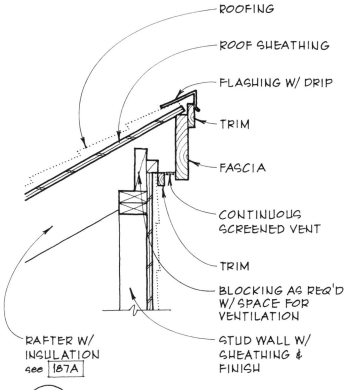

ROOFING

ROOF SHEATHING

FLASHING W/ DRIP

TRIM

FASCIA

CONTINUOUS
SCREENED VENT

TRIM

BLOCKING AS REQ'D
W/ SPACE FOR
VENTILATION

STUD WALL W/
SHEATHING &
FINISH

RAFTER W/
INSULATION
see [187A]

(B) SHED-ROOF EAVE
TOP OF RAFTER @ WALL

NOTES:
DUMMY RAFTERS ARE
RELATIVELY SHORT, SO
A HIGH GRADE OF
MATERIAL MAY BE
USED. CONSIDER USING
THEM IF THE EXPOSED
PART OF THE RAFTER
IS TO BE A DIFFERENT
SIZE THAN THE UNEXPOSED
PART OF THE RAFTER
OR TRUSS; OR
IF EXPOSED RAFTERS
ARE DESIRED WHEN
PLYWOOD I-RAFTERS
ARE USED FOR THE
ROOF STRUCTURE
see [143-146]
FOR ABBREVIATED
EAVES, THE ENTIRE
EAVE ASSEMBLY MAY
BE SHOP-BUILT IN
LENGTHS UP TO
ABOUT 16 FT.

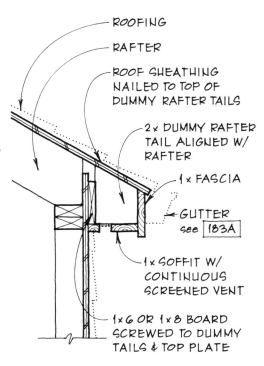

ROOFING

RAFTER

ROOF SHEATHING
NAILED TO TOP OF
DUMMY RAFTER TAILS

2x DUMMY RAFTER
TAIL ALIGNED W/
RAFTER

1x FASCIA

GUTTER
see [183A]

1x SOFFIT W/
CONTINUOUS
SCREENED VENT

1x6 OR 1x8 BOARD
SCREWED TO DUMMY
TAILS & TOP PLATE

ABBREVIATED EAVE

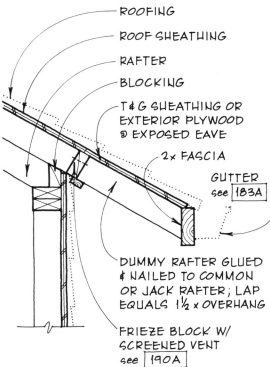

ROOFING

ROOF SHEATHING

RAFTER

BLOCKING

T&G SHEATHING OR
EXTERIOR PLYWOOD
@ EXPOSED EAVE

2x FASCIA

GUTTER
see [183A]

DUMMY RAFTER GLUED
& NAILED TO COMMON
OR JACK RAFTER; LAP
EQUALS 1½ x OVERHANG

FRIEZE BLOCK W/
SCREENED VENT
see [190A]

EXPOSED EAVE

(C) DUMMY RAFTER TAIL

When an overhang is required at the rake, the overhang is made with barge rafters, which stand away from the building and need support. There are several ways to support barge rafters. The roof sheathing alone may be strong enough to support the barge rafters (see 136B), or the ridge board or beam can be designed to support the barge rafters at their upper ends (see 136C), and the fascia may be extended to support the barge rafters at their lower ends (see below). Lookouts or brackets may be also used to support an overhanging rake (see 137A & B).

The roof sheathing can assist in supporting the barge rafter along its length, as shown below.

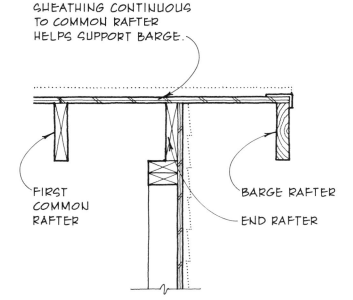

SHEATHING CONTINUOUS TO COMMON RAFTER HELPS SUPPORT BARGE.

FIRST COMMON RAFTER

BARGE RAFTER

END RAFTER

B   **OVERHANGING RAKE**
SUPPORTED BY SHEATHING

END RAFTER (LAST INTERIOR RAFTER)

EXTENDED RIDGE BOARD OR BEAM
see | 136C |

BARGE RAFTER

FASCIA HELPS TO SUPPORT BARGE RAFTER @ ITS LOWER END.

SHEATHING PROVIDES SUPPORT FOR BARGE RAFTER
see | 136B |

NOTE:
VERGE RAFTER NOT SHOWN; FOR DETAILS
see | 138 |

A   **OVERHANGING RAKE**
METHODS OF SUPPORT

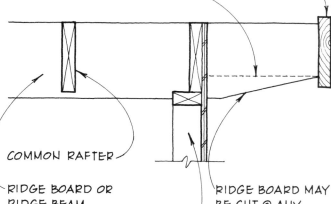

ALTERNATIVE CUT IN RIDGE BOARD ALLOWS FOR BOXED-IN OVERHANGING RAKE.

BARGE RAFTERS MEET @ CENTERLINE OF RIDGE

COMMON RAFTER

RIDGE BOARD OR RIDGE BEAM
see | 123 |

STUD WALL UNDER END COMMON RAFTER

RIDGE BOARD MAY BE CUT @ ANY ANGLE OR SHAPE THAT ALLOWS FOR ATTACHMENT OF BARGE RAFTERS WITHOUT HAVING END EXPOSED BELOW THEM.

C   **OVERHANGING RAKE**
SUPPORTED BY RIDGE BOARD OR BEAM

If the ridge, the fascia and the sheathing together do not provide sufficient support for the barge, lookouts may be added. Lookouts extend from the barge rafter to the first common rafter (or truss) inside the wall. The lookouts are notched through the end rafter at the top of the wall. The size and spacing of lookouts depends on rafter spacing and live loading.

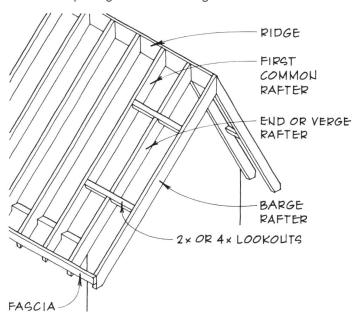

- RIDGE
- FIRST COMMON RAFTER
- END OR VERGE RAFTER
- BARGE RAFTER
- 2x OR 4x LOOKOUTS
- FASCIA

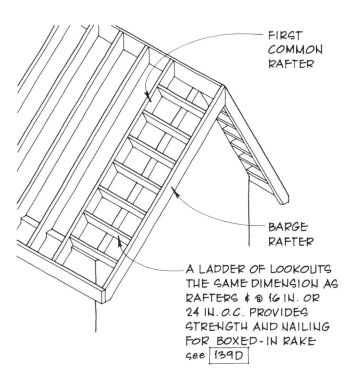

- FIRST COMMON RAFTER
- BARGE RAFTER
- A LADDER OF LOOKOUTS THE SAME DIMENSION AS RAFTERS & @ 16 IN. OR 24 IN. O.C. PROVIDES STRENGTH AND NAILING FOR BOXED-IN RAKE see 139D

(A) OVERHANGING RAKE
SUPPORTED BY LOOKOUTS

Brackets attached to the face of the wall framing can support the barge rafter by means of triangulation.

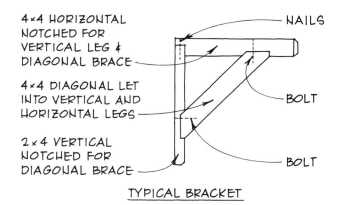

- 4×4 HORIZONTAL NOTCHED FOR VERTICAL LEG & DIAGONAL BRACE
- 4×4 DIAGONAL LET INTO VERTICAL AND HORIZONTAL LEGS
- 2×4 VERTICAL NOTCHED FOR DIAGONAL BRACE
- NAILS
- BOLT
- BOLT

TYPICAL BRACKET

Attaching the bracket to the inside of the barge rafter avoids problems of weathering.

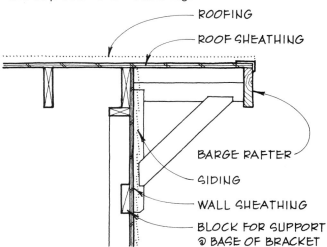

- ROOFING
- ROOF SHEATHING
- BARGE RAFTER
- SIDING
- WALL SHEATHING
- BLOCK FOR SUPPORT @ BASE OF BRACKET

The alternative bracket connection to the barge rafter shown below is common on Craftsman-style buildings. With this detail, moisture collects on top of the bracket, and this contributes to the decay of the bracket and the barge rafter.

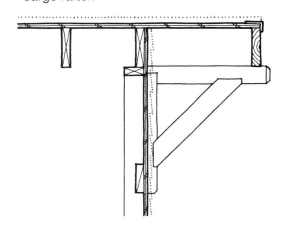

(B) OVERHANGING RAKE
SUPPORTED BY BRACKETS

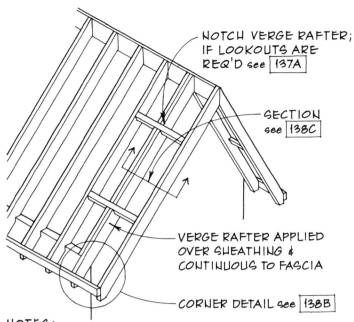

NOTCH VERGE RAFTER;
IF LOOKOUTS ARE
REQ'D see 137A

SECTION
see 138C

VERGE RAFTER APPLIED
OVER SHEATHING &
CONTINUOUS TO FASCIA

CORNER DETAIL see 138B

NOTES:
ROOF SHEATHING MUST BE EXTERIOR-RATED PANEL
OR SOLID (T&G) MATERIAL.
FOR ALTERNATIVE DETAIL W/ TRIM BOARD
see 139A, B &C

 A — **EXPOSED RAKE W/ VERGE RAFTER**
FRAMING

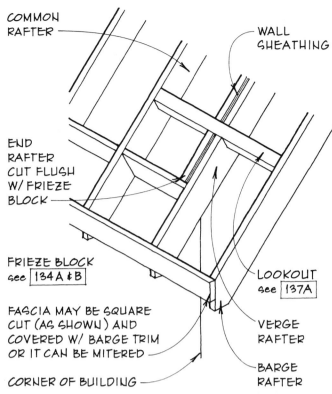

COMMON
RAFTER

WALL
SHEATHING

END
RAFTER
CUT FLUSH
W/ FRIEZE
BLOCK

FRIEZE BLOCK
see 134A & B

LOOKOUT
see 137A

VERGE
RAFTER

FASCIA MAY BE SQUARE
CUT (AS SHOWN) AND
COVERED W/ BARGE TRIM
OR IT CAN BE MITERED

BARGE
RAFTER

CORNER OF BUILDING

 **B** — **EXPOSED RAKE W/ VERGE RAFTER**
CORNER FRAMING

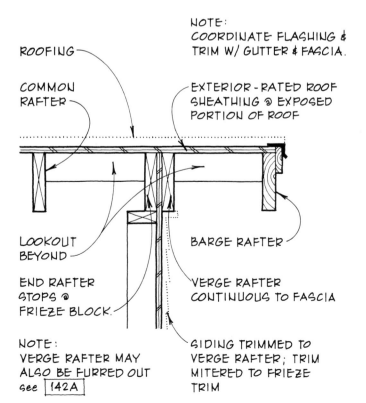

ROOFING

COMMON
RAFTER

NOTE:
COORDINATE FLASHING &
TRIM W/ GUTTER & FASCIA.

EXTERIOR-RATED ROOF
SHEATHING @ EXPOSED
PORTION OF ROOF

LOOKOUT
BEYOND

BARGE RAFTER

END RAFTER
STOPS @
FRIEZE BLOCK

VERGE RAFTER
CONTINUOUS TO FASCIA

NOTE:
VERGE RAFTER MAY
ALSO BE FURRED OUT
see 142A

SIDING TRIMMED TO
VERGE RAFTER; TRIM
MITERED TO FRIEZE
TRIM

 **C** — **EXPOSED RAKE W/ VERGE RAFTER**
SECTION

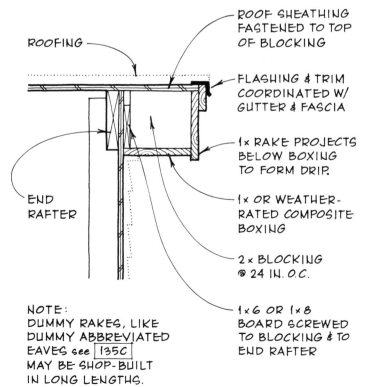

ROOFING

ROOF SHEATHING
FASTENED TO TOP
OF BLOCKING

FLASHING & TRIM
COORDINATED W/
GUTTER & FASCIA

1x RAKE PROJECTS
BELOW BOXING
TO FORM DRIP.

1x OR WEATHER-
RATED COMPOSITE
BOXING

END
RAFTER

2x BLOCKING
@ 24 IN. O.C.

1x6 OR 1x8
BOARD SCREWED
TO BLOCKING & TO
END RAFTER

NOTE:
DUMMY RAKES, LIKE
DUMMY ABBREVIATED
EAVES see 135C
MAY BE SHOP-BUILT
IN LONG LENGTHS.

 D — **DUMMY RAKE**

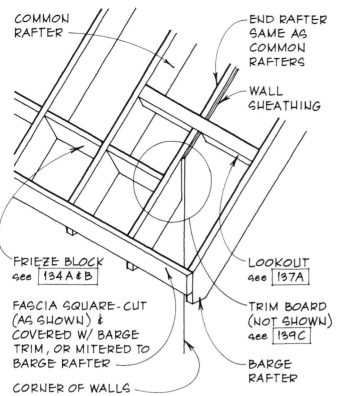

COMMON
RAFTER

END RAFTER
SAME AS
COMMON
RAFTERS

WALL
SHEATHING

FRIEZE BLOCK
see | 134 A & B |

LOOKOUT
see | 137A |

FASCIA SQUARE-CUT
(AS SHOWN) &
COVERED W/ BARGE
TRIM, OR MITERED TO
BARGE RAFTER

TRIM BOARD
(NOT SHOWN)
see | 139C |

CORNER OF WALLS

BARGE
RAFTER

(A) **EXPOSED RAKE W/ TRIM BOARD**
CORNER FRAMING

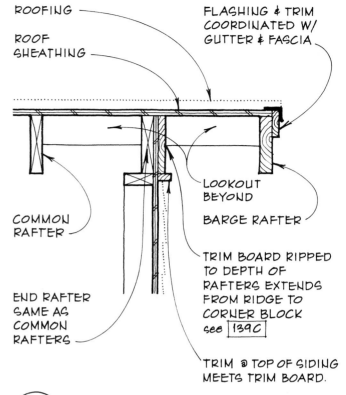

ROOFING

ROOF
SHEATHING

FLASHING & TRIM
COORDINATED W/
GUTTER & FASCIA

COMMON
RAFTER

LOOKOUT
BEYOND

BARGE RAFTER

END RAFTER
SAME AS
COMMON
RAFTERS

TRIM BOARD RIPPED
TO DEPTH OF
RAFTERS EXTENDS
FROM RIDGE TO
CORNER BLOCK
see | 139C |

TRIM @ TOP OF SIDING
MEETS TRIM BOARD.

(B) **EXPOSED RAKE W/ TRIM BOARD**
SECTION

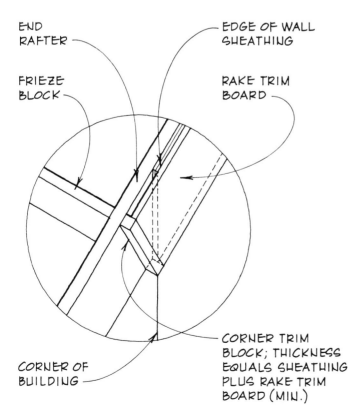

END
RAFTER

EDGE OF WALL
SHEATHING

FRIEZE
BLOCK

RAKE TRIM
BOARD

CORNER OF
BUILDING

CORNER TRIM
BLOCK; THICKNESS
EQUALS SHEATHING
PLUS RAKE TRIM
BOARD (MIN.)

(C) **EXPOSED RAKE W/ TRIM BOARD**
DETAIL @ EAVE

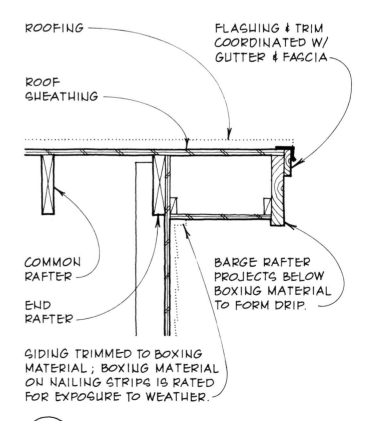

ROOFING

ROOF
SHEATHING

FLASHING & TRIM
COORDINATED W/
GUTTER & FASCIA

COMMON
RAFTER

END
RAFTER

BARGE RAFTER
PROJECTS BELOW
BOXING MATERIAL
TO FORM DRIP.

SIDING TRIMMED TO BOXING
MATERIAL; BOXING MATERIAL
ON NAILING STRIPS IS RATED
FOR EXPOSURE TO WEATHER.

(D) **BOXED-IN RAKE**

The transition from soffited eave to rake can demand some carpentry heroics. Only when the soffit is terminated at the plane of the end wall is the detailing reasonably direct, requiring only that the end of the soffit space be finished. This situation may occur with an abbreviated rake (see below) or with an overhanging rake (see 140A & B). As shown below, the end of the soffit space may be finished with a pork chop or with a layered gable—a continuation of the gable-wall finish over the end of the soffit.

When the soffit extends beyond the plane of the end wall, the rear side of the soffited space (opposite the fascia) must be finished as well as the end. As shown in the drawings below, this may be accomplished most elegantly with a Greek return, or with a simpler soffit return.

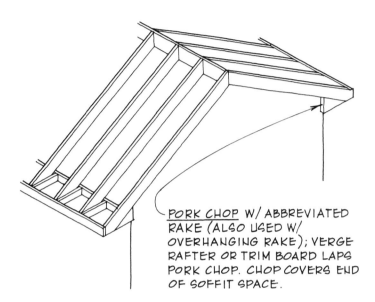

PORK CHOP W/ ABBREVIATED RAKE (ALSO USED W/ OVERHANGING RAKE); VERGE RAFTER OR TRIM BOARD LAPS PORK CHOP. CHOP COVERS END OF SOFFIT SPACE.

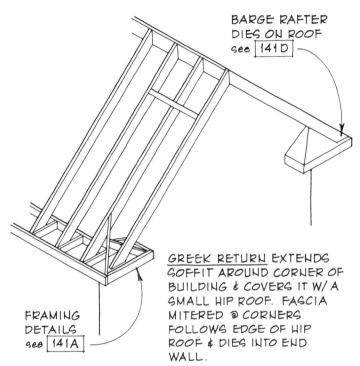

BARGE RAFTER DIES ON ROOF
see | 141D |

FRAMING DETAILS
see | 141A |

GREEK RETURN EXTENDS SOFFIT AROUND CORNER OF BUILDING & COVERS IT W/ A SMALL HIP ROOF. FASCIA MITERED @ CORNERS FOLLOWS EDGE OF HIP ROOF & DIES INTO END WALL.

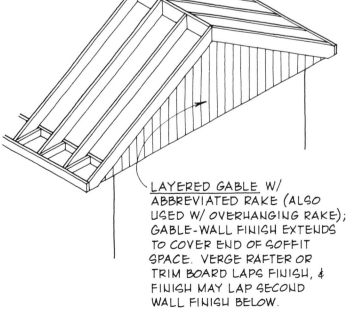

LAYERED GABLE W/ ABBREVIATED RAKE (ALSO USED W/ OVERHANGING RAKE); GABLE-WALL FINISH EXTENDS TO COVER END OF SOFFIT SPACE. VERGE RAFTER OR TRIM BOARD LAPS FINISH, & FINISH MAY LAP SECOND WALL FINISH BELOW.

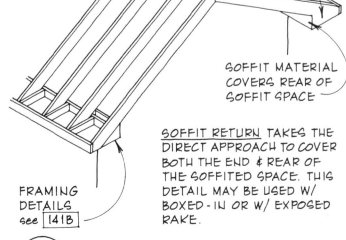

PORK CHOP @ END

SOFFIT MATERIAL COVERS REAR OF SOFFIT SPACE

FRAMING DETAILS
see | 141B |

SOFFIT RETURN TAKES THE DIRECT APPROACH TO COVER BOTH THE END & REAR OF THE SOFFITED SPACE. THIS DETAIL MAY BE USED W/ BOXED-IN OR W/ EXPOSED RAKE.

(A) SOFFITED EAVE/RAKE TRANSITION
ABBREVIATED OR OVERHANGING RAKE

(B) SOFFITED EAVE/RAKE TRANSITION
OVERHANGING RAKE

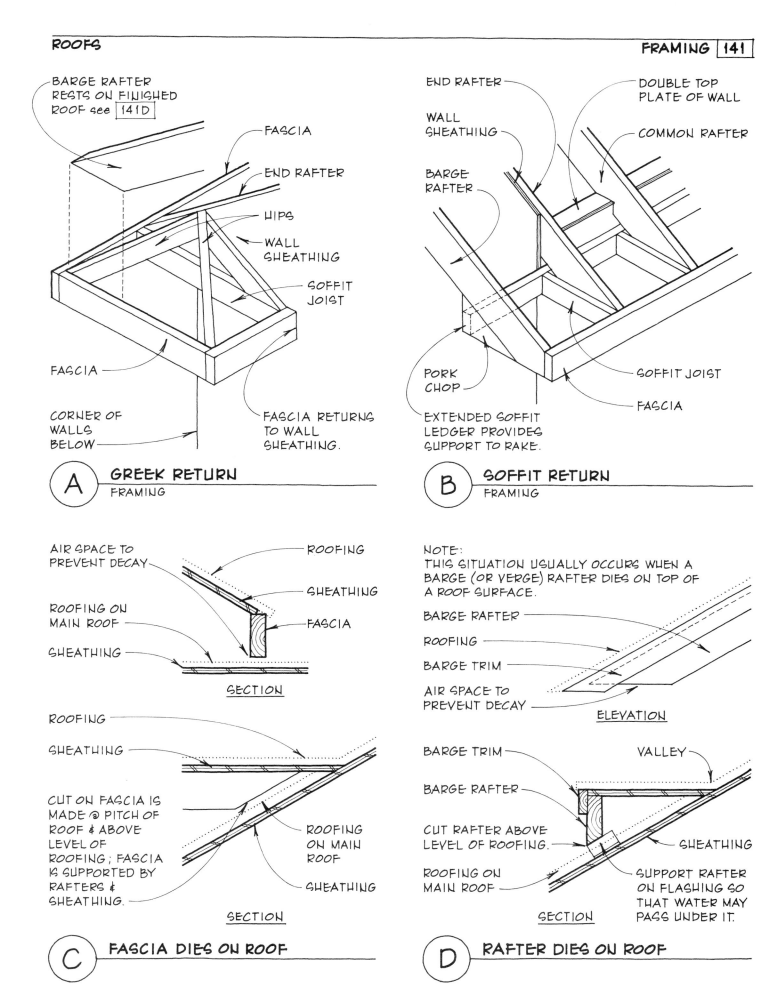

BARGE RAFTER RESTS ON FINISHED ROOF see | 141D |

FASCIA

END RAFTER

HIPS

WALL SHEATHING

SOFFIT JOIST

FASCIA

CORNER OF WALLS BELOW

FASCIA RETURNS TO WALL SHEATHING.

A GREEK RETURN
FRAMING

END RAFTER

WALL SHEATHING

BARGE RAFTER

DOUBLE TOP PLATE OF WALL

COMMON RAFTER

PORK CHOP

SOFFIT JOIST

FASCIA

EXTENDED SOFFIT LEDGER PROVIDES SUPPORT TO RAKE.

B SOFFIT RETURN
FRAMING

AIR SPACE TO PREVENT DECAY

ROOFING

SHEATHING

FASCIA

ROOFING ON MAIN ROOF

SHEATHING

SECTION

ROOFING

SHEATHING

CUT ON FASCIA IS MADE @ PITCH OF ROOF & ABOVE LEVEL OF ROOFING; FASCIA IS SUPPORTED BY RAFTERS & SHEATHING.

ROOFING ON MAIN ROOF

SHEATHING

SECTION

C FASCIA DIES ON ROOF

NOTE:
THIS SITUATION USUALLY OCCURS WHEN A BARGE (OR VERGE) RAFTER DIES ON TOP OF A ROOF SURFACE.

BARGE RAFTER

ROOFING

BARGE TRIM

AIR SPACE TO PREVENT DECAY

ELEVATION

BARGE TRIM

VALLEY

BARGE RAFTER

CUT RAFTER ABOVE LEVEL OF ROOFING.

SHEATHING

ROOFING ON MAIN ROOF

SUPPORT RAFTER ON FLASHING SO THAT WATER MAY PASS UNDER IT.

SECTION

D RAFTER DIES ON ROOF

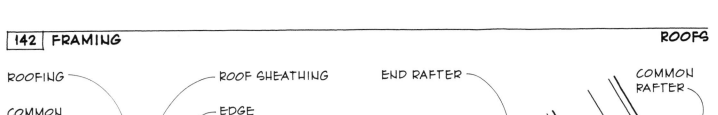

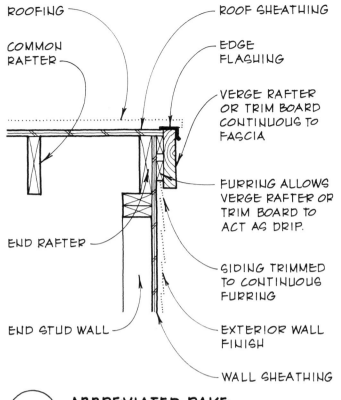

ROOFING

COMMON RAFTER

END RAFTER

END STUD WALL

ROOF SHEATHING

EDGE FLASHING

VERGE RAFTER OR TRIM BOARD CONTINUOUS TO FASCIA

FURRING ALLOWS VERGE RAFTER OR TRIM BOARD TO ACT AS DRIP.

SIDING TRIMMED TO CONTINUOUS FURRING

EXTERIOR WALL FINISH

WALL SHEATHING

(A) ABBREVIATED RAKE

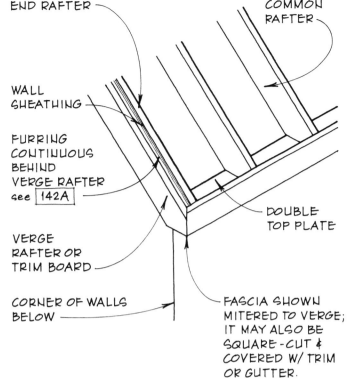

END RAFTER

WALL SHEATHING

FURRING CONTINUOUS BEHIND VERGE RAFTER see 142A

VERGE RAFTER OR TRIM BOARD

CORNER OF WALLS BELOW

COMMON RAFTER

DOUBLE TOP PLATE

FASCIA SHOWN MITERED TO VERGE; IT MAY ALSO BE SQUARE-CUT & COVERED W/ TRIM OR GUTTER.

(B) ABBREVIATED RAKE/EAVE
CORNER FRAMING

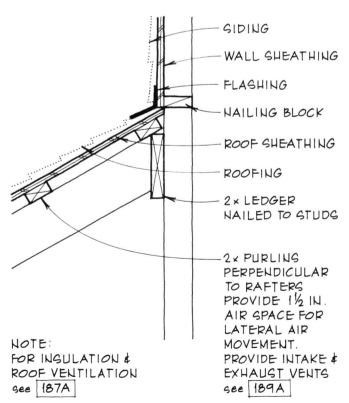

SIDING

WALL SHEATHING

FLASHING

NAILING BLOCK

ROOF SHEATHING

ROOFING

2 × LEDGER NAILED TO STUDS

2 × PURLINS PERPENDICULAR TO RAFTERS PROVIDE 1½ IN. AIR SPACE FOR LATERAL AIR MOVEMENT. PROVIDE INTAKE & EXHAUST VENTS see 189A

NOTE:
FOR INSULATION & ROOF VENTILATION see 187A

(C) TOP OF RAFTER/WALL
SHED ROOF W/ PURLINS

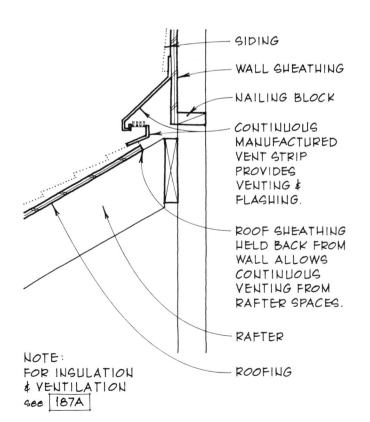

SIDING

WALL SHEATHING

NAILING BLOCK

CONTINUOUS MANUFACTURED VENT STRIP PROVIDES VENTING & FLASHING.

ROOF SHEATHING HELD BACK FROM WALL ALLOWS CONTINUOUS VENTING FROM RAFTER SPACES.

RAFTER

ROOFING

NOTE:
FOR INSULATION & VENTILATION see 187A

(D) TOP OF RAFTER/WALL
SHED ROOF W/ CONTINUOUS VENT STRIP

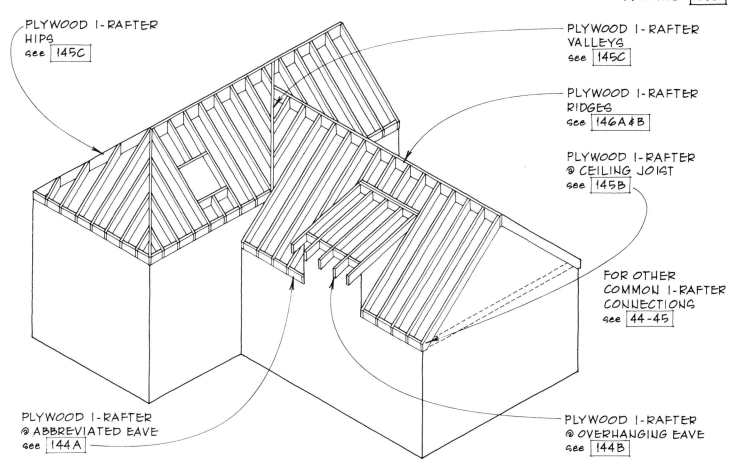

PLYWOOD I-RAFTER
HIPS
see | 145C |

PLYWOOD I-RAFTER
VALLEYS
see | 145C |

PLYWOOD I-RAFTER
RIDGES
see | 146A & B |

PLYWOOD I-RAFTER
@ CEILING JOIST
see | 145B |

FOR OTHER
COMMON I-RAFTER
CONNECTIONS
see | 44-45 |

PLYWOOD I-RAFTER
@ ABBREVIATED EAVE
see | 144A |

PLYWOOD I-RAFTER
@ OVERHANGING EAVE
see | 144B |

The light weight, strength, precision manufacturing and the long lengths that make structural-plywood and other composite framing materials appropriate for floors (see 44A) also indicate their use for rafters. These materials, called I-rafters, are generally stiffer and stronger and can span farther than dimension-lumber rafters of the same size, but they can also cost more, and their appearance is not satisfactory if exposed.

Plywood I-rafters can be attached to each other and to other members with metal straps and hangers, and can be cut on site. They do not have as much strength in compression as lumber rafters and must therefore be stiffened at joints and at other conditions required by manufacturers' specifications and local codes. Many builders find the details required of I-rafter connections at hips, valleys and other locations with compound angles to be more complicated than stick building, so in these locations they are likely to substitute dimension lumber, while using plywood I-rafters for simple framing.

Plywood I-rafters are manufactured items. To perform as designed, they must be installed completely in accordance with the individual manufacturer's instructions. The general framing principles that apply to dimension-lumber roof framing also hold true for plywood I-rafters. The drawings in this section, therefore, emphasize conditions where I-rafters require different detailing from dimension-lumber rafters.

(A)   **PLYWOOD I-RAFTERS**
INTRODUCTION

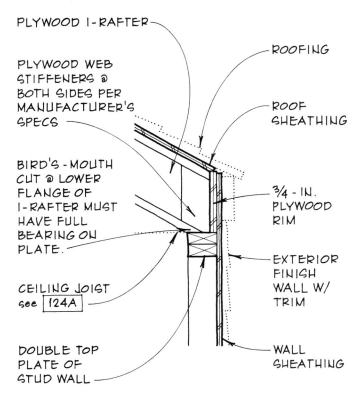

PLYWOOD I-RAFTER

PLYWOOD WEB STIFFENERS @ BOTH SIDES PER MANUFACTURER'S SPECS

BIRD'S-MOUTH CUT @ LOWER FLANGE OF I-RAFTER MUST HAVE FULL BEARING ON PLATE.

CEILING JOIST see | 124A |

DOUBLE TOP PLATE OF STUD WALL

ROOFING

ROOF SHEATHING

3/4-IN. PLYWOOD RIM

EXTERIOR FINISH WALL W/ TRIM

WALL SHEATHING

(A) PLYWOOD I-RAFTER
ABBREVIATED EAVE

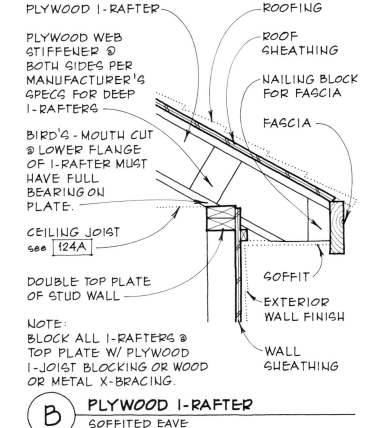

PLYWOOD I-RAFTER

PLYWOOD WEB STIFFENER @ BOTH SIDES PER MANUFACTURER'S SPECS FOR DEEP I-RAFTERS

BIRD'S-MOUTH CUT @ LOWER FLANGE OF I-RAFTER MUST HAVE FULL BEARING ON PLATE.

CEILING JOIST see | 124A |

DOUBLE TOP PLATE OF STUD WALL

NOTE:
BLOCK ALL I-RAFTERS @ TOP PLATE W/ PLYWOOD I-JOIST BLOCKING OR WOOD OR METAL X-BRACING.

ROOFING

ROOF SHEATHING

NAILING BLOCK FOR FASCIA

FASCIA

SOFFIT

EXTERIOR WALL FINISH

WALL SHEATHING

(B) PLYWOOD I-RAFTER
SOFFITED EAVE

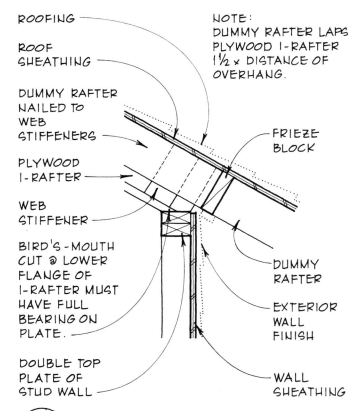

ROOFING

ROOF SHEATHING

DUMMY RAFTER NAILED TO WEB STIFFENERS

PLYWOOD I-RAFTER

WEB STIFFENER

BIRD'S-MOUTH CUT @ LOWER FLANGE OF I-RAFTER MUST HAVE FULL BEARING ON PLATE.

DOUBLE TOP PLATE OF STUD WALL

NOTE:
DUMMY RAFTER LAPS PLYWOOD I-RAFTER 1½ x DISTANCE OF OVERHANG.

FRIEZE BLOCK

DUMMY RAFTER

EXTERIOR WALL FINISH

WALL SHEATHING

(C) PLYWOOD I-RAFTER @ EXPOSED EAVE
EXPOSED DUMMY RAFTER

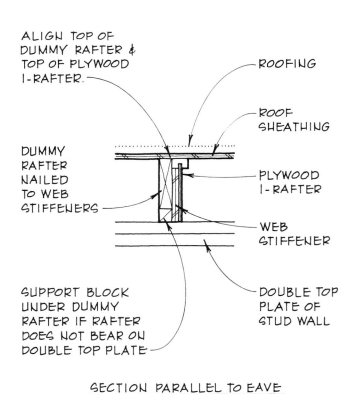

ALIGN TOP OF DUMMY RAFTER & TOP OF PLYWOOD I-RAFTER.

DUMMY RAFTER NAILED TO WEB STIFFENERS

SUPPORT BLOCK UNDER DUMMY RAFTER IF RAFTER DOES NOT BEAR ON DOUBLE TOP PLATE

ROOFING

ROOF SHEATHING

PLYWOOD I-RAFTER

WEB STIFFENER

DOUBLE TOP PLATE OF STUD WALL

SECTION PARALLEL TO EAVE

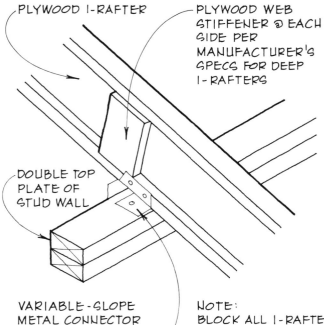

PLYWOOD I-RAFTER

PLYWOOD WEB STIFFENER @ EACH SIDE PER MANUFACTURER'S SPECS FOR DEEP I-RAFTERS

DOUBLE TOP PLATE OF STUD WALL

VARIABLE-SLOPE METAL CONNECTOR ELIMINATES NEED FOR BIRD'S MOUTH ON RAFTERS UP TO 6:12 SLOPE

NOTE:
BLOCK ALL I-RAFTERS @ TOP PLATE W/ PLYWOOD I-JOIST BLOCKING OR WOOD OR METAL X-BRACING.

 A   **PLYWOOD I-RAFTER @ EAVE**
OVERHANGING EAVE / METAL CONNECTOR

NOTE:
COLLAR TIES, LOCATED HIGHER ON THE RAFTER, ARE CONNECTED IN THE SAME FASHION AS THIS DETAIL.

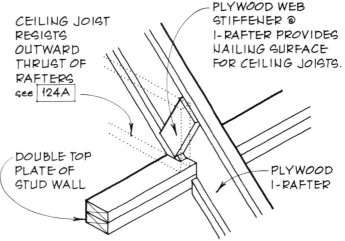

CEILING JOIST RESISTS OUTWARD THRUST OF RAFTERS
see 124A

PLYWOOD WEB STIFFENER @ I-RAFTER PROVIDES NAILING SURFACE FOR CEILING JOISTS.

DOUBLE TOP PLATE OF STUD WALL

PLYWOOD I-RAFTER

NOTE:
BLOCK ALL I-RAFTERS @ TOP PLATE W/ PLYWOOD I-JOIST BLOCKING OR WOOD OR METAL X-BRACING.

 B   **PLYWOOD I-RAFTER/CEILING JOIST**

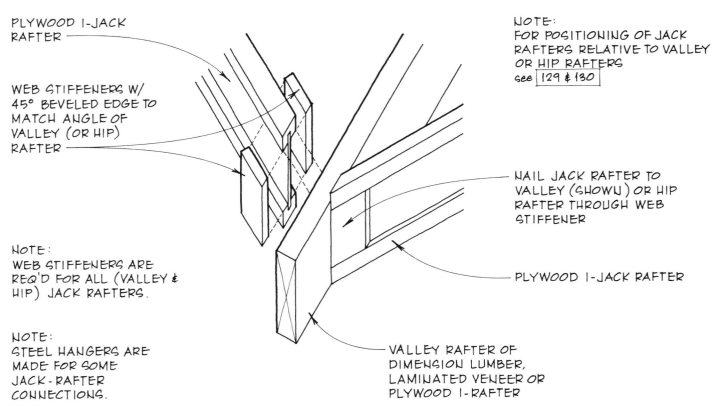

PLYWOOD I-JACK RAFTER

WEB STIFFENERS W/ 45° BEVELED EDGE TO MATCH ANGLE OF VALLEY (OR HIP) RAFTER

NOTE:
WEB STIFFENERS ARE REQ'D FOR ALL (VALLEY & HIP) JACK RAFTERS.

NOTE:
STEEL HANGERS ARE MADE FOR SOME JACK-RAFTER CONNECTIONS.

NOTE:
FOR POSITIONING OF JACK RAFTERS RELATIVE TO VALLEY OR HIP RAFTERS
see 129 & 130

NAIL JACK RAFTER TO VALLEY (SHOWN) OR HIP RAFTER THROUGH WEB STIFFENER

PLYWOOD I-JACK RAFTER

VALLEY RAFTER OF DIMENSION LUMBER, LAMINATED VENEER OR PLYWOOD I-RAFTER

 C   **PLYWOOD I-RAFTER / VALLEY OR HIP**
CONNECTION OF JACK RAFTERS

ROOF SHEATHING

PLYWOOD I-RAFTER

PLYWOOD WEB STIFFENER

METAL I-RAFTER HANGER

2x RIDGE BOARD IS DEEPER THAN PLUMB CUT OF RAFTERS.

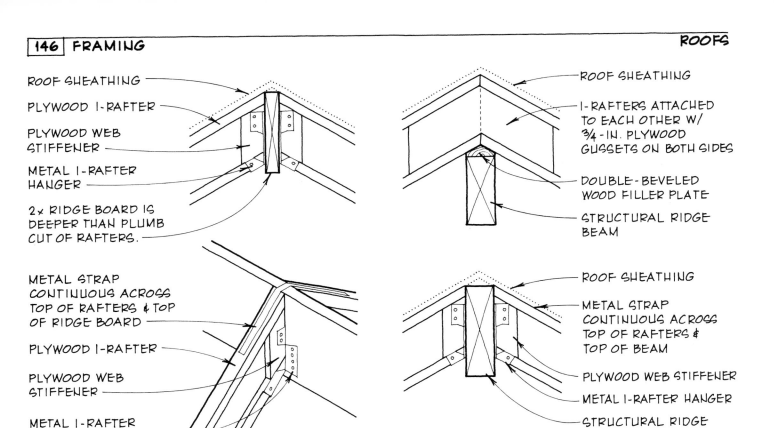

ROOF SHEATHING

I-RAFTERS ATTACHED TO EACH OTHER W/ 3/4-IN. PLYWOOD GUSSETS ON BOTH SIDES

DOUBLE-BEVELED WOOD FILLER PLATE

STRUCTURAL RIDGE BEAM

METAL STRAP CONTINUOUS ACROSS TOP OF RAFTERS & TOP OF RIDGE BOARD

PLYWOOD I-RAFTER

PLYWOOD WEB STIFFENER

METAL I-RAFTER HANGER

ROOF SHEATHING

METAL STRAP CONTINUOUS ACROSS TOP OF RAFTERS & TOP OF BEAM

PLYWOOD WEB STIFFENER

METAL I-RAFTER HANGER

STRUCTURAL RIDGE BEAM

(A) PLYWOOD I-RAFTER / RIDGE
RIDGE BOARD

(B) PLYWOOD I-RAFTER / RIDGE
STRUCTURAL RIDGE BEAM

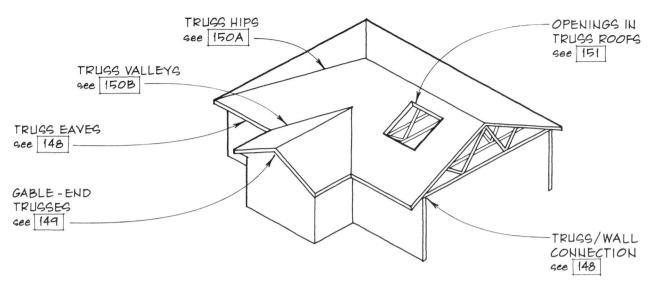

TRUSS HIPS
see | 150A |

OPENINGS IN
TRUSS ROOFS
see | 151 |

TRUSS VALLEYS
see | 150B |

TRUSS EAVES
see | 148 |

GABLE - END
TRUSSES
see | 149 |

TRUSS / WALL
CONNECTION
see | 148 |

Roof trusses, like floor trusses, are a framework of small members (usually 2x4s) that are connected so that they act like a single large member. They are always engineered by the manufacturer.

Engineered roof trusses can span much greater distances than the stick-framed rafter-and-tie system. Long spans (over 40 ft.) are possible with simple trusses so that large open rooms may be designed with roof loads bearing only on the perimeter walls. Interior walls may simply be partition walls and may be repositioned without compromising the roof structure.

A second advantage of roof trusses is the reduction in roof framing labor. Trusses are typically set in place by the delivery truck and may be positioned and fastened in a fraction of the time it would take to frame with rafters and ties.

One major disadvantage of roof trusses is the difficulty of adapting them to complex roof forms. Roofs with vaulted ceilings, unequal plate heights or with numerous hips or valleys are usually easier to build if they are framed with rafters.

Another disadvantage of roof trusses is that the webs of the truss occupy space that could be available for storage or as a full-sized attic. Furthermore, these webs cannot be cut for any future remodeling purposes.

Five common roof truss types are shown in the drawings below.

FINK
TRUSS

FINK TRUSSES SPAN OVER 40 FT.

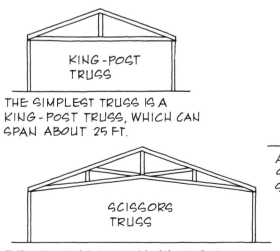

KING - POST
TRUSS

THE SIMPLEST TRUSS IS A KING - POST TRUSS, WHICH CAN SPAN ABOUT 25 FT.

SCISSORS
TRUSS

THE SLOPING BOTTOM CHORDS OF SCISSORS TRUSSES CAN INCREASE INTERIOR VOLUME. SPANS UP TO 40 FT. ARE POSSIBLE.

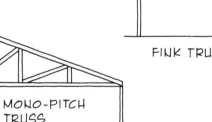

MONO-PITCH
TRUSS

A MONO - PITCH TRUSS, FOR SHED ROOF BUILDINGS, SPANS ABOUT 25 FT.

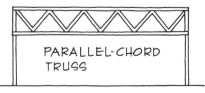

PARALLEL-CHORD
TRUSS

PARALLEL - CHORD TRUSSES ARE FOR FLAT ROOFS; STANDARD SPANS ARE AVAILABLE UP TO 30 FT.

 A **ROOF TRUSSES**
INTRODUCTION

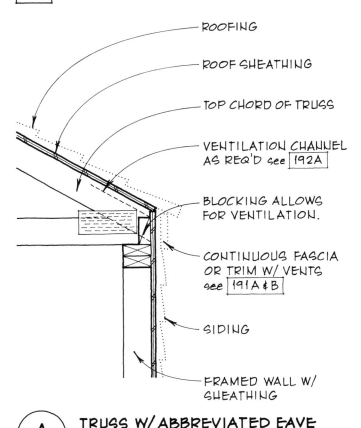

ROOFING

ROOF SHEATHING

TOP CHORD OF TRUSS

VENTILATION CHANNEL AS REQ'D see 192A

BLOCKING ALLOWS FOR VENTILATION.

CONTINUOUS FASCIA OR TRIM W/ VENTS see 191A & B

SIDING

FRAMED WALL W/ SHEATHING

(A) TRUSS W/ ABBREVIATED EAVE

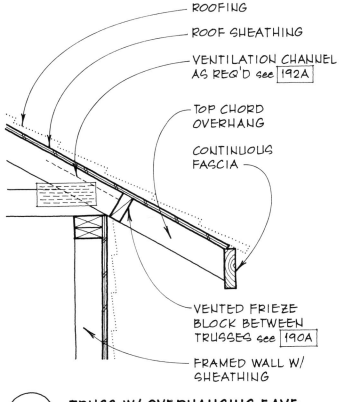

ROOFING

ROOF SHEATHING

VENTILATION CHANNEL AS REQ'D see 192A

TOP CHORD OVERHANG

CONTINUOUS FASCIA

VENTED FRIEZE BLOCK BETWEEN TRUSSES see 190A

FRAMED WALL W/ SHEATHING

(B) TRUSS W/ OVERHANGING EAVE
EXPOSED OR BOXED-IN EAVE

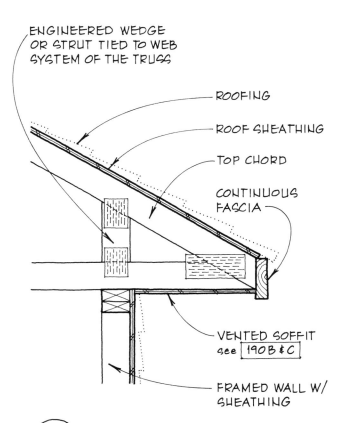

ENGINEERED WEDGE OR STRUT TIED TO WEB SYSTEM OF THE TRUSS

ROOFING

ROOF SHEATHING

TOP CHORD

CONTINUOUS FASCIA

VENTED SOFFIT see 190B & C

FRAMED WALL W/ SHEATHING

(C) TRUSS W/ SOFFITED EAVE
CANTILEVERED TRUSS

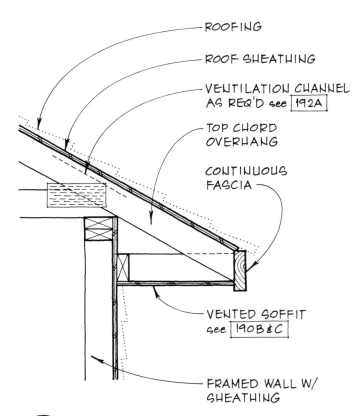

ROOFING

ROOF SHEATHING

VENTILATION CHANNEL AS REQ'D see 192A

TOP CHORD OVERHANG

CONTINUOUS FASCIA

VENTED SOFFIT see 190B & C

FRAMED WALL W/ SHEATHING

(D) TRUSS W/ SOFFITED EAVE
OVERHANGING TRUSS

A gable-end truss transfers the load of the roof to the wall on which it bears through 2x4 struts at 24 in. o.c. The standard gable-end truss is the same size as a standard truss. A gable-end truss can be used with a rake overhang of 12 in. or less when the barge rafter is supported by the roof sheathing. It can also be used with flat 2x4 lookouts let into the truss above the struts. A dropped gable-end truss (see 149B) is shorter than a standard truss by the depth of the lookouts.

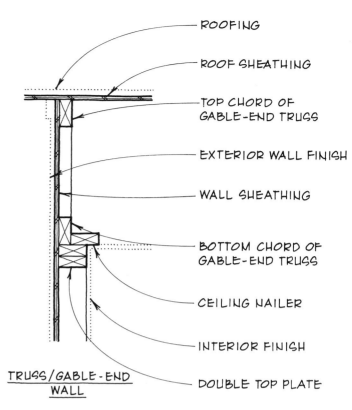

ROOFING

ROOF SHEATHING

TOP CHORD OF GABLE-END TRUSS

EXTERIOR WALL FINISH

WALL SHEATHING

BOTTOM CHORD OF GABLE-END TRUSS

CEILING NAILER

INTERIOR FINISH

DOUBLE TOP PLATE

TRUSS/GABLE-END WALL

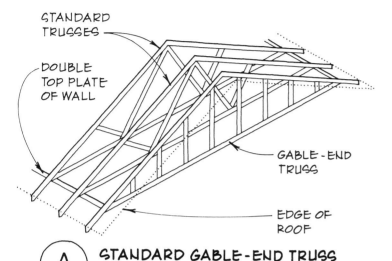

STANDARD TRUSSES

DOUBLE TOP PLATE OF WALL

GABLE-END TRUSS

EDGE OF ROOF

A   STANDARD GABLE-END TRUSS

NOTE:
A DROPPED GABLE-END TRUSS IS SHORTER THAN A STANDARD TRUSS BY THE DEPTH OF THE LOOKOUTS.

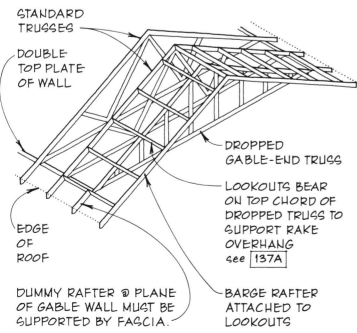

STANDARD TRUSSES

DOUBLE TOP PLATE OF WALL

DROPPED GABLE-END TRUSS

LOOKOUTS BEAR ON TOP CHORD OF DROPPED TRUSS TO SUPPORT RAKE OVERHANG
see 137A

EDGE OF ROOF

DUMMY RAFTER @ PLANE OF GABLE WALL MUST BE SUPPORTED BY FASCIA.

BARGE RAFTER ATTACHED TO LOOKOUTS

B   DROPPED GABLE-END TRUSS

There are several ways to frame a hip roof using trusses. None is simple, so many builders elect to frame hips (even on a truss roof) with rafters (see 130A).

The most common method of framing a hip with trusses is called the step-down system. A series of progressively shallower trusses with flat tops is used to create the end roof pitch of the hip roof. The last of these trusses is the girder truss, which carries the weight of short jack trusses or rafters that complete the roof.

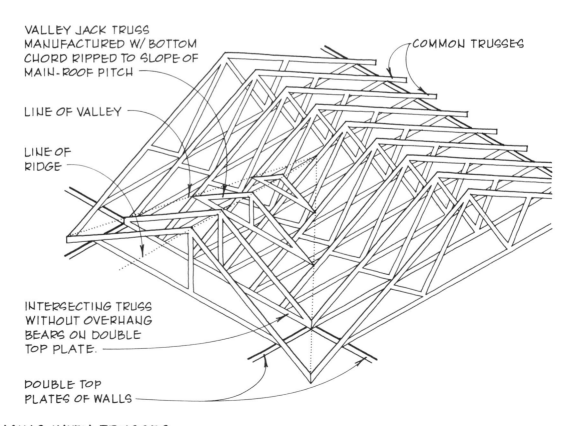

COMMON TRUSS

STEP-DOWN TRUSS

GIRDER TRUSS

JACK TRUSS

DOUBLE TOP PLATE OF WALL

FRAME CORNERS WITH LUMBER HIP AND RAFTERS see 129-130

LINE OF FASCIA

 A HIP FRAMING WITH TRUSSES
STEP-DOWN SYSTEM

Framing a valley with trusses is a simple matter of attaching a series of progressively smaller trusses to the top chords of the trusses of the main roof. The main-roof trusses do not have to be oversized since the only extra weight they will carry is the dead weight of the jack trusses themselves. Simple as this system is, many builders still prefer to frame these roof intersections with dimension lumber as a farmer's valley (see 129A).

VALLEY JACK TRUSS MANUFACTURED W/ BOTTOM CHORD RIPPED TO SLOPE OF MAIN-ROOF PITCH

COMMON TRUSSES

LINE OF VALLEY

LINE OF RIDGE

INTERSECTING TRUSS WITHOUT OVERHANG BEARS ON DOUBLE TOP PLATE.

DOUBLE TOP PLATES OF WALLS

 B VALLEY FRAMING WITH TRUSSES
VALLEY JACK TRUSSES

Rectangular openings for skylights or chimneys may be constructed in a truss roof. Small openings less than one truss space wide may be simply framed between trusses as they would be in a rafter-framed roof (see 127-129). Openings up to three truss spaces wide are made by doubling the trusses to either side of the opening and attaching header and mono or other special trusses to the doubled trusses. Larger openings (more than three truss spaces wide) require specially engineered trusses in place of the doubled trusses. Obviously, it is most efficient if the width and placement of the opening correspond to truss spacing.

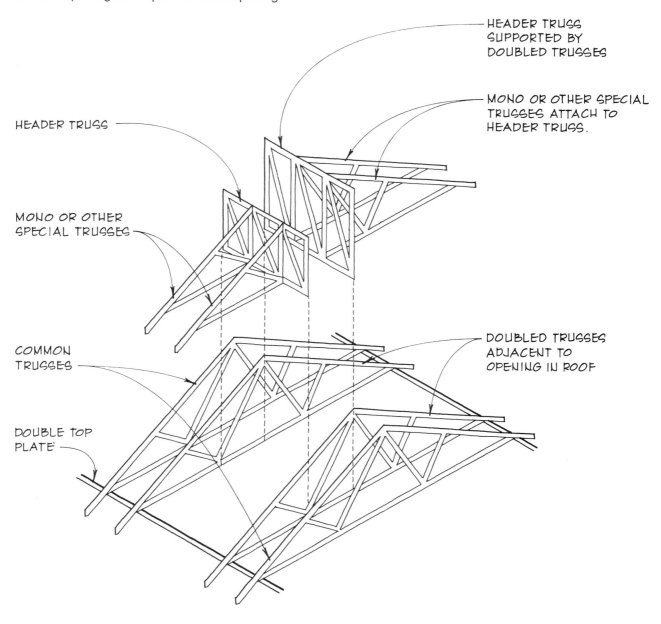

HEADER TRUSS SUPPORTED BY DOUBLED TRUSSES

MONO OR OTHER SPECIAL TRUSSES ATTACH TO HEADER TRUSS.

HEADER TRUSS

MONO OR OTHER SPECIAL TRUSSES

COMMON TRUSSES

DOUBLE TOP PLATE

DOUBLED TRUSSES ADJACENT TO OPENING IN ROOF

A **OPENINGS IN TRUSS ROOF**
HEADERS BETWEEN DOUBLE TRUSSES

Roof sheathing attaches to the surface of the rafters or trusses to form the structural skin of the roof. It spans the rafters to support the roofing and, in the case of panel sheathing such as plywood, acts with the walls to resist horizontal loads. Roof-sheathing material must be coordinated with the roofing itself, since each type of roofing has special requirements.

The two basic types of sheathing are solid sheathing and skip sheathing.

Solid sheathing—Solid sheathing provides a continuous surface at the plane of the roof. This type of sheathing is necessary for composition roofing and built-up roofing, which have no structural capacity themselves. Metal, tile and shingle roofing may also be appplied to solid sheathing. For economic and structural (lateral-load) reasons, solid sheathing is almost always constructed of plywood or other composite panels (see 153A). The plywood acts as a diaphragm to transfer lateral loads at the plane of the roof to the walls. When an exposed ceiling or roof overhang is desired, solid sheathing may also be constructed of solid-wood tongue-and-groove boards (see 154A). Tongue-and-groove sheathing, however, does not act as a diaphragm, so other methods of providing lateral-load stability, such as diagonal bracing, must be employed (see 154A).

Open sheathing—Open sheathing, also called skip sheathing, is composed of boards spaced apart (see 156A). This type of roof sheathing is used under wood shingles and shakes, which usually require ventilation on both sides of the roofing material. Open sheathing may also be chosen for economic reasons, but only if used with roofing systems such as metal and tile, which have the structural capacity to span between sheathing boards. Alternative methods of providing a roof diaphragm, such as diagonal bracing, must be used with open sheathing (see 77).

Combinations, of course, are also possible and often appropriate. For example, solid sheathing at exposed overhangs is often combined with open sheathing on the rest of the roof.

Recommendations—Sheathing recommendations for roofs by roofing types are as follows:

Composition and built-up roofing must be applied to solid sheathing because these roofing materials do not have the structural capacity to span between the boards of open sheathing.

Wood shingle and shake roofing is best applied over open sheathing because the spacing between the open sheathing allows the roofing to breathe from both sides, prolonging its life. Shingle and shake roofs may also be applied to solid sheathing at exposed eaves and rakes and similar locations. In some regions, the common practice is to place an air barrier over open sheathing to keep out wind-driven rain. Consult with local codes and builders for the accepted practice.

Metal and tile roofing may be applied to either solid or open sheathing. Both materials have the structural strength to span across open sheathing, but there is no advantage in having them breathe from both sides.

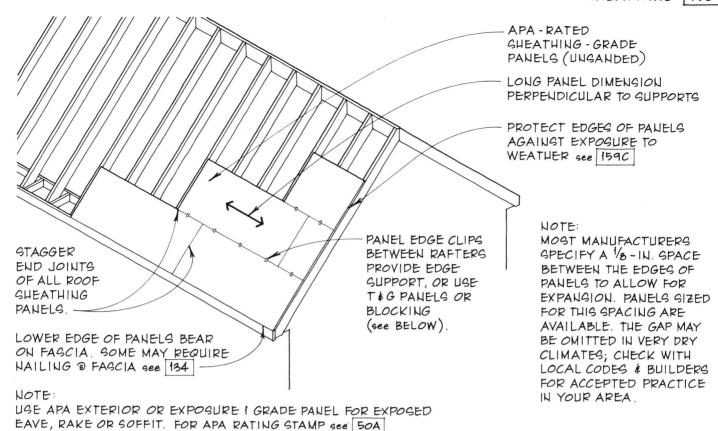

APA - RATED
SHEATHING - GRADE
PANELS (UNSANDED)

LONG PANEL DIMENSION
PERPENDICULAR TO SUPPORTS

PROTECT EDGES OF PANELS
AGAINST EXPOSURE TO
WEATHER see 159C

NOTE:
MOST MANUFACTURERS
SPECIFY A ⅛-IN. SPACE
BETWEEN THE EDGES OF
PANELS TO ALLOW FOR
EXPANSION. PANELS SIZED
FOR THIS SPACING ARE
AVAILABLE. THE GAP MAY
BE OMITTED IN VERY DRY
CLIMATES; CHECK WITH
LOCAL CODES & BUILDERS
FOR ACCEPTED PRACTICE
IN YOUR AREA.

PANEL EDGE CLIPS
BETWEEN RAFTERS
PROVIDE EDGE
SUPPORT, OR USE
T&G PANELS OR
BLOCKING
(see BELOW).

STAGGER
END JOINTS
OF ALL ROOF
SHEATHING
PANELS.

LOWER EDGE OF PANELS BEAR
ON FASCIA. SOME MAY REQUIRE
NAILING @ FASCIA see 134

NOTE:
USE APA EXTERIOR OR EXPOSURE 1 GRADE PANEL FOR EXPOSED
EAVE, RAKE OR SOFFIT. FOR APA RATING STAMP see 50A

Panel installation—Low cost and ease of installation make plywood or non-veneered composite panels the sheathing of choice for most modern roofs. The system provides a structural diaphragm and is appropriate for all but wood shingle or shake roofing, which requires ventilation. The standard panel size is 4 ft. by 8 ft., so rafter or truss spacing that falls on these modules is most practical. Care must be taken to protect panel edges from the weather by the use of trim or edge flashing (see 159C). Sheathing at exposed overhangs must be exterior or exposure 1 rated panels and must be thick enough to hold a nail or other roof fastener without penetration of the exposed underside.

Recommended fastening—Recommended fastening is 6 in. o.c. at edges and 12 in. o.c. in the field (6 in. in the field for supports at 48 in. o.c.). For sheathing spans greater than 24 in., tongue-and-groove edges, lumber blocking or panel edge clips are required at edges between supports; use two clips for supports at 48 in. o.c.

Roof-sheathing spans		
APA rating	**Thickness**	**Maximum span**
12 / 0	5/16 in.	12 in.
16 / 0	5/16 in. to 3/8 in.	16 in.
24 / 0	3/8 in. to 1/2 in.	24 in.
32 / 16	15/32 in. to 5/8 in.	32 in.
48 / 24	23/32 in. to 7/8 in.	48 in.

Notes—Values in the table above are based on APA-rated panels continuous over two or more spans with the long dimension of the panel perpendicular to supports. Verify span with panel rating. (For APA rating stamp, see 50A.)

Spans are based on a 30-lb. live load and 10-lb. dead load, the minimum rated by the American Plywood Association. Check local codes and with design professionals for higher loading such as greater snow loads or higher dead loads of concrete tiles or other heavy roofing. These ratings are minimum. For a more solid roof, reduce spans or increase thickness.

A **SOLID ROOF SHEATHING**
PLYWOOD & NON-VENEERED PANELS

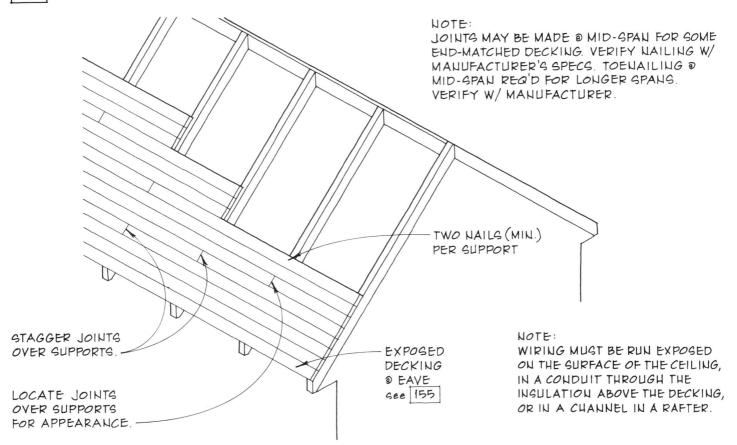

NOTE:
JOINTS MAY BE MADE @ MID-SPAN FOR SOME END-MATCHED DECKING. VERIFY NAILING W/ MANUFACTURER'S SPECS. TOENAILING @ MID-SPAN REQ'D FOR LONGER SPANS. VERIFY W/ MANUFACTURER.

TWO NAILS (MIN.) PER SUPPORT

STAGGER JOINTS OVER SUPPORTS.

LOCATE JOINTS OVER SUPPORTS FOR APPEARANCE.

EXPOSED DECKING @ EAVE see 155

NOTE:
WIRING MUST BE RUN EXPOSED ON THE SURFACE OF THE CEILING, IN A CONDUIT THROUGH THE INSULATION ABOVE THE DECKING, OR IN A CHANNEL IN A RAFTER.

T&G sheathing (decking) is most often used for exposed ceiling applications. It can also be used selectively at exposed eaves or overhanging rakes. Rafters are spaced at wide centers since the decking will span more than 24 in. in most cases (see the chart at right). Since this sheathing material does not provide a diaphragm at the plane of the roof, other means of bracing the roof against horizontal loads must usually be employed. For example, the roof may be braced with metal straps applied to the top of the sheathing or with a thin layer of plywood.

Insulation for an exposed ceiling must be located above the sheathing. Insulation will vary with climate and with roofing material. Rigid insulation is usually the most practical because of its thin profile, but is more expensive than batt insulation. Batts are often chosen for colder climates, where the thickness of either type of insulation (rigid or batts) requires adding a second level of structure above the decking to support the roof (see 192A).

Exposed T&G decking spans	
Nominal thickness	**Approximate span**
2 in.	6.0 ft.
3 in.	10.5 ft.
4 in.	13.5 ft.
5 in.	17.0 ft.

This table assumes a 30-lb. live load for Douglas-fir or southern pine species. The table is for comparison and approximating purposes only. The actual span capacity depends on roof pitch, species, live-load values and end-joint pattern.

A **SOLID ROOF SHEATHING**
EXPOSED T & G DECKING

ROOFING

RIGID INSULATION OVER TEMPERATURE-CONTROLLED SPACE

T&G EXPOSED DECKING

VAPOR BARRIER BETWEEN INSULATION & DECKING CONTINUOUS TO INSIDE OF WALL & CAULKED AROUND RAFTERS

FURRING STRIPS &/OR PLYWOOD SHEATHING OVER EXPOSED EAVE

FRIEZE BLOCK

T&G DECKING EXPOSED @ EAVE

INSULATION

NAILING BLOCK FOR FINISH WALL

ROOFING

FURRING OVER RIGID INSULATION NAILED TO DECKING

RIGID INSULATION OVER TEMPERATURE-CONTROLLED SPACE

T&G EXPOSED DECKING

VAPOR BARRIER BETWEEN INSULATION & DECKING CONTINUOUS TO INSIDE OF WALL & CAULKED AROUND RAFTERS

FURRING STRIPS @ SAME SPACING AS STRIPPING OVER EXPOSED EAVE

T&G DECKING EXPOSED @ EAVE

INSULATION

FRIEZE BLOCK

NAILING BLOCK FOR FINISH WALL

Metal or composition roofing may be applied directly over rigid insulation on T&G sheathing. For this construction, fasteners must be sized to penetrate through the insulation but not through the decking.

Preformed metal roofing—Preformed metal roofing may be applied directly to the insulation over a layer of 15-lb. or 30-lb. felt. If the insulation is over 3½ in. thick, wooden nailers equal to the thickness of the insulation and parallel to the decking are recommended to provide a stable surface for roof fasteners. Nailers should be located 3 ft. to 5 ft. o.c., depending on the profile of the metal roofing.

Composition roofing—Composition roofing may also be applied directly if the insulation board is strong enough to withstand the rigors of the roofing process. Most asphalt-shingle manufacturers, however, will not honor their warranty unless the shingles are applied to a ventilated roof. Unventilated shingles can get too hot and deteriorate prematurely. The addition of vertical furring strips and sheathing over the insulation with vents at the top and bottom of the assembly will satisfy the requirement for ventilation.

Wood or tile roofing requires another layer of material over the insulation. In some cases, it may be more economical to substitute non-rigid insulation.

Wood shingles or shakes—Wood shingles and shakes last longer if they are allowed to breathe from both sides, so they should be raised on furring strips above the level of the insulation. The furring strips may be nailed through the rigid insulation to the decking, or they may be attached directly to the decking between rows of insulation. The spaces and cracks between the shakes or shingles will usually provide adequate ventilation.

Ceramic or concrete tiles—Ceramic and concrete tiles, like shingles, commonly require furring strips. The furring strips should be spaced according to the length of the tiles (see 177B, 178 and 179).

A EXPOSED T&G DECKING @ EAVE
METAL OR COMPOSITION ROOF

B EXPOSED T&G DECKING @ EAVE
WOOD OR TILE ROOF

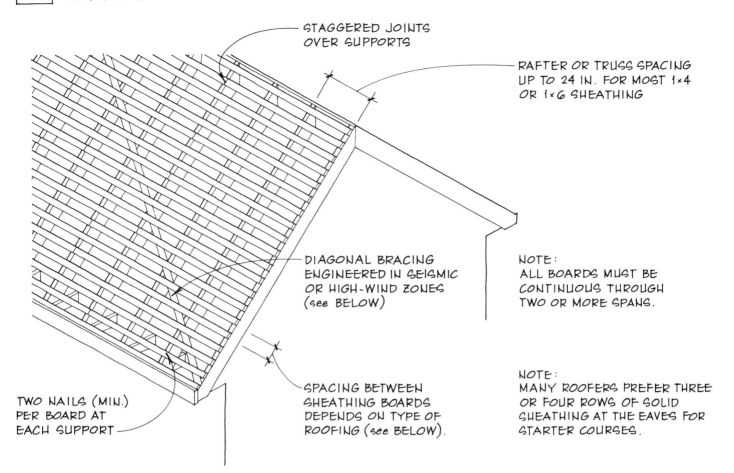

STAGGERED JOINTS
OVER SUPPORTS

RAFTER OR TRUSS SPACING
UP TO 24 IN. FOR MOST 1×4
OR 1×6 SHEATHING

DIAGONAL BRACING
ENGINEERED IN SEISMIC
OR HIGH-WIND ZONES
(see BELOW)

NOTE:
ALL BOARDS MUST BE
CONTINUOUS THROUGH
TWO OR MORE SPANS.

TWO NAILS (MIN.)
PER BOARD AT
EACH SUPPORT

SPACING BETWEEN
SHEATHING BOARDS
DEPENDS ON TYPE OF
ROOFING (see BELOW).

NOTE:
MANY ROOFERS PREFER THREE
OR FOUR ROWS OF SOLID
SHEATHING AT THE EAVES FOR
STARTER COURSES.

Open, or skip, sheathing is usually made with 1x4 or 1x6 boards nailed horizontally to the rafters with a space between the boards. Since this sheathing material does not provide a diaphragm at the plane of the roof, other means of bracing the roof against horizontal loads must be employed. Let-in wooden bracing or metal strap bracing applied to the top or bottom surface of the rafters will suffice in most cases. This bracing must be engineered in seismic or high-wind zones or for very large roofs. Bracing may sometimes be omitted on hip roofs because the shape of the roof provides the bracing.

Spacing for skip sheathing depends on the type of roofing. The ability of the sheathing to span between supports depends on the spacing and on the type of roofing applied over it. Check with local codes and with roofers for accepted local practices.

Wood shingles or shakes require spacing equal to the exposure of the shingles or shakes—usually about 5 in. for shingles to 10 in. for shakes. The sheathing is usually 1x4.

Concrete tiles, depending on the type, may be installed on open sheathing spaced in the 12-in. to 14-in. range. The roofing material is heavy, so 1x6 or 1x8 or 2x4 sheathing is practical.

Preformed metal roofing is lightweight and runs continuously in the direction of the rafters. In most cases, 1x6 sheathing @ 24 in. o.c. is adequate.

(A) OPEN ROOF SHEATHING

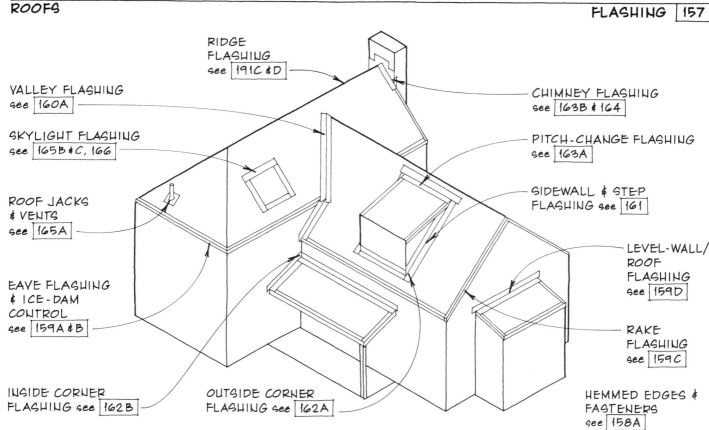

VALLEY FLASHING
see [160A]

SKYLIGHT FLASHING
see [165B & C, 166]

ROOF JACKS
& VENTS
see [165A]

EAVE FLASHING
& ICE-DAM
CONTROL
see [159A & B]

INSIDE CORNER
FLASHING see [162B]

RIDGE
FLASHING
see [191C & D]

OUTSIDE CORNER
FLASHING see [162A]

CHIMNEY FLASHING
see [163B & 164]

PITCH-CHANGE FLASHING
see [163A]

SIDEWALL & STEP
FLASHING see [161]

LEVEL-WALL/
ROOF
FLASHING
see [159D]

RAKE
FLASHING
see [159C]

HEMMED EDGES &
FASTENERS
see [158A]

Flashing is a necessary component of most roofing systems. Flashing makes the roof watertight at edges, openings and bends in the roof where the roofing material cannot perform the job alone.

Flashing materials and details must be coordinated with the roofing material to make a durable and waterproof roof. Although design principles are transferable from one type of roofing to another, proportions of materials may vary. For example, the details drawn in this section show a thin-profile roofing material such as asphalt or wood shingles, but flashing for thicker roofing materials such as tile, shake or metal will have different proportions. Some of these special flashings can be found with the details for the particular roofing type. (For a discussion of flashing materials, see 99A.)

You may want to use different flashing materials for roofs than for walls, because roofs are constantly exposed to the weather and, in most cases, are replaced much more frequently than walls. Moreover, roof flashing itself is not always replaced at the same time as the roof. Chimney or wall flashing may not be easily changed when the building is re-roofed, so it should be made of materials like copper or stainless

steel, which may last as long as the building. Valley or pitch-change flashing, will be easy to replace at the time of re-roofing if the original roof is removed. This flashing may be made of material with a life span equivalent to the roof itself.

The flashing and its fasteners must be compatible with each other and with the roofing material itself. For example, flashing and fasteners for metal roofs must be compatible with the roofing metal to avoid galvanic corrosion. Flashing may be isolated from other materials with 30-lb. felt or bituminous paint.

The basic principle of roof flashing is to have the roofing, the flashing and other materials overlap each other like shingles. Water running down the surface of the roof should always be directed by the flashing across the surface of the roof. Gravity will then work to direct water down the roof away from the gaps filled by the flashing. If this principle is followed, only wind-driven rain can force water through the roofing to the waterproof underlayment (see 167A), which acts as a second line of defense. Each detail may have local variations to account for such weather-related factors. All flashing materials, therefore, should be discussed with local sheet-metal contractors or roofers.

A **ROOF FLASHING**
INTRODUCTION

Hemmed edges—One very important detail for roof flashing is the hemmed edge, which folds back on itself about ½ in.

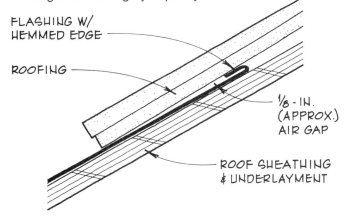

This fold makes the flashing thicker at the edge, which, aside from forming a stronger and neater edge when exposed, helps control the flow of water on roofs, as shown in the drawings on this page. Tucked under roofing, the turned-up hemmed edge creates an air gap that prevents moisture from migrating between the roofing and flashing by capillary action.

FLASHING W/
HEMMED EDGE

ROOFING

⅛-IN.
(APPROX.)
AIR GAP

ROOF SHEATHING
& UNDERLAYMENT

A hemmed edge also works when it is horizontal, as in sidewall flashing (see 161A & B), where the hemmed edge not only resists capillary action but also forms a barrier to water running down the flashing and keeps it from running onto the roof sheathing.

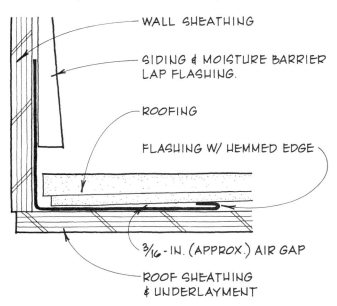

WALL SHEATHING

SIDING & MOISTURE BARRIER
LAP FLASHING.

ROOFING

FLASHING W/ HEMMED EDGE

³⁄₁₆-IN. (APPROX.) AIR GAP

ROOF SHEATHING
& UNDERLAYMENT

Turned down and lapped over roofing, the hemmed edge creates an air gap under the flashing that discourages capillary action. The hemmed edge can also form a seal on smooth surfaces such as skylight glass, which is only made more complete by the presence of water adhering by surface tension to the two surfaces.

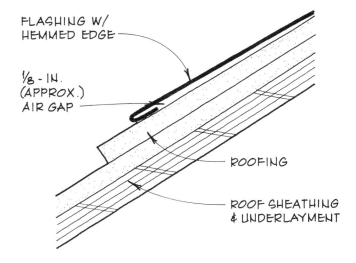

FLASHING W/
HEMMED EDGE

⅛-IN.
(APPROX.)
AIR GAP

ROOFING

ROOF SHEATHING
& UNDERLAYMENT

Fasteners—Flashing is usually nailed to the structure. Nails are located at the edge of the flashing to avoid punctures in the flashing where it is designed to keep moisture from entering. Care must be taken to select nails that will not cause galvanic corrosion.

Another method of attaching flashing is the cleat, a small metal clip usually made of the same material as the flashing itself. Cleats fasten flashing to the roof without puncturing the flashing and allow for expansion and contraction of flashing metal without dislodging of fasteners. Cleats may also be used to make concealed connections of flashing.

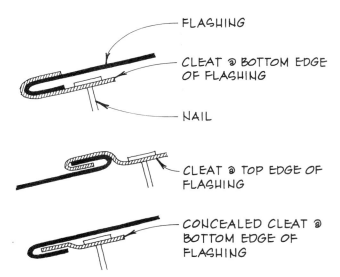

FLASHING

CLEAT @ BOTTOM EDGE
OF FLASHING

NAIL

CLEAT @ TOP EDGE OF
FLASHING

CONCEALED CLEAT @
BOTTOM EDGE OF
FLASHING

ROOF FLASHING
HEMMED EDGES & FASTENERS

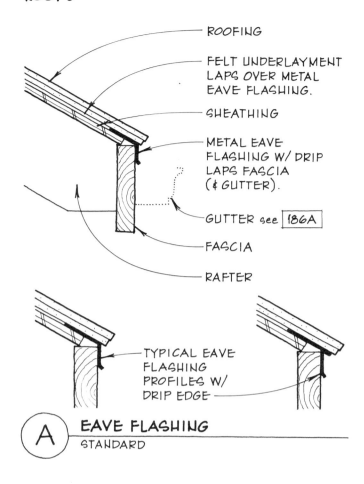

ROOFING

FELT UNDERLAYMENT LAPS OVER METAL EAVE FLASHING.

SHEATHING

METAL EAVE FLASHING W/ DRIP LAPS FASCIA (& GUTTER).

GUTTER see 186A

FASCIA

RAFTER

TYPICAL EAVE FLASHING PROFILES W/ DRIP EDGE

 A EAVE FLASHING
STANDARD

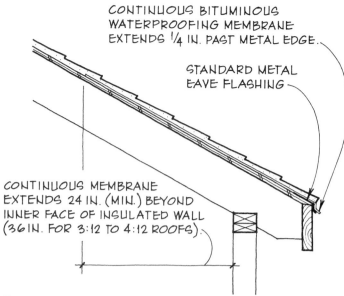

CONTINUOUS BITUMINOUS WATERPROOFING MEMBRANE EXTENDS 1/4 IN. PAST METAL EDGE.

STANDARD METAL EAVE FLASHING

CONTINUOUS MEMBRANE EXTENDS 24 IN. (MIN.) BEYOND INNER FACE OF INSULATED WALL (36 IN. FOR 3:12 TO 4:12 ROOFS).

NOTE:
THIS EAVE FLASHING IS REQ'D BY CODE IN MANY AREAS WITH COLD WINTERS, BUT SHOULD BE CONSIDERED A BACKUP STRATEGY BECAUSE ICE DAMS CAN BE PREVENTED W/ ADEQUATE INSULATION AND VENTILATION see 187 & 188

B EAVE FLASHING
COLD CLIMATE

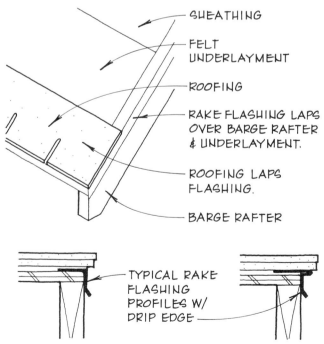

SHEATHING

FELT UNDERLAYMENT

ROOFING

RAKE FLASHING LAPS OVER BARGE RAFTER & UNDERLAYMENT.

ROOFING LAPS FLASHING.

BARGE RAFTER

TYPICAL RAKE FLASHING PROFILES W/ DRIP EDGE

NOTE:
METAL & TILE ROOFS HAVE SPECIAL RAKE FLASHINGS see 181C OR 179 B & C

C RAKE FLASHING

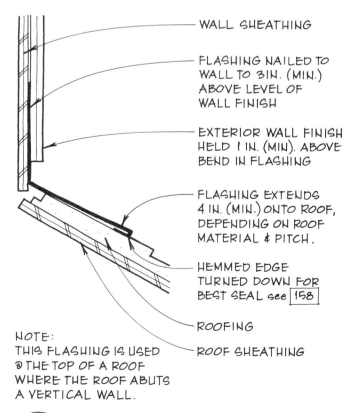

WALL SHEATHING

FLASHING NAILED TO WALL TO 3 IN. (MIN.) ABOVE LEVEL OF WALL FINISH

EXTERIOR WALL FINISH HELD 1 IN. (MIN.) ABOVE BEND IN FLASHING

FLASHING EXTENDS 4 IN. (MIN.) ONTO ROOF, DEPENDING ON ROOF MATERIAL & PITCH.

HEMMED EDGE TURNED DOWN FOR BEST SEAL see 158

ROOFING

ROOF SHEATHING

NOTE:
THIS FLASHING IS USED @ THE TOP OF A ROOF WHERE THE ROOF ABUTS A VERTICAL WALL.

D LEVEL WALL FLASHING

Valleys on roofs, like valleys in the landscape, collect the runoff of all the slopes above them. To handle such a concentration of water, valleys must be carefully flashed. Except when using roofing materials that can bend (see 171B and 173B & C), valleys are usually flashed with metal flashing.

Open valley flashing is the most common and may be used with virtually all roofing materials. An open valley allows the runoff water to flow within the confines of the exposed metal flashing rather than over the roofing material itself.

Cleats at 2 ft. o.c. fasten valley flashing to the roof without puncturing the flashing and allow for expansion and contraction of flashing metal without dislodging fasteners (see 158A). Without cleats, flashing is wider and is nailed at the outer edges.

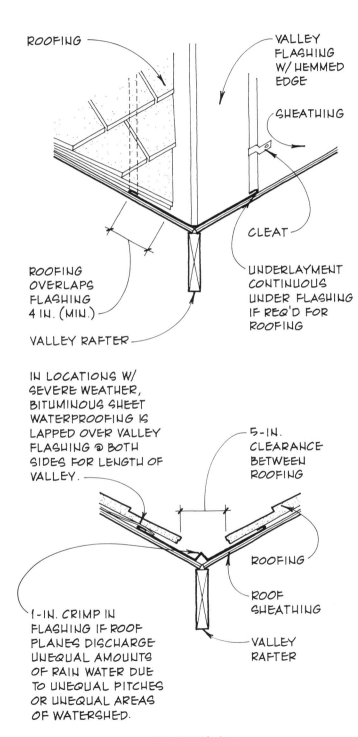

NOTE:
BITUMINOUS SHEET WATERPROOFING LAPS VALLEY FLASHING IN LOCATIONS W/ SEVERE WEATHER see SECTION A-A @ LOWER RIGHT

VALLEY FLASHING EXTENDS FULL LENGTH OF VALLEY.

UNDERLAYMENT

ROOFING

ROOFING

VALLEY FLASHING W/ HEMMED EDGE

SHEATHING

CLEAT

UNDERLAYMENT CONTINUOUS UNDER FLASHING IF REQ'D FOR ROOFING

ROOFING OVERLAPS FLASHING 4 IN. (MIN.)

VALLEY RAFTER

IN LOCATIONS W/ SEVERE WEATHER, BITUMINOUS SHEET WATERPROOFING IS LAPPED OVER VALLEY FLASHING @ BOTH SIDES FOR LENGTH OF VALLEY.

5-IN. CLEARANCE BETWEEN ROOFING

ROOFING

ROOF SHEATHING

VALLEY RAFTER

1-IN. CRIMP IN FLASHING IF ROOF PLANES DISCHARGE UNEQUAL AMOUNTS OF RAIN WATER DUE TO UNEQUAL PITCHES OR UNEQUAL AREAS OF WATERSHED.

VALLEY BETWEEN ROOFING IS WIDER AT EAVE THAN AT TOP, ESPECIALLY IN AREAS OF EXTREME COLD. TYPICAL VALLEY IS 5 IN. TO 6 IN. WIDE @ TOP & INCREASES @ 1/8 IN. PER LINEAR FOOT OF VALLEY.

NOTES:
FOR VALLEY FLASHING OF ASPHALT SHINGLES see 173B & C
FOR ROLL ROOFING WITHOUT FLASHING see 171B

SECTION A-A

 A VALLEY FLASHING

Sidewall flashing is a single-piece flashing installed before the roofing to create a flashing channel against the wall (see 161B). This type of flashing is adequate for most situations and allows easy re-roofing.

Step flashing is a multiple-piece flashing that is woven in with the courses of roofing material (see 161C). This flashing is best for severe weather conditions. It may present some re-roofing difficulties, especially if the type of roofing material is changed.

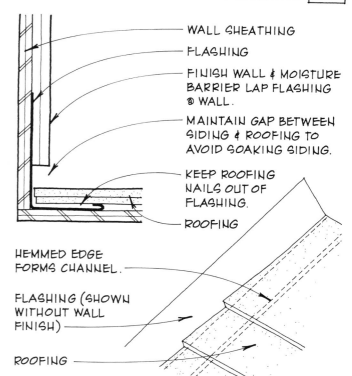

WALL SHEATHING

FLASHING

FINISH WALL & MOISTURE BARRIER LAP FLASHING @ WALL.

MAINTAIN GAP BETWEEN SIDING & ROOFING TO AVOID SOAKING SIDING.

KEEP ROOFING NAILS OUT OF FLASHING.

ROOFING

HEMMED EDGE FORMS CHANNEL.

FLASHING (SHOWN WITHOUT WALL FINISH)

ROOFING

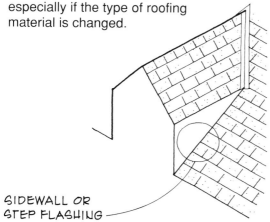

SIDEWALL OR STEP FLASHING

A SIDEWALL & STEP FLASHING
INTRODUCTION

B SIDEWALL FLASHING

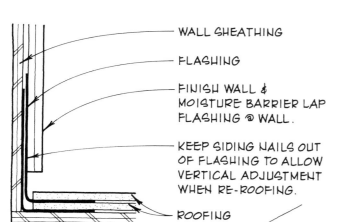

WALL SHEATHING

FLASHING

FINISH WALL & MOISTURE BARRIER LAP FLASHING @ WALL.

KEEP SIDING NAILS OUT OF FLASHING TO ALLOW VERTICAL ADJUSTMENT WHEN RE-ROOFING.

ROOFING

FLASHING

ROOFING

SHEATHING

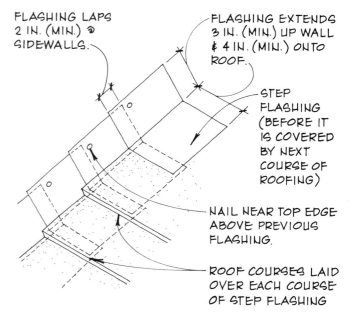

FLASHING LAPS 2 IN. (MIN.) @ SIDEWALLS.

FLASHING EXTENDS 3 IN. (MIN.) UP WALL & 4 IN. (MIN.) ONTO ROOF.

STEP FLASHING (BEFORE IT IS COVERED BY NEXT COURSE OF ROOFING)

NAIL NEAR TOP EDGE ABOVE PREVIOUS FLASHING.

ROOF COURSES LAID OVER EACH COURSE OF STEP FLASHING

NOTES:
STEP-FLASHING PIECES ARE 2 IN. LONGER THAN ROOF COURSING EXPOSURE & ARE INSTALLED WITH THE ROOFING MATERIAL, ONE COURSE AT A TIME. EXTERIOR WALL FINISH & MOISTURE BARRIER WILL LAP STEP FLASHING. FLASHING DIMENSIONS DEPEND ON ROOFING MATERIAL AND PITCH.

C STEP FLASHING

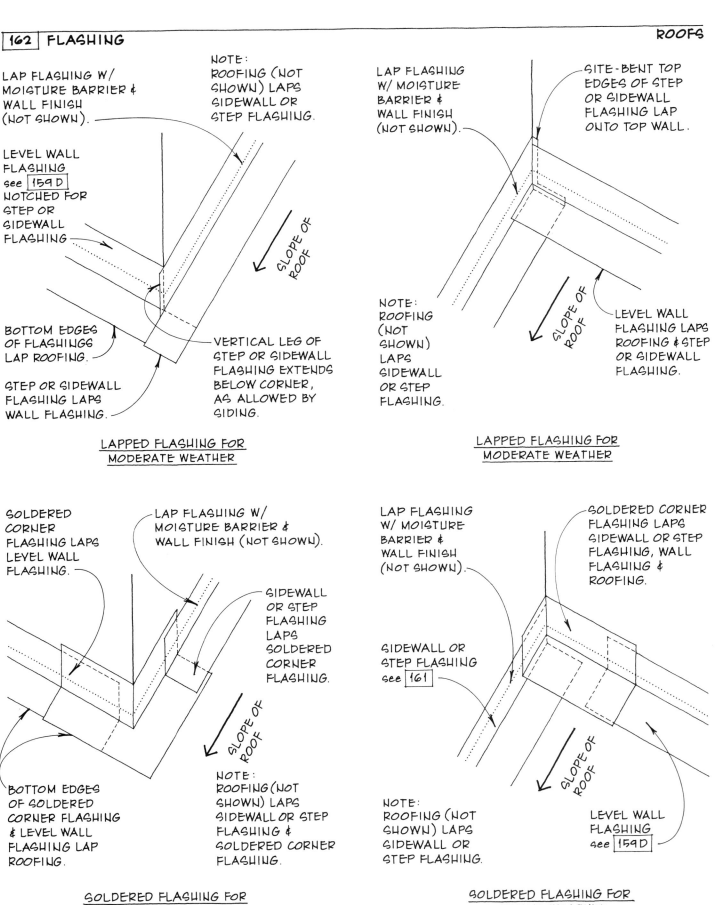

LAP FLASHING W/ MOISTURE BARRIER & WALL FINISH (NOT SHOWN).

NOTE: ROOFING (NOT SHOWN) LAPS SIDEWALL OR STEP FLASHING.

LEVEL WALL FLASHING see 159D NOTCHED FOR STEP OR SIDEWALL FLASHING

SLOPE OF ROOF

BOTTOM EDGES OF FLASHINGS LAP ROOFING.

STEP OR SIDEWALL FLASHING LAPS WALL FLASHING.

VERTICAL LEG OF STEP OR SIDEWALL FLASHING EXTENDS BELOW CORNER, AS ALLOWED BY SIDING.

LAPPED FLASHING FOR MODERATE WEATHER

LAP FLASHING W/ MOISTURE BARRIER & WALL FINISH (NOT SHOWN).

SITE-BENT TOP EDGES OF STEP OR SIDEWALL FLASHING LAP ONTO TOP WALL.

NOTE: ROOFING (NOT SHOWN) LAPS SIDEWALL OR STEP FLASHING.

SLOPE OF ROOF

LEVEL WALL FLASHING LAPS ROOFING & STEP OR SIDEWALL FLASHING.

LAPPED FLASHING FOR MODERATE WEATHER

SOLDERED CORNER FLASHING LAPS LEVEL WALL FLASHING.

LAP FLASHING W/ MOISTURE BARRIER & WALL FINISH (NOT SHOWN).

SIDEWALL OR STEP FLASHING LAPS SOLDERED CORNER FLASHING.

SLOPE OF ROOF

BOTTOM EDGES OF SOLDERED CORNER FLASHING & LEVEL WALL FLASHING LAP ROOFING.

NOTE: ROOFING (NOT SHOWN) LAPS SIDEWALL OR STEP FLASHING & SOLDERED CORNER FLASHING.

SOLDERED FLASHING FOR EXTREME WEATHER

A   OUTSIDE CORNER FLASHING

LAP FLASHING W/ MOISTURE BARRIER & WALL FINISH (NOT SHOWN).

SOLDERED CORNER FLASHING LAPS SIDEWALL OR STEP FLASHING, WALL FLASHING & ROOFING.

SIDEWALL OR STEP FLASHING see 161

SLOPE OF ROOF

NOTE: ROOFING (NOT SHOWN) LAPS SIDEWALL OR STEP FLASHING.

LEVEL WALL FLASHING see 159D

SOLDERED FLASHING FOR EXTREME WEATHER

B   INSIDE CORNER FLASHING

The flashing detail at left applies to both reduced pitch (shown) and increased pitch. Reduced pitch-change flashing can be avoided in favor of a cleaner detail by bending asphalt shingles or by soaking or steaming and bending wood shingles. The pitch change can also be made gradual by adding a strip of sheathing at the bend in the roof (see below) so that stiffer roofing materials such as wood shingles and shakes, tiles and slates can make the transition without flashing.

LOCATE FLASHING FASTENERS @ UPPER EDGE OF FLASHING.

LOCATE ROOFING FASTENERS ABOVE FLASHING.

ROOFING STOPS ABOVE BREAK IN FLASHING.

ATTACH LOWER EDGE OF FLASHING W/ CLEATS TO AVOID PUNCTURING FLASHING.

ROOFING

SHEATHING

PITCH-CHANGE FRAMING see | 126B |

LENGTH OF UPPER LEG OF FLASHING DEPENDS ON ROOFING MATERIAL & SLOPE.

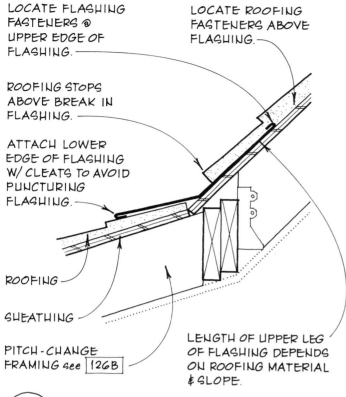

EXTRA SHEATHING

FURRING @ 16 IN. OR 24 IN. O.C.

ROOFING

SHEATHING

RAFTERS

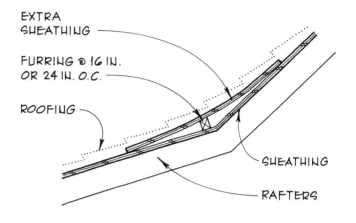

 A   PITCH-CHANGE FLASHING

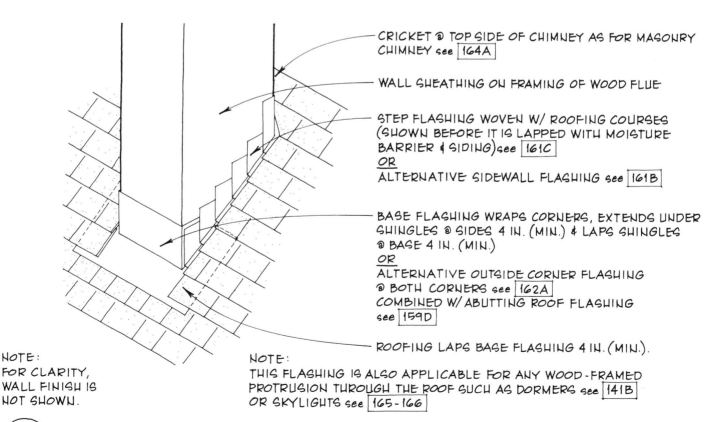

CRICKET @ TOP SIDE OF CHIMNEY AS FOR MASONRY CHIMNEY see | 164A |

WALL SHEATHING ON FRAMING OF WOOD FLUE

STEP FLASHING WOVEN W/ ROOFING COURSES (SHOWN BEFORE IT IS LAPPED WITH MOISTURE BARRIER & SIDING) see | 161C |
OR
ALTERNATIVE SIDEWALL FLASHING see | 161B |

BASE FLASHING WRAPS CORNERS, EXTENDS UNDER SHINGLES @ SIDES 4 IN. (MIN.) & LAPS SHINGLES @ BASE 4 IN. (MIN.)
OR
ALTERNATIVE OUTSIDE CORNER FLASHING @ BOTH CORNERS see | 162A |
COMBINED W/ ABUTTING ROOF FLASHING see | 159D |

ROOFING LAPS BASE FLASHING 4 IN. (MIN.).

NOTE:
FOR CLARITY, WALL FINISH IS NOT SHOWN.

NOTE:
THIS FLASHING IS ALSO APPLICABLE FOR ANY WOOD-FRAMED PROTRUSION THROUGH THE ROOF SUCH AS DORMERS see | 141B | OR SKYLIGHTS see | 165-166 |

 B   CHIMNEY FLASHING
WOOD-FRAMED FLUE

The flashing for a masonry chimney is best made of permanent materials such as copper or stainless steel. The flashing fits to the roof using the same principles as flashing for wood-framed flues (see 163B). The top edge of this flashing is then lapped with a counterflashing that is set into the mortar joints between masonry units. Because of the complex shapes, many of the pieces in chimney flashing cannot be folded but must be soldered or welded.

A chimney located in the slope of the roof will require a cricket (also called a saddle), a ridged connection between chimney and roof that directs water away from the chimney. Most crickets may be formed with exterior-grade plywood; larger crickets may need to be framed like a typical roof. The entire surface of the cricket is flashed, as shown in the drawing below.

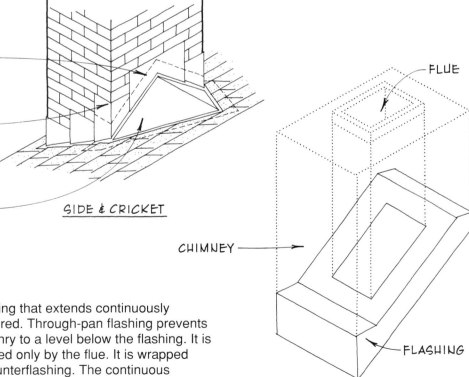

STEP FLASHING WOVEN WITH ROOFING COURSES see 161C

COUNTERFLASHING SET IN MORTAR 1 IN. (MIN.) @ TOP EDGE, LAPS ITSELF 2 IN. (MIN.) & LAPS STEP OR OTHER SIDE FLASHING 4 IN. (MIN.)

SOLDERED BASE FLASHING WRAPS CORNERS, IS SET IN MORTAR 2 IN. (MIN.) @ TOP EDGE, EXTENDS UNDER SHINGLES @ SIDES 4 IN. (MIN.) AND LAPS SHINGLES @ BASE 4 IN. (MIN.). THIS CAN ALSO BE MADE WITH TWO PIECES — A BASE FLASHING WITH COUNTERFLASHING SET IN MORTAR

ROOFING LAPS BASE FLASHING 4 IN. (MIN.).

SIDE & BASE

COUNTERFLASHING SET IN MORTAR & CUT TO SLOPE OF CRICKET

SOLDERED COUNTERFLASHING CONTINUOUS AROUND CORNER LAPS CRICKET.

SOLDERED CRICKET WRAPS CORNERS, EXTENDS UNDER ROOFING 6 IN. (MIN.) AND TURNS UP AGAINST CHIMNEY 4 IN. (MIN.).

STEP FLASHING (NOT VISIBLE) WOVEN WITH ROOFING COURSES see 161C

SIDE & CRICKET

FLUE

CHIMNEY

FLASHING

THROUGH-PAN FLASHING

In severe climates, a through-pan flashing that extends continuously through the chimney should be considered. Through-pan flashing prevents water from migrating through the masonry to a level below the flashing. It is made of lead or copper and is penetrated only by the flue. It is wrapped down at the edges, where it acts as counterflashing. The continuous flashing through the chimney does weaken the masonry bond, so this flashing should not be used in earthquake or hurricane zones.

A **CHIMNEY FLASHING**
MASONRY

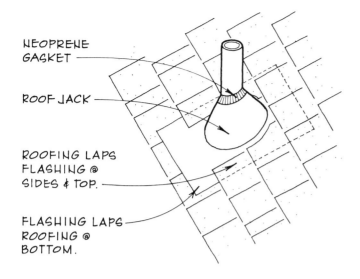

NEOPRENE GASKET

ROOF JACK

ROOFING LAPS FLASHING @ SIDES & TOP.

FLASHING LAPS ROOFING @ BOTTOM.

Most skylights are manufactured with a complete flashing package and instructions for installation in a rough opening in the roof framing. Some are available with a kit to adapt the flashing to unusual roofing materials or pitches. Skylights are available in fixed or operable types with screens and/or sun-shade devices. Rough-opening sizes are specified and usually correspond with standard rafter spacing.

Many fixed skylights require a flashed curb to which the manufactured skylight is attached. With these skylights, the curb must be flashed like any other large penetration of the roofing surface, such as a chimney or dormer (see 163A). Site-built curbless skylights are fixed and appear flush with the roof (see 166A). Some codes prohibit these skylights because of the requirement for a curb.

For skylight framing, see 128A & B.

Modern roof jacks are typically fitted with neoprene gaskets sized to seal plumbing vents and other roof penetrations. Jacks are woven in with roofing materials where possible. Jacks for metal roofs pose special problems (see 180).

 A   **ROOF JACKS AND VENTS**

 B   **SKYLIGHT FLASHING**
                                      NOTES

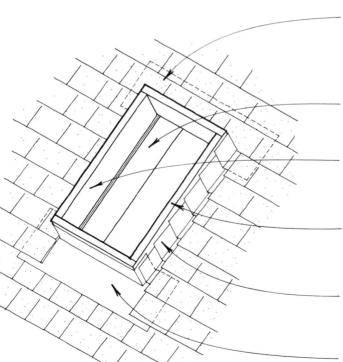

SOLDERED TOP FLASHING WRAPS CORNERS, EXTENDS UNDER ROOFING @ TOP EDGE 6 IN. (MIN.) & SIDE EDGES 4 IN. (MIN.) & TURNS UP AGAINST CURB.

RAFTER FORMS SIDE OF ROUGH OPENING.

2 × CURB FRAMED ON TOP OF ROOF SHEATHING & PERPENDICULAR TO THE ROOF

SMOOTH SURFACE WOOD CURB SEALED & READY FOR APPLICATION OF SKYLIGHT

STEP FLASHING WOVEN W/ ROOFING COURSES see | 161B |

SOLDERED (OR FOLDED) BASE FLASHING WRAPS CORNERS, EXTENDS UNDER SHINGLES @ SIDES 4 IN. (MIN.) & LAPS SHINGLES @ BASE 4 IN. (MIN.).

 C   **SKYLIGHT CURB FLASHING**
                                      FOR USE W/ MANUFACTURED SKYLIGHT

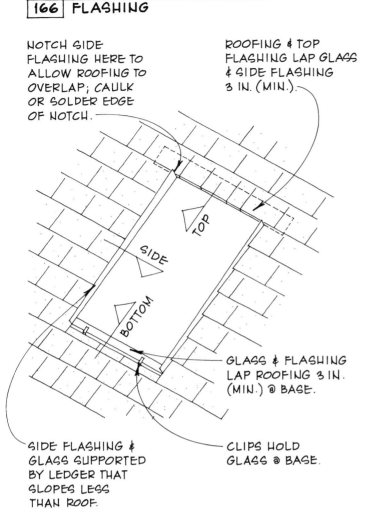

NOTCH SIDE FLASHING HERE TO ALLOW ROOFING TO OVERLAP; CAULK OR SOLDER EDGE OF NOTCH.

ROOFING & TOP FLASHING LAP GLASS & SIDE FLASHING 3 IN. (MIN.).

TOP

SIDE

BOTTOM

SIDE FLASHING & GLASS SUPPORTED BY LEDGER THAT SLOPES LESS THAN ROOF.

GLASS & FLASHING LAP ROOFING 3 IN. (MIN.) @ BASE.

CLIPS HOLD GLASS @ BASE.

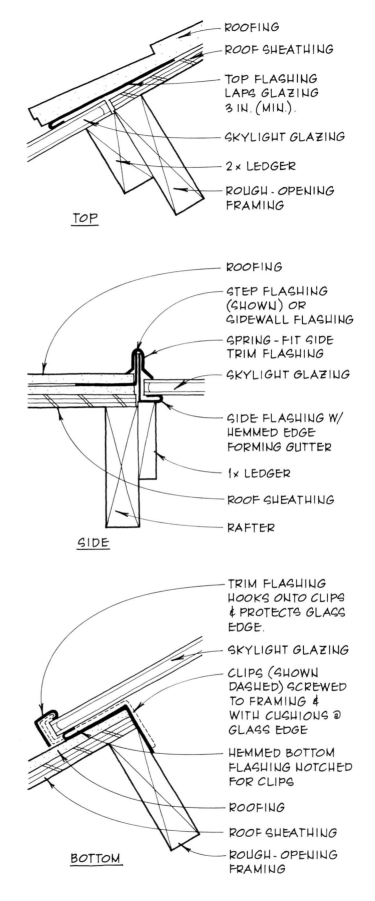

TOP

ROOFING
ROOF SHEATHING
TOP FLASHING LAPS GLAZING 3 IN. (MIN.).
SKYLIGHT GLAZING
2× LEDGER
ROUGH-OPENING FRAMING

SIDE

ROOFING
STEP FLASHING (SHOWN) OR SIDEWALL FLASHING
SPRING-FIT SIDE TRIM FLASHING
SKYLIGHT GLAZING
SIDE FLASHING W/ HEMMED EDGE FORMING GUTTER
1× LEDGER
ROOF SHEATHING
RAFTER

BOTTOM

TRIM FLASHING HOOKS ONTO CLIPS & PROTECTS GLASS EDGE.
SKYLIGHT GLAZING
CLIPS (SHOWN DASHED) SCREWED TO FRAMING & WITH CUSHIONS @ GLASS EDGE
HEMMED BOTTOM FLASHING NOTCHED FOR CLIPS
ROOFING
ROOF SHEATHING
ROUGH-OPENING FRAMING

A site-built curbless skylight is woven in with the roofing. Its bottom edge laps the roofing, and its top edge is lapped by roofing. This means that the skylight itself must be at a slightly lower pitch than the roof. Ledgers at the sides of the rough opening provide the support at this lower pitch. If built properly, there is no need for any caulking of these skylights except at the notch at the top of the side flashing. Insulated glass should limit condensation on the glazing, but any condensation that does form can weep out through the clip notches in the bottom flashing. In extremely cold climates, the side flashing should be thermally isolated from the other flashing to prevent condensation on the flashing itself.

Curbless skylights are especially practical at the eave edge of a roof, where the lower edge of the skylight does not have to lap the roofing. This condition, often found in attached greenhouses, will simplify the details on this page because the slope of the skylight can be the same as the roof. The top and side details above right are suitable in such a case. Codes that require curbs preclude the use of these skylights.

 A **CURBLESS SKYLIGHT**

With the exception of wood roofs, which are now made with lower-grade material than in the past, today's roofing materials will last longer than ever before, and can be installed with less labor. Composite materials now take the place of most natural roofing materials, including wood shingle and slate.

The selection of a roofing material must be carefully coordinated with the design and construction of the roof itself. Some factors to consider are the type of roof sheathing (see 152-156), insulation (see 187-193) and flashing (see 157-166). For example, some roofing materials perform best on open sheathing, but others require solid sheathing. Some roofing materials may be applied over rigid insulation; others may not.

Many roofing materials require a waterproof underlayment to be installed over solid sheathing before roofing is applied. Underlayment, usually 15-lb. felt, which can be applied quickly, is often used to keep the building dry until the permanent roofing is applied. In the case of wood shakes, the underlayment layer is woven in with the roofing courses and is called interlayment (see 176A).

Other considerations for selecting a roofing material include cost, durability, fire resistance and slope (the pitch of the roof).

Cost—Considering both labor and materials, the least expensive roofing is roll roofing (see 170-171). Next in the order of expense are asphalt shingles (see 172-173), followed by preformed metal (see 180), wood shingles (see 174-175), shakes (see 176-177) and tile (see 178-179). Extremely expensive roofs such as slate and standing-seam metal are not discussed in depth in this book.

Durability—As would be expected, the materials that cost the most also last the longest. Concrete-tile roofs are typically warranteed for 50 years. Shake and shingle roofs can last as long under proper conditions but are never warranteed. Preformed metal and asphalt shingles are warranteed in the 20-year to 25-year range.

Fire resistance—Tile and metal are the most resistant to fire, but fiberglass-based asphalt shingles and roll roofing can also be rated in the highest class for fire resistance. Wood shakes and shingles can be chemically treated to resist fire, but are not as resistant as other types of roofing.

Slope—The slope of a roof is measured as a proportion of rise to run of the roof. A 4-in-12 roof slope, for example, rises 4 in. for every 12 in. of run.

There are wide variations among roofing manufacturers, but in general, the slope of a roof can be matched to the type of roofing. Flat roofs (⅛-in-12 to ¼-in-12) are roofed with a built-up coating or with a single ply membrane (see 168-169). Shallow-slope roofs (1-in-12 to 4-in-12) are often roofed with roll roofing. Special measures may be taken to allow asphalt shingles on a 2-in-12 slope and wood shingles or shakes on a 3-in-12 slope, and some metal roofs may be applied to 1-in-12 slopes. Normal-slope roofs (4-in-12 to 12-in-12) are the slopes required for most roofing materials. Some materials such as built-up roofing are designed for lower slopes and may not be applied to normal slopes.

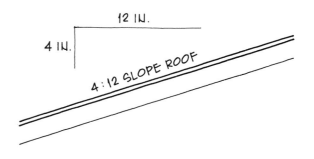

12 IN.

4 IN.

4 : 12 SLOPE ROOF

Flat roofs aren't actually flat, but must slope to drain water or manufacturers will not guarantee their products. The actual slope depends on the application, but most manufacturers recommend ¼ in. per ft. The slope may be achieved with the framing of the roof (see 131A) or with tapered insulation. Water is usually contained at the edges of a flat roof with a curb or a wall and directed to a central drain (see 169B) or scupper at the edge of the roof (see 59D). A continuous gutter at the edge of a flat roof can also collect the water. Also see the section on porches and decks (54-62).

The selection of an appropriate roofing system for a flat roof can be complicated. As with all roofs, climate is one factor. But the fact that a flat roof is covered with a large continuous waterproof membrane presents some special technical problems, such as expansion and contraction. If the roof is going to be used for a terrace or walkway, the effects of foot traffic must also be considered. For these reasons, a flat roof is best selected by a design professional and constructed by a reputable roofing contractor.

There are several application methods for flat roofs:

Built-up roof—A built-up roof is composed of several layers of asphalt-impregnated felt interspersed with coats of hot tar (bitumen) and capped with gravel. This traditional and effective method is in widespread use. The application is technical and should be performed by professional roofers. Warranties range from one to five years.

Single-ply roof—A more recent development in roofing, the single-ply roof is less labor intensive and more elastic than the built-up roof. The single-ply roof is applied as a membrane and glued, weighted with gravel ballast or mechanically fastened to the roof. Seams are glued with adhesive or heat sealed. Single-ply roofs are usually applied to large areas, but, like the built-up roof, can also cover small areas. Application is technical; warranties start at five years.

Liquid-applied roof—Liquid-applied roofing polymerizes from chemicals suspended in volatile solvents to form a watertight elastomeric membrane that adheres to the sheathing. Application is usually in several coats using brush, roller or spray. Liquid-applied roofs are practical for small areas, where they may be applied by an untrained person without specialized tools; their flexibility allows them to be applied without the cant strips required of built-up roofs (see 168B & C).

A | FLAT ROOFING

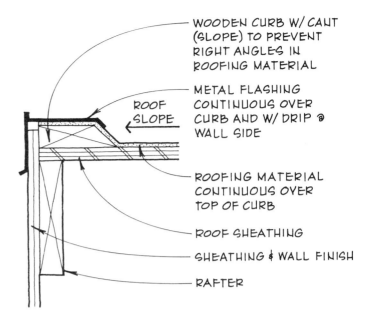

WOODEN CURB W/ CANT (SLOPE) TO PREVENT RIGHT ANGLES IN ROOFING MATERIAL

METAL FLASHING CONTINUOUS OVER CURB AND W/ DRIP @ WALL SIDE

ROOF SLOPE

ROOFING MATERIAL CONTINUOUS OVER TOP OF CURB

ROOF SHEATHING

SHEATHING & WALL FINISH

RAFTER

NOTE:
THIS CURB IS GENERALLY USED IN CONJUNCTION W/ A SCUPPER WHEN THE ROOF SLOPES TOWARD THE OUTSIDE EDGE OF THE BUILDING. FOR SCUPPER see 59D

B | FLAT ROOF EDGE W/ CURB

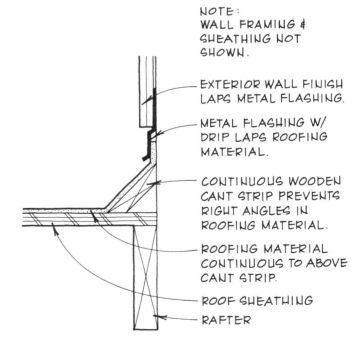

NOTE:
WALL FRAMING & SHEATHING NOT SHOWN.

EXTERIOR WALL FINISH LAPS METAL FLASHING.

METAL FLASHING W/ DRIP LAPS ROOFING MATERIAL.

CONTINUOUS WOODEN CANT STRIP PREVENTS RIGHT ANGLES IN ROOFING MATERIAL.

ROOFING MATERIAL CONTINUOUS TO ABOVE CANT STRIP.

ROOF SHEATHING

RAFTER

C | FLAT ROOF EDGE @ WALL

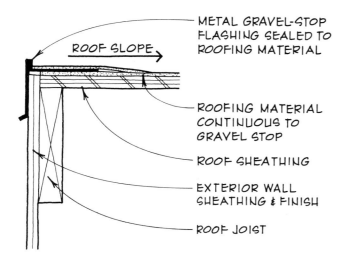

ROOF SLOPE

METAL GRAVEL-STOP
FLASHING SEALED TO
ROOFING MATERIAL

ROOFING MATERIAL
CONTINUOUS TO
GRAVEL STOP

ROOF SHEATHING

EXTERIOR WALL
SHEATHING & FINISH

ROOF JOIST

NOTE:
THIS DETAIL IS GENERALLY USED WHEN THE ROOF
SLOPES AWAY FROM THE EDGE TOWARD A
CENTRAL DRAIN see 169B

 A FLAT ROOF EDGE W/ GRAVEL STOP

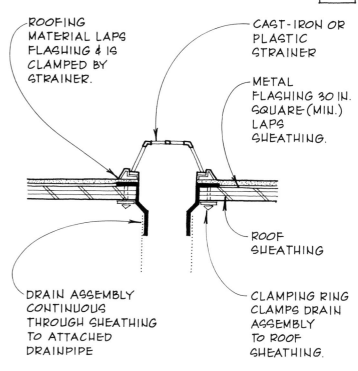

ROOFING
MATERIAL LAPS
FLASHING & IS
CLAMPED BY
STRAINER.

CAST-IRON OR
PLASTIC
STRAINER

METAL
FLASHING 30 IN.
SQUARE (MIN.)
LAPS
SHEATHING.

ROOF
SHEATHING

CLAMPING RING
CLAMPS DRAIN
ASSEMBLY
TO ROOF
SHEATHING.

DRAIN ASSEMBLY
CONTINUOUS
THROUGH SHEATHING
TO ATTACHED
DRAINPIPE

 B FLAT ROOF DRAIN

Roll roofing is an inexpensive roofing for shallow-pitch roofs (1-in-12 to 4-in-12). The 36-in. wide by 36-ft. long rolls are made with a fiberglass or organic felt base that is impregnated with asphalt and covered on the surface with mineral granules similar to asphalt shingles. Several colors are available. Roll roofing weighs 55 lb. to 90 lb. per square (100 sq. ft.). (The 90-lb. felt used for roll roofing is three times heavier than the 30-lb. felt used for underlayment.) The average life expectancy for roll roofing ranges from 10 to 15 years; fiberglass-base roofing is the longest lasting. Fiberglass-base rolls are also more resistant to fire.

Roll roofing must be applied over solid sheathing and does not require underlayment. It is easily nailed in place without using any specialized equipment.

There are two basic types of roll roofing, single coverage and double coverage.

Single coverage—Single-coverage roofing rolls are uniformly surfaced with mineral granules and are applied directly to the roof sheathing with only a 2-in. to 4-in. lap, which is sealed with roofing adhesive. The rolls may be applied parallel to the eaves or to the rake. The roofing may be applied using the concealed-nail method (see 170B) or the exposed-nail method (not shown). A minimum pitch of 2-in-12 is required for the exposed-nail method. Single coverage is the least expensive and the least durable of the roll-roofing methods.

Double coverage—Double-coverage rolls are half surfaced with mineral granules and half smooth. The smooth part of the roll is called the selvage. The rolls are lapped over each other so that the surfaced portion of each roll laps over the smooth portion of the previous course. Each course of roofing is sealed to the previous course with either cold asphalt adhesive or hot asphalt. In this fashion, the roof is covered with a double layer of felt. The final double layer of felt weighs 110 lb. to 140 lb. per square. Double-coverage roofing is more expensive than single-coverage roofing, but it makes a more durable roof. Double-coverage roll roofing may be applied with the courses paralled to the eave or to the rake (see 171A).

(A) ROLL ROOFING
INTRODUCTION

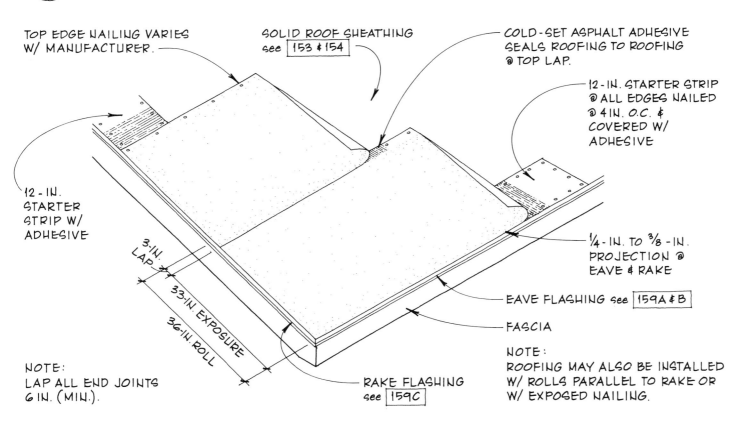

TOP EDGE NAILING VARIES W/ MANUFACTURER.

SOLID ROOF SHEATHING see | 153 & 154 |

COLD-SET ASPHALT ADHESIVE SEALS ROOFING TO ROOFING @ TOP LAP.

12-IN. STARTER STRIP @ ALL EDGES NAILED @ 4 IN. O.C. & COVERED W/ ADHESIVE

12-IN. STARTER STRIP W/ ADHESIVE

3-IN. LAP

33-IN. EXPOSURE

36-IN. ROLL

¼-IN. TO ⅜-IN. PROJECTION @ EAVE & RAKE

EAVE FLASHING see | 159A & B |

FASCIA

NOTE: ROOFING MAY ALSO BE INSTALLED W/ ROLLS PARALLEL TO RAKE OR W/ EXPOSED NAILING.

NOTE: LAP ALL END JOINTS 6 IN. (MIN.).

RAKE FLASHING see | 159C |

(B) SINGLE-COVERAGE ROLL ROOFING
CONCEALED-NAIL METHOD

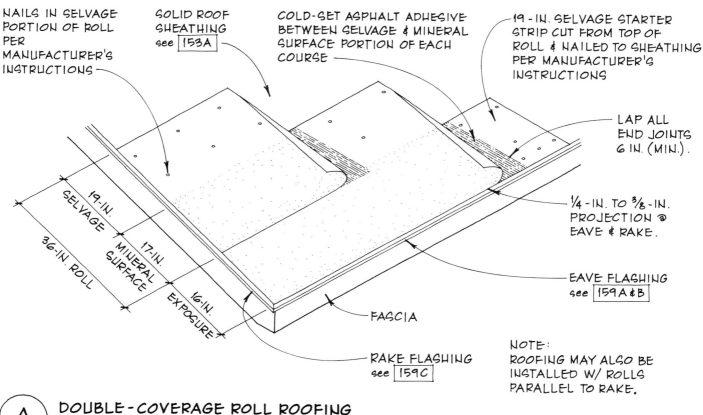

NAILS IN SELVAGE PORTION OF ROLL PER MANUFACTURER'S INSTRUCTIONS

SOLID ROOF SHEATHING see | 153A |

COLD-SET ASPHALT ADHESIVE BETWEEN SELVAGE & MINERAL SURFACE PORTION OF EACH COURSE

19-IN. SELVAGE STARTER STRIP CUT FROM TOP OF ROLL & NAILED TO SHEATHING PER MANUFACTURER'S INSTRUCTIONS

LAP ALL END JOINTS 6 IN. (MIN.).

1/4-IN. TO 3/8-IN. PROJECTION @ EAVE & RAKE.

EAVE FLASHING see | 159A & B |

19-IN. SELVAGE
17-IN. MINERAL SURFACE
16-IN. EXPOSURE
36-IN. ROLL

FASCIA

RAKE FLASHING see | 159C |

NOTE:
ROOFING MAY ALSO BE INSTALLED W/ ROLLS PARALLEL TO RAKE.

(A) DOUBLE-COVERAGE ROLL ROOFING

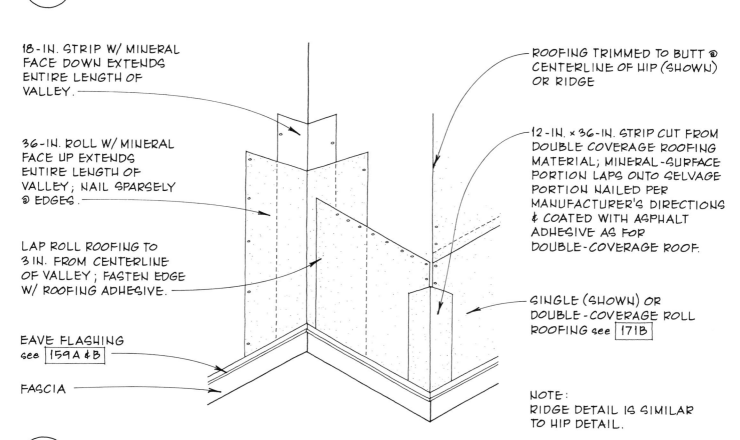

18-IN. STRIP W/ MINERAL FACE DOWN EXTENDS ENTIRE LENGTH OF VALLEY.

36-IN. ROLL W/ MINERAL FACE UP EXTENDS ENTIRE LENGTH OF VALLEY; NAIL SPARSELY @ EDGES.

LAP ROLL ROOFING TO 3 IN. FROM CENTERLINE OF VALLEY; FASTEN EDGE W/ ROOFING ADHESIVE.

EAVE FLASHING see | 159A & B |

FASCIA

ROOFING TRIMMED TO BUTT @ CENTERLINE OF HIP (SHOWN) OR RIDGE

12-IN. × 36-IN. STRIP CUT FROM DOUBLE COVERAGE ROOFING MATERIAL; MINERAL-SURFACE PORTION LAPS ONTO SELVAGE PORTION NAILED PER MANUFACTURER'S DIRECTIONS & COATED WITH ASPHALT ADHESIVE AS FOR DOUBLE-COVERAGE ROOF.

SINGLE (SHOWN) OR DOUBLE-COVERAGE ROLL ROOFING see | 171B |

NOTE:
RIDGE DETAIL IS SIMILAR TO HIP DETAIL.

(B) ROLL-ROOFING VALLEY & HIP (OR RIDGE)
DOUBLE OR SINGLE COVERAGE

Composite asphalt shingles are almost the perfect roofing material. They are inexpensive, waterproof, lightweight and easily cut and bent. That is why asphalt shingles are so popular nationwide. They are available in a wide range of colors and textures, some with extra thickness to imitate shakes, slate or other uneven materials. There is also a range of quality, with warranties from 15 to 30 years.

Asphalt shingles are made with a fiberglass or organic felt base that is impregnated with asphalt and covered on the surface with granulated stone or ceramic material, which gives it color. Fiberglass shingles are more durable and more resistant to fire.

Asphalt shingles must be applied over a solid sheathing covered with 15-lb. felt underlayment. They are easily nailed in place using no specialized equipment. Many roofing contractors, however, use air-driven staples.

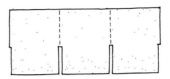

STANDARD FIELD SHINGLES HAVE 3 TABS & WEIGH 235 LB. PER SQUARE (100 SQ. FT.).

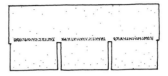

STANDARD FIELD SHINGLES MAY BE CUT INTO 3 PIECES TO MAKE HIP OR RIDGE SHINGLES.

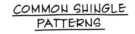

SELF-SEALING ADHESIVE AVAILABLE ON TOP SIDE OF SHINGLES TO PROTECT AGAINST WIND.

ALTERNATIVE PATTERNS AVAILABLE W/ SOME THICKER TABS TO RESEMBLE MORE NATURAL ROOFS.

COMMON SHINGLE PATTERNS

OTHER LESS COMMON PATTERNS ARE ALSO AVAILABLE.

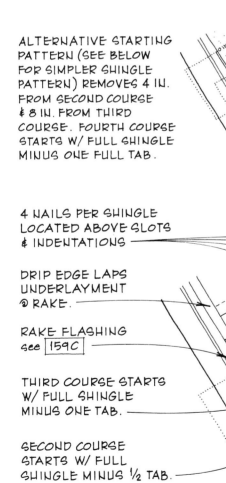

ALTERNATIVE STARTING PATTERN (SEE BELOW FOR SIMPLER SHINGLE PATTERN) REMOVES 4 IN. FROM SECOND COURSE & 8 IN. FROM THIRD COURSE. FOURTH COURSE STARTS W/ FULL SHINGLE MINUS ONE FULL TAB.

4 NAILS PER SHINGLE LOCATED ABOVE SLOTS & INDENTATIONS

DRIP EDGE LAPS UNDERLAYMENT @ RAKE.

RAKE FLASHING see 159C

THIRD COURSE STARTS W/ FULL SHINGLE MINUS ONE TAB.

SECOND COURSE STARTS W/ FULL SHINGLE MINUS ½ TAB.

FIRST COURSE STARTS W/ FULL SHINGLE.

SOLID ROOF SHEATHING see 153-155

CODES IN COLD CLIMATES OFTEN REQUIRE A 36-IN. STARTER STRIP OF BITUMINOUS WATERPROOFING see 159B

15-LB. FELT UNDERLAYMENT LAPPED OVER EAVE FLASHING see 159A

STARTER COURSE W/ TABS CUT OFF TO BE OFFSET 3 IN.

EAVE FLASHING see 159A&B

FOR HIP, VALLEY & RIDGE DETAILS see 173

A ASPHALT-SHINGLE ROOFING

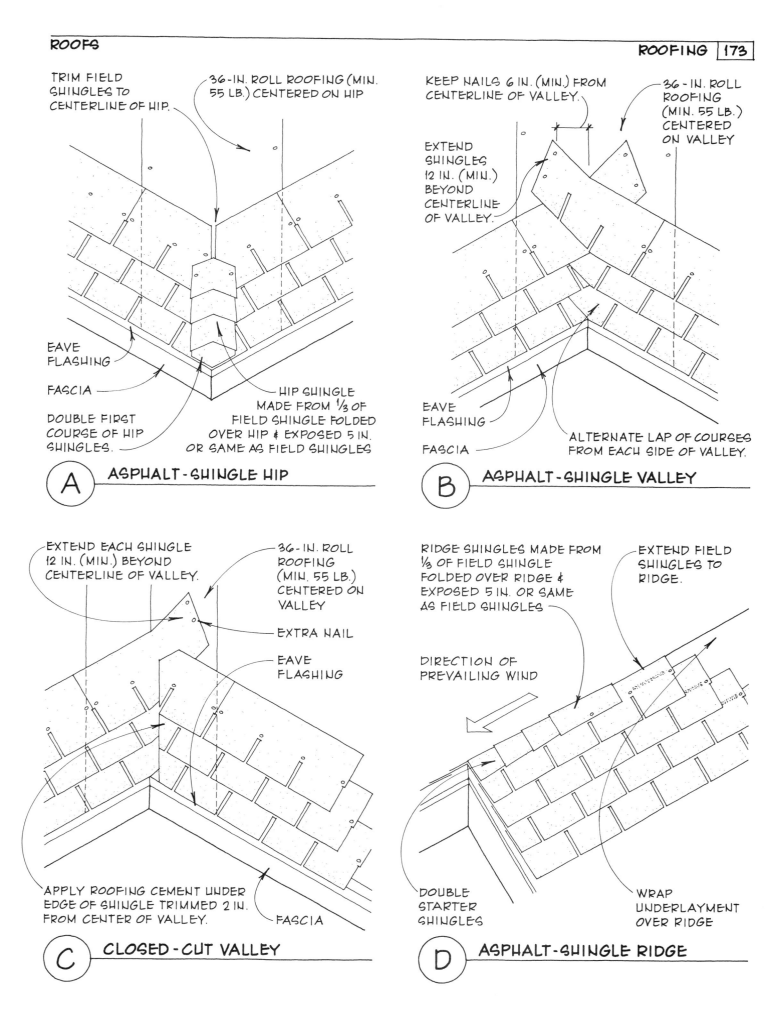

TRIM FIELD SHINGLES TO CENTERLINE OF HIP.

36-IN. ROLL ROOFING (MIN. 55 LB.) CENTERED ON HIP

EAVE FLASHING

FASCIA

DOUBLE FIRST COURSE OF HIP SHINGLES.

HIP SHINGLE MADE FROM 1/3 OF FIELD SHINGLE FOLDED OVER HIP & EXPOSED 5 IN. OR SAME AS FIELD SHINGLES

A ASPHALT-SHINGLE HIP

KEEP NAILS 6 IN. (MIN.) FROM CENTERLINE OF VALLEY.

36-IN. ROLL ROOFING (MIN. 55 LB.) CENTERED ON VALLEY

EXTEND SHINGLES 12 IN. (MIN.) BEYOND CENTERLINE OF VALLEY.

EAVE FLASHING

FASCIA

ALTERNATE LAP OF COURSES FROM EACH SIDE OF VALLEY.

B ASPHALT-SHINGLE VALLEY

EXTEND EACH SHINGLE 12 IN. (MIN.) BEYOND CENTERLINE OF VALLEY.

36-IN. ROLL ROOFING (MIN. 55 LB.) CENTERED ON VALLEY

EXTRA NAIL

EAVE FLASHING

APPLY ROOFING CEMENT UNDER EDGE OF SHINGLE TRIMMED 2 IN. FROM CENTER OF VALLEY.

FASCIA

C CLOSED-CUT VALLEY

RIDGE SHINGLES MADE FROM 1/3 OF FIELD SHINGLE FOLDED OVER RIDGE & EXPOSED 5 IN. OR SAME AS FIELD SHINGLES

EXTEND FIELD SHINGLES TO RIDGE.

DIRECTION OF PREVAILING WIND

DOUBLE STARTER SHINGLES

WRAP UNDERLAYMENT OVER RIDGE

D ASPHALT-SHINGLE RIDGE

For centuries, wood shingles have been used extensively for roofing, and they continue to be very popular. However, with the advent of the asphalt shingle, they have recently lost their dominance as a roofing material. Furthermore, their use continues to decline because of cost increases and a drop in the quality of the raw materials.

Roof shingles are made predominantly from clear western red cedar, but are also available in redwood and cypress. They are sawn on both sides to a taper, and have a uniform butt thickness. Standard shingles are 16 in. long; 18-in. and 24-in. lengths are also available. Widths are random, usually in the 3-in. to 10-in. range. There are several grades of wood shingles; only the highest grade should be used for roofing.

In most cases, wood shingles will last longer if applied over skip sheathing (see 156A) because they will be able to breathe and dry out from both sides and therefore be less susceptible to rot and other moisture-related damage. Use solid sheathing and underlayment, however, for low pitch (3-in-12 and 3½-in-12) and in areas of severe wind-driven snow (see 159B).

Chemically treated fire-rated shingles are available. They must be installed over solid sheathing that is covered with a plastic-coated steel foil.

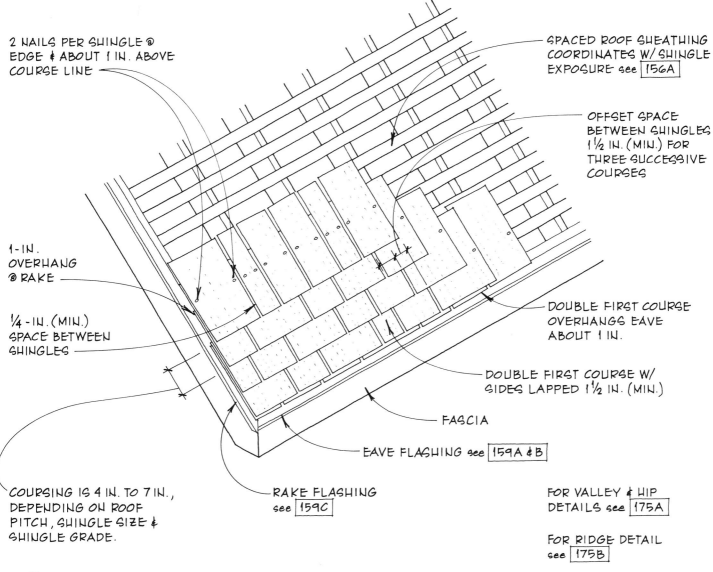

2 NAILS PER SHINGLE @ EDGE & ABOUT 1 IN. ABOVE COURSE LINE

SPACED ROOF SHEATHING COORDINATES W/ SHINGLE EXPOSURE see | 156A |

OFFSET SPACE BETWEEN SHINGLES 1½ IN. (MIN.) FOR THREE SUCCESSIVE COURSES

1-IN. OVERHANG @ RAKE

¼-IN. (MIN.) SPACE BETWEEN SHINGLES

DOUBLE FIRST COURSE OVERHANGS EAVE ABOUT 1 IN.

DOUBLE FIRST COURSE W/ SIDES LAPPED 1½ IN. (MIN.)

FASCIA

EAVE FLASHING see | 159A & B |

COURSING IS 4 IN. TO 7 IN., DEPENDING ON ROOF PITCH, SHINGLE SIZE & SHINGLE GRADE.

RAKE FLASHING see | 159C |

FOR VALLEY & HIP DETAILS see | 175A |

FOR RIDGE DETAIL see | 175B |

(A) WOOD-SHINGLE ROOFING

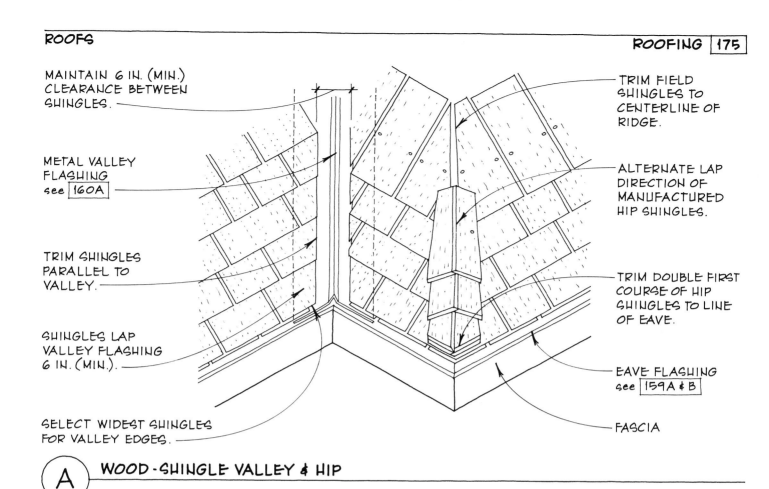

MAINTAIN 6 IN. (MIN.) CLEARANCE BETWEEN SHINGLES.

METAL VALLEY FLASHING see | 160A |

TRIM SHINGLES PARALLEL TO VALLEY.

SHINGLES LAP VALLEY FLASHING 6 IN. (MIN.).

SELECT WIDEST SHINGLES FOR VALLEY EDGES.

TRIM FIELD SHINGLES TO CENTERLINE OF RIDGE.

ALTERNATE LAP DIRECTION OF MANUFACTURED HIP SHINGLES.

TRIM DOUBLE FIRST COURSE OF HIP SHINGLES TO LINE OF EAVE.

EAVE FLASHING see | 159A & B |

FASCIA

A WOOD-SHINGLE VALLEY & HIP

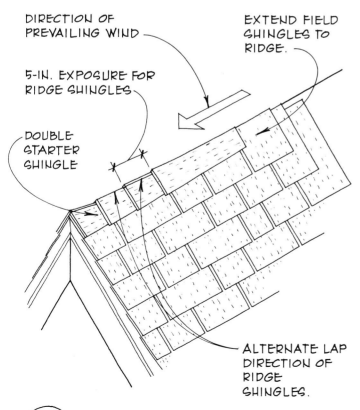

DIRECTION OF PREVAILING WIND

EXTEND FIELD SHINGLES TO RIDGE.

5-IN. EXPOSURE FOR RIDGE SHINGLES

DOUBLE STARTER SHINGLE

ALTERNATE LAP DIRECTION OF RIDGE SHINGLES.

B WOOD-SHINGLE RIDGE

Wood shakes are popular for their rustic look and their durability. They are made from the same materials as wood shingles, but they are split to achieve a taper instead of being sawn. Shakes may have split faces and sawn backs or be taper-split with both sides having a split surface. In either case, the split side is exposed to the weather because it has small smooth grooves parallel to the grain that channel rainwater down the surface of the shake. Standard shakes are 18 in. or 24 in. long and come in heavy or medium thickness.

Wood shakes may be applied over open sheathing (see 156A) or solid sheathing (see 153A). The courses of shakes are usually alternated with an interlayment of 30-lb. felt that retards the penetration of moisture through the relatively large gaps between shakes. Solid sheathing and cold-climate eave flashing (see 159B) are recommended in areas of wind-driven snow.

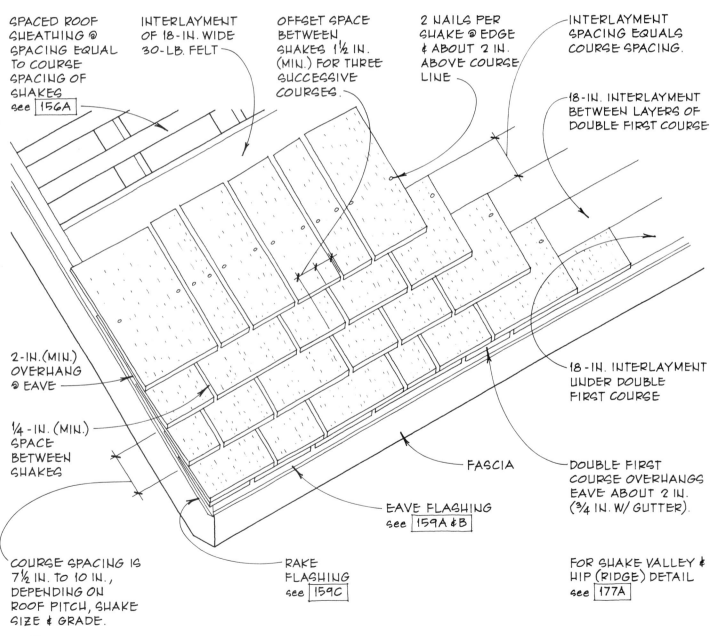

SPACED ROOF SHEATHING @ SPACING EQUAL TO COURSE SPACING OF SHAKES see |156A|

INTERLAYMENT OF 18-IN. WIDE 30-LB. FELT

OFFSET SPACE BETWEEN SHAKES 1½ IN. (MIN.) FOR THREE SUCCESSIVE COURSES.

2 NAILS PER SHAKE @ EDGE & ABOUT 2 IN. ABOVE COURSE LINE

INTERLAYMENT SPACING EQUALS COURSE SPACING.

18-IN. INTERLAYMENT BETWEEN LAYERS OF DOUBLE FIRST COURSE

2-IN. (MIN.) OVERHANG @ EAVE

¼-IN. (MIN.) SPACE BETWEEN SHAKES

18-IN. INTERLAYMENT UNDER DOUBLE FIRST COURSE

FASCIA

DOUBLE FIRST COURSE OVERHANGS EAVE ABOUT 2 IN. (¾ IN. W/ GUTTER).

EAVE FLASHING see |159A & B|

COURSE SPACING IS 7½ IN. TO 10 IN., DEPENDING ON ROOF PITCH, SHAKE SIZE & GRADE.

RAKE FLASHING see |159C|

FOR SHAKE VALLEY & HIP (RIDGE) DETAIL see |177A|

 A WOOD-SHAKE ROOFING

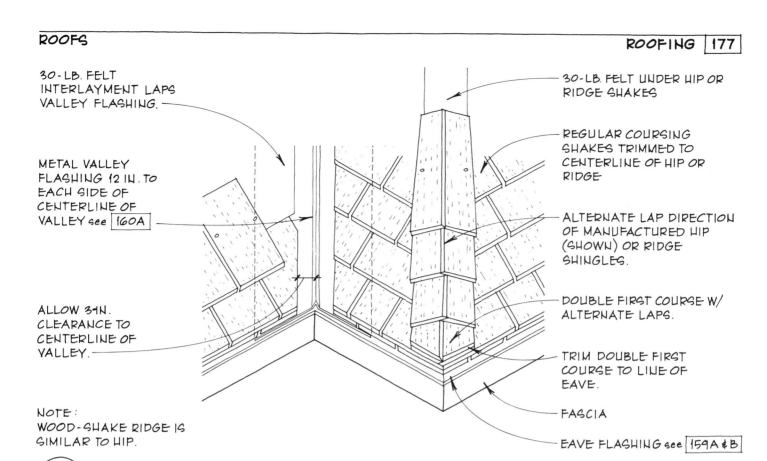

30-LB. FELT INTERLAYMENT LAPS VALLEY FLASHING.

METAL VALLEY FLASHING 12 IN. TO EACH SIDE OF CENTERLINE OF VALLEY see 160A

ALLOW 3-IN. CLEARANCE TO CENTERLINE OF VALLEY.

NOTE: WOOD-SHAKE RIDGE IS SIMILAR TO HIP.

30-LB. FELT UNDER HIP OR RIDGE SHAKES

REGULAR COURSING SHAKES TRIMMED TO CENTERLINE OF HIP OR RIDGE

ALTERNATE LAP DIRECTION OF MANUFACTURED HIP (SHOWN) OR RIDGE SHINGLES.

DOUBLE FIRST COURSE W/ ALTERNATE LAPS.

TRIM DOUBLE FIRST COURSE TO LINE OF EAVE.

FASCIA

EAVE FLASHING see 159A & B

(A) WOOD-SHAKE VALLEY & HIP

Clay tiles have been used in warm climates for centuries. Their use is still common in the southern extremes of this country, but they have recently been superseded by concrete tiles, which cost less but have better quality control.

Concrete tiles are made from high-density concrete coated with a waterproof resin. They are available in a variety of shapes and colors. Most tile patterns fall in the range of 16 in. to 18 in. long and 9 in. to 13 in wide. Tiles weigh from 6 lb. to 10½ lb. per square foot (psf), which is about 2½ to 5 times the weight of asphalt

shingles. Most roofs must be structured to support snow loads averaging 30 psf, which is considerably in excess of the weight of the tiles, so the cost of stronger framing to support a tile roof is seldom a factor.

The cost of concrete tiles themselves is high compared to other common roofing materials, but most concrete tile-roof systems are warranteed for 50 years.

Most manufacturers recommend installing the tiles on solid sheathing with 30-lb. felt underlayment and pressure-treated nailing battens under each course. Course spacing is usually about 13 in., and can be adjusted to make courses equal on each slope of roof.

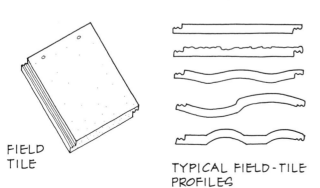

FIELD TILE

TYPICAL FIELD-TILE PROFILES

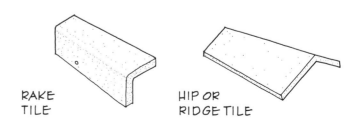

RAKE TILE

HIP OR RIDGE TILE

(B) CONCRETE TILE ROOFING
INTRODUCTION & TYPES OF TILE

2 NON-CORROSIVE NAILS @ TOP OF EACH TILE

NOTE:
ADJUST TILE COURSE EXPOSURE @ EACH ROOF SLOPE TO MAKE COURSES EQUAL.

BARGE RAFTER

TOP OF RAKE TILES BUTT TO BOTTOM OF FIELD TILES

RAKE TILES LAP FIELD TILES see 179B

FOR METAL-TRIMMED RAKE DETAIL see 179C

NAIL RAKE TILES @ SIDE.

TRIM HEAD OF BOTTOM RAKE TILE SO THAT TILE IS FLUSH W/ EAVE.

1×2 PRESSURE-TREATED BATTENS NAILED TO FACE OF UNDERLAYMENT

30-LB. FELT UNDERLAYMENT OVER SOLID SHEATHING; FELT LAPPED 2½ IN. @ HORIZONTAL JOINTS, 6 IN. @ JOINTS PARALLEL TO SLOPE

TILE COURSES LAP ABOUT 3 IN.

STAGGER JOINTS BETWEEN TILES ON ALTERNATE COURSES.

FIRST COURSE OF TILES W/ LOWER EDGE ELEVATED BY STARTER TILE, METAL CLOSURE STRIP OR FASCIA see 179A

EAVE DETAIL see 179A

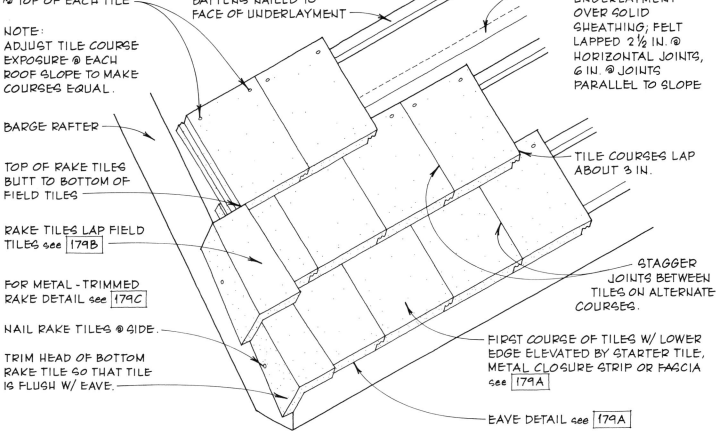

(A) CONCRETE-TILE ROOFING

CUT CONCRETE TILES PARALLEL TO VALLEY.

VALLEY FLASHING see 160

NOTE:
RIDGE TILES ARE SIMILAR TO HIP TILES, BUT ANGLE DIFFERS FOR STEEP PITCHES.

BUTT HIP TILES TO BOTTOM OF EACH COURSE OF FIELD TILES; NAIL EACH HIP TILE @ TOP.

MANUFACTURED HIP TILES CONFORM TO SLOPE OF ROOF.

HIP TILES LAP EACH OTHER BY SAME AMOUNT AS FIELD TILES.

CUT FIRST HIP TILE TO LINE OF EAVE.

EAVE DETAIL see 179A

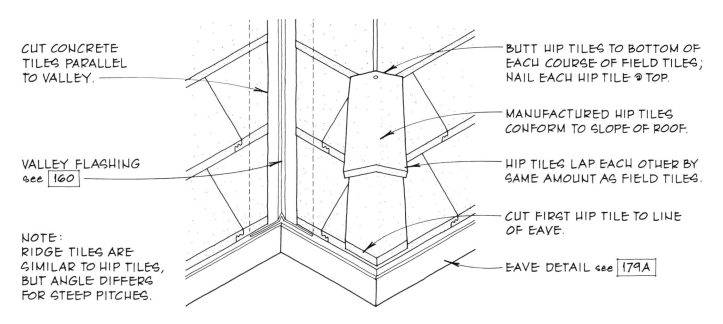

(B) CONCRETE-TILE VALLEY & HIP

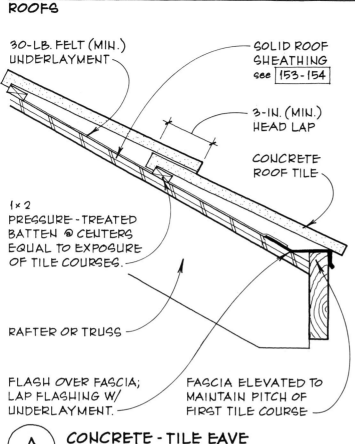

30-LB. FELT (MIN.) UNDERLAYMENT

SOLID ROOF SHEATHING see 153-154

3-IN. (MIN.) HEAD LAP

CONCRETE ROOF TILE

1×2 PRESSURE-TREATED BATTEN @ CENTERS EQUAL TO EXPOSURE OF TILE COURSES.

RAFTER OR TRUSS

FLASH OVER FASCIA; LAP FLASHING W/ UNDERLAYMENT.

FASCIA ELEVATED TO MAINTAIN PITCH OF FIRST TILE COURSE

Ⓐ CONCRETE-TILE EAVE

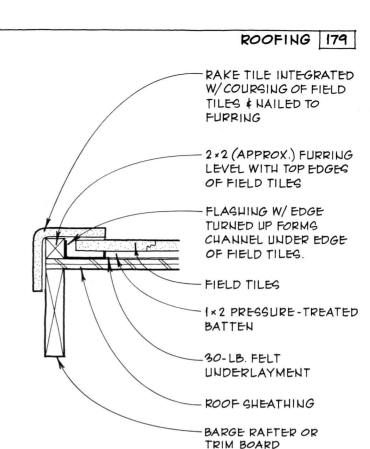

RAKE TILE INTEGRATED W/ COURSING OF FIELD TILES & NAILED TO FURRING

2×2 (APPROX.) FURRING LEVEL WITH TOP EDGES OF FIELD TILES

FLASHING W/ EDGE TURNED UP FORMS CHANNEL UNDER EDGE OF FIELD TILES.

FIELD TILES

1×2 PRESSURE-TREATED BATTEN

30-LB. FELT UNDERLAYMENT

ROOF SHEATHING

BARGE RAFTER OR TRIM BOARD

Ⓑ CONCRETE-TILE RAKE
TILE RAKE

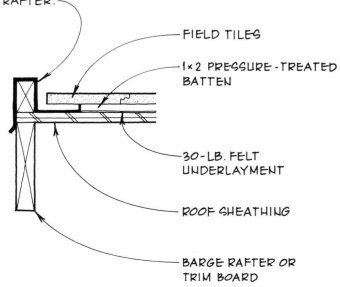

FLASHING W/ EDGE TURNED UP FORMS CHANNEL UNDER EDGE OF FIELD TILES & W/ DRIP @ BARGE RAFTER.

FIELD TILES

1×2 PRESSURE-TREATED BATTEN

30-LB. FELT UNDERLAYMENT

ROOF SHEATHING

BARGE RAFTER OR TRIM BOARD

Ⓒ CONCRETE-TILE RAKE
METAL RAKE

Low-cost metal roofs of aluminum or galvanized steel have been used for some time on agricultural and industrial buildings. The rolled metal panels are lightweight, long-lasting and extremely simple to install. New panel patterns and new finishes have made metal roofing popular for residential and commercial buildings. A baked-on or porcelain enamel finish is often guaranteed for 20 years, and the galvanized steel or aluminum over which it is applied will last for another 20 years in most climates.

Rolled-metal sheets are typically 2 ft. to 3 ft. wide and are factory-cut to the full length of the roof from eave to ridge. Because of the difficulty of field cutting at angles, metal roofs are best suited to simple shed or gable roofs without extensive valleys and hips. Small openings such as vents should be kept to a minimum and collected wherever possible into single openings. (Vents are best located at the ridge, where they are most easily flashed with the ridge flashing.)

The width of metal roofs should be carefully coordinated with the width of roofing panels so that rake trim, dormers, skylights and other interruptions of the simple system will be located at an uncut factory edge.

Because the metal roofing itself has structural capacity, it is possible to install the roofing over purlins, which are 2xs spaced 2 ft. to 4 ft. apart. Most metal roofing panels will span 4 ft. or more, so the load on each purlin is great, and the design of the purlins that support the roofing is a critical factor.

A wide range of finish colors is available with coordinated flashing and trim metal. Translucent fiberglass or plastic panels that match the profile of some metal roofing patterns are also available as skylights.

Choose fasteners and flashing that are compatible with the roofing in order to avoid corrosive galvanic action. Care must also be taken to avoid condensation, which can occur on metal roofs. In extreme climates, where proper ventilation of the roofing system does not suffice, a fiberboard backing covered with 30-lb. felt parallel to the roofing panels will insulate the roofing from moisture-laden air and provide protection from what little condensation does occur.

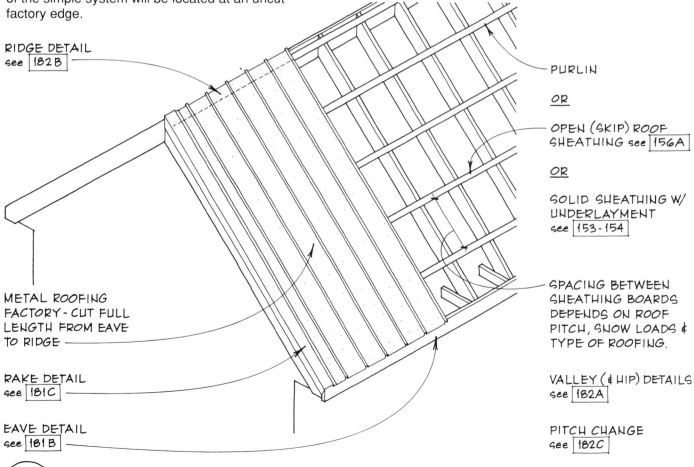

RIDGE DETAIL
see | 182 B |

PURLIN

OR

OPEN (SKIP) ROOF
SHEATHING see | 156A |

OR

SOLID SHEATHING W/
UNDERLAYMENT
see | 153-154 |

SPACING BETWEEN
SHEATHING BOARDS
DEPENDS ON ROOF
PITCH, SNOW LOADS &
TYPE OF ROOFING.

METAL ROOFING
FACTORY-CUT FULL
LENGTH FROM EAVE
TO RIDGE

RAKE DETAIL
see | 181C |

EAVE DETAIL
see | 181 B |

VALLEY (& HIP) DETAILS
see | 182A |

PITCH CHANGE
see | 182C |

 (A) PREFORMED METAL ROOFING

RIBBED ROOFING

SCREW (OR NAIL) W/ NEOPRENE WASHER LOCATED IN FLAT (VALLEY) PART OF ROOFING PROMOTES TIGHT SEAL OF WASHER.

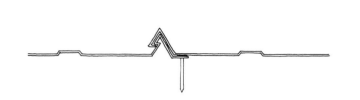

SNAP-TOGETHER ROOFING

SUBSEQUENT PIECE SNAP-FASTENS TO EDGE OF PIECE PREVIOUSLY NAILED. FLAT-HEAD NAIL IS COVERED SO NEOPRENE WASHER IS UNNECESSARY. SECTIONS ARE NARROWER FOR THIS TYPE.

CORRUGATED ROOFING

SCREW (OR NAIL) W/ NEOPRENE WASHER IS LOCATED ON RIDGE OF CORRUGATION BECAUSE VALLEYS ARE NOT WIDE OR FLAT ENOUGH. IT'S DIFFICULT TO ADJUST TENSION OF NAIL OR SCREW.

NOTE:
SOME MANUFACTURERS RECOMMEND NEOPRENE TAPE @ JOINTS.

 A **METAL ROOFING TYPES**
PROFILES

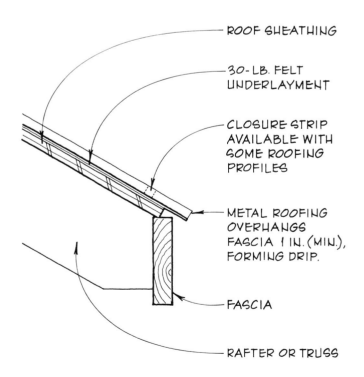

- ROOF SHEATHING
- 30-LB. FELT UNDERLAYMENT
- CLOSURE STRIP AVAILABLE WITH SOME ROOFING PROFILES
- METAL ROOFING OVERHANGS FASCIA 1 IN. (MIN.), FORMING DRIP.
- FASCIA
- RAFTER OR TRUSS

 B **METAL-ROOF EAVE**

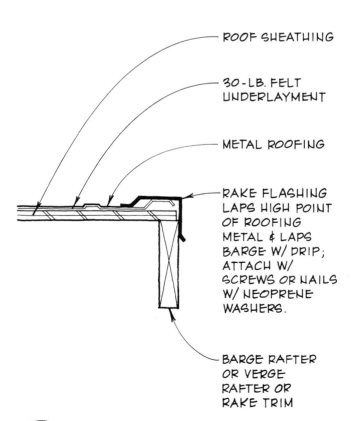

- ROOF SHEATHING
- 30-LB. FELT UNDERLAYMENT
- METAL ROOFING
- RAKE FLASHING LAPS HIGH POINT OF ROOFING METAL & LAPS BARGE W/ DRIP; ATTACH W/ SCREWS OR NAILS W/ NEOPRENE WASHERS.
- BARGE RAFTER OR VERGE RAFTER OR RAKE TRIM

 C **METAL-ROOF RAKE**

TYPICAL VALLEY
FLASHING
see 160A

METAL
ROOFING

HIP FLASHING LAPS 6 IN.
(MIN.) TO EACH SIDE OF
CENTERLINE OF HIP; ATTACH
W/ SCREWS OR NAILS W/
NEOPRENE WASHERS.

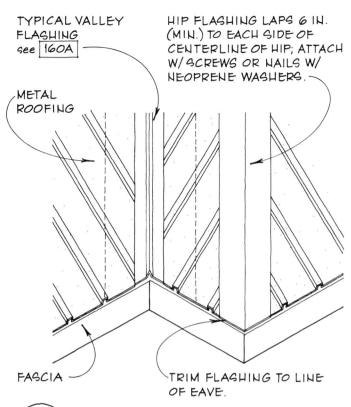

FASCIA

TRIM FLASHING TO LINE
OF EAVE.

(A) METAL-ROOF VALLEY & HIP

FLASHING LAPS
ROOFING 6 IN. (MIN.).

METAL RIDGE
FLASHING MADE FROM
SAME MATERIAL AS
ROOFING

CLOSURE FLASHING
@ TOP OF METAL
ROOFING KEEPS
OUT INSECTS &
WIND-DRIVEN RAIN;
FLASHING LAPS 30-LB.
FELT UNDERLAYMENT.

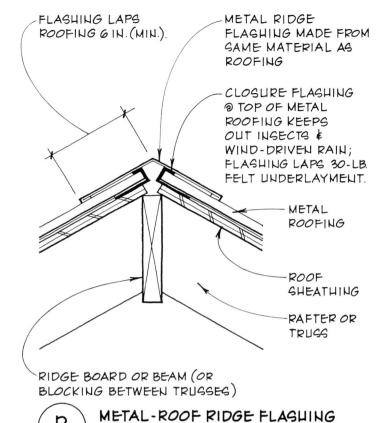

METAL
ROOFING

ROOF
SHEATHING

RAFTER OR
TRUSS

RIDGE BOARD OR BEAM (OR
BLOCKING BETWEEN TRUSSES)

(B) METAL-ROOF RIDGE FLASHING

30-LB. FELT UNDERLAYMENT
EXTENDS UP BEYOND END
OF LOWER ROOFING PANEL.

BEAD OF CAULKING OR
SEALANT @ TOP EDGE OF
LOWER ROOFING PANEL
FORMS A DAM AGAINST
WIND-DRIVEN RAIN.

TOP ROOFING PANEL NESTS
AGAINST LOWER PANEL,
FORMING TIGHT SEAL.

SHEATHING

LOWER ROOFING PANEL
EXTENDS 3 IN. (MIN.)
BEYOND INTERSECTION
W/ TOP PANEL.

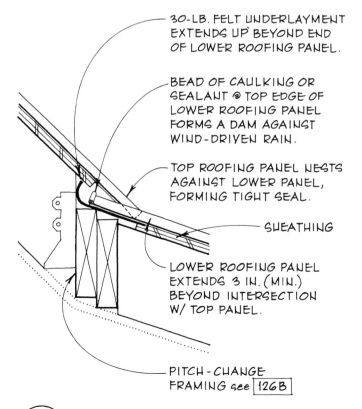

PITCH-CHANGE
FRAMING see 126B

(C) METAL-ROOF PITCH CHANGE

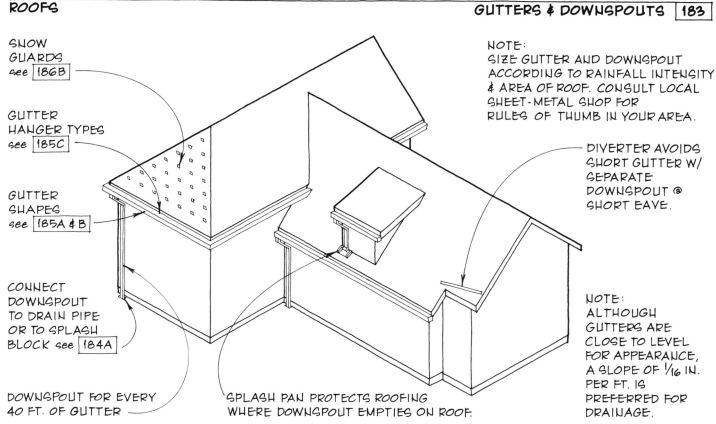

SNOW
GUARDS
see | 186B |

GUTTER
HANGER TYPES
see | 185C |

GUTTER
SHAPES
see | 185A & B |

CONNECT
DOWNSPOUT
TO DRAIN PIPE
OR TO SPLASH
BLOCK see | 184A |

DOWNSPOUT FOR EVERY
40 FT. OF GUTTER

SPLASH PAN PROTECTS ROOFING
WHERE DOWNSPOUT EMPTIES ON ROOF.

NOTE:
SIZE GUTTER AND DOWNSPOUT
ACCORDING TO RAINFALL INTENSITY
& AREA OF ROOF. CONSULT LOCAL
SHEET-METAL SHOP FOR
RULES OF THUMB IN YOUR AREA.

DIVERTER AVOIDS
SHORT GUTTER W/
SEPARATE
DOWNSPOUT @
SHORT EAVE.

NOTE:
ALTHOUGH
GUTTERS ARE
CLOSE TO LEVEL
FOR APPEARANCE,
A SLOPE OF 1/16 IN.
PER FT. IS
PREFERRED FOR
DRAINAGE.

The collection of rainwater by gutters at the eave of a roof prevent it from falling to the ground, where it can splash back onto the building and cause discoloration and decay, or where it can seep into the ground, causing settling or undermining of the foundation. Gutters also protect people passing under the eaves from a cascade of rainwater. In areas of light rainfall, gutters may be eliminated if adequate overhangs are designed and a rock bed is placed below the eaves to control the water and prevent splashback.

Most wood-framed buildings are fitted with site-formed aluminum or galvanized steel gutters with a baked-enamel finish. Continuous straight sections of site-formed gutters are limited only by the need for expansion joints (see 184A) and by the ability of workers to carry the sections without buckling them. Very long sections can be manufactured without joints, the most common location of gutter failures.

Vinyl gutters, although more expensive, are popular with owner-builders because they are more durable and can be installed without specialized equipment.

Downspouts conduct the water from the gutter to the ground, where it should be collected in a storm drain and carried away from the building to be dispersed on the surface, deposited in a dry well or directed to a storm sewer system.

The problem of water freezing in gutters and downspouts may be solved with heat tapes.

Snow sliding off a roof can cause real problems — especially over porches, decks and garages. The problem of sliding snow may be solved by keeping the snow on the roof with snow clips that project from the roofing surface to hold the snow mechanically in place (see 186B).

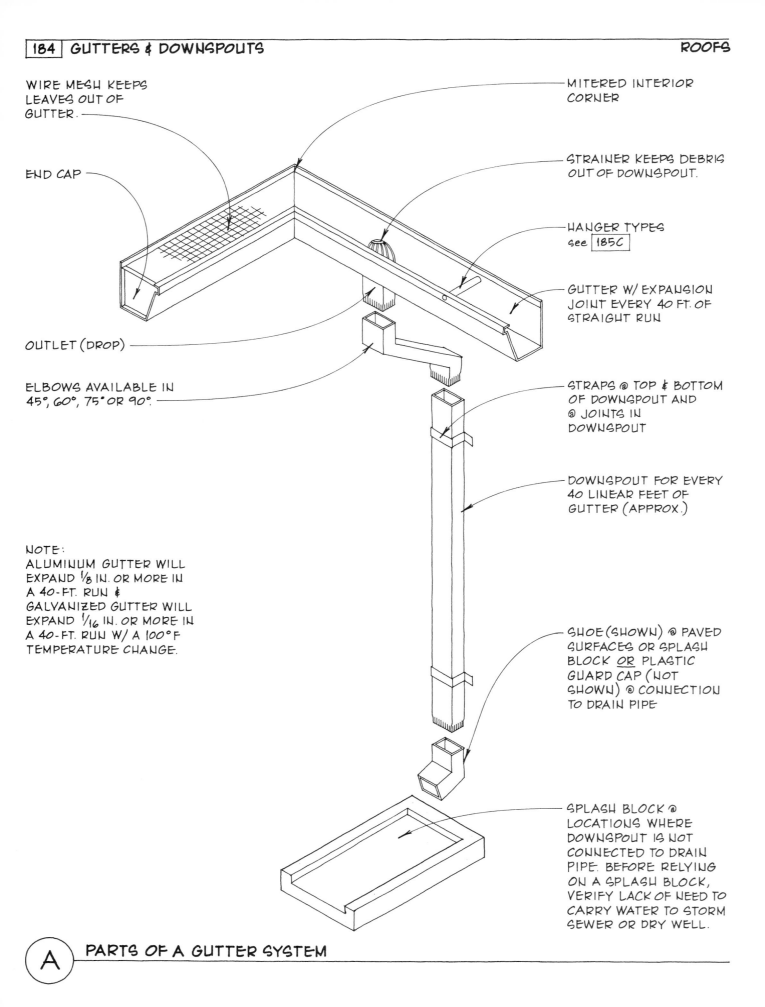

WIRE MESH KEEPS LEAVES OUT OF GUTTER.

END CAP

OUTLET (DROP)

ELBOWS AVAILABLE IN 45°, 60°, 75° OR 90°.

NOTE:
ALUMINUM GUTTER WILL EXPAND 1/8 IN. OR MORE IN A 40-FT. RUN & GALVANIZED GUTTER WILL EXPAND 1/16 IN. OR MORE IN A 40-FT. RUN W/ A 100°F TEMPERATURE CHANGE.

MITERED INTERIOR CORNER

STRAINER KEEPS DEBRIS OUT OF DOWNSPOUT.

HANGER TYPES
see 185C

GUTTER W/ EXPANSION JOINT EVERY 40 FT. OF STRAIGHT RUN

STRAPS @ TOP & BOTTOM OF DOWNSPOUT AND @ JOINTS IN DOWNSPOUT

DOWNSPOUT FOR EVERY 40 LINEAR FEET OF GUTTER (APPROX.)

SHOE (SHOWN) @ PAVED SURFACES OR SPLASH BLOCK OR PLASTIC GUARD CAP (NOT SHOWN) @ CONNECTION TO DRAIN PIPE

SPLASH BLOCK @ LOCATIONS WHERE DOWNSPOUT IS NOT CONNECTED TO DRAIN PIPE. BEFORE RELYING ON A SPLASH BLOCK, VERIFY LACK OF NEED TO CARRY WATER TO STORM SEWER OR DRY WELL.

A   PARTS OF A GUTTER SYSTEM

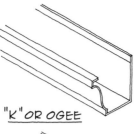

"K" OR OGEE

OGEE IS THE MOST COMMON GUTTER SHAPE. AVAILABLE IN SITE-FORMED ALUMINUM OR GALVANIZED IN A VARIETY OF SIZES, IT IS ALSO MADE IN UNPAINTED GALVANIZED STEEL OR COPPER.

WOODEN GUTTER

WOODEN GUTTERS ARE USED EXTENSIVELY IN THE NORTHEAST. THEY ARE DIFFICULT TO JOIN @ CORNERS OR FOR LONG LENGTHS & ARE PRONE TO DECAY.

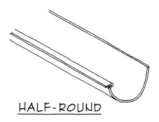

BEVELED

SAME AS OGEE, EXCEPT NOT SO COMMON

CONCEALED GUTTER

CONCEALED GUTTERS OF VARIABLE SHAPES & SIZES MAY BE DESIGNED TO FIT BEHIND THE FASCIA OR WITHIN THE SLOPE OF A ROOF. THESE ARE ALWAYS CUSTOM MADE & ARE THEREFORE EXPENSIVE. UPPER EDGE OF GUTTER IS TYPICALLY LAPPED BY ROOFING; LOWER EDGE CAPS FASCIA.

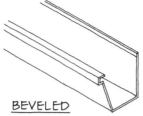

HALF-ROUND

HALF-ROUND GUTTER CANNOT BE SITE-FORMED; IT IS AVAILABLE IN VINYL OR UNPAINTED GALVANIZED STEEL OR COPPER.

 A GUTTER SHAPES

 B SPECIAL GUTTERS

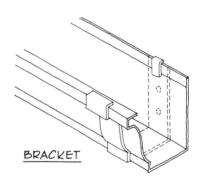

BRACKET

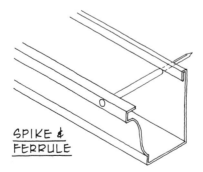

SPIKE & FERRULE

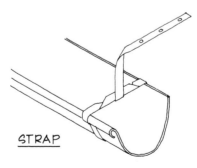

STRAP

BRACKET HANGERS ARE AVAILABLE FOR ALL TYPES OF GUTTER; SCREW TO FASCIA OR (WITH LONGER SCREWS) TO RAFTER TAILS.

SPIKE & FERRULE HANGERS ARE USED W/ BEVELED OR OGEE GUTTERS; SPIKE TO FASCIA OR TO RAFTER TAILS. THE NEED FOR EXPANSION JOINTS IS GREATEST WITH THIS TYPE OF CONNECTOR (MAXIMUM RUN WITHOUT JOINT IS 40 FT.).

STRAP HANGERS ARE USED W/ METAL HALF-ROUND GUTTERS; NAIL OR SCREW TO ROOF SHEATHING OR THROUGH SHEATHING TO TOP OF RAFTER. UNCOMMON, ARCHAIC.

 C GUTTER HANGERS

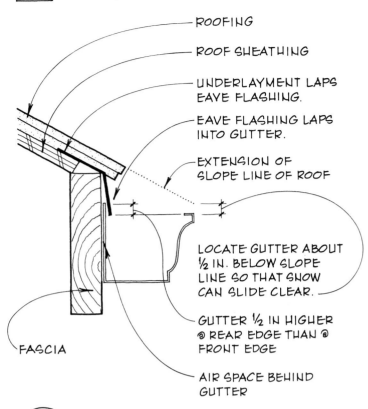

ROOFING

ROOF SHEATHING

UNDERLAYMENT LAPS EAVE FLASHING.

EAVE FLASHING LAPS INTO GUTTER.

EXTENSION OF SLOPE LINE OF ROOF

LOCATE GUTTER ABOUT ½ IN. BELOW SLOPE LINE SO THAT SNOW CAN SLIDE CLEAR.

GUTTER ½ IN HIGHER @ REAR EDGE THAN @ FRONT EDGE

AIR SPACE BEHIND GUTTER

FASCIA

NOTES:
FASCIA IS SHOWN PLUMB FOR EASE OF INSTALLATION OF COMMON GUTTERS. SQUARE-CUT RAFTER TAILS WORK WHERE THERE ARE NO GUTTERS OR WHERE HALF-ROUND GUTTERS ARE HUNG FROM STRAP HANGERS see 185C

FASCIA IS GENERALLY 2x MATERIAL FOR EASE OF INSTALLATION OF COMMON GUTTERS. GUTTERS MAY BE HUNG FROM 1x FASCIA, BUT SPIKES MUST BE LOCATED AT RAFTERS & FASCIA PREDRILLED TO PREVENT SPLITTING. BRACKETS SHOULD BE LOCATED NEAR RAFTERS.

(A) GUTTER/EAVE

Snow guards are metal protrusions that are integrated with the roofing to prevent snow from sliding off the roof. They are either clipped to the top edge of the roofing material (tiles and slate) or are nailed integral with it (shakes and shingles). Snow guards are used at the rate of 10 to 30 guards per square, depending on roof steepness.

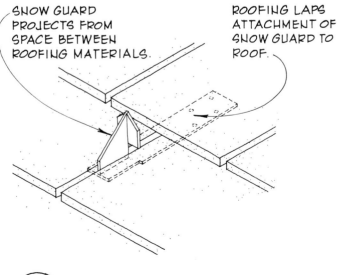

SNOW GUARD PROJECTS FROM SPACE BETWEEN ROOFING MATERIALS.

ROOFING LAPS ATTACHMENT OF SNOW GUARD TO ROOF.

(B) SNOW GUARDS

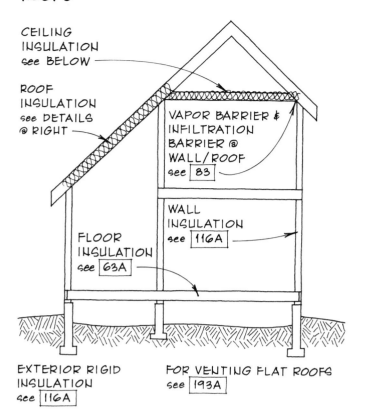

CEILING
INSULATION
see BELOW

ROOF
INSULATION
see DETAILS
@ RIGHT

VAPOR BARRIER &
INFILTRATION
BARRIER @
WALL/ROOF
see 83

WALL
INSULATION
see 116A

FLOOR
INSULATION
see 63A

EXTERIOR RIGID
INSULATION
see 116A

FOR VENTING FLAT ROOFS
see 193A

Most heat is potentially lost or gained through the roof, so ceilings and roofs are generally more heavily insulated than floors or walls. Building codes in most climates require R-30 in roofs. The temperature difference between the two sides of a roof or ceiling can cause condensation when warm, moist interior air hits cold surfaces in the roof assembly. It is therefore important to place a vapor barrier on the warm side of the insulation (see the drawing at right) and, in most cases, to ventilate the roof (see 188).

Ceiling insulation—Ceiling insulation consists typically of either fiberglass batts placed between ceiling joists before the ceiling is applied or loose-fill insulation blown (or poured) into place in the completed attic space. The loose-fill type has the advantage of filling tightly around trusses and other interruptions of the attic space and of being able to fill to any depth. With either type, the vapor barrier should be located on the warm side of the insulation.

When trusses or shallow rafters restrict the depth of insulation at the edges of the ceiling, ventilation channels may be needed (see 189A). Baffles may also be required to keep insulation from obstructing roof intake vents.

Roof insulation—Roof insulation may be fiberglass batts or rigid insulation. If the rafters are deep enough, batts are the most economical. When the rafters do not have adequate depth for batts, rigid insulation must be fit between the rafters. In both cases, a 1-in. air space must be provided above the insulation for ventilating the roof.

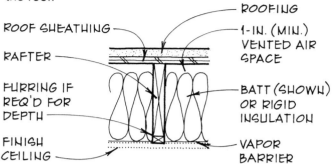

ROOF SHEATHING
RAFTER
FURRING IF REQ'D FOR DEPTH
FINISH CEILING
ROOFING
1-IN. (MIN.) VENTED AIR SPACE
BATT (SHOWN) OR RIGID INSULATION
VAPOR BARRIER

When the rafters are exposed to the living space below, the roof must be insulated from above. Rigid insulation is typically used because of its compactness and/or its structural value. Some roofing materials may be applied directly to the rigid insulation (e.g. membrane roofing on flat roofs); others will require additional structure and/or an air space for ventilation.

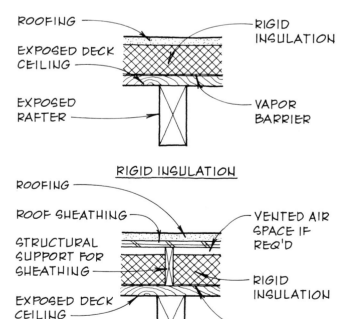

ROOFING
EXPOSED DECK CEILING
EXPOSED RAFTER
RIGID INSULATION
VAPOR BARRIER

RIGID INSULATION

ROOFING
ROOF SHEATHING
STRUCTURAL SUPPORT FOR SHEATHING
EXPOSED DECK CEILING
EXPOSED RAFTER
VENTED AIR SPACE IF REQ'D
RIGID INSULATION
VAPOR BARRIER

RIGID INSULATION W/ AIR SPACE & STRUCTURAL SUPPORT

 A CEILING & ROOF INSULATION

VENTING HIPS
see 130A

THROUGH-ROOF
VENTS see 189A

RIDGE VENTS
see 191C & D

GABLE VENTS
see 189A

FASCIA
VENTS
see 191B

VENTING AN
ABUTTING
ROOF
see 142C & D

SOFFIT VENTS
see 190B & C, 191A

FRIEZE VENTS
see 190A

Roofs and attics must be vented to prevent heat buildup in summer and to minimize condensation in winter. Condensation is reduced primarily by the installation of a vapor barrier (see 187). In addition, winter ventilation is necessary in cold climates to prevent escaping heat from melting snow that can re-freeze and cause structural or moisture damage.

The best way to ventilate a roof or attic is with both low (intake) and high (exhaust) vents, which together create convection currents. Codes recognize this by allowing the ventilation area to be cut in half if vents are placed both high and low. Most codes allow the net free ventilating area to be reduced from $1/150$ to $1/300$ of the area vented if half of the vents are 3 ft. above the eave line, with the other half at the eave line.

A special roof, called the cold roof, is designed to ventilate vaulted ceilings in extremely cold climates (see 192A).

Passive ventilation using convection will suffice for almost every winter venting need, but active ventilation is preferred in some areas for the warm season. Electric-powered fan ventilators improve summer cooling by moving more air through the attic space to remove the heat that has entered the attic space through the roof. The use of fans should be carefully coordinated with the intake and exhaust venting discussed in this section so that the flow of air through the attic is maximized.

Some roofing materials (e.g. shakes, shingles and tile), are self-venting if applied over open sheathing. These roof assemblies can provide significant ventilation directly through voids in the roof itself. Check with local building officials to verify the acceptance of this type of ventilation.

A ROOF & ATTIC VENTING

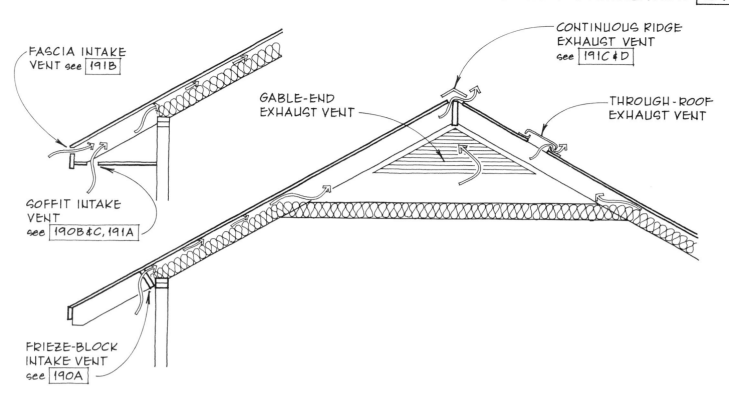

FASCIA INTAKE VENT see 191B

CONTINUOUS RIDGE EXHAUST VENT see 191C & D

GABLE-END EXHAUST VENT

THROUGH-ROOF EXHAUST VENT

SOFFIT INTAKE VENT see 190B & C, 191A

FRIEZE-BLOCK INTAKE VENT see 190A

Intake vents—Intake vents are commonly located either in a frieze block or in a soffit or fascia. They are usually screened to keep out birds and insects. The screening itself impedes the flow of air, so the vent area should be increased to allow for the screen (by a factor of 1.25 for ⅛-in. mesh screen, 2.0 for 1/16-in. screen). The net venting area of all intake vents together should equal about half the total area of vents.

Vent channels may be applied to the underside of the roof sheathing in locations where the free flow of air from intake vents may be restricted by insulation. The vent channels provide an air space by holding the insulation away from the sheathing. These channels should be used only for short distances, such as at the edge of an insulated ceiling.

Exhaust vents—If appropriately sized and balanced with intake vents, exhaust vents should remove excess moisture in winter. There are three types of exhaust vents: the continuous ridge vent, the gable-end vent and the through-roof exhaust vent.

The continuous ridge vent is best for preventing summer heat buildup because it is located highest on the roof and theoretically draws ventilation air evenly across the entire underside of the roof surface. Ridge vents can be awkward looking, but they can also be fairly unobtrusive if detailed carefully (see 191C & D). (Another type of ridge vent, the cupola, is also an effective ventilator, but is difficult to waterproof against wind-driven rain.)

The gable-end vent is a reasonably economical exhaust vent. Gable-end vents should be located across the attic space from one another. They are readily available in metal, vinyl or wood, and in round, rectangular or triangular shapes. Because the shape of gable-end vents can be visually dominant, they may be emphasized as a design feature of the building.

The through-roof exhaust vent is available as the "cake pan" type illustrated above or the larger rotating turbine type, available in many sizes. Through-roof vents are usually shingled into the roof and are useful for areas difficult to vent with a continuous ridge vent or a gable-end vent.

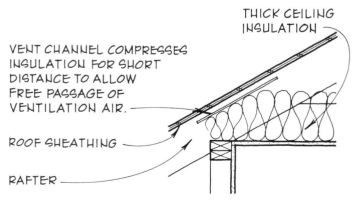

THICK CEILING INSULATION

VENT CHANNEL COMPRESSES INSULATION FOR SHORT DISTANCE TO ALLOW FREE PASSAGE OF VENTILATION AIR.

ROOF SHEATHING

RAFTER

A INTAKE & EXHAUST ROOF VENTS

NOTCH TOP OF FRIEZE BLOCK.

FOLD SCREEN & STAPLE TO BACK OF FRIEZE BLOCK.

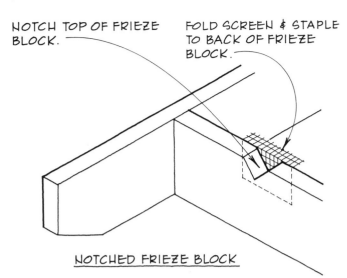

NOTCHED FRIEZE BLOCK

RIP FRIEZE BLOCK TO ALLOW CONTINUOUS VENT @ TOP.

FOLD SCREEN, PRESS UP TO SHEATHING & STAPLE TO BACK OF FRIEZE BLOCK.

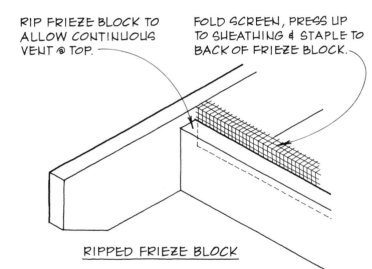

RIPPED FRIEZE BLOCK

BORE ROUND VENT HOLE(S) NEAR TOP OF FRIEZE BLOCK.

STAPLE SCREEN TO BACK OF FRIEZE BLOCK

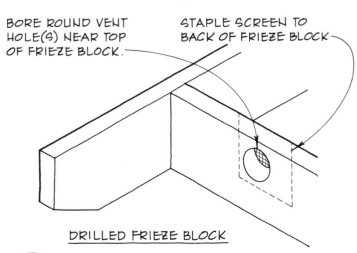

DRILLED FRIEZE BLOCK

A **FRIEZE-BLOCK INTAKE VENTS**
THREE TYPES

FASCIA

RAFTER TAIL OR TOP CHORD OF TRUSS

SOFFIT JOIST

SOFFIT

SOFFIT NAILING LEDGER

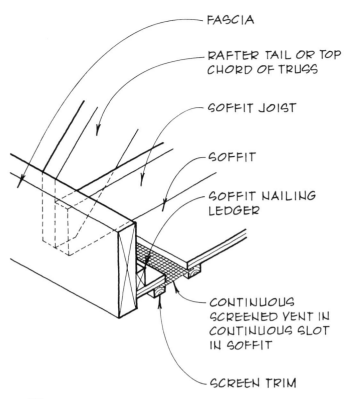

CONTINUOUS SCREENED VENT IN CONTINUOUS SLOT IN SOFFIT

SCREEN TRIM

B **SOFFIT INTAKE VENT**
SCREENED

FASCIA

RAFTER TAIL OR TOP CHORD OF TRUSS

SOFFIT JOIST

SOFFIT NAILING LEDGER

SOFFIT

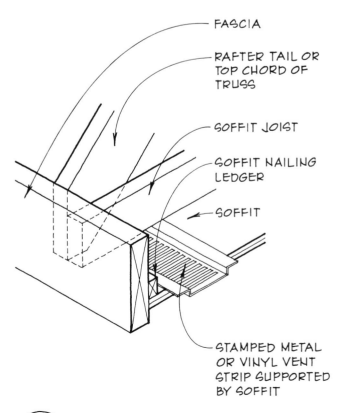

STAMPED METAL OR VINYL VENT STRIP SUPPORTED BY SOFFIT

C **SOFFIT INTAKE VENT**
STAMPED

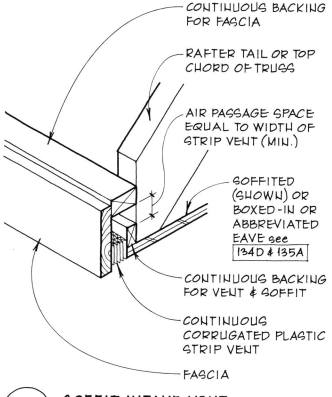

CONTINUOUS BACKING FOR FASCIA

RAFTER TAIL OR TOP CHORD OF TRUSS

AIR PASSAGE SPACE EQUAL TO WIDTH OF STRIP VENT (MIN.)

SOFFITED (SHOWN) OR BOXED-IN OR ABBREVIATED EAVE see
134D & 135A

CONTINUOUS BACKING FOR VENT & SOFFIT

CONTINUOUS CORRUGATED PLASTIC STRIP VENT

FASCIA

(A) SOFFIT INTAKE VENT
CORRUGATED STRIP

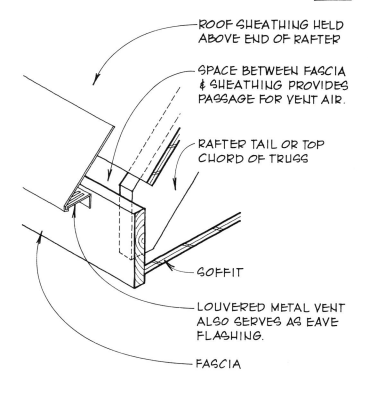

ROOF SHEATHING HELD ABOVE END OF RAFTER

SPACE BETWEEN FASCIA & SHEATHING PROVIDES PASSAGE FOR VENT AIR.

RAFTER TAIL OR TOP CHORD OF TRUSS

SOFFIT

LOUVERED METAL VENT ALSO SERVES AS EAVE FLASHING.

FASCIA

(B) FASCIA INTAKE VENT
STARTER

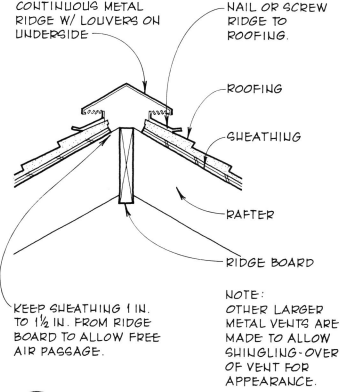

CONTINUOUS METAL RIDGE W/ LOUVERS ON UNDERSIDE

NAIL OR SCREW RIDGE TO ROOFING.

ROOFING

SHEATHING

RAFTER

RIDGE BOARD

KEEP SHEATHING 1 IN. TO 1½ IN. FROM RIDGE BOARD TO ALLOW FREE AIR PASSAGE.

NOTE:
OTHER LARGER METAL VENTS ARE MADE TO ALLOW SHINGLING-OVER OF VENT FOR APPEARANCE.

(C) RIDGE EXHAUST VENT
METAL

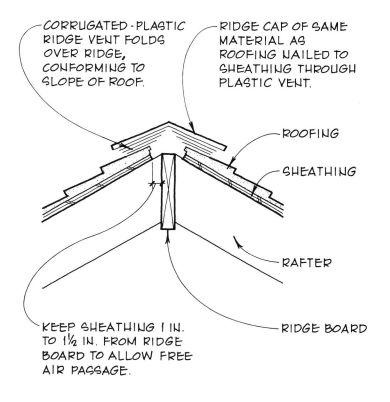

CORRUGATED-PLASTIC RIDGE VENT FOLDS OVER RIDGE, CONFORMING TO SLOPE OF ROOF.

RIDGE CAP OF SAME MATERIAL AS ROOFING NAILED TO SHEATHING THROUGH PLASTIC VENT.

ROOFING

SHEATHING

RAFTER

RIDGE BOARD

KEEP SHEATHING 1 IN. TO 1½ IN. FROM RIDGE BOARD TO ALLOW FREE AIR PASSAGE.

(D) RIDGE EXHAUST VENT
CORRUGATED PLASTIC

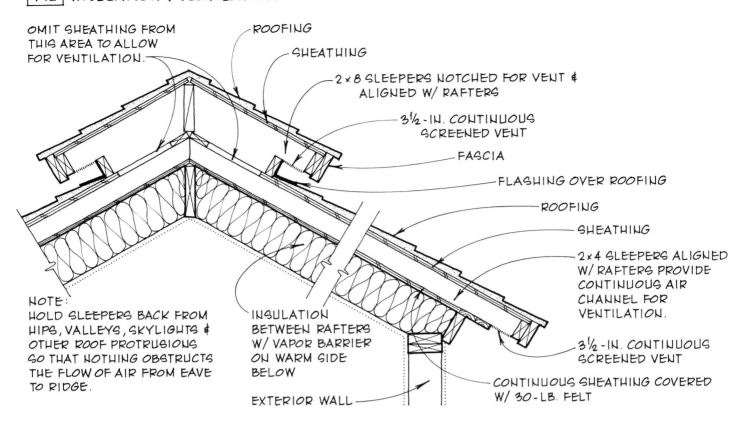

OMIT SHEATHING FROM THIS AREA TO ALLOW FOR VENTILATION.

ROOFING

SHEATHING

2 × 8 SLEEPERS NOTCHED FOR VENT & ALIGNED W/ RAFTERS

3½-IN. CONTINUOUS SCREENED VENT

FASCIA

FLASHING OVER ROOFING

ROOFING

SHEATHING

2 × 4 SLEEPERS ALIGNED W/ RAFTERS PROVIDE CONTINUOUS AIR CHANNEL FOR VENTILATION.

3½-IN. CONTINUOUS SCREENED VENT

CONTINUOUS SHEATHING COVERED W/ 30-LB. FELT

INSULATION BETWEEN RAFTERS W/ VAPOR BARRIER ON WARM SIDE BELOW

EXTERIOR WALL

NOTE:
HOLD SLEEPERS BACK FROM HIPS, VALLEYS, SKYLIGHTS & OTHER ROOF PROTRUSIONS SO THAT NOTHING OBSTRUCTS THE FLOW OF AIR FROM EAVE TO RIDGE.

The cold roof is a way to protect vaulted ceilings in cold climates from the formation of ice dams. A cold roof is a double-layer roof with the upper layer vented and the lower layer insulated. The vented layer promotes continuous unrestricted air flow from eave to ridge across the entire area of the roof. This flow of cold air removes any heat that escapes through the insulated layer below. The entire outer roof surface is thus maintained at the temperature of the ambient air, thereby preventing the freeze-thaw cycle caused by heat escaping through the insulation of conventional roofs.

The typical cold roof is built with sleepers aligned over rafters and with continuous eave vents and ridge vents (called a "Boston ridge"), as shown in the drawing above. A 3½-in. air space has been found to provide adequate ventilation, but a 1½-in. space does not. The sleepers must be held away from obstructions such as skylights, vents, hips and valleys to allow air to flow continuously around them.

A modified cold roof with extra deep rafters to provide deeper than normal ventilation space but without the double-layer ventilation system can work, but it does not provide protection against condensation, which can form above the insulation in the ventilation space.

 COLD ROOF

Flat roofs, like sloped roofs, require ventilation to prevent heat buildup and to minimize condensation. The principles of ventilation are the same for flat roofs as for sloped roofs, but flat roofs have some particular ventilation requirements due to their shape. On a flat roof, a low intake vent can rarely be balanced by a high exhaust vent (3 ft. min. above the intake vent). The net free ventilating area therefore cannot usually be reduced from $1/150$ of the area of the roof.

Flat-roof ventilators are commonly of the continuous strip type, located at a soffit, or a series of small vents scattered across the roof. Parapet walls can also provide effective ventilation for flat roofs (see 193B).

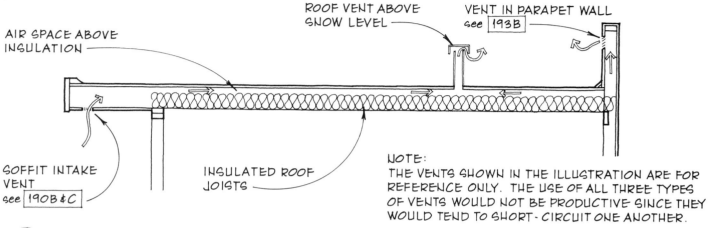

ROOF VENT ABOVE SNOW LEVEL

VENT IN PARAPET WALL
see 193B

AIR SPACE ABOVE INSULATION

SOFFIT INTAKE VENT
see 190B & C

INSULATED ROOF JOISTS

NOTE:
THE VENTS SHOWN IN THE ILLUSTRATION ARE FOR REFERENCE ONLY. THE USE OF ALL THREE TYPES OF VENTS WOULD NOT BE PRODUCTIVE SINCE THEY WOULD TEND TO SHORT-CIRCUIT ONE ANOTHER.

 A FLAT-ROOF VENTING

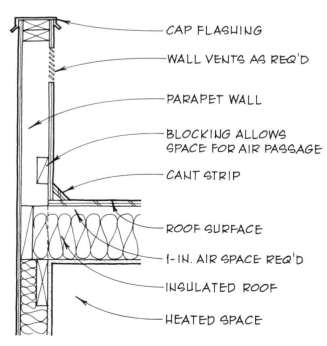

CAP FLASHING

WALL VENTS AS REQ'D

PARAPET WALL

BLOCKING ALLOWS SPACE FOR AIR PASSAGE

CANT STRIP

ROOF SURFACE

1-IN. AIR SPACE REQ'D

INSULATED ROOF

HEATED SPACE

NOTE:
IT MAY BE USEFUL TO BE ABLE TO VENT AN INSULATED ROOF (OR DECK) THROUGH A PARAPET WALL IN ORDER TO GET CROSS VENTILATION.

 B VENTED PARAPET WALL
2×4 OR 2×6 WALL

STAIRS

5

S tairs do not really support or protect a building in the same way as foundations, floors, walls and roofs but this book would be incomplete without them. Stairs are the vertical connectors of the parts of the building. Most buildings require a few steps just to enter the main floor, and stairs connect any internal levels. A well-designed and well-built staircase can contribute immeasurably to the function and beauty of a building.

STAIR DIMENSIONS

More than most other parts of a building, stairs need to be proportioned to the human body for safety. The height (rise) and depth (run) of the individual step must be in a comfortable relationship for the average person and must be manageable for people who are infirm or disabled. Building codes prescribe a range of dimensions for rise and run, a minimum width for stairways, the location of handrails, and minimum head clearance over stairs. The numbers vary depending on the location of the stair, the building type and the specific code; the typical requirements are outlined as follows:

Rise and run—Rise and run of stairs are governed by building codes, which may vary. Minimum unit rise is typically 4 in. and maximum is 7 in., except for residential stairs, which can have a unit rise of 8 in. For residential stairs, however, a comfortable rise is about 7 in. Minimum unit run is 11 in., except for residential stairs, which can have 9-in. treads.

Generally, wider treads have shallower risers. Here are two useful rules of thumb for the rise/run relationship:

rise + run = 17 in. to 18 in.
run + twice the rise = 24 in. to 26 in.

Both for safety and for code compliance, it is important to make each riser of a stair the same height. Most codes allow only ⅜-in. variance between the tallest and shortest riser in a flight of stairs. The maximum

total rise between floors or landings is typically 12 ft. Landings must be as deep as the width of the stairway but need not exceed 44 in. if the stair has a straight run.

Stair width—The width of stairways is also defined by building codes. Minimum width is usually 36 in., except for residential stairs, which may sometimes be as narrow as 30 in. Minimum widths are measured inside finished stairwells, so rough openings must allow for finished wall surfaces.

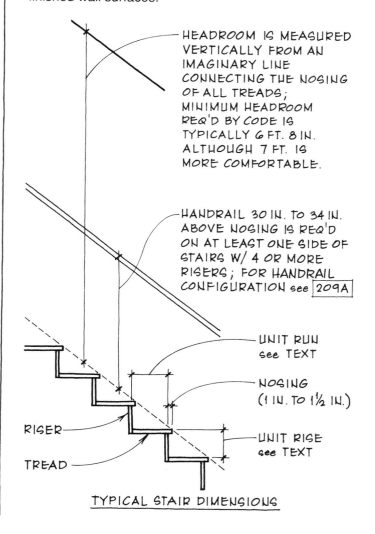

HEADROOM IS MEASURED VERTICALLY FROM AN IMAGINARY LINE CONNECTING THE NOSING OF ALL TREADS; MINIMUM HEADROOM REQ'D BY CODE IS TYPICALLY 6 FT. 8 IN. ALTHOUGH 7 FT. IS MORE COMFORTABLE.

HANDRAIL 30 IN. TO 34 IN. ABOVE NOSING IS REQ'D ON AT LEAST ONE SIDE OF STAIRS W/ 4 OR MORE RISERS; FOR HANDRAIL CONFIGURATION see 209A

UNIT RUN see TEXT

NOSING (1 IN. TO 1½ IN.)

UNIT RISE see TEXT

RISER

TREAD

TYPICAL STAIR DIMENSIONS

STAIR CONFIGURATION

The shape or configuration of a stairway is determined primarily by the circulation patterns of a building and by available space. Virtually any configuration of stairway may be constructed using the standard details of this chapter by merely breaking the stairway into smaller pieces and reassembling them. Several typical configurations that are worthy of note are shown in the drawings that follow; for clarity, these drawings do not show railings.

Straight-run stair—The straight-run stair is the most economical standard stairway from the standpoint of efficiency of floor space taken up by the stairway itself. The straight-run stair works best in two-story buildings.

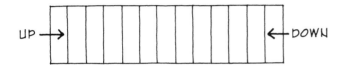

The bottom and top steps are separated horizontally from each other by the entire length of the stairway, so a multi-story building with stacked stairways requires circulation space on each floor to get from the top step of one flight to the bottom step of the next.

U-shaped stair—The U-shaped stair, also called a switchback stair, has a landing about half a flight up, and the flights run in opposite directions. The area of the stairway is increased over a straight-run stair by

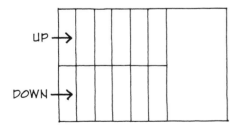

the area of the landing (less one step), but the top step of one flight is adjacent to the bottom step of the next. This arrangement saves circulation space at each floor level and makes this stair more efficient overall for multi-story buildings than the straight-run stair.

L-shaped stair—The L-shaped stair is not so common as the straight or U-shaped stair because it lacks the simplicity of the straight-run stair and the efficiency of the U-shaped stair. It can, however, be useful in tight

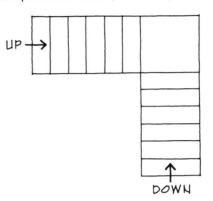

spots, as it takes up less floor space than a U-shaped stair and requires less length than a straight-run stair. The framing of the opening in the floor for this stairway can be atypical because of its L-shape. A framed wall under one side of the floor projecting into the L or a column under the floor at the bend in the L is the common way to support this floor.

Winder stairs at the bend in the L (or at the bend in a U-shaped stair) are common, but for reasons of safety, should not be allowed to be less than 6 in. deep at the narrow end (verify with local codes).

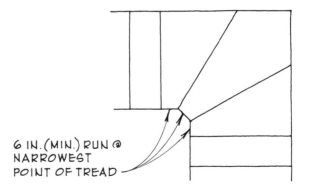

6 IN. (MIN.) RUN @ NARROWEST POINT OF TREAD

Spiral stair—A spiral stair saves space. It is most appropriate for accessing mezzanines and lofts where furniture and other large items may actually be hoisted from floor to floor by means other than the stairway. Spiral stairs usually have special code requirements that are somewhat less restrictive than standard stairs. They are usually prefabricated, often of metal or wood kits. Their details are idiosyncratic and not included in this book.

STRUCTURE

Stairs may be classified into two basic structural types: continuously supported and freestanding.

Continuously supported stairs—Continuously supported stairs are commonly used as interior stairs. Both sides of the stairway are supported by wall framing, so calculations of spanning capacities are not necessary. These stairs are site-built in some regions, but are predominantly prefabricated in others.

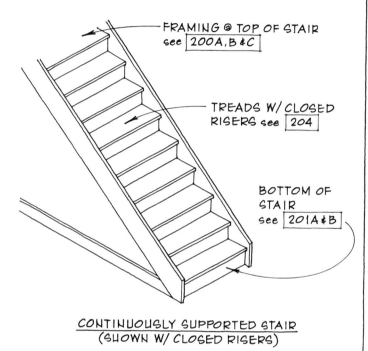

CONTINUOUSLY SUPPORTED STAIR
(SHOWN W/ CLOSED RISERS)

Freespanning stairs—Freespanning stairs have the structural capacity to span from the bottom stair to the top stair without intermediate support. The freespanning stair is commonly used as an exterior stair between floors or landing levels or in conjunction with porches and decks. It is often also seen as an access stair to basements and attics. The strength of a freespanning stair is usually in the carriages (stringers) that support the treads, although the handrail may also contribute to the strength of the stair. Freespanning stairs, like continuously supported stairs, may be site-built or prefabricated. Some freespanning stairs have only a single central support.

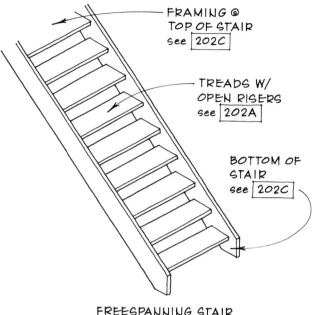

FREESPANNING STAIR
(SHOWN W/ OPEN RISERS)

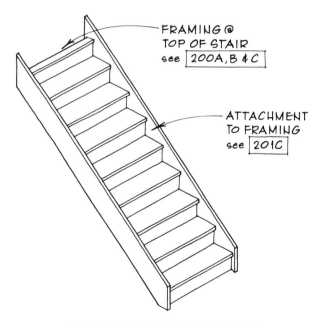

PREFABRICATED CUSTOM STAIR
(MAY BE FREESPANNING OR
CONTINUOUSLY SUPPORTED)

INTERIOR AND EXTERIOR STAIRS

The basic structure of the stair depends primarily on whether the stairway is to be located inside or outside and whether it is to be protected from the weather or not. The wood-stair details discussed in this chapter can be employed for either interior or exterior stairways, although the location will suggest basic detailing differences due to the fact that one is protected from the weather and the other isn't.

Interior stairs—Interior stairs are usually more refined than exterior stairs (because, like the rest of the building, interior stairs are more detailed). Interior stairways may be the showcase of a building and so are often located near the entry and used as a major circulation route. They may also provide the opportunity to connect more than one floor with natural light.

Exterior stairs—Exterior stairs (see 210) have the same minimum proportional requirements as interior stairs, but they are generally built less steep. The treads need to be deeper and risers shallower outdoors to make the stairs safer when wet or covered with snow or ice. Materials on exterior stairs must also be chosen with the weather in mind. Weather-resistant materials such as concrete, masonry and metal are sound choices for stairs exposed to the elements. Heavy timber or pressure-treated wood is often chosen for a wood stair out of doors. Special attention should be paid to non-skid surfaces for treads exposed to the weather.

Some exterior stairs are supported directly on the ground, in which case they are usually called steps (see 211-213). Ground-supported steps follow the contours of sloping sites to provide easy access to porches or entrances or as connections between terraces and other landscape elements.

ADDITIONAL DECISIONS

There are several other design decisions to make regarding both interior and exterior stairs. The primary decisions concern whether the risers are open (see 202A) or closed (see 204) and the design of the balustrade (see 206-208) and the handrail (see 209).

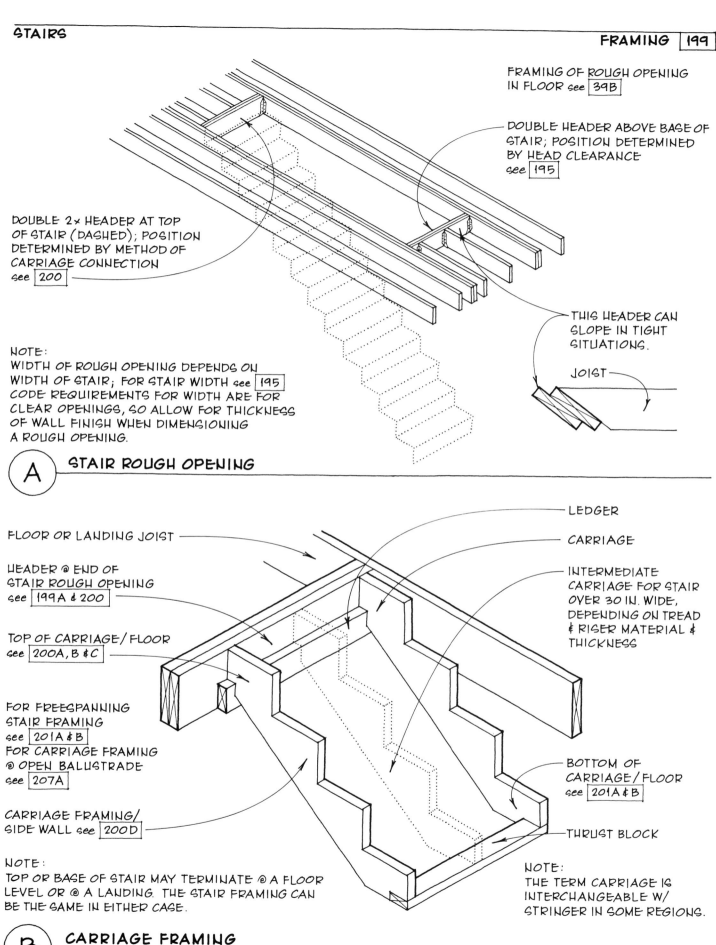

FRAMING OF ROUGH OPENING
IN FLOOR see 39B

DOUBLE HEADER ABOVE BASE OF
STAIR; POSITION DETERMINED
BY HEAD CLEARANCE
see 195

DOUBLE 2x HEADER AT TOP
OF STAIR (DASHED); POSITION
DETERMINED BY METHOD OF
CARRIAGE CONNECTION
see 200

THIS HEADER CAN
SLOPE IN TIGHT
SITUATIONS.

JOIST

NOTE:
WIDTH OF ROUGH OPENING DEPENDS ON
WIDTH OF STAIR; FOR STAIR WIDTH see 195
CODE REQUIREMENTS FOR WIDTH ARE FOR
CLEAR OPENINGS, SO ALLOW FOR THICKNESS
OF WALL FINISH WHEN DIMENSIONING
A ROUGH OPENING.

(A) STAIR ROUGH OPENING

LEDGER

CARRIAGE

FLOOR OR LANDING JOIST

HEADER @ END OF
STAIR ROUGH OPENING
see 199A & 200

INTERMEDIATE
CARRIAGE FOR STAIR
OVER 30 IN. WIDE,
DEPENDING ON TREAD
& RISER MATERIAL &
THICKNESS

TOP OF CARRIAGE/FLOOR
see 200A, B & C

FOR FREESPANNING
STAIR FRAMING
see 201A & B
FOR CARRIAGE FRAMING
@ OPEN BALUSTRADE
see 207A

BOTTOM OF
CARRIAGE/FLOOR
see 201A & B

THRUST BLOCK

CARRIAGE FRAMING/
SIDE WALL see 200D

NOTE:
TOP OR BASE OF STAIR MAY TERMINATE @ A FLOOR
LEVEL OR @ A LANDING. THE STAIR FRAMING CAN
BE THE SAME IN EITHER CASE.

NOTE:
THE TERM CARRIAGE IS
INTERCHANGEABLE W/
STRINGER IN SOME REGIONS.

(B) CARRIAGE FRAMING
CONTINUOUSLY SUPPORTED STAIR

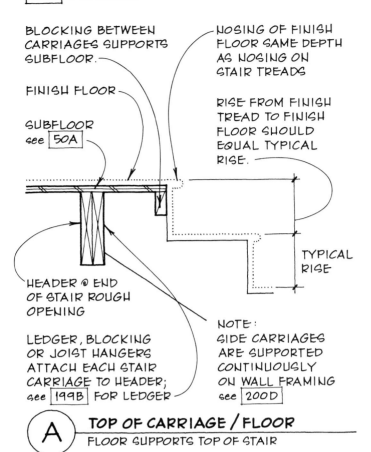

BLOCKING BETWEEN CARRIAGES SUPPORTS SUBFLOOR.

FINISH FLOOR

SUBFLOOR see |50A|

NOSING OF FINISH FLOOR SAME DEPTH AS NOSING ON STAIR TREADS

RISE FROM FINISH TREAD TO FINISH FLOOR SHOULD EQUAL TYPICAL RISE.

TYPICAL RISE

HEADER @ END OF STAIR ROUGH OPENING

LEDGER, BLOCKING OR JOIST HANGERS ATTACH EACH STAIR CARRIAGE TO HEADER; see |199B| FOR LEDGER

NOTE: SIDE CARRIAGES ARE SUPPORTED CONTINUOUSLY ON WALL FRAMING see |200D|

(A) TOP OF CARRIAGE / FLOOR
FLOOR SUPPORTS TOP OF STAIR

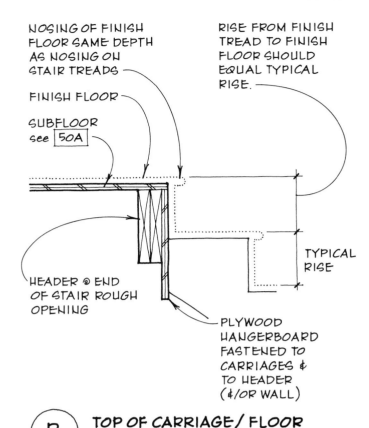

NOSING OF FINISH FLOOR SAME DEPTH AS NOSING ON STAIR TREADS

FINISH FLOOR

SUBFLOOR see |50A|

RISE FROM FINISH TREAD TO FINISH FLOOR SHOULD EQUAL TYPICAL RISE.

TYPICAL RISE

HEADER @ END OF STAIR ROUGH OPENING

PLYWOOD HANGERBOARD FASTENED TO CARRIAGES & TO HEADER (&/OR WALL)

(B) TOP OF CARRIAGE / FLOOR
HANGERBOARD SUPPORTS TOP OF STAIR

FINISH FLOOR

SUBFLOOR see |50A|

NOSING OF FINISH FLOOR SAME DEPTH AS NOSING ON STAIR TREADS

RISE FROM FINISH TREAD TO FINISH FLOOR SHOULD EQUAL TYPICAL RISE.

TYPICAL RISE

HEADER @ END OF STAIR ROUGH OPENING

LEDGER OR BLOCKING BETWEEN CARRIAGES ATTACH EACH STAIR CARRIAGE TO HEADER.

(C) TOP OF CARRIAGE / FLOOR
WALL SUPPORTS TOP OF STAIR

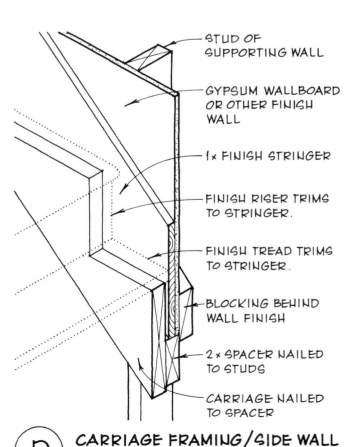

STUD OF SUPPORTING WALL

GYPSUM WALLBOARD OR OTHER FINISH WALL

1x FINISH STRINGER

FINISH RISER TRIMS TO STRINGER.

FINISH TREAD TRIMS TO STRINGER.

BLOCKING BEHIND WALL FINISH

2 x SPACER NAILED TO STUDS

CARRIAGE NAILED TO SPACER

(D) CARRIAGE FRAMING / SIDE WALL
CONTINUOUSLY SUPPORTED STAIR

2× THRUST BLOCK
NAILED TO SUBFLOOR
& NOTCHED INTO
CARRIAGES

RISE FROM FINISH
FLOOR TO FIRST TREAD
EQUALS TYPICAL RISE.

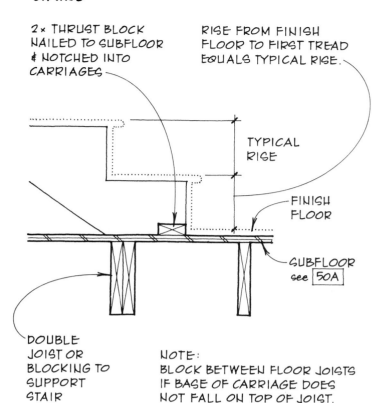

TYPICAL
RISE

FINISH
FLOOR

SUBFLOOR
see | 50A |

DOUBLE
JOIST OR
BLOCKING TO
SUPPORT
STAIR

NOTE:
BLOCK BETWEEN FLOOR JOISTS
IF BASE OF CARRIAGE DOES
NOT FALL ON TOP OF JOIST.

(A) **BOTTOM OF CARRIAGE / FLOOR**
     SINGLE FLIGHT

NOTE:
SIDE CARRIAGES MAY
BE HUNG FROM
HEADER OR ATTACHED
TO WALL FRAMING.

RISE FROM FINISH
FLOOR TO FIRST TREAD
EQUALS TYPICAL RISE.

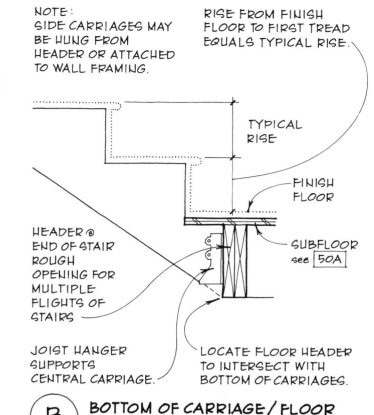

TYPICAL
RISE

FINISH
FLOOR

HEADER @
END OF STAIR
ROUGH
OPENING FOR
MULTIPLE
FLIGHTS OF
STAIRS

SUBFLOOR
see | 50A |

JOIST HANGER
SUPPORTS
CENTRAL CARRIAGE.

LOCATE FLOOR HEADER
TO INTERSECT WITH
BOTTOM OF CARRIAGES.

(B) **BOTTOM OF CARRIAGE / FLOOR**
     INTERMEDIATE FLIGHT

EXTEND
HOUSED
STRINGER
see | 205B |
TO MEET
BASE
MOLDING.

TOP NOSING OF
PREFABRICATED
STAIR TYPICALLY
HAS RABBET ON
UNDERSIDE TO
ADJUST
THICKNESS TO
THAT OF FINISH
FLOOR.

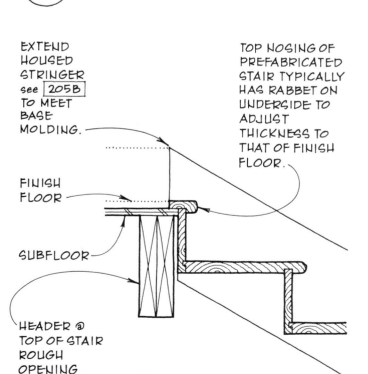

FINISH
FLOOR

SUBFLOOR

HEADER @
TOP OF STAIR
ROUGH
OPENING

SECTION @
TOP OF STAIR

NOTES:
ALIGN TOP NOSING FLUSH W/ FINISH FLOOR OR
ALIGN TOP NOSING FLUSH W/ SUBFLOOR FOR WALL-
TO-WALL CARPETING; BOTTOM RISER BEARS ON
SUBFLOOR.

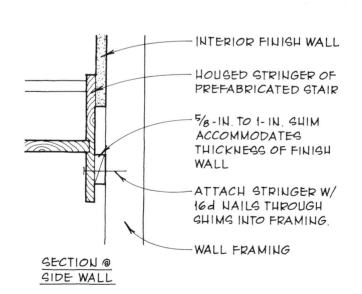

INTERIOR FINISH WALL

HOUSED STRINGER OF
PREFABRICATED STAIR

⅝-IN. TO 1-IN. SHIM
ACCOMMODATES
THICKNESS OF FINISH
WALL

ATTACH STRINGER W/
16d NAILS THROUGH
SHIMS INTO FRAMING.

WALL FRAMING

SECTION @
SIDE WALL

(C) **PREFABRICATED STAIR**

NOTE:
TREADS FOR OPEN-RISER
STAIRS MUST BE ABLE TO SPAN
FULL WIDTH OF STAIRWAY.

ATTACHMENT OF TREADS
TO CARRIAGE MAY BE WITH:

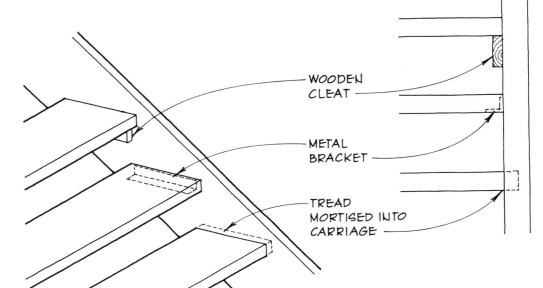

WOODEN CLEATS
SCREWED TO
STRUCTURAL CARRIAGE;

OR

METAL BRACKET LET INTO
END OF TREAD SO THAT
BRACKET IS CONCEALED
FROM ABOVE (& DOES NOT
PROJECT BELOW);

OR

MORTISED TREAD, WHICH
PROVIDES CONCEALED
CONNECTION FOR
APPEARANCE; SCREW
TREADS THROUGH
CARRIAGE OR GLUE &
TOENAIL FROM
UNDERSIDE INTO
CARRIAGE.

WOODEN
CLEAT

METAL
BRACKET

TREAD
MORTISED INTO
CARRIAGE

ELEVATION

(A) TREADS W/ OPEN RISERS

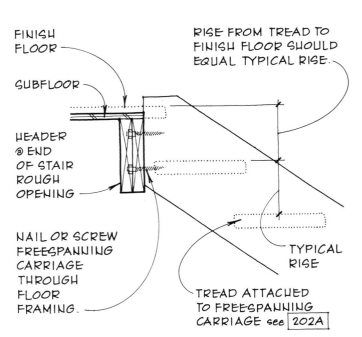

FINISH
FLOOR

SUBFLOOR

RISE FROM TREAD TO
FINISH FLOOR SHOULD
EQUAL TYPICAL RISE.

HEADER
@ END
OF STAIR
ROUGH
OPENING

NAIL OR SCREW
FREESPANNING
CARRIAGE
THROUGH
FLOOR
FRAMING.

TYPICAL
RISE

TREAD ATTACHED
TO FREESPANNING
CARRIAGE see | 202A |

NOTE:
A FREESTANDING CARRIAGE LEFT EXPOSED
REQUIRES A CONCEALED OR CLEAN BOLTED
CONNECTION TO THE FLOOR (OR LANDING)
@ THE TOP & BOTTOM OF THE CARRIAGE.

(B) TOP OF CARRIAGE/FLOOR
FREESPANNING STAIR

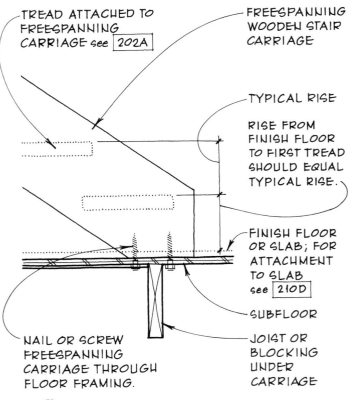

TREAD ATTACHED TO
FREESPANNING
CARRIAGE see | 202A |

FREESPANNING
WOODEN STAIR
CARRIAGE

TYPICAL RISE

RISE FROM
FINISH FLOOR
TO FIRST TREAD
SHOULD EQUAL
TYPICAL RISE.

FINISH FLOOR
OR SLAB; FOR
ATTACHMENT
TO SLAB
see | 210D |

SUBFLOOR

JOIST OR
BLOCKING
UNDER
CARRIAGE

NAIL OR SCREW
FREESPANNING
CARRIAGE THROUGH
FLOOR FRAMING.

(C) BOTTOM OF CARRIAGE/FLOOR
FREESPANNING STAIR

Finish landings must be at least as deep as the
stairway is wide (automatic in the case
of an L-shaped stair). Set the landing
height so that the finish-floor level
corresponds to the rise of
the stair.

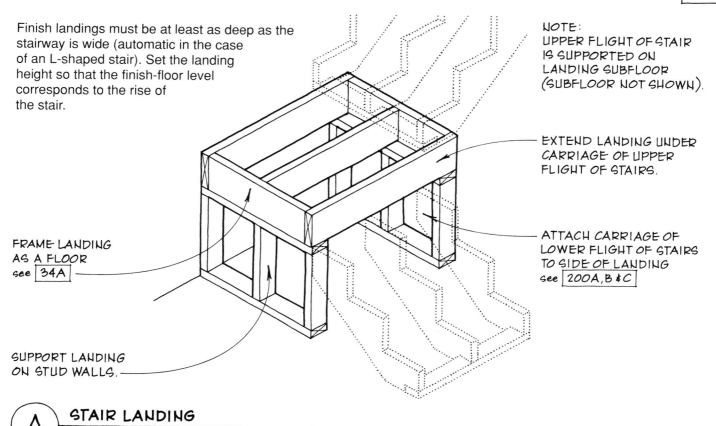

NOTE:
UPPER FLIGHT OF STAIR
IS SUPPORTED ON
LANDING SUBFLOOR
(SUBFLOOR NOT SHOWN).

EXTEND LANDING UNDER
CARRIAGE OF UPPER
FLIGHT OF STAIRS.

ATTACH CARRIAGE OF
LOWER FLIGHT OF STAIRS
TO SIDE OF LANDING
see 200A, B & C

FRAME LANDING
AS A FLOOR
see 34A

SUPPORT LANDING
ON STUD WALLS.

(A) STAIR LANDING

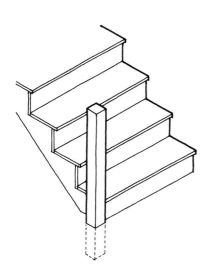

STAIRS

NEWEL POST
(OR 4×4 POST @
BASE OF CLOSED
RAILING)

LAG OR BOLT NEWEL
TO STAIR CARRIAGE;
PLACE BOLT AS HIGH
AS PRACTICAL.

FINISH FLOOR

LAG OR BOLT
NEWEL TO
BLOCKING
BETWEEN FLOOR
JOISTS; PLACE ONE
BOLT AS LOW AS
POSSIBLE.

FLOOR-JOIST
SYSTEM

IF THE FIRST FLOOR
IS A SLAB, BOLT A
METAL POST
ANCHOR TO THE
SLAB & PASS THE
NEWEL THROUGH
THE FIRST TREAD TO
THE POST ANCHOR.

The newel post must be firmly
anchored to resist the force of a
person swinging around it. The
most effective way to anchor the
newel (or the framing of a closed rail)
is to pass it through the subfloor and bolt
or lag it to the floor framing. For balustrades
and handrails, see 206-209.

(B) NEWEL-POST FRAMING

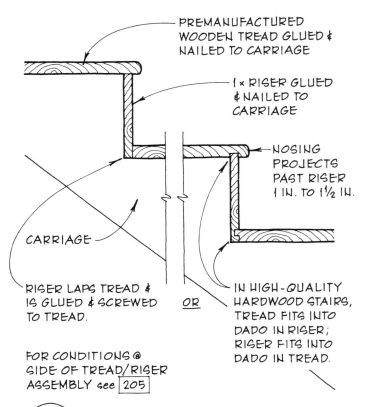

PREMANUFACTURED WOODEN TREAD GLUED & NAILED TO CARRIAGE

1 × RISER GLUED & NAILED TO CARRIAGE

NOSING PROJECTS PAST RISER 1 IN. TO 1½ IN.

CARRIAGE

RISER LAPS TREAD & IS GLUED & SCREWED TO TREAD.

IN HIGH-QUALITY HARDWOOD STAIRS, TREAD FITS INTO DADO IN RISER; RISER FITS INTO DADO IN TREAD.

FOR CONDITIONS @ SIDE OF TREAD/RISER ASSEMBLY see 205

A **EXPOSED FINISH TREAD & RISER**
2 ALTERNATIVES W/ NO SUB-TREAD

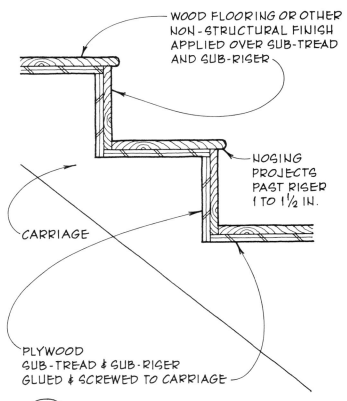

WOOD FLOORING OR OTHER NON-STRUCTURAL FINISH APPLIED OVER SUB-TREAD AND SUB-RISER

NOSING PROJECTS PAST RISER 1 TO 1½ IN.

CARRIAGE

PLYWOOD SUB-TREAD & SUB-RISER GLUED & SCREWED TO CARRIAGE

B **EXPOSED FINISH TREAD & RISER**
W/ SUB-TREAD

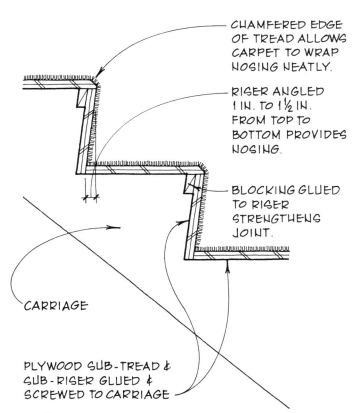

CHAMFERED EDGE OF TREAD ALLOWS CARPET TO WRAP NOSING NEATLY.

RISER ANGLED 1 IN. TO 1½ IN. FROM TOP TO BOTTOM PROVIDES NOSING.

BLOCKING GLUED TO RISER STRENGTHENS JOINT.

CARRIAGE

PLYWOOD SUB-TREAD & SUB-RISER GLUED & SCREWED TO CARRIAGE

C **CARPETED TREAD & RISER**

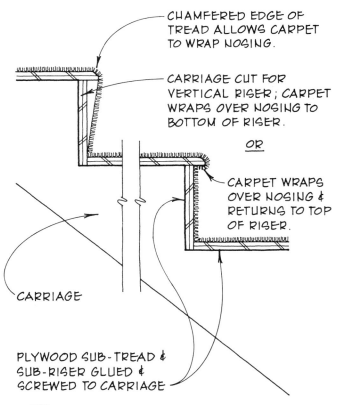

CHAMFERED EDGE OF TREAD ALLOWS CARPET TO WRAP NOSING.

CARRIAGE CUT FOR VERTICAL RISER; CARPET WRAPS OVER NOSING TO BOTTOM OF RISER.

OR

CARPET WRAPS OVER NOSING & RETURNS TO TOP OF RISER.

CARRIAGE

PLYWOOD SUB-TREAD & SUB-RISER GLUED & SCREWED TO CARRIAGE

D **CARPETED TREAD & RISER**
2 ALTERNATIVES

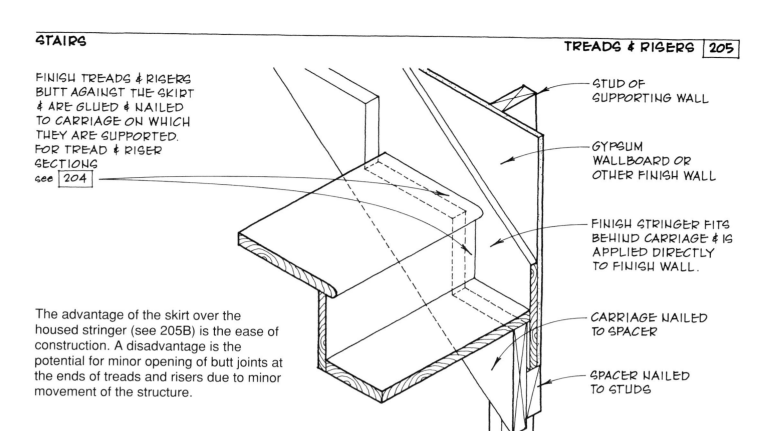

FINISH TREADS & RISERS
BUTT AGAINST THE SKIRT
& ARE GLUED & NAILED
TO CARRIAGE ON WHICH
THEY ARE SUPPORTED.
FOR TREAD & RISER
SECTIONS
see | 204 |

STUD OF
SUPPORTING WALL

GYPSUM
WALLBOARD OR
OTHER FINISH WALL

FINISH STRINGER FITS
BEHIND CARRIAGE & IS
APPLIED DIRECTLY
TO FINISH WALL.

CARRIAGE NAILED
TO SPACER

SPACER NAILED
TO STUDS

The advantage of the skirt over the
housed stringer (see 205B) is the ease of
construction. A disadvantage is the
potential for minor opening of butt joints at
the ends of treads and risers due to minor
movement of the structure.

A) FINISH STRINGER (SKIRT) @ FINISH WALL

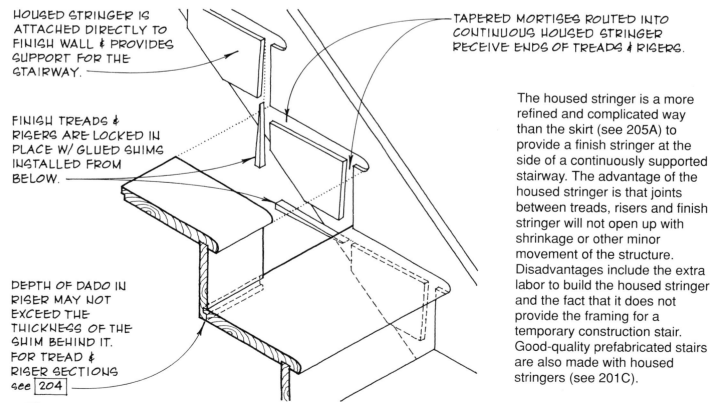

HOUSED STRINGER IS
ATTACHED DIRECTLY TO
FINISH WALL & PROVIDES
SUPPORT FOR THE
STAIRWAY.

TAPERED MORTISES ROUTED INTO
CONTINUOUS HOUSED STRINGER
RECEIVE ENDS OF TREADS & RISERS.

FINISH TREADS &
RISERS ARE LOCKED IN
PLACE W/ GLUED SHIMS
INSTALLED FROM
BELOW.

DEPTH OF DADO IN
RISER MAY NOT
EXCEED THE
THICKNESS OF THE
SHIM BEHIND IT.
FOR TREAD &
RISER SECTIONS
see | 204 |

The housed stringer is a more
refined and complicated way
than the skirt (see 205A) to
provide a finish stringer at the
side of a continuously supported
stairway. The advantage of the
housed stringer is that joints
between treads, risers and finish
stringer will not open up with
shrinkage or other minor
movement of the structure.
Disadvantages include the extra
labor to build the housed stringer
and the fact that it does not
provide the framing for a
temporary construction stair.
Good-quality prefabricated stairs
are also made with housed
stringers (see 201C).

B) HOUSED STRINGER @ FINISH WALL

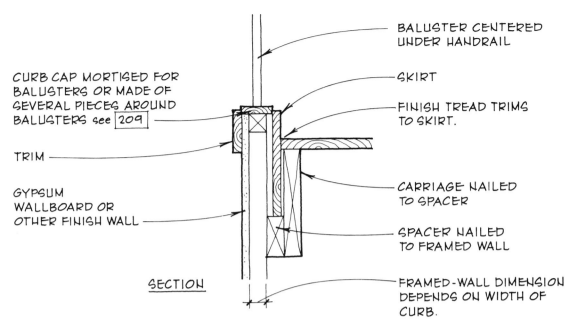

CURB CAP MORTISED FOR BALUSTERS OR MADE OF SEVERAL PIECES AROUND BALUSTERS see | 209 |

TRIM

GYPSUM WALLBOARD OR OTHER FINISH WALL

BALUSTER CENTERED UNDER HANDRAIL

SKIRT

FINISH TREAD TRIMS TO SKIRT.

CARRIAGE NAILED TO SPACER

SPACER NAILED TO FRAMED WALL

FRAMED-WALL DIMENSION DEPENDS ON WIDTH OF CURB.

SECTION

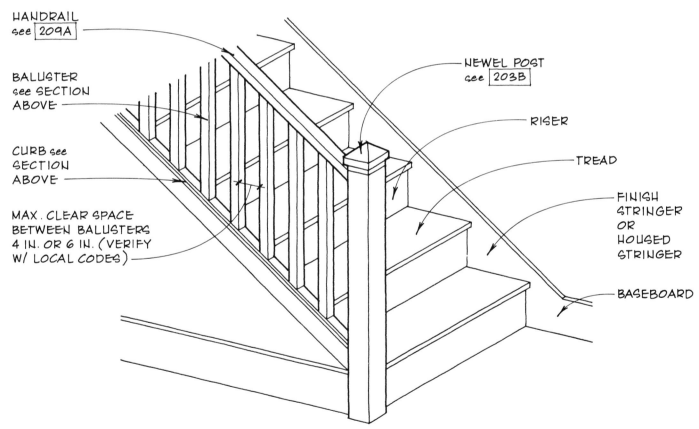

HANDRAIL see | 209A |

BALUSTER see SECTION ABOVE

CURB see SECTION ABOVE

MAX. CLEAR SPACE BETWEEN BALUSTERS 4 IN. OR 6 IN. (VERIFY W/ LOCAL CODES)

NEWEL POST see | 203B |

RISER

TREAD

FINISH STRINGER OR HOUSED STRINGER

BASEBOARD

In an open balustrade with a curb, the treads and risers are constructed on carriages and finished on both sides with a skirt, just as if the stairway were constructed between two walls. The skirt on the open side of the stairway forms one side of the curb. This simple construction has a similar aesthetic effect as the more technically difficult open balustrade without a curb (see 207).

OPEN BALUSTRADE
W/ CURB

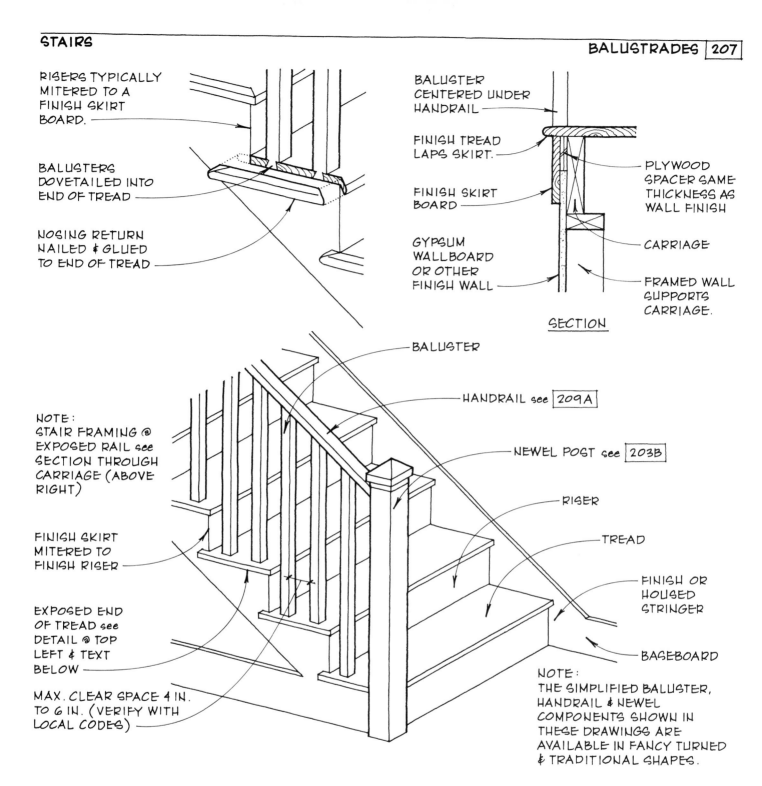

RISERS TYPICALLY MITERED TO A FINISH SKIRT BOARD.

BALUSTERS DOVETAILED INTO END OF TREAD

NOSING RETURN NAILED & GLUED TO END OF TREAD

BALUSTER CENTERED UNDER HANDRAIL

FINISH TREAD LAPS SKIRT.

FINISH SKIRT BOARD

GYPSUM WALLBOARD OR OTHER FINISH WALL

PLYWOOD SPACER SAME THICKNESS AS WALL FINISH

CARRIAGE

FRAMED WALL SUPPORTS CARRIAGE.

SECTION

BALUSTER

HANDRAIL see 209A

NEWEL POST see 203B

RISER

TREAD

FINISH OR HOUSED STRINGER

BASEBOARD

NOTE:
STAIR FRAMING @ EXPOSED RAIL see SECTION THROUGH CARRIAGE (ABOVE RIGHT)

FINISH SKIRT MITERED TO FINISH RISER

EXPOSED END OF TREAD see DETAIL @ TOP LEFT & TEXT BELOW

MAX. CLEAR SPACE 4 IN. TO 6 IN. (VERIFY WITH LOCAL CODES)

NOTE:
THE SIMPLIFIED BALUSTER, HANDRAIL & NEWEL COMPONENTS SHOWN IN THESE DRAWINGS ARE AVAILABLE IN FANCY TURNED & TRADITIONAL SHAPES.

In this traditional treatment of the open balustrade, the balusters rest on the treads, and the ends of the treads are exposed and finished. The balusters may be attached to the treads in four ways: toenailing, doweling, mortising or sliding dovetail (see the detail at top left). The exposed ends of the treads may be finished in one of the following two ways. The treads may be cantilevered and rounded or chamfered like the nose of the tread (this will expose end grain). Alternatively, the treads may be capped with a finish piece called a nosing return, which is mitered at the corner and matches the profile of the nosing (see the detail at top left). This is the most refined finish treatment and is usually used in conjunction with mortised or sliding dovetail balusters.

(A) OPEN BALUSTRADE
WITHOUT CURB

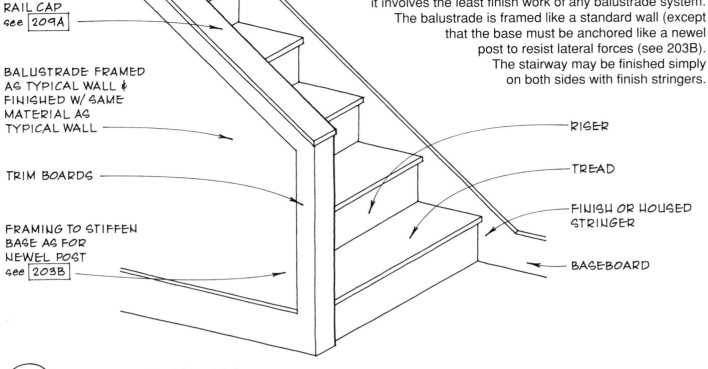

RAIL CAP
see 209A

BALUSTRADE FRAMED
AS TYPICAL WALL &
FINISHED W/ SAME
MATERIAL AS
TYPICAL WALL

TRIM BOARDS

FRAMING TO STIFFEN
BASE AS FOR
NEWEL POST
see 203B

The closed balustrade is very economical to build because it involves the least finish work of any balustrade system. The balustrade is framed like a standard wall (except that the base must be anchored like a newel post to resist lateral forces (see 203B). The stairway may be finished simply on both sides with finish stringers.

RISER

TREAD

FINISH OR HOUSED
STRINGER

BASEBOARD

A CLOSED BALUSTRADE

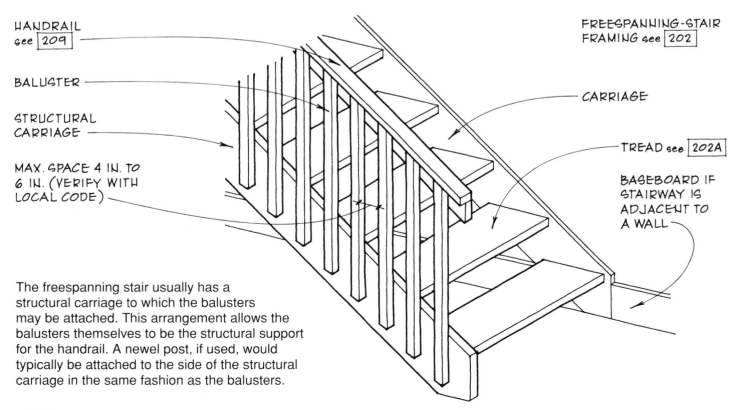

HANDRAIL
see 209

BALUSTER

STRUCTURAL
CARRIAGE

MAX. SPACE 4 IN. TO
6 IN. (VERIFY WITH
LOCAL CODE)

FREESPANNING-STAIR
FRAMING see 202

CARRIAGE

TREAD see 202A

BASEBOARD IF
STAIRWAY IS
ADJACENT TO
A WALL

The freespanning stair usually has a structural carriage to which the balusters may be attached. This arrangement allows the balusters themselves to be the structural support for the handrail. A newel post, if used, would typically be attached to the side of the structural carriage in the same fashion as the balusters.

B FREESPANNING - STAIR BALUSTRADE

Handrails provide stability and security for the young, the old, the blind and the infirm. In addition, handrails are a safety feature for anyone who uses a stairway — one of the most likely and dangerous places for people to trip and fall.

In terms of safety, the most important design feature of a handrail is its ability to be grasped, especially in an emergency. The 1½-in. to 2-in. round rail is the most effective in this regard, as it allows the thumb and fingers to curl around and under the rail. Other shapes are allowable by code, but are less graspable.

The height of the handrail is usually specified by code. Most codes fall within the range of 29 in. to 36 in. above the nosing of the stairs. If the handrail is against a wall, a 1½-in. space is required between the handrail and the wall.

The tops and bottoms of handrails should be designed so as to avoid snagging clothing. For this reason, many codes require returning handrails to the wall at both top and bottom.

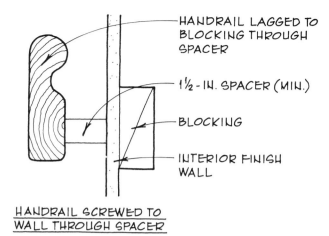

HANDRAIL LAGGED TO BLOCKING THROUGH SPACER

1½-IN. SPACER (MIN.)

BLOCKING

INTERIOR FINISH WALL

HANDRAIL SCREWED TO WALL THROUGH SPACER

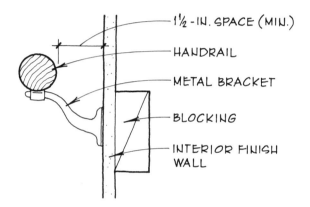

1½-IN. SPACE (MIN.)

HANDRAIL

METAL BRACKET

BLOCKING

INTERIOR FINISH WALL

HANDRAIL ATTACHED TO WALL W/ METAL BRACKETS

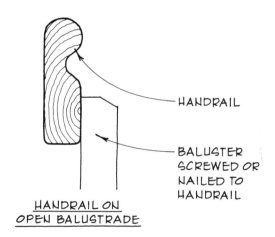

HANDRAIL

BALUSTER SCREWED OR NAILED TO HANDRAIL

HANDRAIL ON OPEN BALUSTRADE

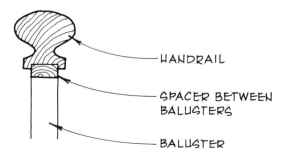

HANDRAIL

SPACER BETWEEN BALUSTERS

BALUSTER

TRADITIONAL HANDRAIL ON OPEN BALUSTRADE

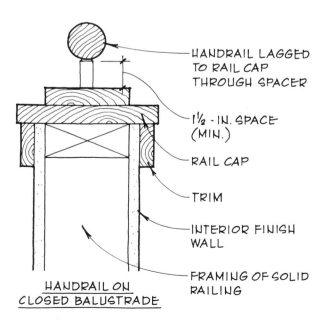

HANDRAIL LAGGED TO RAIL CAP THROUGH SPACER

1½-IN. SPACE (MIN.)

RAIL CAP

TRIM

INTERIOR FINISH WALL

FRAMING OF SOLID RAILING

HANDRAIL ON CLOSED BALUSTRADE

A   HANDRAILS

Exterior wood stairs should be built of weather-resistant species such as cedar or redwood or of pressure-treated lumber. Simple connections that minimize joints between boards are less likely to retain moisture. Where joints must occur, it is best to minimize the area of contact between pieces so that moisture will drain and the lumber can breathe.

Most exterior wooden stairs are freespanning. For long runs of stairs, the continuous unnotched carriage is usually required for strength (see 210B). Short runs of stairs may be strong enough with a notched carriage (see 210C), as, of course, are wooden stairs built between two parallel concrete or masonry walls.

Open risers are often employed in exterior wooden stairs, but solid risers, common on traditional porches, are useful to stiffen the treads. For wood porches, see 62.

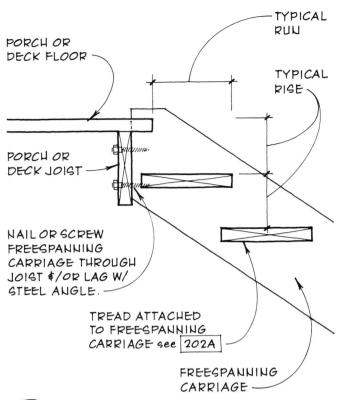

PORCH OR DECK FLOOR

PORCH OR DECK JOIST

TYPICAL RUN

TYPICAL RISE

NAIL OR SCREW FREESPANNING CARRIAGE THROUGH JOIST &/OR LAG W/ STEEL ANGLE.

TREAD ATTACHED TO FREESPANNING CARRIAGE see 202A

FREESPANNING CARRIAGE

A | **EXTERIOR WOOD STAIRS**
INTRODUCTION

B | **EXTERIOR WOOD STAIRS**
UNNOTCHED CARRIAGE / WOOD PORCH

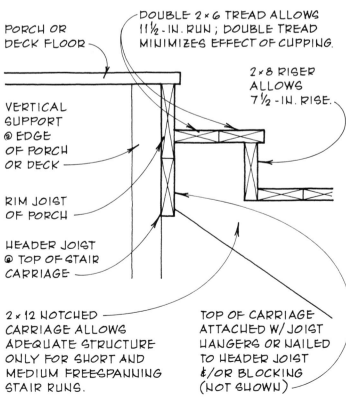

PORCH OR DECK FLOOR

DOUBLE 2×6 TREAD ALLOWS 11½-IN. RUN; DOUBLE TREAD MINIMIZES EFFECT OF CUPPING.

2×8 RISER ALLOWS 7½-IN. RISE.

VERTICAL SUPPORT @ EDGE OF PORCH OR DECK

RIM JOIST OF PORCH

HEADER JOIST @ TOP OF STAIR CARRIAGE

2×12 NOTCHED CARRIAGE ALLOWS ADEQUATE STRUCTURE ONLY FOR SHORT AND MEDIUM FREESPANNING STAIR RUNS.

TOP OF CARRIAGE ATTACHED W/ JOIST HANGERS OR NAILED TO HEADER JOIST &/OR BLOCKING (NOT SHOWN)

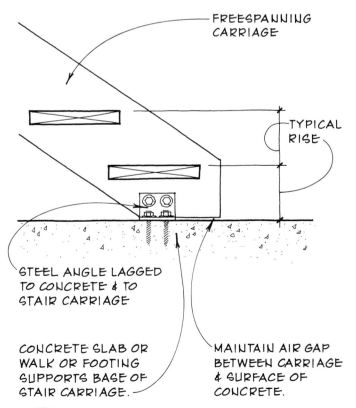

FREESPANNING CARRIAGE

TYPICAL RISE

STEEL ANGLE LAGGED TO CONCRETE & TO STAIR CARRIAGE

CONCRETE SLAB OR WALK OR FOOTING SUPPORTS BASE OF STAIR CARRIAGE.

MAINTAIN AIR GAP BETWEEN CARRIAGE & SURFACE OF CONCRETE.

C | **EXTERIOR WOOD STAIRS**
NOTCHED CARRIAGE / WOOD PORCH

D | **EXTERIOR WOOD STAIRS**
FREESPANNING CARRIAGE @ GROUND

Dry-set brick steps are supported on a bed of compacted gravel on the ground and are laid dry without concrete or mortar. The bricks must be contained at the edges or they will separate. A 2x decay-resistant header used as a riser will contain the bricks at each step.

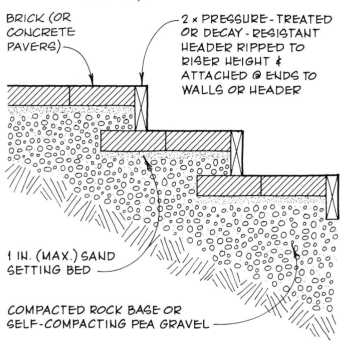

BRICK (OR CONCRETE PAVERS)

2 × PRESSURE-TREATED OR DECAY-RESISTANT HEADER RIPPED TO RISER HEIGHT & ATTACHED @ ENDS TO WALLS OR HEADER

1 IN. (MAX.) SAND SETTING BED

COMPACTED ROCK BASE OR SELF-COMPACTING PEA GRAVEL

The sides of the steps may be contained with 2x headers the same height as the riser, as shown below. These side headers may be staked to the ground so that they contain the step at the sides on their own.

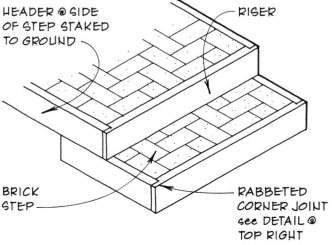

HEADER @ SIDE OF STEP STAKED TO GROUND

RISER

BRICK STEP

RABBETED CORNER JOINT see DETAIL @ TOP RIGHT

DRY-SET EXTERIOR STEPS
BRICK

The rabbeted riser/side-header joint is nailed from two directions to lock the joint together.

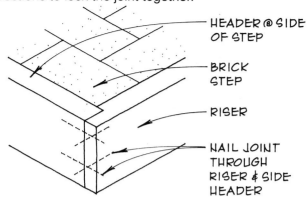

HEADER @ SIDE OF STEP

BRICK STEP

RISER

NAIL JOINT THROUGH RISER & SIDE HEADER

The sides of the brick steps may also be contained between two masonry or concrete walls.

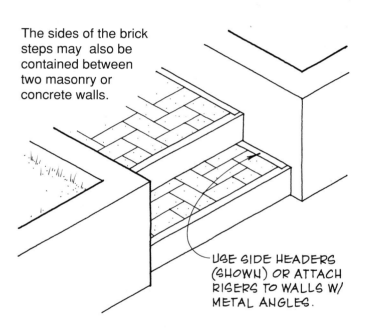

USE SIDE HEADERS (SHOWN) OR ATTACH RISERS TO WALLS W/ METAL ANGLES.

A third alternative is to contain the sides of the steps with decay-resistant stringers at the slope of the steps. The risers may be attached directly to the stringers.

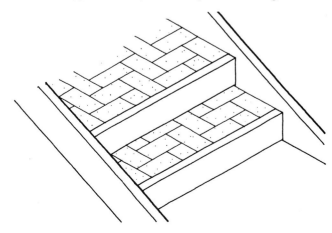

Dry-set concrete paver steps, like dry-set brick steps, are supported on a bed of compacted gravel on the ground and are laid dry without concrete or mortar. Because of their size, large pavers like the ones shown here are more stable than bricks. For this reason, paver stairs may be constructed without containment at the riser; some paver stairs are even constructed without containment at the sides.

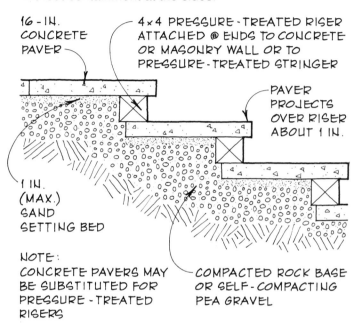

16 - IN. CONCRETE PAVER

4×4 PRESSURE - TREATED RISER ATTACHED @ ENDS TO CONCRETE OR MASONRY WALL OR TO PRESSURE - TREATED STRINGER

PAVER PROJECTS OVER RISER ABOUT 1 IN.

1 IN. (MAX.) SAND SETTING BED

NOTE: CONCRETE PAVERS MAY BE SUBSTITUTED FOR PRESSURE - TREATED RISERS

COMPACTED ROCK BASE OR SELF - COMPACTING PEA GRAVEL

Most paver stairs are contained at the sides with walls or stringers, as shown below.

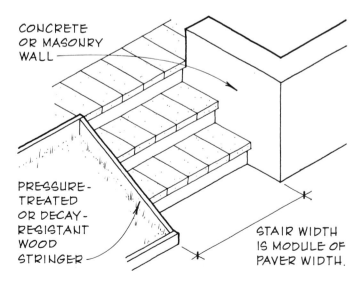

CONCRETE OR MASONRY WALL

PRESSURE - TREATED OR DECAY - RESISTANT WOOD STRINGER

STAIR WIDTH IS MODULE OF PAVER WIDTH.

Paver stairs may also be contained at all edges like brick stairs with 2x risers and side headers (see 211).

A) **DRY-SET EXTERIOR STEPS**
CONCRETE PAVERS

Concrete steps are durable and can be reasonably inexpensive, especially if they are built along with other concrete work. They should be adequately supported on a foundation and should be reinforced. Handrails or handrail supports may be cast into the steps or into the walks, porches or terraces adjacent to them. The steps may be covered with a masonry or other veneer.

The main problem with concrete steps is that they are difficult to repair if anything should go wrong with them. The usual problem is settling due to the extreme weight of the steps themselves and to the fact that they are often constructed on fill. The safest way to avoid settling is to provide for the porch and steps a footing that is below the frost line with a foundation wall above. This footing and foundation wall system may be an integral part of the foundation of the main structure (see the detail below), or it may be independent of the main structure with an expansion joint adjacent to the main structure that will allow the porch to move slightly without cracking (see 213A & B). Alternatively, concrete steps may be built independent of the main structure and adjacent to a wooden porch (see 213C). All methods are expensive, but will avoid costly maintenance in the long run.

For areas where building on backfill cannot be avoided, a wooden porch with a lightweight wood stair that can be easily re-leveled is the most practical (see 210C).

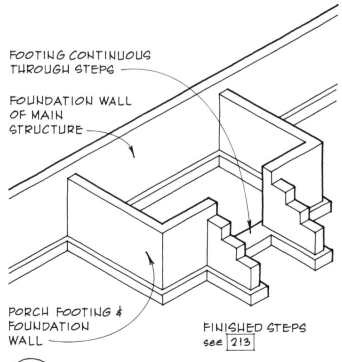

FOOTING CONTINUOUS THROUGH STEPS

FOUNDATION WALL OF MAIN STRUCTURE

PORCH FOOTING & FOUNDATION WALL

FINISHED STEPS see | 213 |

B) **CONCRETE STEPS**

NOTE:
ELEMENTS OF THE DETAILS ON THIS PAGE MAY BE COMBINED
IN VARIOUS WAYS TO MEET THE NEEDS OF SPECIFIC
SITUATIONS.

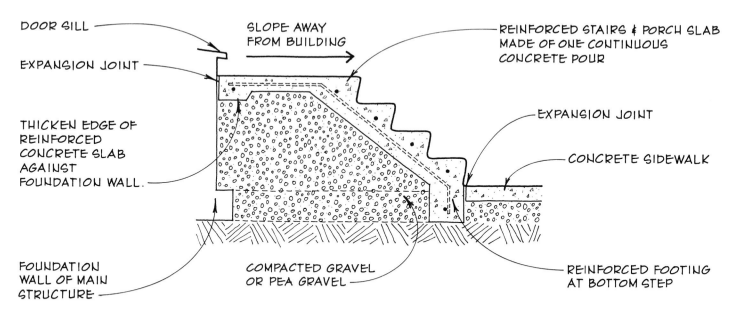

DOOR SILL

EXPANSION JOINT

THICKEN EDGE OF
REINFORCED
CONCRETE SLAB
AGAINST
FOUNDATION WALL.

SLOPE AWAY
FROM BUILDING

REINFORCED STAIRS & PORCH SLAB
MADE OF ONE CONTINUOUS
CONCRETE POUR

EXPANSION JOINT

CONCRETE SIDEWALK

FOUNDATION
WALL OF MAIN
STRUCTURE

COMPACTED GRAVEL
OR PEA GRAVEL

REINFORCED FOOTING
AT BOTTOM STEP

(A) CONCRETE STEPS ON GRAVEL
@ CONCRETE PORCH

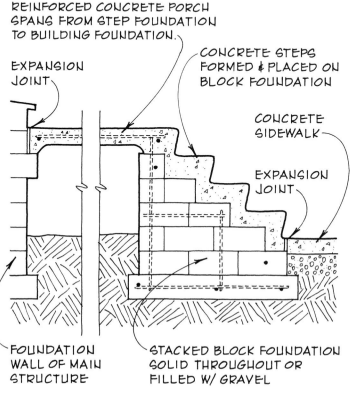

REINFORCED CONCRETE PORCH
SPANS FROM STEP FOUNDATION
TO BUILDING FOUNDATION.

EXPANSION
JOINT

CONCRETE STEPS
FORMED & PLACED ON
BLOCK FOUNDATION

CONCRETE
SIDEWALK

EXPANSION
JOINT

FOUNDATION
WALL OF MAIN
STRUCTURE

STACKED BLOCK FOUNDATION
SOLID THROUGHOUT OR
FILLED W/ GRAVEL

(B) CONCRETE STEPS ON BLOCK
@ CONCRETE PORCH

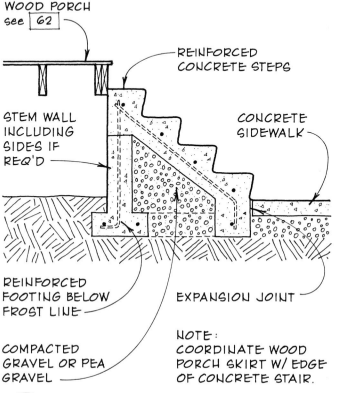

WOOD PORCH
see | 62 |

REINFORCED
CONCRETE STEPS

STEM WALL
INCLUDING
SIDES IF
REQ'D

CONCRETE
SIDEWALK

REINFORCED
FOOTING BELOW
FROST LINE

EXPANSION JOINT

COMPACTED
GRAVEL OR PEA
GRAVEL

NOTE:
COORDINATE WOOD
PORCH SKIRT W/ EDGE
OF CONCRETE STAIR.

(C) CONCRETE STEPS @ WOOD PORCH
ON BLOCK OR GRAVEL

LEGEND

CONCRETE

GRAVEL FILL

UNDISTURBED SOIL

SAND FILL

RIGID INSULATION

BATT INSULATION

MASONRY – BRICK OR
CONCRETE BLOCK

CONTINUOUS STRUCTURAL
FRAMING MEMBER

BLOCKING (NOT CONTINUOUS)

WOOD FINISH MATERIAL

PLYWOOD OR OTHER
STRUCTURAL PANEL

STUCCO OR GYPSUM
WALL BOARD (G.W.B.)

MATERIAL BURIED IN ANOTHER
MATERIAL, e.g., REBAR IN CONCRETE

FUTURE CONSTRUCTION

LIST OF ABBREVIATIONS

&	AND
@	AT
APPROX.	APPROXIMATE(LY)
FT.	FOOT/FEET
F.F.L.	FINISH FLOOR LEVEL
H	HEIGHT
IN.	INCH(ES)
LVL	LAMINATED-VENEER LUMBER
MAX.	MAXIMUM
MIN.	MINIMUM
#	NUMBER
O.C.	ON CENTER
‖	PARALLEL
⊥	PERPENDICULAR

LB.	POUNDS
PSF	POUNDS PER SQUARE FOOT
PSI	POUNDS PER SQUARE INCH
P.T.	PRESSURE TREATED
REBAR	REINFORCING STEEL
REQ'D	REQUIRED
SQ. FT.	SQUARE FOOT/FEET
T & G	TONGUE AND GROOVE
TYP.	TYPICAL
W	WIDTH
W/	WITH
W.W.M.	WELDED WIRE MESH

RESOURCES

TRADE AND PROFESSIONAL ASSOCIATIONS

American Concrete Institute
22400 W. Seven-Mile Road
Detroit, MI 48219
(313) 532-2600

American Institute of Architects
1735 New York Avenue, N.W.
Suite 700
Washington, DC 20006
(202) 626-7300

American Plywood Association
P.O. Box 11700
Tacoma, WA 98411
(206) 565-6600

Brick Institute of America
11490 Commerce Park Drive
Reston, VA 22091
(703) 620-0010

Forest Products Laboratory
Forest Service, USDA, P.O. Box 5130
Madison, WI 53705
(608) 257-2211

National Association of Home Builders
15th and M Streets, N.W.
Washington DC 20005
(800) 368-5242

National Concrete Masonry Association
2302 Horsepen Road
Herndon, VA 22071-3406
(703) 435-4900

National Forest Products Association
1250 Connecticut Avenue, N.W.
Suite 200
Washington, DC 20036
(202) 463-2700

National Roofing Contractors Association
O'Hare International Center
10255 W. Higgins Road
Suite 600
Rosemont, IL 60018
(708) 299-9070

Northeastern Lumber Manufacturers' Association
P.O. Box 87A
Cumberland Center, ME 04021
(207) 829-6901

Sheet Metal and Air Conditioning Contractors
National Association
4201 Lafayette Center Drive
Chantilly, VA 22021
(703) 803-2980

Small Homes Council
University of Illinois at Urbana-Champaign
One East St. Mary's Road
Champaign, IL 61820
(217) 333-1801

Southern Forest Products Association
P.O. Box 52468
New Orleans, LA 70152
(504) 443-4464

Western Wood Products Association
Yeon Building
522 S.W. 5th Avenue
Portland, OR 97204
(503) 224-3930

FURTHER READING

Allen, Edward. *Fundamentals of Building Construction.* New York: John Wiley & Sons, 1986.

American Institute of Architects. *Architectural Graphic Standards.* 8th ed. New York: John Wiley & Sons, 1988.

Dietz, Albert. *Dwelling House Construction.* 5th ed. Cambridge, Mass.: M.I.T. Press, 1991.

Fine Homebuilding. Bimonthly magazine. Newtown, Conn.: The Taunton Press (P.O. Box 5506, 63 South Main Street, Newtown, CT 06470-5506).

Riechers, A. F. *The Full Length Roof Framer.* Palo Alto, Calif.: Self published (Box 405, Palo Alto, CA 94302).

PRODUCT INFORMATION

Sweet's Catalogue File. New York: McGraw-Hill, updated annually.

Thomas Register of American Manufacturers and Thomas Register Catalog File. New York: Thomas Publishing Company, updated annually.

INDEX

Editor/Layout Artist: Joanne Bouknight
Designer: Deborah Fillion
Copy/Production Editor: Ruth Dobsevage

Typeface: Helvetica

Printer: Arcata Graphics/Kingsport, Tennessee